Lectures on the Acts of the Apostles

Lectures on the Acts of the Apostles

John Dick

Solid Ground Christian Books
Birmingham, Alabama USA

Solid Ground Christian Books
2090 Columbiana Rd, Suite 2000
Birmingham, AL 35216
205-443-0311
sgcb@charter.net
http://solid-ground-books.com

Lectures on the Acts of the Apostles

John Dick (1764-1833)

Taken from 1857 edition by Robert Carter & Brothers, New York, NY

Solid Ground Classic Reprints

First printing of new edition August 2005

Cover work by Borgo Design, Tuscaloosa, AL
Contact them at nelbrown@comcast.net

Cover image is entitled The Apostles Preaching the Gospel, and was done by Gustave Dore from The Dore Bible Gallery.

ISBN: 1-59925-010-1

PREFACE.

The following Lectures were first published in two volumes, which appeared at different times. The original design of the Author, was to illustrate the principal events in the history of the Church, from the ascension of Christ to the meeting of the Council of Jerusalem. He was afterwards induced to extend the selection of passages to the end of the Book; and of these the chief subject is Paul, to whose labours and sufferings the narrative confines our attention. The Lectures have been revised, and are now presented to the Public in one volume.

CONTENTS

LECTURE I.
THE RESURRECTION OF CHRIST, HIS LAST INTERVIEW WITH HIS DISCIPLES, AND HIS ASCENSION TO HEAVEN. 7

LECTURE II.
THE DAY OF PENTECOST. 20

LECTURE III.
THE FORMATION AND ORDER OF THE PRIMITIVE CHURCH. . . . 31

LECTURE IV.
THE LAME MAN CURED BY PETER AND JOHN. 46

LECTURE V.
PETER AND JOHN EXAMINED BY THE COUNCIL. 58

LECTURE VI.
ANANIAS AND SAPPHIRA. 72

LECTURE VII.
THE COUNSEL OF GAMALIEL. 85

LECTURE VIII.
THE INSTITUTION OF DEACONS, AND THE HISTORY OF STEPHEN. . . 98

LECTURE IX.
THE MARTYRDOM OF STEPHEN. 111

LECTURE X.
THE HISTORY OF SIMON MAGUS. 123

LECTURE XI.
THE CONVERSION OF THE ETHIOPIAN EUNUCH. 136

LECTURE XII.
THE CONVERSION OF PAUL. 149

LECTURE XIII.
THE CONVERSION OF CORNELIUS. 163

LECTURE XIV.
HEROD AND PETER. 176

LECTURE XV.
PAUL AND BARNABAS IN LYSTRA. 190

LECTURE XVI.
THE COUNCIL OF JERUSALEM. 202

LECTURE XVII.
THE MISSION OF PAUL AND SILAS TO MACEDONIA. 220

LECTURE XVIII.
THE CONVERSION OF THE JAILOR OF PHILIPPI. 234

LECTURE XIX.
PAUL AND SILAS IN THESSALONICA AND BEREA. 248

LECTURE XX.
PAUL IN ATHENS. 261

LECTURE XXI.
PAUL IN CORINTH. 276

LECTURE XXII.
PAUL IN EPHESUS. 290

LECTURE XXIII.
THE UPROAR IN EPHESUS. 304

LECTURE XXIV.
THE LAST INTERVIEW OF PAUL WITH THE ELDERS OF EPHESUS. . . 319

LECTURE XXV.
PAUL IN JERUSALEM. 335

LECTURE XXVI.
PAUL BEFORE THE COUNCIL. 349

LECTURE XXVII.
PAUL BEFORE FELIX. 363

LECTURE XXVIII.
PAUL BEFORE FESTUS AND AGRIPPA. 377

LECTURE XXIX.
PAUL IN MALTA AND ROME. 393

LECTURES, &c.

LECTURE I.

THE RESURRECTION OF CHRIST; HIS LAST INTERVIEW WITH HIS DISCIPLES; AND HIS ASCENSION TO HEAVEN.

Acts i. 1—11.

We are prompted by curiosity to inquire into the origin of nations, to trace their progress from rudeness to refinement, and to mark the steps by which they rose to eminence in power, in wealth, and in knowledge. To these subjects the researches of profane history are directed; and while its pages communicate instruction and entertainment to every reader, they particularly engage the attention of the statesman, who derives from them a more extensive acquaintance with mankind, and is enabled to add to his experience the accumulated wisdom of ages.

To a Christian the history of the Church must appear more worthy of notice than the revolutions of empire. A society, towards which Providence has, in all ages, exercised a particular care, presents an interesting object of inquiry; and must exhibit, in the detail of events, admirable proofs of the power, and wisdom, and goodness of God. Its history is the history of religion; of the accomplishment of a long series of prophecies; of the execution of a scheme, to which all the other parts of the divine administration are subservient.

The early periods of the history of nations are generally enveloped in fable; and although the truth could be discovered through the veil which conceals it, would, for the most part, present little that is worthy to be known. The human race may be considered as then in a state of infancy. Their ideas are few and gross, their manners are barbarous, and their knowledge of arts is confined to some simple operations performed without elegance or skill. The history of the first age of the Christian Church is more instructive and engaging than that of any subsequent period. It is splendid, because it is miraculous; it is edifying, as it records many noble examples of faith, charity, patience, and zeal; it arrests the attention and touches the heart, by displaying the triumph of the gospel over the combined malice and wisdom of the world.

As a record of the Acts, or proceedings of the Apostles, in collecting and modelling the Church, this book forms a valuable portion of Scripture. It contains information upon subjects of great importance; the miraculous manner in which those simple and unlettered men were qualified for their arduous work; the means by which the Church was founded, and rose to a holy temple in the Lord; the rapidity with which the gospel was propagated; the opposition which was made to it by Jews and Gentiles; and the causes to which its unexampled success should be ascribed. The narrative is written in a plain and artless manner; and our pleasure in perusing it suffers no abatement from the suspicion of misinformation, or partiality in the writer.

The historian, as we learn from the introductory verses, was the same person who published the Gospel, which, from the earliest ages, has been uniformly attributed to Luke. He was alive during the events which he records, was an eye-witness of many of them, and inquired, we may believe, into the rest, with the same diligence which he used in compiling his Gospel. Although he was not one of the Apostles, yet he lived in habits of intimate correspondence with them; and the Church has, from the beginning, received his writings as of equal authority with theirs.

I propose to deliver a course of Lectures on some passages of this book, selecting such as relate the more remarkable events in the history of the primitive Church. Of those passages it is not my intention to give a minute explanation, but to illustrate the principal topics, and to deduce such instructions as they seem to suggest. Conformably to this plan, I shall at this time confine your attention to three points, to which the verses now read have a reference; the resurrection of our Lord Jesus Christ from the dead; his last interview with his disciples; and his ascension to heaven.

I. The first point which claims our notice in this passage, is the resurrection of our Saviour, of which Luke makes mention in the third verse. "To whom also," that is, to the Apostles whom he had chosen, "he showed himself alive after his passion, by many infallible proofs, being seen of them forty days." The resurrection of Christ is an article of great importance in our religion, the foundation upon which its other doctrines rest, and by which the faith and hope of his followers are sustained. "If Christ be not risen," says Paul, "then is our preaching vain, and your faith is also vain. Yea, and we are found false witnesses of God; because we have testified of God, that he raised up Christ; whom he raised not up, if so be that the dead rise not. For if the dead rise not, then is not Christ raised. And if Christ be not raised, your faith is vain; ye are yet in your sins. Then they also which have fallen asleep in Christ are perished." Such evidence, as should leave no doubt in the cautious and inquisitive mind, was necessary to establish a fact upon which so much depended. Luke affirms, that Jesus showed himself alive to his disciples, "after his passion," that is, after his sufferings and death, by many "infallible proofs." The word signifies signs, tokens, or evidences, which were so numerous and decisive, that it was impossible for those who saw them to be mistaken. He refers to the frequent appearance of Christ, of which not less than eight are recorded by the Evangelists, besides many more which may have taken place during the forty days between his resurrection and ascension; and to the methods which he used to convince the disciples, by calling upon them "to handle him and see, that a spirit had not flesh and bones as he had," and by eating, drinking, and conversing with them in a familiar manner.

It is vain to insinuate, that the Apostles might be imposed upon by the power of imagination, which the eagerness of their wishes and expectations had excited, and might thus fancy that they saw what had no real existence. It does not appear that they actually expected the resurrection of their Master; but, on the contrary, there is reason to think, that they had almost given over all hope of that event. When the women, who had been at the sepulchre, told them of it, their words seemed as "idle tales;" and the two disciples on the road to Emmaus may be supposed to have expressed the sentiments and feelings of their brethren, when they said, "We trusted that it had been he which should have redeemed Israel;" manifestly using the language of disappointment and despondency. In such a state of mind, there was no room for imagination to operate. It will be still more evident, that they were not under its influence, if we consider, that some of the appearances were made, not to a solitary individual, but to several of the disciples at once, in one instance to five hundred brethren, who could not all have been deluded at the same moment by a phantom of their own brain; that the appearances were not transient, but lasted for a considerable time, so that the spectators had full leisure to examine them; that some of them were sudden, or without warning, and others were the consequence of previous appointment; that they frequently took place, not in the night when the mind is more subject to illusion, but in the day when the disciples were composed, and all their senses were awake; and that the interviews were not distant and silent, but Jesus familiarly associated with the Apostles, and gave all the satisfaction which the most incredulous among them could demand. From these circumstances, there does not remain the slightest ground to suspect that the Apostles themselves were deceived; and the only question now to be determined is, whether they have deceived us.

Infidels object, that the Apostles, who were interested persons were the only witnesses of the resurrection, and that Jesus did not show himself to the Sanhedrim and the inhabitants of Jerusalem, as he ought to have done, that the reality of the event might be placed beyond dispute. They affirm, that on this account the whole narrative is suspicious. There is one important circumstance, which, perhaps, they willingly forget, that the enemies of Jesus were the first and immediate witnesses of the resurrection, that event having taken place, according to Matthew, in the presence of the Roman soldiers, not before the eyes of the disciples. Sufficient reasons have been assigned why he did not appear to the rulers and people of the Jews, which your time will not permit me fully to state. It may be remarked, that although this demand had been complied with, and our Lord had resorted after his resurrection to the temple, and walked in the streets of Jerusalem, it is by no means certain that the purpose which is pretended would have been gained. We have no ground to think, that the Jews, who would not believe the testimony of Moses and the Prophets, nor the evidence of our Saviour's miracles, would have believed, although they had seen him risen from the dead. But upon the supposition, that they had been convinced by this last and seemingly irresistible proof, the truth of his resurrection would have been as much perplexed as ever by the cavils of free-thinkers. We should have been told of the superstition and credulity of the Jews, and of their national pride, which disposed them fondly to embrace any story that seemed to realise their boasted hopes of the Messiah; and whereas now the testimony of the Apostles is corroborated by the trying and perilous circumstances in which they were placed, the whole would then have been represented as an imposture, concerted between them and their countrymen, and first promulgated where it was sure to be received, and no person had either inclination or power to detect it. I shall only farther observe, that if there be satisfactory proof that Christ did appear to the Apostles, we are bound to acquiesce in their solemn testimony; and that nothing can be more unreasonable than to demand more evidence than is sufficient, or to reject sufficient evidence, because it is not presented in that form which we prefer.

After this general observation, I may appeal to every unprejudiced person, whether there is any thing in the narrative of this transaction, in its general complexion, or its particular parts, which gives countenance to the suspicion of imposture; or rather, whether it does not bear unequivocal marks of simplicity, candour, and the sacred love of truth. Let it be farther considered, that the testimony of the Apostles was given in public, and before the persons who were above all concerned to detect a falsehood, and possessed the means of detecting it; that it was consistent and uniform, there not being a single instance of retractation or variation among the witnesses; that no motive can be assigned for their conduct if it was false, as in that case they could not expect to be believed, and the only prospect before them was that of persecution and death in this world, without the hope of a recompense in the next; that they did not require men to give credit to their simple testimony, but appealed, in confirmation of it, to miracles wrought, as they affirmed, by the power of him who had been raised from the dead; and, finally, that this testimony was believed by thousands of Jews and Gentiles, although their prejudices against it were the strongest imaginable. I challenge all the infidels in the world to produce a single fact, in the whole compass of history, supported by more decisive evidence.

I shall subjoin a remark upon the qualifications of the Apostles. What made those babblers so eloquent; those ignorant and illiterate men so profoundly skilled in the mysteries of redemption; those cowards so courageous, as to despise every danger, and maintain the truth amidst the most terrible sufferings? This change could not have been effected by their Master, if he was still lying in the grave;

and it is, therefore, a proof that he had risen from it, and performed the promise which we shall immediately proceed to consider.

II. Our attention is next called to the interview, which took place between our Lord and his disciples prior to his ascension. It is mentioned in the sixth verse: "When they therefore were come together, they asked of him, saying, Lord, wilt thou at this time restore again the kingdom to Israel." It seems to be the same meeting to which the historian refers in the fourth verse. "And being assembled together with them, he commanded them, that they should not depart from Jerusalem, but wait for the promise of the Father, which, saith he, ye have heard of me." We are informed, that during the forty days which he spent upon earth after his resurrection, he spoke to his disciples of "the things pertaining to the kingdom of God;" explaining to them, as far as they were able to bear it, the nature of that dispensation which he was about to introduce. But still the old leaven of Jewish prejudices, and carnal ideas of the Messiah's reign, fermented in their minds. Although they had beheld his poverty and humility, and had seen him put to death in the most ignominious manner, they had not abandoned the fond and flattering thought, that he would assume the character of a temporal monarch, and establish the dominion of the chosen people over the tributary nations. Such were the notions with respect to the purpose of his mission and the nature of his kingdom, which their countrymen had adopted from the magnificent language of prophecy, describing his spiritual power and glory by metaphors and similitudes borrowed from the wealth and grandeur of earthly potentates. To the remaining influence of these notions upon their minds, after all his instructions, we must attribute the question which the disciples put to him, "Lord, wilt thou at this time restore again the kingdom to Israel?" "Is the time now come, when thou wilt deliver thy people from the oppression of a foreign yoke, and give them the empire of the world?"

To this question Jesus did not return a direct answer, but one which implied a reproof of that vain curiosity which had led them to propose it. "It is not for you to know the times, and the seasons, which the Father hath put in his own power." These words import, that the revolutions in the civil and religious state of the world were predetermined by God, as they are all brought to pass by his providence; that he only knows the order and series of events; and that, except in those instances in which he has revealed them to us in the word of prophecy, we should beware of attempting to discover his secrets, and to draw aside the veil which hangs over futurity. Let man remember the limited nature of his faculties, and the dependent condition of his mind. Let him be thankful for what he does know, and content to remain ignorant of what his Maker has been pleased to conceal.

This answer, being a rebuke to their unhallowed curiosity, was calculated to discourage the Apostles. That they might not be dejected, and no disagreeable impression might be left upon their minds, our Lord subjoined a promise, well fitted to comfort them. "But ye shall receive power, after that the Holy Ghost is come upon you; and ye shall be witnesses unto me, both in Jerusalem, and in all Judea, and in Samaria, and unto the uttermost part of the earth." In the fourth verse, "he commanded them that they should not depart from Jerusalem, but wait for the promise of the Father." What he teaches them, in both verses, to expect, is the Holy Ghost, in a more abundant measure of his influences than they had yet received, to qualify them for the duties of the Apostleship. They were appointed to be "witnesses" of Christ to the world; to bear public testimony to Jews and Gentiles, concerning his doctrine, his miracles, his death, and his resurrection. With this view, they had been admitted to attend him from the commencement of his ministry to the present moment; and had enjoyed frequent meetings, and intimate conversation with him, since his return from the grave. But now it was farther necessary, that they should be furnished with more profound knowledge of the mysteries of the kingdom than they yet possessed, with higher capacity for reasoning, with a talent for public speaking, with the gift of tongues, with a power to work miracles for the confirmation of their testimony, with zeal, courage, meekness, prudence, and unwearied perseverance. Without these qualifications, they would have been unfit for the office which their Master had conferred upon them. This, then, is a promise of "power," of such vigour of mind, of such intellectual and spiritual endowments, as should fully prepare them for their various and difficult duties.

The promise, for which they were commanded to wait, our Saviour called "the promise of the Father," to inform his disciples, that it is the Father who sends the Holy Ghost, to give effect to the death of his Son in the conversion and sanctification of sinners;

but chiefly, because his faithfulness was pledged for the mission of the Spirit in many passages of the Old Testament, particularly in he following words, which were fulfilled on the day of Pentecost: "And it shall come to pass afterward, that I will pour out my Spirit upon all flesh, and your sons and your daughters shall prophesy, your old men shall dream dreams, your young men shall see visions; and also upon the servants and upon the handmaids, in those days, will I pour out my Spirit."

From the mention of the promise of the Spirit, Jesus takes occasion to point out to the disciples the difference between his own administration and that of his forerunner. "For John truly baptized with water; but ye shall be baptized with the Holy Ghost not many days hence." The Baptist, although greater than the Prophets, could only sprinkle his disciples with water, to signify their purification from the guilt and defilement of sin; but Jesus was able to communicate the Spirit himself in his regenerating influences, and miraculous gifts. To apply the means of salvation is the province of the ministers of religion; but the wisest and holiest of them can contribute nothing to their efficacy. The source of spiritual life and power is the invisible Head of the Church, "from whom all the body, by joints and hands, having nourishment ministered, and knit together, increaseth with the increase of God." The blessings of grace are entrusted to his disposal; and he gives or withholds them at his pleasure.

That our Saviour when he made this promise, claimed no power of which he was not possessed, the disciples were soon to be convinced by experience. They were commanded to wait at Jerusalem till the promise should be performed. Accordingly, we know that more than ten days did not elapse between this meeting and the day of Pentecost, when the Holy Ghost descended upon them.

The interview now described took place immediately before his ascension; and the historian proceeds to relate the event.

III. "And when he had spoken these things, while they beheld, he was taken up, and a cloud received him out of their sight." Jesus had now fulfilled all the designs of his mission. He had declared the counsels of God to mankind; he had offered himself upon the cross as a sacrifice for sin; and having triumphed over death, he had given his disciples sufficient opportunity to assure themselves of the truth of the fact. "I have glorified thee on the earth; I have finished the work which thou gavest me to do." There was no reason therefore, why he should prolong his stay. It was necessary that the great High Priest of our profession, having made atonement for his people, should go into the most holy place, to present his blood and make intercession for them. It was necessary, that the Lord and King of the Church, having vanquished his enemies, after a hard and bloody conflict, should ascend his throne and receive the sceptre of universal dominion. He had forewarned the disciples of his departure, both before and after his death; and lest they should suppose, when they heard of his resurrection, that he meant to associate with them as formerly, he sent his message to them by Mary Magdalene: "I ascend unto my Father, and your Father, and to my God, and your God." Accordingly, "when he had spoken these things," given them all the instructions which they needed, or were able to bear, "he was taken up while they beheld, and a cloud received him out of their sight." It appears from these words, which represent him as passive in his ascension, that it was effected by the power of his Father, who had engaged to reward his humiliation, by exalting him to glory; that it was not sudden, but gradual, the disciples having full leisure to observe his ascent from the earth; and, lastly, that when he had risen to a certain height in the air, a cloud intervened, and concealed him from their sight. They had seen enough to qualify them to be witnesses of the fact.

This event, however honourable to their Lord, and joyful to themselves, had they understood its design, could not fail to affect the disciples in a disagreeable manner, in the first moments of surprise, and while they were not acquainted with the important purposes to be served by the ascension. To his personal presence they had conceived a warm attachment, founded in esteem of his excellencies, and experience of his friendship. From his lips they had heard discourses replenished with wisdom and grace; and by his hand they had seen works of the most wonderful and beneficent nature performed. He had been their counsellor in difficulties, and their comforter in sorrow. To be deprived in a moment of his company; to be left alone in the midst of numerous and implacable enemies; to have the prospect of labours, and sufferings, and death, without their Master at their head, without their condescending and affectionate Saviour to advise and encourage them; these were circumstances sufficient to have discomposed the firmest mind, and which would have almost excused the Apostles, had they given way to lamentation and dejection. We are informed that they "looked steadfastly towards heaven, as he went up," continuing to gaze long after the cloud had concealed him. It was a look of astonishment and grief for the sudden loss of all that was dear to them; it was a look of eager desire to be again gratified with a sight of their Master.

They did not, however, remain long in this uncomfortable state. "Behold two men stood by them in white apparel; which also said, Ye men of Galilee, why stand ye gazing up into heaven? This same Jesus, which is taken up from you into heaven, shall so come, in like manner as ye have seen him go into heaven." There is no doubt that these men in appearance were angels; and the splendour of their dress was a sign by which they must have been immediately known to be heavenly messengers. They were a part of that illustrious retinue, which came from the celestial regions to attend our Lord in his ascension, and to heighten the glory of his triumph. Thousands, and ten thousands of angels accompanied him as he passed from earth to heaven, celebrating his praises. "The chariots of God are twenty thousand, even thousands of angels: the Lord is among them as in Sinai, in the holy place. Thou hast ascended on high, thou hast led captivity captive." To the sorrowful disciples, the words of the angels were full of comfort. They seem to suggest a resemblance between the ascension of Jesus and his second appearance, and in this way have been frequently explained. But I rather think, that nothing more is intended than to assert, that as certainly as he had ascended to heaven, he would descend from it, at the time appointed by his Father; and that the Apostles should entertain no more doubt of the one event than of the other. Between the ascension and his coming at the end of the world, there is no great similarity of circumstances, unless we should choose to say, that as he departed in a cloud, so with clouds he will return, and that as he was now accompanied by angels, so the same glorious spirits will be his attendants and ministers, when he appears in the character of universal Judge.

But the chief thing to which the angels called the attention of the disciples, and ours should be directed, is the certainty of his second coming; for this is an event, which, although an object of dreadful expectation to the unbelieving and impenitent, is fraught with hope and joy to those who love and obey the truth. The person who shall appear, will be "that same Jesus who was taken up into heaven," clothed with the same nature, sustaining the same relations to us, animated with the same love, and carrying on the same gracious design. Ten thousand tongues will hail him with accents of exultation and triumph. "Lo, this is our God, we have waited for him, and he will save us: this is the Lord, we have waited for him, we will be glad, and rejoice in his salvation." Then shall the disciples be again gathered to their Master, and the sheep to their Shepherd. Oh! how joyful the meeting, so long promised, so eagerly expected? It will be the day of the gladness of his heart, to behold around him those for whom he died upon the cross, and has ever since ministered in heaven: it will be a source of ineffable felicity to them, to see him whose glory was the subject of their contemplations in this world, to be taken under his immediate care, to be admitted to the most intimate fellowship with him, and to know that no event shall ever separate them again.

Such was the comfortable prospect which the words of the angels gave to the disciples; and we need not wonder, that their fears and sorrows were dispelled, and that, as we are informed in another place, "they returned to Jerusalem with great joy; and were continually in the temple, praising and blessing God."

I conclude with the following reflections upon the passage.

First, We follow no cunningly devised fable, when we receive the gospel as an authentic record of the character and doctrine of Jesus Christ. It is confirmed by "infallible proofs," by ample and luminous evidence, which is sufficient to convince every ingenuous mind, every man who examines it with a candid, dispassionate temper. You may be assured, my brethren, that it is not for want of evidence that the gospel is in any instance rejected. Difficulties, indeed, there may be, which are apt to perplex ill-informed and superficial observers; but the chief objection to it, an objection level to the comprehension of every depraved heart, is its holiness. "Men hate the light, because their deeds are evil." This will appear to be no false charge, if you consider, that there is scarcely any thing that infidels believe, for which they have half the evidence that can be produced in favour of the truth of Christianity. It is not, therefore, to reason that their unbelief should be attributed, but to some other cause; a corrupt taste, an impatience of restraint, a wish to live without any law to control them, or any fear to disturb them in their pleasure

In the second place, Christians may place unbounded confidence in their Redeemer, who having conquered their enemies, and triumphed over death and the grave, has ascended, in the most glorious manner, to heaven, where he sways the sceptre of universal government, and bearing his people, and all their interests upon his heart, makes continual intercession for them in the presence of his Father. Why should you be afraid to draw near to the throne of God, and to present your supplications? Is not the merit of our great High Priest sufficient to counterbalance your demerit? And shall not the efficacy of his prayers ensure the acceptance and success of yours, notwithstanding the imperfection which adheres to your best duties? Why should you be discouraged by adverse dispensations of providence, by the power and threatenings of your adversaries, by the afflictions of the Church, by the uproar and confusion of the nations? Is not he who reigns the friend and patron of the righteous, under whose protection they are safe, and by whose almighty agency, and unerring wisdom, the perplexities and turmoils of the present scene shall issue in perfect order and eternal felicity?

Lastly, The attention and the hope of Christians are now directed to the second appearance of their Saviour. The ancient Church looked for his coming in the flesh; we, according to his promise, look for his coming in glory. "Lift up your heads with joy, believers; for the day of your redemption draweth nigh." To them alone who are waiting for him, will he appear for salvation; but there is not an eye which shall not see him in the clouds, nor a knee which shall not bow before him. How alarming will be the sight, how mortifying the homage, to infidels and blasphemers of his gospel, to the enemies of his grace, to the despisers of his institutions, to the transgressors of his laws? Professed disciples of the Son of Man, are you prepared to go forth and meet him? To what class of mankind do you belong? to that which, standing on his right hand, shall be invited to enter into his kingdom? or to that which, being ranged on the left, shall be condemned to darkness and everlasting woe? Ask your consciences the important question; and that it may be satisfactorily answered, call in the assistance of the infallible word, by which we shall be finally judged. "Behold he cometh with clouds, and every eye shall see him." Happy are they who can say, with holy and earnest desire, "Even so, come Lord Jesus."

LECTURE II.

THE DAY OF PENTECOST.

Chap. ii. 1—13.

The promise of the Holy Ghost, which our Saviour made to the disciples at his last interview with them, was well fitted to reconcile their minds to his departure, and to encourage them in the view of the various and difficult duties of the Apostolical office. There was but a short interval between his ascension and the performance of the promise; an event of great importance in the history of the Church, and of which the passage now read gives an account.

The first point which requires our notice, is the time when "the promise of the Father," as it is termed, was performed. We are told in the first verse, that it was when "the day of Pentecost was fully come."—Pentecost is a Greek word signifying the fiftieth day, and is the name of that grand festival which the Israelites were commanded to celebrate fifty days after the passover, in commemoration of the giving of the law. God having delivered his people from Egypt, led them through the Red Sea into the wilderness, where they were conducted, by easy marches, to the spot which he had chosen for displaying the tokens of his Majesty. There he descended on the top of Sinai, a rugged and barren mountain; and from the midst of darkness and devouring fire, proclaimed his law with a voice which filled with terror the immense multitude assembled at its base. At the same time, he enjoined, by the ministry of Moses, that system of ordinances and statutes, which was the foundation of the civil and ecclesiastical polity of the Jews. That a law, published with such solemnity by God himself, should not pass away like the transient institutions of men, but should remain through all ages as a monument of the divine goodness to their nation, and as the rule of their worship and obedience, was an idea natural enough to men, who could not, as an Apostle observes, "steadfastly look to the end of it;" or were ignorant of its typical design. But it was destined to give place to a new and better dispensation. Aaron and his sons were to retire from the altar, when a priest of another order should appear, and by a more excellent sacrifice than that of rams and bullocks, make a true atonement for the sins of the people. That priest had now come, and by the oblation of himself, "had perfected for ever them that are sanctified." The veil had been rent from the top to the bottom; and the glory had departed from the temple of Jerusalem. A law was to go forth from Zion, by which the law from Sinai should be superseded; the pompous ritual of Moses was to be succeeded by a system of worship, simple and spiritual. It was with a design to signify this change, that Pentecost was chosen for the effusion of the Holy Ghost upon the Apostles of Christ. On the anniversary of the promulgation of the ancient law, they were enabled to publish the good news of the reign of the Messiah, not to the inhabitants of Jerusalem alone, but, in their own language, "to men of every nation under heaven." And, surely, to every reflecting mind it is evident, that the interposition of God himself, in a miraculous manner, to qualify the Apostles, at this particular time, to preach a new religion, was an unequivocal declaration, that the old religion, having served its purpose, was to be no longer obligatory. Thus Pentecost was again rendered illustrious as the commencement of a new era. Besides the reason now given for the choice of this day, we may conceive Divine Wisdom to have pitched upon it, with a view to the opportunity which it afforded, of speedily conveying tidings of salvation to many distant parts of the earth, by means of the strangers who were assembled at the feast.

Our attention is next called to the subjects of this miracle, or the persons upon whom the Holy Ghost descended. "They were all with one accord in one place." Some suppose, that the historian refers to the hundred and twenty disciples mentioned in the fifteenth verse of the preceding chapter, among whom there were several women; and they add, that if the women be included, the prophecy of Joel, afterwards quoted, was literally fulfilled. "Your sons and your daughters shall prophesy:—and on my servants, and on my handmaidens, I will pour out in those days of my Spirit." Others maintain, that the reference goes no farther back than the last verse of the first chapter, in which mention is made of Matthias and the eleven Apostles; and they consider the fourteenth verse of this chapter, which informs us that Peter stood up with the eleven, as supporting this opinion. It seems, indeed, to be more probable than the other, because it was not to all the disciples, but to the Apostles, that Christ made the promise which was now performed; and because the gift of tongues, being intended as a qualification for preaching the gospel, there is no ground to imagine that it was bestowed upon women, to whom that office was never assigned by any but some wild enthusiast.

Let us now consider the account of the miracle. In the first place, we must take notice of the symbols, or external signs of it, which were two; the one addressed to the eye, and the other to the ear. We read, in the second verse, that "suddenly there came a sound from heaven, as of a rushing mighty wind, and it filled all the house where they were sitting." It is remarkable, that in the two languages in which the Scriptures are written, as well as in some others, the word which signifies spirit, signifies also breath or wind. For the use of the same term to denote two ideas so distinct, different reasons may be assigned. Perhaps the men who spoke those languages in remote ages, were so gross and ignorant as to form no conception of an immaterial soul, or of any living principle in man besides the air which he breathes; or from the penury of language which compels us to apply words expressive of sensible objects to intellectual and spiritual things, they gave the same name to the soul, and to the breath or air, because it is by the air that human life is sustained. Be this as it may, we are authorised to consider air in motion as a sort of emblem of the Holy Spirit and his operations. When speaking on this subject to Nicodemus, our Lord used the following comparison. "The wind bloweth where it listeth, and thou hearest the sound thereof, but canst not tell whence it cometh, and whither it goeth; so is every one that is born of the Spirit." At a meeting with his disciples after his resurrection, "he breathed on them, and said unto them, Receive ye the Holy Ghost." To the Apostles therefore, a wind from heaven was a significant sign; a sign which must have immediately suggested the idea of the spirit and his influences, and have led them to expect that now the promise of their Saviour should be performed.

It may be thought, that a gentle breeze would have been a more proper emblem of the Holy Ghost than a loud and violent wind; that it would have accorded better with the purpose of his descent and with the mild and gracious nature of the new dispensation. But this fancy will be dismissed as soon as we reflect, that his coming was to be productive of the most astonishing effects, in endowing the minds of the Apostles with extraordinary powers, and in bearing down the opposition made to the truth, by ignorance and prejudice, by the wisdom of philosophers, and the policy of statesmen ; and that nothing could more aptly represent the energy by which these effects should be produced, than "a rushing mighty wind." At the same time, the noise served to collect together the people to witness the miracle. It was confined to a particular spot, and filled the house in which the Apostles were assembled.

The other sign which accompanied this miracle is described in the third verse. "And there appeared unto them cloven tongues, like as of fire, and it sat upon each of them. When John announced the approach of the Messiah, he said to the people, " He shall baptize you with the Holy Ghost, and with fire ;" by which we are not to understand some thing distinct from the Holy Ghost, but his influences, which are represented under the metaphor of fire, on account of the resemblance between the properties of the one and of the other. Fire, then, was an emblem equally significant as wind, which must have likewise recalled to the minds of the Apostles the promise of their Lord. The fire appeared in the form of tongues, cloven, or divided at top; and a flame of this figure rested upon the head of each of the Apostles. The shape of the flame was emblematical of the nature of the miracle, which consisted in enabling them to speak " with other tongues," or to speak languages which they had never learned ; and the division of the flame pointed out the variety of those languages. But why, it may be asked, were the tongues of fire ? To intimate, I answer, that in the languages which the Apostles were now enabled to speak, they should communicate to the world that heavenly doctrine, which, like fire, both illuminates and purifies ; or rather to signify, that their tongues, touched as with a live-coal from the altar, should utter strains of glowing eloquence, not fashioned, it might be, according to the rules observed by the orators of Greece and Rome, but capable of producing far nobler effects ; eloquence, which would terrify the boldest, and alarm the most careless sinner ; which would humble the proud, comfort the dejected, inspire the timid with invincible courage, and, with an energy unknown to philosophy, kindle the living fire of devotion in the coldest and most unfeeling heart.

After this account of the signs, we proceed to inquire into the nature, of the miracle. "And they were all filled with the Holy Ghost, and began to speak with other tongues, as the Spirit gave them utterance." The general effect is manifest, namely, the communication of the knowledge of languages, with which the Apostles were formerly unacquainted; but it does not appear, whether the same languages were imparted to them all, or to one was given the knowledge of some, and to another, the knowledge of others. The Holy Ghost could "divide to every one of them severally as he pleased;" but as they were all destined to preach to different nations, there can be no doubt that they were all furnished with a diversity of tongues.

Language is composed of articulate sounds, which, when uttered by the mouth, or represented by characters or letters, signify certain ideas. The connexion between the sounds and the things which they signify is arbitrary, not founded in nature, but in convention; and, consequently, a sound can convey no information to the hearer till he have learned its meaning. Hence the acquisition of a foreign language requires close application and frequent practice. Much time must be spent, before a person can be acquainted with the signification of the great variety of sounds which are used in any country, and be able to understand them as soon as they are pronounced. It is still more difficult to attain the power of speaking a foreign language fluently and accurately; or to become so familiar with its words, as instantly to call them up, to express the ideas, which arise in the mind. What increases the difficulty is, that, in all languages, the same word has sometimes a variety of meanings, so that, if it be not skilfully used, it may suggest a sense very different from that which it was our intention to express; and that there is a mode peculiar to every language of combining and arranging its words, without observing which, a stranger shall speak unintelligibly to the natives. Those who have engaged in the study of languages can attest, that it is an arduous task, when one aims at a thorough acquaintance with them; and although, after much labour, some may be able to understand, with considerable ease, a book written in a foreign tongue, yet there is not one in twenty who is capable of carrying on conversation in it with facility. It may be added, that the sounds of a foreign language are, in some instances, so different from those to which we have been accustomed, that we feel ourselves at a loss to pronounce them; and that, unless we begin to learn in an early period of life, when our organs are flexible, we can hardly ever speak in such a manner as to please the ear of a native.

These remarks are intended to show you the astonishing nature of the miracle which was performed on the day of Pentecost. The Apostles were illiterate men, who understood no language but that of their own country, and could speak it only according to the rude dialect of Galilee. They had never thought of learning the languages of foreigners; and it is probable, that even the names of some of the nations, mentioned in the following verses, had not reached their ears. Yet, in a moment were those men inspired with the knowledge of an immense number of words, which they had never heard before, and with the knowledge not only of the words, but of the connected ideas, and of the structure, the arrangement, and the peculiar phrases of the languages to which they belonged. At the same time, their organs were rendered capable of adapting themselves to sounds different from each other, as well as from those to which they had been familiarized from their infancy. Notwithstanding this diversity, there was not the smallest confusion in their minds, nor were they in danger of mixing the words of different languages together; but they spoke each as distinctly, as if they had been acquainted with it alone.

It may be safely affirmed, that there is not a more remarkable miracle recorded in the New Testament. It will not, however, appear incredible to any person, who considers, on the one hand, that the cause was adequate to the effect, for it was produced by that Being who made the tongue of man, and was the original Author of language; and, on the other, that it was necessary to qualify the Apostles for executing their commission to preach the gospel to every creature. Without the gift of tongues their ministrations must have been confined to their own countrymen; for it is not probable, that at their time of life, and with their habits, they could have acquired, by ordinary means, a single foreign language so perfectly, as to be able to deliver a discourse in it upon the subject of religion. We have been informed, by the missionaries in Otaheite, that after a residence of several years among the natives, in a situation the most advantageous of all for learning a language, they have not yet ventured to preach or pray publicly in the language of the country.

In the following verses, the historian relates the impression which the miracle made upon the multitude. "And there were dwelling at Jerusalem, Jews, devout men, out of every nation under heaven. Now when this was noised abroad, the multitude came together, and were confounded, because that every man heard them speak in his own language. And they were all amazed, and marvelled, saying one to another, Behold, are not all these which speak Galileans? And how hear we every man in our own tongue wherein we were born? Parthians, and Medes, and Elamites, and the dwellers in Mesopotamia, and in Judea, and Cappadocia, in Pontus, and Asia, Phrygia, and Pamphylia, in Egypt, and in the parts of Libya about Cyrene, and strangers of Rome, Jews and proselytes, Cretes and Arabians, we do hear them speak in our tongues the wonderful works of God." It is probable, that the sound of the "rushing mighty wind" alarmed the persons in the neighbourhood, and drew them to the place from which it proceeded; and the report having spread through the city, a great number of spectators was speedily assembled. The Apostles immediately began to exercise the gift of tongues, as they observed in the crowd strangers from very different parts of the earth. These had now come to Jerusalem to celebrate the feast of Pentecost, or, as the original term may import, had taken up their residence there, in the expectation, as some think, of the appearance of the Messiah. After the Babylonian captivity, many of the Jews remained in the countries in which they had sojourned during its continuance; and by subsequent revolutions they were dispersed over all the East, and through almost every province of the Roman empire. Hence, although they retained their religion and their peculiar manners, they unavoidably adopted the language of the natives. Together with the Jews of the dispersion, there were present also, on this occasion, several persons of heathen extraction, who, being convinced of the unity of God, and of the divine authority of the law of Moses, had received the seal of circumcision, and were incorporated with the peculiar people. These were the proselytes mentioned in the end of the tenth verse.

How great must have been the astonishment of this mixed multitude, to hear themselves unexpectedly addressed in the languages of the countries from which they respectively came: The assembly was composed of strangers from at least fourteen different nations; and every man heard the Apostles speak in his own tongue. The speakers, they perceived, were Galileans, common men, from a part of the country reputed the most unpolished and illiterate. The sacred historian uses three words to describe the state of their minds. They were "confounded;" they were "amazed;" and they "marvelled." At first they were so affected by the extraordinary nature of the event, that they could only gaze with silent wonder; but afterwards they gave vent to their feelings in words; and they began to inquire into the meaning of the miracle. "They were all amazed, and were in doubt, saying one to another, What meaneth this?" It was manifest that the hand of God was in the event, and that there must be some end worthy of so unusual an interposition. What that end was, they were at a loss to conceive; but perhaps some suspicion, some confused apprehension of it arose in their minds. They heard the Apostles speaking "the wonderful works of God;" proclaiming the incarnation, the doctrine, the death, the resurrection, and the ascension of the Lord Jesus. Comparing this account with the miracle, of which they were now witnesses, they began to doubt, whether he might not be the Messiah, and this extraordinary scene might not be a preliminary step to the establishment of his kingdom. In this perplexity they were desirous to know the real design of the miracle.

But a part of the audience did not discover so favourable a disposition. They attempted to turn the affair into ridicule, and imputed to intoxication what was manifestly the effect of supernatural influence. "Others mocking, said, These men are full of new wine." Some commentators suppose these mockers to have been inhabitants of Jerusalem, who understood no foreign language, and represent them as acting from ignorance rather than from malice. But the testimony of the strangers was sufficient to have convinced such persons, that there was a real miracle in the case; and it might have been easily known, that the Apostles were sober, from the gravity of their appearance and gestures. The true reason of this calumnious charge is to be found in their opposition to Christ and his religion, which they heard his ministers proclaiming; for it appears from the ninth verse, that besides the languages of foreigners they spoke likewise that of Judea. As the Pharisees, when they saw the miracles of Jesus, malignantly ascribed them to the assistance of Satan; so these men sought to evade this proof of his resurrection and ascension, by pronouncing all that passed to be the effect of intemperance. The evidence in favour of the gospel may be sufficient to convince the understandings of some men, whose hatred to it is so great, that they will neither acknowledge its divine authority, nor abstain from impertinent cavils against it. Infidels sometimes tell us, that it is vain to appeal to the miracles of the New Testament, of which we have no knowledge but by questionable testimony; and that miracles should be wrought in every age, to give men an opportunity of seeing and examining them. But there is no reason to expect, that if this demand should be complied with, their hostility to our religion would cease. The infidels in the first ages of Christianity, are a specimen of the unbelievers of our times. With the most splendid proofs of divine interposition before their eyes, the former continued to contradict and blaspheme; and what ground have we to think that the latter would be more ready to yield? Their opposition proceeds, not from want of evidence, but from want of candour; a temper of mind upon which arguments and demonstration are thrown away. A mind full of prejudice, a heart attached to the world and its pleasures, will always find something to object to a religion which teaches the purest morality, and requires, from those who embrace it, the sacrifice of their corrupt propensities, and unhallowed gratifications.

I shall close this discourse with the following reflections.

Let us, sinners of the Gentiles, consider our interest in this miraculous dispensation, and the obligations which we are under to be thankful for it. It was preparatory to the accomplishment of the gracious designs of heaven towards the nations of the world, who were perishing without a vision, but to whom the salvation of God was now to be revealed. When the law was published from Sinai, it was delivered to the Israelites in their own language, because they were alone to enjoy the benefit of it; but the new law from Sion was promulgated in a diversity of languages, to signify that it was intended to be universal. "Every man was now to hear in his own tongue, the wonderful works of God." "Let us sing a new song to the Lord, because he hath done marvellous things. The Lord hath made known his salvation: his righteousness hath he openly showed in the sight of the heathen."

The event, recorded in this passage, leads us to reflect upon the means by which the Christian religion was established in the earth. "Not by might, nor by power, but by my Spirit, saith the Lord." The first missionaries were destitute of all natural qualifications for their arduous work; and the world was adverse to the reception of the faith. But the same Spirit, who endowed them with supernatural gifts, subdued, by his secret influence, the prejudices, and purified the hearts, of their hearers. The obstacle to the propagation of the gospel, arising from a diversity of languages, was removed when there rested upon each of the Apostles "cloven tongues, like as of fire ;" but there remained other obstacles, of a moral nature, more formidable, which it was still less in the power of human means to surmount. Had the Holy Ghost operated only in a supernatural manner upon the minds of the Apostles, and by miraculous works, the new religion would not have made its way in the earth, opposed as it was by superstition, by philosophy, by the power of the state, and by all the corrupt passions of the soul. But the gospel was the ministration of the Spirit, in his graces as well as in his gifts, in his regeneration as well as in his miraculous virtue. Hence it was "mighty through God to pull down strong holds, and to bring every thought into captivity to Christ."

Lastly, "If the word spoken by angels was steadfast, and every transgression and disobedience received a just recompense of reward; how shall we escape if we neglect so great salvation, which at the first began to be spoken by the Lord, and was confirmed unto us by them that heard him ; God also bearing them witness, both with signs and wonders, and with divers miracles, and gifts of the Holy Ghost, according to his own will ?" These words are full of alarm to open infidels and to secret unbelievers. To the former they announce the certainty, and the dreadful nature of the punishment which awaits them, if they persist in rejecting and vilifying a religion, stamped with such characters of truth. Your sneers and cavils cannot make that false which is true ; and if the gospel is true, as we know it to be, and the best and most enlightened men, in all ages, have believed, think for a moment what will be your doom ! If the gospel is true, so are its threatenings ; and they are awful beyond conception. To the other class of persons, who are secret unbelievers, but call themselves disciples of Jesus, the words of the Apostle suggest matter of serious consideration. You profess to give credit to the gospel, but you do not cordially assent to its doctrines, nor embrace its promises, nor submit to its authority, nor cultivate that holiness of heart and life which it enjoins. Shall a salvation, in its nature so desirable, in the means of its accomplishment so wonderful, be safely despised ? Shall the Son of God be rejected with impunity ? Shall men trample upon his blood, and refuse the testimony of his Spirit, and yet run no hazard ? Is it nothing to call the God of truth a liar? nothing to disregard the wonders of his grace and power? Of all sins, unbelief is the greatest; and persistence in it will terminate in unavoidable and irretrievable ruin. Be persuaded to reflect seriously upon your guilt and danger, and to seek from God the influences of his Holy Spirit, to enlighten your minds and regenerate your hearts, that receiving the Lord Jesus Christ, and "setting to your seal that God is true," you may now obtain an interest in the "great salvation," and may be admitted to the full enjoyment of it in the world to come.

LECTURE III

THE FORMATION AND ORDER OF THE PRIMITIVE CHURCH.

Chap. ii. 37—47.

As the passage now read refers to the preceding part of the chapter, it is necessary to take a summary view of its contents. Our Lord having, according to his promise, poured out the Holy Ghost upon the Apostles, on the day of Pentecost, a mixed multitude of natives and strangers were collected, to whom they published, in their respective languages, "the wonderful works of God." Some were astonished, and eagerly inquired into the cause of that extraordinary event; while others, from malignity against Jesus and his religion, affirmed that the Apostles were intoxicated. To satisfy the inquiries of the one class, and to repel the accusation of the other, Peter rose with his brethren; and having first shown, by a reference to the national manners, that the supposition of drunkenness at so early an hour was destitute of all probability, he informed the audience, that the event which had now taken place was the fulfilment of a prophecy long since delivered by Joel. He then proceeded to the main purpose of his speech, to prove that Jesus of Nazareth is the Messiah. With this view, having reminded them of the miracles performed by our Saviour during his public ministry, which were the seal of heaven affixed to his commission, he boldly charges his hearers with the atrocious crime of putting him to death; but affirms that God had restored him to life, and that it was not possible that death should have retained him under its dominion. This fact, which was the point at issue between the Jews, and the Apostles, he establishes by an argument, the validity of which they would hardly venture to dispute; by an appeal to a prophecy of David. After some reasoning, intended to convince them that the passage which he had cited could not be applied to the Prophet himself, he again asserts the resurrection of

Christ; and he calls upon the house of Israel, who had been favoured with sensible evidence of his exaltation, to acknowledge "that God had made that same Jesus, whom they had crucified, both Lord and Christ." The effect produced by this discourse is worthy of notice.

It awakened compunction, and an eager inquiry with respect to the course which it was necessary for them to pursue. "Now when they heard this, they were pricked in their hearts, and said unto Peter, and to the rest of the Apostles, Men and brethren, what shall we do?" The sentence of death was reluctantly pronounced upon our Lord by the Roman governor, whose conscience attested the innocence of the prisoner at his bar, but who was prevailed upon, by the clamours and menaces of the multitude, to disregard its admonitions. The people, the dupes of their priests and rulers, had conceived the most violent prejudice against Christ as an impostor, and were persuaded that they discovered fervent zeal for the glory of God, and the honour of their holy religion, when they demanded his crucifixion. Some women followed him in the way to Calvary with tears and lamentations; but the deluded, infuriated crowd, beheld his cruel sufferings without pity. In how different a light did their conduct now appear to them, when the evidence of the Messiahship of Jesus flashed conviction on their minds! If ever confusion, remorse, and terror, rushed at once into the bosom of a sinner with irresistible force, it was at this moment, when the Jews learned, that the deceiver whom they had nailed to the cross, the blasphemer whose blood they had shed, was the Redeemer promised to the Church, the Son of the living God, the Lord of heaven and earth. What a crime had they committed! The annals of human guilt could not furnish another of equal atrocity. How dreadful was the punishment which they had reason to expect! Now they remembered their own imprecation, "His blood be on us, and on our children;" and they trembled lest its weight should press them down to the lowest hell. Alarmed and perplexed, tortured with a consciousness of guilt, and dreading the just vengeance of heaven, from which they knew not how to escape, they say to Peter and the rest of the Apostles, "Men and brethren, what shall we do?" They were anxious to hear from these ambassadors of Jesus, whether there was any hope of pardon for so great a crime, any means of protection from the wrath which was ready to overwhelm them.

To this question, Peter, in the name of his brethren, returned the following answer. "Repent, and be baptized every one of you, in the name of Jesus Christ, for the remission of sins, and ye shall receive the gift of the Holy Ghost." One general remark must occur to every person who considers this answer, that the Jews are directed to Jesus himself for the remission of their sins. That blood only, which they had impiously shed, could wash them from guilt; and thus what is true in reference to sinners in general, was particularly illustrated in the case of those men, that "his blood speaketh better things than that of Abel," crying to God for the pardon, not for the punishment, of his enemies and murderers. The particular course which he directs them to take, is repentance and baptism. Repentance cannot here signify remorse and sorrow for sin, for these feelings were already working in their breasts. Nor does it mean the relinquishment of their sins, and the amendment of their lives, because, although reformation will be the undoubted result of contrition of heart, yet there was not time to carry good resolutions into effect prior to baptism, to which the repentance here enjoined was a previous step. The penitent Jews appear to have been immediately baptized. In the present case, therefore, repentance is equivalent to that complete change of views and dispositions which is implied in the cordial reception of the gospel, and consists in a perception of the excellencies of the character of Christ, an approbation of the plan of salvation by his righteousness, and a reliance upon his obedience and blood as the foundation of our acceptance and our hopes. Such sentiments and exercises of mind are very different from those to which the hearers of Peter were accustomed, who had "gone about to establish their own righteousness;" and from those, which are familiar to a natural man, who sees no comeliness or beauty in the Saviour for which he should be desired, and disdains "to submit to the righteousness of God." Yet, till this change, to which the heart is so adverse, and which can be effected only by supernatural power, be experienced, we have no interest in the redemption of Christ; for although God has "set him forth as a propitiation for sin," he becomes actually such to a sinner, only "through faith in his blood."

With repentance, baptism in the name, or by the authority of Christ, is conjoined; and Peter required it from his hearers for the three following reasons: first, as a solemn and public declaration of the change of their views and dispositions, the baptism of Christ being, like that of John, a baptism of repentance; secondly, as a testimony of their subjection to Jesus, by whom this ordinance was appointed; and, lastly, as a sign and seal of the new covenant, by which the remission of sins is represented to all, and confirmed to those who belong to that covenant.

To encourage his hearers to comply with this exhortation, he subjoined the following declaration or promise. "And ye shall receive the gift of the Holy Ghost." When in this book the Holy Ghost is said to be given, the meaning frequently is, that his extraordinary gifts were communicated. This is evident from the cases of those in Samaria who received the word, of Cornelius and his company, and of the disciples of John, who were baptized at Ephesus; and it is observable, that in two of those cases, the persons immediately began to speak with tongues. From these examples, as well as from the consideration, that the words were spoken just after the descent of the Spirit, we may conceive Peter to have assured the Jews, that they should participate of the miraculous gifts which had been conferred upon the Apostles. Yet, as we have no reason to think, notwithstanding the liberal distribution of such gifts in the primitive Church, that they were imparted to every person who believed; it seems proper to interpret the words as referring likewise to the sanctifying influences and comforts of the Spirit, and to consider the Apostle as holding out a promise of these to all, and of extraordinary endowments to such among them as God should be pleased to qualify, in this manner, for the manifestation and establishment of the truth.

"For the promise," he adds, "is unto you, and to your children, and to all that are afar off, even as many as the Lord our God shall call." Many commentators suppose, that he alludes to the promise which God made to Abraham, that "he would be a God unto him, and to his seed after him," with a design to convince the Jews, that by embracing the new religion, they should lose none of the privileges which they enjoyed under the old. The same promise was continued, and gave them and their children a right to baptism, the present seal of the covenant, as both had formerly received the seal of circumcision. If, however, we should rather understand the promise to be that of the Holy Ghost, which the connexion seems to suggest, the same argument may be deduced from it; for if the spirit is promised, not to believers alone, but to their seed, it follows that their seed are taken into the covenant of God, and, consequently, are entitled to that ordinance which represents our participation of its blessings. "Can any man forbid water, that these should not be baptized, which have received the Holy Ghost as well as we?" The Jews were plainly given to understand, that the new dispensation in which they were required to acquiesce, was of an enlarged and liberal nature. Its ample treasury of grace was opened to enrich them and their families; and it is farther suggested, that the Gentiles, although they were now "afar off," should be admitted to a share, when in his own time, "the Lord their God should call them."

To this exhortation he added "many other words;" the purport of which was to excite them "to save themselves from that untoward generation." This character is descriptive of the perverseness with which the unbelieving Jews opposed all the methods of divine grace. Our Saviour had formerly illustrated their conduct by the capriciousness and pettishness of children. "Whereunto shall I liken this generation? It is like unto children sitting in the markets, and calling unto their fellows, and saying, We have piped unto you, and ye have not danced; we have mourned unto you, and ye have not lamented. For John came neither eating nor drinking, and they say, He hath a devil. The Son of Man came eating and drinking, and they say, Behold a man gluttonous, and a wine-bibber, a friend of publicans and sinners." They were offended at the austerity of the Baptist, and imputed it to the influence of an unsocial, melancholy demon; they were equally displeased with the more open and familiar manners of our Lord, and advanced against him a charge of intemperance and licentiousness. A more complete description of frowardness was never given than the following, in the first Epistle to the Thessalonians. "The Jews," says Paul, "both killed the Lord Jesus, and their own Prophets, and have persecuted us; and they please not God, and are contrary to all men." Whatever means were employed for their good, the effect was still the same, obstinate resistance or sullen contempt. Over this incorrigible race the judgments of heaven were impending. There was indeed, a season allowed for repentance, during which the gospel would be preached to them; but as soon as it should expire, unmingled vengeance would overwhelm the ungodly nation. Peter exhorts the awakened Jews to flee from the wrath to come. Joel had long ago foretold the terrors of the day of the Lord, and the salvation of those who should believe. "I will show wonders in the heavens, and in the earth, blood and fire, and pillars of smoke. The sun shall be turned into darkness, and the moon into blood, before the great and the terrible day of the Lord. And it shall come to pass, that whosoever shall call on the name of the Lord shall be delivered: for in mount Zion and in Jerusalem shall be deliverance, as the Lord hath said, and in the remnant whom the Lord shall call."

The success of Peter's sermon is pointed out in the next verse. "Then they that gladly received his word were baptized: and the same day there were added unto them about three thousand souls." Their "receiving his word gladly," signifies their believing and embracing, with joy and gratitude, the tidings of salvation through the crucified Jesus. Such is the reception, which the gospel will not fail to meet with from those, who are awakened to perceive and feel their need of its comforts. A philosopher, a speculatist, who looks upon it merely as a theory, may coolly sit down and discuss its evidence; but the bosom of a convinced and trembling sinner throbs with emotions of desire and transport, when he hears its gracious declarations; and he hastens to lay hold of the offered mercy with the same eagerness, with which a criminal, shuddering under the suspended axe of the executioner, accepts the unexpected pardon of his prince. Their obedience to the gospel was manifested by submission to the ordinance of baptism, in which they at once expressed their faith in Christ, and recognised him as the Lord of their consciences.

We may stop, for a few moments, to consider this transaction as a proof of the sincerity of those converts, of their full conviction of the truth of the gospel. To an acknowledgement of Christ and his religion, the prejudices of education, the example of their friends, the authority of their rulers, and the sacred institutions of Moses, as they were then explained, presented powerful obstacles. They could not become his disciples without the renunciation of early and favourite opinions, and without a sacrifice of principle; and there was every reason to expect, that they should incur the reproaches of their countrymen, as apostates, and experience other effects of their intolerant zeal. Yet these considerations did not deter them from assuming the badge of Christianity; from standing forth as the marked objects of the hatred and scorn of their brethren. And how shall we account for their conduct? It can be explained on no other principle than an irresistible conviction of the truth, a firm belief of the threatenings and promises of the Apostles, the exertion of that almighty energy upon their hearts, which " brings every thought into captivity to Christ." To these causes we attribute the conversion of those Jews; and we perceive to what extent they operated from the number of the converts. By the accession of three thousand persons, our Saviour was pleased to encourage the Apostles, at their outset; and to give a specimen of the rapid success which should afterwards attend the publication of the gospel.

We have seen how the Christian Church was formed. We are next presented with a view of the conduct of its members, in reference to the doctrines and institutions of the gospel. " And they continued steadfastly in the Apostles' doctrine, and fellowship, and in breaking of bread, and in prayers." Each of these particulars deserves to be distinctly considered.

The first is their continuance in " the doctrine of the Apostles." It sometimes happens, that by an artful representation of an object, and a dexterous appeal to his passions, a person is induced to adopt an opinion which he formerly reprobated, and which, upon calm reflection, he will renounce. In the midst of a multitude, a man is hardly master of himself, and is often hurried away by a sympathetic feeling with those around him to form resolutions, which in his cool moments he may see reason to retract. There are instances, too, in which sentiments are embraced, in the hope that they shall be held without trouble or inconvenience, but are abandoned as soon as they are found to be incompatible with reputation and personal safety. The converted Jews had undergone a very sudden change of their views. At the same meeting, at which the pathetic address of Peter operated so strongly upon them, they solemnly declared themselves disciples of Jesus. Yet neither the reflections which they had afterwards leisure to make upon their conduct, nor the difficulties which they soon experienced to be inseparable from their new profession, created any regret at the step which they had taken. The gospel, the more they examined it, appeared the more worthy of all acceptation. Its evidence was strengthened every day by the miracles which were performed before their eyes; and from what passed in their own minds, they felt the same need of its comforts as ever, the same delightful calm, the same ineffable happiness, arising from the belief of its declarations and promises. They continued, therefore, steadfast in the doctrine of the Apostles, fully convinced of its truth, and assured by experience of its excellence.

Luke mentions, in the second place, their steadfastness "in fellowship;" by which is meant the communion of saints in the exercise of evangelical love. The gospel is not a selfish religion. It requires, indeed, every man to take care of his own salvation, and shows it to be of such importance, as to be truly worthy of his care; but it teaches him, at the same time, to take an interest in the temporal and spiritual welfare of his Christian brethren. Upon the basis of brotherly love is reared a system of duties, from the cheerful and conscientious performance of which there results great benefit to the Church, and much honour to religion. By exhorting one another daily, by instructing, and reproving, and comforting, and assisting one another in all good things, Christians fulfil the law of Christ, and act as partakers of the same Spirit, and children of the same Father. In these labours of love the new converts were employed; for, in believing the gospel, they had imbibed that pure spirit of benevolence, which is now so little known, but in those days made the Gentiles say, "Behold how the Christians love one another."

Farther, they continued steadfastly in "the breaking of bread." This phrase does not necessarily mean the Lord's supper, as we shall afterwards see; but being introduced among the religious duties of the primitive Church, it seems, in the present case, to signify that institution, the whole being denominated from a part. Perhaps, the celebration of that solemn ordinance is particularly mentioned, because it was a public and explicit testimony of their attachment to the Saviour, a recognition of their baptismal engagements, an avowal that they gloried in the cross of Christ, which was a stumbling block to their unbelieving countrymen. It is evident that they frequently commemorated his death; but how often they were thus employed, it is impossible to ascertain from this passage. No man in his senses can suppose, that they observed the ordinance as often as they performed the duties of fellowship, and offered up either secret or social prayer. I can find nothing in the New Testament, from which any determinate rule for our conduct can be collected. The arguments for the weekly celebration of the sacred supper, founded on some incidental expressions, are too feeble to authorise the strong and peremptory conclusions which have been drawn from them. Evidence much more ample and decisive would be requisite to justify any religious party, in pronouncing this practice to be a mark of Apostolic purity, and erecting it into a standard, to which other Christians are bound to conform.*

In the last place, we are informed that they continued steadfastly "in prayer." The gospel humbles man, by showing him his meanness and infirmity. It draws him off from presumptuous confidence in himself, and directs him to place his trust and hope in God. Prayer is therefore the natural exercise of a genuine Christian. It

---

* Nothing more can be inferred from this passage, than that the Lord's supper was one of the evangelical institutions, which the disciples were steadfast in observing. The words of Christ, "As often as ye eat this bread, and drink this cup," mean only, " When ye eat and drink, ye show forth my death ;" as if I should say to a friend, " As often as you come to this part of the country, I shall be happy to see you in my house ;" I mean, when he comes, without any reference to the number of times. The chief argument for the weekly celebration of it is drawn from these words, "And upon the first day of the week, when the disciples came together to break bread, Paul preached unto them; Acts xx. 7, from which it is manifest, say the advocates for this opinion, that the Lord's supper was a stated part of the worship of the Church, and that there is the same evidence for the weekly celebration of it as for the observance of the Christian Sabbath. Nay, so distinguished a place did this ordinance occupy in the regular service, that it is mentioned as the main purpose of the meeting. I acknowledge, that the words do imply that it was the main purpose; but for this very reason I conclude, that it was not the usual design of coming together; for I have yet to learn, that the Lord's supper is so much to be preferred to prayer, and praise, and the preaching of the word, as to be the principal cause of holding religious assemblies. Where does the Scripture say or insinuate any such thing ? If there be any purpose for which in preference to others Christians should meet on the first day of the week, it is to hear the gospel, the great appointed mean of promoting the life of God in the soul. Scripture will bear me out in this assertion. When men begin to be zealous about any thing, they often become extravagant, and are not satisfied till they have put it out of its place, and exalted it above all other things. Since then it is agreed, that "to break bread" was the chief intention of the meeting at Troas, I conclude, that the intention was special, not common ; because it cannot be proved from Scripture, or history, or the nature of the ordinance, that to eat the Lord's supper ever was, or ever ought to be, at all times, the principal reason for assembling on the Sabbath. The disciples at Troas probably embraced the opportunity of commemorating the death of Christ, while they enjoyed the presence and ministrations of Paul; and hence this ordinance is represented to have been, because it really was, the design of this meeting. From the words of Paul to the Corinthians, 1 Cor. xi. 17, 20, " You come together not for the better, but for the worse," compared with what he afterwards says, " When ye come together,—this is not to eat the Lord's supper," it has been inferred, that always when they met, they observed this ordinance, because otherwise there would be no force in his argument, that their coming together was for the worse. This is very feeble reasoning. Join the two passages together, and the meaning obviously is, " When you come together, and eat in the riotous manner afterwards described, you come together for the worse." Nothing is asserted but the pernicious consequences of such assemblies; there is not a word about their frequency. I do not, at present, inquire what was the practice of the Church after the death of the Apostles, as I am examining only the arguments from Scripture.

is the language of his necessities. It is the voice of his faith imploring relief from the all-sufficiency of his Maker. It is the mean of bringing almighty power to his aid; of deriving from the infinite stores of divine goodness the supply of his wants. Hence the prayer of a Christian is not an occasional exclamation in a moment of alarm, or the effervescence of transient desire; but is founded in a habitual disposition of mind, a permanent sense of weakness and dependence. It constitutes a part of his daily exercise, without which his spiritual life could no more be preserved than his natural life could be sustained without food. By continuing in prayer, the new converts discovered the ardour of their piety, and were enabled to persevere, amidst difficulties and dangers, in the profession of the truth, and in obedience to the institutions of Christ.

I have given what appears to me to be the genuine sense of this passage; and in doing so have paid no regard to the opinion of some writers, that it is a description of the procedure of the first Christians in their religious assemblies. The opinion receives no countenance from the passage itself, would not occur to an impartial reader unacquainted with the theories of disputants, and is chiefly adopted with a view to establish a favourite point, that the Lord's supper was a stated part of the worship of the primitive Church. But if we take the liberty to explain the Scriptures as we please, there is no doubt that we may prove from them any fancy however extravagant.

Let us now consider the love of the primitive Christians, as displayed in the liberality with which they supplied the necessities of their poor brethren. " And all that believed were together, and had all things common, and sold their possessions and goods, and parted them to all men, as every man had need." The expression, " all that believed were together," does not mean that they were assembled in one place, but that they were united in mind and affection, according to the sense which it bears in some other places of Scripture. " They had all things common." It has been supposed, that there was a real community of goods among the Christians of Jerusalem; or that every man, renouncing all right to his property, delivered it over to a public stock, to which all had an equal claim. It appears, however, from the story of Annanias and Sapphira, that the disciples were under no obligation, or were bound by no positive law, to dispose of their property for the benefit of the Church; and that after it was sold, they could retain the whole, or any part of the price, provided that they did not, like those unhappy persons, practice dissimulation and deceit: and it is farther evident from the passage before us, that although in many instances they laid down the price at the feet of the Apostles, entrusting them with the distribution, yet they sometimes reserved it in their own hands, and gave it to the indigent, according to their own ideas of their need. These considerations seem to prove, that there was not an actual community of goods in the primitive Church, but that, in consequence of the fervent charity which united the hearts and interests of the disciples, "no man," as Luke informs us in the fourth chapter, "said that ought of the things which he possessed was his own," or appropriated them solely to his own use, but readily parted with them for the supply of others. "They parted them to all men, as every man had need." All things were common, because they were at the service of every man who wanted them. On this ground, one of the Fathers said long after, "Among us Christians all things are common," although the practice of selling possessions, and distributing the price to the poor, was discontinued. There is no evidence, that the conduct of the Church of Jerusalem was followed by any other Church, even in the Apostolic age; but so far as it is an example of generous love, triumphing over the selfish affections, and exciting men to seek the welfare of others as well as their own, it is worthy to be imitated to the end of the world.

The words, upon which I shall next make some observations, are contained in the forty-sixth verse, where we are told, that "they continued daily in the temple, and breaking bread from house to house, did eat their meat with gladness and singleness of heart." Attempts have been made to prove, that "breaking bread" here signifies the celebration of the Lord's supper; and it has been inferred, that there was not only a weekly, but a daily observance of that solemn rite in the primitive Church. This, indeed, is sometimes the meaning of the phrase; but partaking of the Lord's supper is nowhere denoted by the familiar expression of "eating our meat." I am persuaded, that to a plain reader, who had no darling notion to support, it would never occur that any thing more was intended, than to inform us how the first Christians conducted themselves in their private intercourse. Prompted by brotherly love, they embraced opportunities of frequently meeting together at their common meals; and, on such occasions, they manifested the influence of the gospel, as well as in the more solemn services of religious worship.

Joy and innocence presided at their frugal repasts. But it was joy different from that which wine inspires, flowing from an assurance of the favour of God, a sense of his love, which gives a relish to the homeliest fare, and the triumphant hope of immortality. " Go thy way, eat thy bread with joy, and drink thy wine with a merry heart; for God now accepteth thy works." At those happy meetings, envy and jealousy did not rankle in the bosoms of the guests, nor were purposes of revenge concealed under the deceitful smile of friendship. All duplicity was banished, and their hearts, purified by divine grace, admitted no sentiments but those of honest, undissembled affection. At their tables they sealed their mutual love, and anticipated the pure felicity, which will circulate from breast to breast in the blessed company, who shall eat bread in the kingdom of God.

I shall farther take notice only of the sentiments with which the rising Church was regarded by the Jews. It was at once the object of veneration and of esteem. It is said, in the forty-third verse, that " fear came upon every soul." With respect to external circumstances, the disciples were a despicable company, composed of persons, for the most part, in the lower classes of society, with some illiterate fishermen and publicans at their head. Yet there were such tokens of the presence and power of God in this assembly, that the spectators could not avoid being impressed with awe. The miracles performed by the Apostles astonished the beholders; and although they did not always produce conviction, made them afraid to treat the disciples with disrespect. " Many wonders and signs were done by the Apostles." At the same time, the character of the first professors of the faith was so amiable, their manners were so pure, and their charity was so unbounded, that they conciliated the good-will of all around them. " They were in favour with the people." Their faith the people might not approve, but their virtues they could not refuse to commend. " He is a good man," said the heathens of a peaceable, beneficent neighbour, " but he is a Christian." The doctrines of our religion may seem mysterious and perplexed, and some of its precepts may be accounted severe; but when it is embodied, if I may speak so, in the conduct of its genuine friends; when it puts on the lovely aspect of meekness, gentleness, and goodness, the hearts of its enemies bear an unequivocal testimony in its favour, and sometimes their lips unwittingly pronounce its eulogium.

Such were the sentiments with which the Jews beheld the primitive Christians; and the impression made upon their minds contributed, through the divine blessing, to bring many of them to the knowledge of the truth. The Church was a growing society. It received daily accessions. The power of God was exerted to carry into effect his purpose of grace with respect to such of the Jewish nation as he had chosen to eternal life. " The Lord added to the Church daily such as should be saved."

I shall conclude with two or three reflections upon the passage.

First, We have before us the pure and perfect model of a Christian Church. The primitive Church was composed of persons awakened and enlightened by the truth, who, having entered into its communion by baptism, continued regular and steadfast in the ordinances and commandments of Christ, and were united by sincere and ardent love. How dissimilar are those societies, the members of which are associated from the mere accident of local situation, or from caprice and prejudice, without knowledge, and without principle; societies made up of such loose and light materials, that a breath of novelty shall blow them asunder, and the most frivolous offence shall occasion their disunion; societies, which having no common purpose, no mutual bond of connexion, are a chaos of discordant elements, in which envy, jealousy, pride, selfishness, calumny, and evil surmisings, produce perpetual agitation and war? Alas! my brethren, we have all departed, more or less, from the Apostolical standard; and we are not likely to return to it, notwithstanding the schemes of improvement which the fertile invention of the present times is almost daily suggesting, till, as in former days, the Spirit be poured out from on high. Then " the wilderness and the solitary place shall be glad, and the desert shall rejoice and blossom as the rose."

In the second place, The mighty efficacy of the word of God is manifest in the sudden and complete conversion of the Jews. " Is not my word like as a fire? saith the Lord: and like a hammer, that breaketh the rock in pieces?" Let it not be supposed, that as the occasion was peculiar, the power exerted was unusual, and ought not to be looked for again. " The Lord's hand is not shortened that it cannot save." " The residue of the Spirit is with him;" and the same effects are still produced in the conversion of every sinner. Some of the prejudices which influenced the Jews may not be entertained by persons educated in a Christian country; but there are other prejudices equally effectual in blinding the mind, and fortifying the heart against conviction, which it is therefore as difficult to overcome. Did we consider how powerful is the dominion of pride, how firmly the interests of sin are established, and how fascinating is the influence of the world, we should be convinced, that the same energy is exerted in modern conversions, as in those which took place in the beginning of the gospel. Hence, in the most unpromising times, we may hope that the interests of religion shall be maintained; and we should never despair of the ultimate triumph of truth over error. The gospel is "mighty through God" to subdue all opposition. When "the Lord shall send the rod of his strength out of Zion, the people shall be willing in the day of his power."

In the last place, We are presented with a powerful argument for the truth of the resurrection and exaltation of Christ. Let it only be admitted, that many of the Jews were converted to Christianity soon after its publication; and this is a fact which no man will venture to dispute. By what means, I ask, was their conversion effected? The Apostles, who addressed them were men of no learning, of no influence, and unskilled in the arts of sophistry and eloquence. And what did they require their hearers to believe? Did they not tell them, that the man whom they had crucified a few weeks before was the Son of God; that there was no way of salvation but by his blood; and that God had raised him from the grave, and exalted him to his right hand in heaven? These were not palatable truths. The Jews could not assent to them, without acknowledging themselves to be the vilest wretches upon earth, guilty beyond all other men, and deserving severer punishment; and without giving up their agreeable dreams, their soothing prospects of worldly grandeur. We cannot suppose, then, that they would receive those truths without evidence so strong, as to force conviction upon their minds. That they did receive them, we know; and we learn from this chapter on what grounds they were satisfied. The account is consistent and probable. Infidelity can give no other, which shall not be liable to unanswerable objections. Assuming, then, that the Holy Ghost was poured out upon the Apostles, and that they were enabled to speak with new tongues, and to work miracles before the eyes of their countrymen, we may demand, by whom the Spirit was sent. Was it not, as they affirmed, by Jesus of Nazareth, who had suffered as a malefactor without the gates of Jerusalem? And could he have sent him, if he had been still lying in the grave? Did it not hence appear, that he had triumphed over death, and was now proceeding to establish that kingdom which he had shed his blood to obtain? Christians, the Lord is risen indeed. "He hath ascended up on high, and led captivity captive." Infidels may cavil and blaspheme; but assured by evidence, from which they perversely turn away their eyes, that he lives and reigns, we hail him Lord of all. "And he must reign, till all his enemies be put under his feet." "Arise, O Lord, and let thine enemies be scattered; but let them that love thee be as the sun, when he goeth forth in his might."

LECTURE IV.

THE LAME MAN CURED BY PETER AND JOHN.

Chap. iii. 1—16.

The Apostles were commissioned to promulgate a religion, which, notwithstanding its intrinsic excellence, the world was ill disposed to receive. To the Jews, superstitiously attached to the ritual of Moses, and persuaded of its perpetuity, it appeared in the light of an impious heresy; a bold attempt to substitute the crude notions of an upstart teacher in the room of the oracles of heaven. On the part of the Gentiles, accustomed to pompous ceremonies, and the unrestrained license, in which the ancient systems of idolatry indulged their votaries, its pure doctrines, and simple institutions were calculated to excite sentiments of aversion and contempt. The prejudices, with which the gospel had to contend, were not likely to be removed by the character and qualifications of its first preachers. They were not men who could command respect by their talents and their rank. They were poor and illiterate; they had sat at the feet of no Jewish doctor, and frequented the school of no heathen philosopher. Coming from the lips of such men, the religion of Jesus must have presented itself under new disadvantages, in consequence of the awkward manner, and unpolished style, in which they may be conceived to have delivered it. Whence, then, did it succeed? What precautions were taken to prevent it from being rejected by universal consent? To the fishermen and publicans of Galilee, upon whom had devolved the important office of converting the world, Jesus communicated powers of an extraordinary kind, by which they were better qualified for their work than if they had possessed the treasures of human learning and eloquence. While, by the descent of the Holy Ghost, they were inspired with the knowledge of foreign languages, and could address every man in his own tongue upon the subject of their mission, they were enabled to perform such wonderful works as awakened the attention of the spectators, and were undoubted evidences of the divine authority of their doctrine. Incidental mention is made of their miracles towards the close of the preceding chapter. "Many wonders and signs were done by the Apostles." In the passage now read, one is selected as a specimen; and as it was accompanied with several important circumstances, which throw light upon the general design of miracles, and the character of the Apostles, it deserves to be particularly considered.

The occasion of performing this miracle was a visit paid by two of the Apostles, Peter and John, to the temple, for the purpose of devotion. "Now Peter and John went up together into the temple, at the hour of prayer, being the ninth hour." The Jews had stated hours of prayer, the third, the sixth, and the ninth, corresponding to nine in the morning, twelve at noon, and three in the afternoon, according to our division of the day. Two of those hours coincided with the appointed times of offering the daily sacrifices, when those pious Israelites, who resided in Jerusalem, resorted to the temple, that while the smoke ascended from the altar and the censers of the priests, they might present the nobler oblation of holy supplications and thanksgivings. The Apostles, in this instance, complied with the practice of their country, without any intention to bind Christians in succeeding ages, to fixed hours of religious worship, or to represent any particular place as rendering prayer more acceptable to God. Our Churches are quite different from the temple, which was a consecrated house, the chosen habitation of the God of Israel. It is probable, too, that they had another reason for going up to it at this time, namely, to embrace the opportunity of addressing the people, when a considerable number was assembled.

The person, upon whom the miracle was performed, was afflicted with a lameness, incurable by any means which human skill could employ; for it did not proceed from an accidental dislocation of the joints, which might have been reduced, nor from temporary debility, which would have been gradually removed as he regained his strength, but from an original defect, or derangement of the parts. He was therefore a fit subject for displaying a supernatural power with which the Apostles were endowed by their Master, because, among those who were acquainted with the case, there could be no question, if a cure was performed, whether it had been effected by ordinary or miraculous means. There was no room for discussion with respect to what nature itself could do, or what surprising effects might be produced upon the bodily frame, by the force of imagination, by sudden and violent emotions of fear and joy, or by hope calling forth some latent energy, and dissipating, as by magic influence, the langour or infirmity which had long oppressed the patient. The interposition of heaven would be too evident to be obscured by plausible theories and sophistical cavils. Even if his lameness might have been cured in infancy, it had now acquired an inveteracy which the most perfect art should have laboured in vain to subdue. His situation was well known to the inhabitants of Jerusalem; for being unable to work for his subsistence, and having no friends who could or would support him, he was carried daily to one of the gates of the temple, at which he lay imploring the compassion and charity of passengers. The place was well chosen, as it may be justly expected, that if our hearts shall ever be disposed to relieve the necessities of our brethren, it will be in those moments when they are awake to religious sentiments, and we are going to implore from our heavenly Father mercy to ourselves. "And a certain man, lame from his mother's womb, was carried, whom they laid daily at the gate of the temple, which is called Beautiful, to ask alms of them that entered into the temple."

It is not a matter of any importance to inquire upon what gate of the temple the epithet Beautiful was bestowed. It was probably a gate of which Josephus informs us, that it surpassed all the rest in the richness of its materials, and the splendour of its ornaments; and, from the purpose for which it was chosen by the lame man, it seems to have been the principal entrance. The mention of its name, however, suggests some observations which it may be useful to state, upon the marks of truth to be found in the record of the miracles of the gospel. When a story is told in general terms, without date, or place, or any circumstance which an inquirer might lay hold of to ascertain its reality, there is reason to suspect it to be a fiction, or at least, that the writer knows nothing about it but by vague and uncertain tradition. But when an event is related with a detail of particulars, with a specification of the time when, and the spot on which, it happened, and of the witnesses who were present, we are induced to believe that the narrator was fully assured of its truth, and considered it as capable of bearing the strictest investigation. There is always some truth, it has been remarked, where there is considerable particularity.* If we apply this remark to the miracles recorded in the New Testament, we shall perceive a strong presumption at least of their credibility. The time when, and the persons upon whom, they were performed, are mentioned; the witnesses are described by their names, by their station, or by some other circumstance which sufficiently distinguishes them, and even the enemies of Jesus Christ and his religion are appealed to for the truth of the relation; and all this was done, while the witnesses, whether friends or enemies, were alive.

In the present case, Luke does not content himself with saying, that on a certain occasion, the Apostles, somewhere in Judea, cured a lame man; but he points out the individual by such marks as are equivalent to giving his name. He is represented as a sort of public person, having been often seen by those who frequented the temple; the gate at which he was wont to lie is specified; and thus an opportunity was given to every reader at that time to bring the narrative to the test. No reason can be conceived why Luke has inserted, in a history so concise, a circumstance apparently of so little importance, as his being laid at the gate of the temple called Beautiful, but his knowledge that what he was writing was true, and his willingness to subject it to the most scrupulous examination. Impostors do not write in this manner. They dread inquiry, and use every precaution to elude it.

The lame man begged alms from all the passengers, from the poor as well as from the rich; and perhaps he often found, that the former were more ready to give their mite than the latter to bestow their larger sums. The mitred priest might have passed him without notice, while the humble mechanic stopped to share with him the scanty earnings of his industry. There was nothing in the appearance of Peter and John to encourage him to expect much from them, for in their dress and manner they were evidently persons of the lowest rank; yet the cripple, as soon as he saw them, began the wonted tale of distress, entreating them, we may presume, to help him for the sake of the God whom they were about to adore. And as their attention was attracted by his piteous story, he hoped to see them draw forth from their little store

---

* Paley's View of the Evidences of Christianity, vol. i. 332—334.

something to relieve his necessities. His expectation was the more excited by the words of the Apostles, requiring him to look upon them, which he construed as an intimation of their purpose to give alms; whereas their design was to fix his attention upon the miracle which they intended to perform. "Who seeing Peter and John about to go into the temple, asked an alms. And Peter fastening his eyes upon him, with John, said, Look on us. And he gave heed unto them, expecting to receive something of them."

But how must the poor man have been surprised and disappointed on hearing the following declaration from Peter? "Silver and gold have I none." "What," he might have said, "have you indeed no money? Why, then, did you excite my expectation? Might you not have passed on, as many others have done, without giving heed to my petition? Surely it is enough that misery is left to pine away in neglect; it is the wantonness of cruelty to pour into its cup the bitter ingredient of mockery." "No;" said Peter, "I have neither silver nor gold; but I have something better to give; in the name of Jesus Christ of Nazareth, rise up and walk." This was a new kind of alms, of which the cripple had no expectation. All the physicians in Judea could not have imparted vigour to his limbs; and how could he presume, that these plain, uneducated men, were possessed of superior skill! But it is not by their own skill that they accomplish the cure; the miracle is performed in the name of Jesus of Nazareth. "Who is he?" might the lame man have replied. "Is he not the same person who was lately crucified without the gates of the city; over whose fall the priests and rulers exulted; and whose name is never mentioned but in terms of reproach and execration?" But he had not leisure to reason in this manner; for no sooner had Peter commanded him to rise, than "he took him by the right hand, and lift him up; and immediately his feet and ankle-bones received strength." Observe the simple yet authoritative manner in which the miracle is performed. No solemn preparations are made, no mystic ceremonies are used, which might work upon the imagination of the patient, and excite his reverence and admiration of the persons of the Apostles. By a few words, pronounced in a serious unaffected manner, the effect is produced. It is thus that divine power is exerted. It stands in no need of any artifice to set it off, of any ostentatious display to raise the wonder of the beholders.

Its works are sufficient to awaken, by their own grandeur, the strongest emotions of astonishment and awe.

"Silver and gold have I none." The apostles were poor when they connected themselves with Christ; and it was not in the hope of improving their circumstances that they became his disciples; for what could they expect from a Master who had not "where to lay his head?" They were, indeed, furnished with powers of an extraordinary nature, which, in the hands of persons of different views, would have been converted into means of accumulating wealth. Willingly, we may believe, would those have loaded them with gifts, whom they rescued from the languor of sickness, and the agonies of pain; and those to whose arms they had brought back their beloved friends from the grave. But their Lord enjoined a disinterested exercise of their miraculous powers. "Freely ye have received, freely give." The missionaries resembled the Author of our religion, who wrought many miracles to relieve the distresses of others, and sometimes to supply their bodily necessities, but never exerted his power to provide for his own wants, except in a single instance, when Peter was sent to draw a fish out of the sea, with a piece of money in its mouth, to be applied to the payment of tribute. There were other opportunities of acquiring riches, which they might have improved, if these had possessed any charms in their eyes. The new converts of Christianity, under the influence of the most generous love to their brethren, sold their possessions, and laid the price at the feet of the Apostles, who thus became sole trustees of large sums of money. Their characters were free from suspicion; and such was the confidence placed in their integrity, that no disciple would have thought it necessary to demand an account of their management. Here, then, was an occasion, which private interest, had any regard to it lurked in their breasts, would not have neglected. And how often has avarice, carefully concealing itself under a cloak of religion and disinterested zeal, secretly stretched out its hand to appropriate that wealth which it affected to despise? "My vow of poverty," said a monk, "has brought me a revenue of a hundred thousand crowns." How great do the Apostles appear! how high do they rise in the estimation of every man who can appreciate moral worth, when they hold up hands which no bribe had touched, no unlawful gain had polluted! Dispensing the treasures of the Church under the control of no superintendent, and without the fear of a reckoning, they could say with a clear conscience, "Silver and gold have we none." Certainly, such men were sincere; it was from conviction that they preached the resurrection of Jesus; and if they be suspected of a design to deceive, there is an end to all confidence in human testimony.

I cannot pass on to the sequel of the story, without calling your attention, for a few moments, to a heathen miracle, which has been confidently brought forth to confront the miracles of the gospel.* Let us compare it with the miracle now under consideration, that we may perceive on which side the strength of the evidence lies. It is related by a celebrated Roman historian, that when Vespasian was in Alexandria, a lame man applied to him for a cure, pretending that he had been directed to make the application by Serapis, one of the Gods of the Egyptains. The emperor at first treated the request with derision; but being urged by the earnest petitions of the man, and the flattery of his followers, he commanded some physicians to inquire into the case, who reported, that the lameness was such as might be removed by means of a due degree of force; and added, that if the attempt should not succeed, the laughter of the public would not be turned against him, but against the credulous sufferer. By these representations, Vespasian was induced to make a trial, and a cure immediately ensued.† But what is there in this silly story, which can be reasonably opposed to the miracle before us! The performer was a mighty prince, by the terror of whose power any exact inquiry into the transaction was prevented. The spectators were his friends and partisans, who were eager to have his title to the throne confirmed by the Gods, and a superstitious populace, disposed implicitly to believe whatever reflected honour upon their favourite Deity. The lameness itself was doubtful. It was confessed by competent judges to be curable by ordinary means; and there is reason to suspect that it was a mere pretence. The whole seems to have been an imposture, contrived and carried on for political purposes. Is it necessary to point out the difference of the miracle which we are now considering? As the subject of it had been a cripple from his birth, there could be no deception in the case. The persons who performed the miracle were

---

* Hume's Essays, vol. ii. 137.

† Tacit. Hist. iv. 81. Tacitus and Suetonius, in whose life of Vespasian we find the same account, relate another miracle, performed upon a blind man, which is liable to the same objections. In vita Vespas. cap. 7.

poor unfriended men; and the cause, which it was meant to serve, was unpopular. It was performed at the gate of the temple, which was under the jurisdiction of the enemies of Christ; and the priests and rulers were interested, for the credit of their religion, and the vindication of their conduct in putting our Saviour to death, to detect the fraud, if any had been practised. Every circumstance renders the one miracle suspicious; and every circumstance demonstrates the truth of the other. No person, I will venture to say, would think of bringing the former into competition with the latter, except one who is so blinded by his malice against the gospel, as to be incapable of distinguishing the degrees of evidence, or is determined to contend against it in spite of his convictions.

The following description is picturesque. "And he leaping up, stood, and walked, and entered with them into the temple, walking, and leaping, and praising God." The sacred historian writes without art; but by following nature, and drawing from the life, he has finished a painting, in which the emotions of the soul, in a moment of sudden joy, are represented with truth. Some men, however, can admire nothing of this nature, unless they find it in a heathen or a profane author; their taste is partial as well as their judgment. We see the lame man trying his new powers. He stands, he leaps, he walks, he follows his benefactors into the temple, and mingles with the demonstrations of his joy the praises of God, by whose power he had been cured. He felt a pleasure in the use of his limbs, which he could not conceal. His gestures and motions were those of a man, whom unexpected happiness has almost rendered frantic. Thus the words of the Prophet were literally fulfilled. "Then shall the lame man leap as an hart."

He was instantly recognised by the people in the temple. "And all the people saw him walking and praising God. And they knew that it was he who sat for alms at the beautiful gate of the temple: and they were filled with wonder and amazement at that which had happened unto him." They were not long in suspense with respect to the persons by whom this unquestionable miracle was performed; for the man "held Peter and John," with a design to point them out to the people, or, perhaps, in the present tumult of his mind, not well knowing what he did. A crowd was immediately collected, and gazed upon them with wonder and reverence, as men high in favour with heaven, who had rendered themselves worthy, by the piety of their lives, to be invested with extraordinary powers. This was a situation which would have been hazardous to most men, and from which few would have made their escape with safety. Admiration is apt to make us forget ourselves and our duty, and often stimulates vanity to advance the most arrogant pretensions and to act with extravagance. Almost upon every mind it exercises some degree of influence; but it operates, with peculiar force, upon those to whom it is new, whose condition in life seemed to preclude them from the hope of distinction, and who find themselves suddenly brought out of obscurity to be the objects of public notice and applause. This was exactly the temptation to which the apostles were exposed. Men, who had spent the former part of their lives in a humble station, and in manual labour, are looked upon as beings of a superior order; and the wondering populace are disposed to give them all the glory of the miracle. Had there been any latent spark of vanity in their bosoms, the breath of admiration would have kindled it into a flame. But they, who had already resisted the allurements of avarice, now triumph over the charms of ambition. Instead of appropriating the respect and homage of the multitude, they transfer them to their Master. " And when Peter saw it, he answered unto the people, Ye men of Israel, why marvel ye at this? or why look ye so earnestly on us, as though by our own power, or holiness, we had made this man to walk?" He repels the supposition that they had performed this miracle by their own power, or had obtained power to perform it by their holiness. Their office was merely ministerial; and it was not in consideration of their personal merit, or with an intention to exalt them in the eyes of others, that authority had been delegated to them. Miraculous powers were not conferred for show, or as the reward of obedience; but solely for the purpose of verifying a divine commission, or attesting a revelation from heaven.

The design of the present miracle is expressed by the Apostle himself. " The God of Abraham, and of Isaac, and of Jacob, the God of our fathers hath glorified his Son Jesus: whom ye delivered up, and denied him in the presence of Pilate, when he was determined to let him go. But ye denied the Holy One and the Just, and desired a murderer to be granted unto you, and killed the Prince of Life, whom God hath raised from the dead; whereof we are witnesses. And his name, through faith in his name, hath made this man strong, whom ye see and know; yea, the faith which is by him, hath given him this perfect soundness, in the presence of you all." Jesus of Nazareth lately appeared among them, calling himself the Messiah, and the Son of God. His claims were not admitted by the Jewish nation. They were opposed with violence; and the contest issued in his death, under the imputed crimes of imposture and blasphemy. God had interposed to vindicate the character of Christ, and had reversed the sentence of his unjust and impious judges, by raising him from the dead. It was to prove the truth of this event, to attest it in such a manner, that those who had not seen it might have sufficient ground to believe it, that the power of working miracles was granted to the Apostles. They did not, therefore, perform them in their own name, nor by a simple invocation of the God of Israel, but in the name of Jesus; pointing him out as the Author of those wonderful works, the source of the power by which they were effected. It was in this way that the use of his limbs was restored to the lame man. Was it not an obvious inference from this view of the case, that Jesus of Nazareth was the very person whom he had announced himself to be, the expected Saviour of Israel? Had he been still in the state of the dead, he could have imparted no extraordinary powers to his disciples; nor would there have been more virture in his name than in that of any other deceased malefactor. It being manifest, then, that he had triumphed over death, and was invested with sovereign authority, the house of Israel were bound to acknowledge him as the Messiah, and to embrace his religion. Thus the Apostles acted the part of faithful servants, concerned only for the glory of their Master, and willing to retire from view, that he alone might be contemplated and admired. "Look not earnestly on us; but consider Jesus, whom the God of your fathers hath glorified."

But why does Peter, when addressing the Jews on the subject of this miracle, introduce the mention of their crime, mixing reproaches with his reasoning? This is not the manner of an artful deceiver. He would have soothed and flattered his audience, and by avoiding every offensive term, by using soft and palliating language, would have endeavoured to remove their prejudices, and to render them favourably disposed. What but a conviction of the truth, and firm confidence in the patronage of heaven, could have induced the Apostle to bring forward a subject so unwelcome and ungrateful to the feelings of his hearers? "Jesus of Nazareth was the Son of God, but ye delivered him up, and pursued him with unrelenting hostility, against the remonstrances of his judge: he was the Prince of Life, but ye killed him." It was not merely from zeal for his beloved Master, that this unseasonable and dangerous honesty, as politicians would have called it, proceeded, but from a concern for the best interests of his countrymen. They were chargeable with a crime of the most aggravated nature, of which their consciences did not at present accuse them, because they were unacquainted with the real character of him whom they had nailed to the cross. It was the wish of Peter to make them sensible of the atrocity of that action, to apprize them of the danger to which they were exposed, and, while they trembled at the thought of divine vengeance, to conduct them for safety to that blood which they had impiously shed. And what fitter opportunity could he have chosen for his purpose than the present, when they were astonished at the miracle wrought in the name of the crucified Jesus, which demonstrated, that, although men had rejected and condemned him, he was the object of the approbation of God? The hearts of the Jews were in a state susceptible of the feelings of remorse and fear. Now, their guilt could be held up to view, with the best prospect of alarming their consciences; and it might be hoped, that an exhortation to repentance would be tendered with effect. Accordingly, it appears that Peter did not speak to them in vain; for we are informed, in the next chapter, that "many of them which heard the word believed; and the number of the men was about five thousand."

And now, my brethren, since the God of Abraham, Isaac, and Jacob, has glorified his Son; since he has testified his approbation of him by many "infallible proofs," let us consider, that we are under an obligation to embrace his gospel with the full consent of our minds. Our persuasion of its truth should be in proportion to the evidence. Why were so many miracles performed, and for what reason were they recorded, but that they who saw them, and we who read the account, should believe that Jesus is the Christ, the Son of the living God? That a man shall be savingly convinced of the truth of the gospel by external evidence, it would betray ignorance of the Scriptures to affirm; but that evidence is sufficient to produce a rational conviction of the divine origin of Christianity, to prove that the gospel is indeed the testimony of God, which ought to be believed, and to establish our faith against the suggestions of Satan, and the objections of his coadjutors among men. Let us pray, that the account of the evidence with which our religion was confirmed, may have its due effect upon our minds; and that what has been fully attested, we may be disposed to receive with an undoubting assent.

Let us learn from the passage now explained, to join together prayers and alms, that both may come up as a memorial before God; to do good to our brethren with the means which we possess, distributing our worldly substance to relieve their necessities, or bestowing upon them our sympathy, attendance, consolations, and instructions, in imitation of the Apostles, who gave what they had; and, finally, to ascribe to Jesus Christ the glory of all our qualifications and good actions, never daring to arrogate to ourselves any portion of the praise, or to thrust ourselves forward as objects of notice and commendation, but endeavouring to fix our own attention, and that of others, upon his grace, which has "wrought all our works in us." Do we profess firmly to believe, and cordially to embrace the gospel? It is only by submitting to its institutions, by obeying its laws, by displaying its spirit in our temper and conduct, that we can prove our regard to it to be sincere. It will be evident that we have received the truth in love, when we imitate the noble examples which are set before us, and above all, that of our Redeemer; when we cultivate the dispositions which our religion requires; when devotion, humility, and charity, exert their united influence upon our hearts. Let us then go forth and practise in the world what we assemble to learn in the Church. In the present age, when the distinguishing truths of the gospel are boldly called in question, and its evidence is rejected by many as defective, let us come forward as its friends, not only by argumentation, which often fails to convince, because the heart is indisposed, but by exhibiting in our lives its amiable character, by cultivating those mild virtues which it inspires. The Apostles enforced their instructions by example, made proselytes by the purity of their manners and their deeds of beneficence, as well as by their miracles. Let us do likewise; and while religion shall be exhibited in its native excellence, and shown to be worthy of its author Jesus Christ, and of God, who is said to have patronised it, in a visible manner, at its first publication, we shall enjoy the esteem of the wise and good, the testimony of conscience in our favour, and, what is best of all, the approbation of our Saviour and Lord. "Whosoever shall confess me before men, him will I confess also before my Father which is in heaven."

LECTURE V.

PETER AND JOHN EXAMINED BY THE COUNCIL.

Chap. iv. 1—22.

In the last Lecture, I considered the miracle performed by the Apostles upon a lame man, who lay at the gate of the temple called Beautiful, and illustrated part of the discourse which they delivered, on that occasion, to the people. Although the opportunity was tempting to vanity, as it would have been easy to pass themselves for extraordinary persons upon the wondering multitude; yet these honest and humble disciples of Jesus disclaimed the honour of the cure, and transferred all the glory of it to their Master. Their minds were too strongly convinced of his excellence and dignity, and their hearts were too sensible of his love, to permit them to harbour any purpose but that of exalting him in the eyes of their countrymen, and gaining them over to his religion. With this view, they boldly affirmed, in the presence of his murderers, that he was the Holy One and the Just; and called upon them to acknowledge him as the great Prophet, whom the Church was bound implicitly to obey.

In the mean time, intelligence of these proceedings was conveyed to the men in power, by some of their zealous partisans, who had mingled with the crowd, and in whom the miracle and doctrine of the Apostles had awakened no sentiments but those of hostility. Alarmed at the information, the priests, the captain of the temple, and the Sadducees came in haste, and laid violent hands upon Peter and John, and committed them to prison. The situation of affairs was so serious as to call for some prompt and decisive measure. We are told, that " they were grieved, because the Apostles taught the people, and preached through Jesus the resurrection from the dead." On looking back to their discourse, we do not observe this doctrine mentioned; but the resurrection of Jesus himself is expressly affirmed, and that of his followers is an obvious and necessary inference from it. Both were alike offensive to the rulers of the Jews; the one, because it disclosed a secret which they had taken great pains to conceal, and defeated their design in putting our Saviour to death; the other, because it was opposed to the doctrine of the Sadducees, who maintained, that death terminates the existence of man, and, consequently, that his body is consigned to the grave, under a sentence of eternal imprisonment. It is not improbable that Peter and John had introduced the latter subject in their address to the people; for their discourses are not always given at full length, but, in some cases at least, we have only the principal topics, or an abridgment of what they delivered.

But the priests and Sadducees, although they hastened to the place with all the speed of affronted pride, and irritated zeal, came too late to prevent the effect which they dreaded. The seeds of heresy, as these churchmen would have said, were already sown, and had taken deep root in the hearts of many of the Jews. The Apostles had infused their own sentiments into the breasts of their hearers. The word of God, delivered by these Galilean fishermen with much simplicity, but with the earnestness of conviction, and in the demonstration of the Spirit, had made an impression, which not all the arts of sophistry, nor all the terrors of persecution, could afterwards erase. " Howbeit, many of them which heard the word believed; and the number of the men was about five thousand." This number is quite distinct from the three thousand converted on the day of Pentecost; and it would be idle to spend time in proving what is plain to every reader. These are all the remarks which I think it necessary to make upon the four introductory verses. Let us proceed to the account of the appearance of Peter and John before the council.

" And it came to pass on the morrow, that their rulers, and elders, and scribes, and Annas the high-priest, and Caiaphas, and John, and Alexander, and as many as were of the kindred of the high-priest, were gathered together at Jerusalem." This seems to be a description of the Sanhedrim, or the supreme council of the Jewish nation, which was composed of the High-Priest, as president, the Elders of the people, and the Scribes who were learned in the law. As its jurisdiction extended to all causes relating to religion, we perceive for what reason it was assembled on this occasion. A new sect had appeared, which threatened to overthrow the established faith, and purposed to erect upon its ruins the doctrines and institutions of Jesus of Nazareth. When the members of this council *condemned him to be crucified,* they flattered themselves that his cause would be buried in the same grave with himself. But three full days had not elapsed, when the report of his resurrection, brought by the very men whom they had stationed to watch his sepulchre, filled them with perplexity and terror. Yet, instead of yielding to the evidence, of which it was impossible to entertain any suspicion, these obstinate sinners, resolved, it should seem, to brave heaven itself, contrived a story, which, they hoped, would retain the people in their error. "Say ye, His disciples came by night, and stole him away while we slept." Thus their minds were again at rest. At rest, did I say? No; they might force their countenances to be cheerful, and repeat, with an air of confidence, the charge of imposture against Christ; but their hearts misgave them, and they secretly trembled at the name which they publicly blasphemed.

The time passed on, and for several weeks nothing more was heard about him, or his disciples, till suddenly it was rumoured abroad, that they had appeared in Jerusalem on the day of Pentecost, and were addressing, in their respective languages, strangers from every country under heaven. This surprising information must have stirred up afresh all the fears of the Sanhedrim, whose minds were ill at ease; but as we hear of no measure adopted by them on the occasion, they perhaps persuaded themselves, that it was only a sudden burst of zeal on the part of the followers of Jesus, which had been magnified into a miracle by the credulity of the populace. But now, finding that the Apostles persisted in maintaining the resurrection of their Master, that they were attracting the attention of the public, that they were becoming popular, that converts to their cause were fast multiplying, and that they were actually performing miracles in confirmation of their doctrine, they judged it high time to bestir themselves, and to make some great effort to save their honour and interests, which were in imminent danger.

The council was assembled; and Peter and John having been brought out of prison, and placed at the bar, the president demanded, with a stern countenance, we may presume, and in an authoritative tone, "By what power, or by what name, have ye done this?"

The question was not necessary for the information of the judges, who knew well that they were disciples of Jesus; but they wished to draw from their own lips a confession, upon which they could found their proceedings; or they hoped, that overawed by the presence of so high and venerable an assembly, they would make a retractation. And had fear induced the Apostles to dissemble, and to attribute the miracle, not to Jesus of Nazareth, but to the God of Israel, their declaration would have been triumphantly published, as an everlasting check to the progress of Christianity. But Peter and John were not to be intimidated. They knew that they had truth on their side; and, according to the promise of their Saviour, they received, on this trying occasion, extraordinary assistance. "Then Peter, filled with the Holy Ghost, said unto them, Ye rulers of the people, and elders of Israel, if we this day be examined of the good deed done to the impotent man, by what means he is made whole; be it known unto you, and to all the people of Israel, that by the name of Jesus Christ of Nazareth, whom ye crucified, whom God raised from the dead, even by him doth this man stand here before you whole." "The question relates to the cure of the lame man; and you inquire by what means it has been effected. Know, then, that we have performed it by no power or holiness of our own, by no demoniacal or magical influence, nor simply, like the Prophets, in the name of Jehovah, the God of our fathers; but in the name, and by the authority, of Jesus our Master, with a design to prove that he is the Son of God, and the Messiah." You observe no evasion in this answer, no reluctance to bring out the truth, no attempt to palliate it, although Peter knew that it was in the highest degree offensive to his audience. There is a studied plainness and explicitness in his words, manifestly indicating a mind, which, instead of being ashamed, gloried in the truth, and was careless of the personal consequences which might flow from the publication of it. Not content with simply avowing it, he ventures upon a direct accusation of his judges. It was not a time to flatter: the glory of his Master, the dignity of the Apostolical office, and the real interest of those whom he addressed, forbade such complaisance. "Whom ye crucified." "By that same man, with whose innocent blood your hands are yet stained, has this incontrovertible miracle been performed. We are only his ministers. In vain did you combine against him. In vain, while Providence permitted you to carry your malice so far, did you nail him to the cross. You could not defeat the purposes of heaven, and prevent his entrance into his glory and his kingdom. The right hand of his Father restored the life which you wickedly took away, and has invested the insulted and rejected Saviour with all power in heaven and earth." Every word was a sharp arrow, piercing the hearts of those enemies of the King. Oh! the torture which they must have felt, while those contemptible men braved them to the face, and compelled them to hear their own shame and condemnation. The order of things is reversed. The prisoners at the bar are the accusers; and the judges on the bench are the self-convicted criminals.

"This is the stone, which was set at nought of you builders, which is become the head of the corner." The priests and rulers had often sung these words of the Psalmist, and felt, or thought that they felt, holy indignation against the froward and impious men, whose conduct they describe. They never suspected, that the portrait, which they surveyed with so much detestation, was drawn for themselves. "But you," said the Apostle, "are the builders, who have refused to admit that stone which is now the head of the corner." It was incumbent upon them, as ministers of God, and workers together with him, to contribute their endeavours to carry on that structure, which he purposed to erect for the glory of his mercy and wisdom. In prosecution of this design, they were required, when Jesus Christ, who was described in prophecy as "the stone which God should lay in Zion," came into the world, to assign to him his proper place in the building, by acknowledging him to be the Messiah, and calling upon the people to believe in him, and to submit to his authority. But, without regarding the evidence of his divine mission, and inquiring into his qualifications for saving them from sin and death, they opposed his pretensions, because he wanted external splendour, because he promised neither wealth nor worldly honours to his followers, because he did not offer to deliver the nation from the Roman yoke, and to give them the empire of the world. For these reasons the builders threw this stone aside as useless. "But God's thoughts were not as their thoughts; neither were his ways as their ways." The despised and neglected stone he raised to the most elevated and important place in the building. Upon the crucified Saviour he conferred glory and authority, constituting him the head of the Church, the centre of union to his people, the bond which connects Jews and Gentiles, and composes of both one holy temple in the Lord. "The man," said the Apostle, "whom you treated with contempt, and put to death in an ignominious manner, is seated at the right hand of the Father, and is entitled to the homage and obedience of angels and men."

It was manifest, then, that Jesus was the only Saviour; and, consequently, that no person could reject him but at his peril. "Neither is there salvation in any other: for there is none other name under heaven given among men, whereby we must be saved." Some suppose the meaning of these words to be, that the name of Jesus was the only name which had virtue, when pronounced, to effect miraculous cures; and that there is a literal reference to the question of the Sanhedrim, "By what name have ye done this?" They think that the council in their question, and Peter in his answer, had respect to a notion which prevailed among the Jews, and other nations that there was a power in certain names, to cure diseases. This foolish opinion was adopted by some of the more superstitious Fathers of the Church.* Although, however, it be true, that the use of any other name than that of Jesus would have proved inefficient in an attempt to work a miracle; yet I apprehend, that the words before us contain a higher and more important sense. Salvation signifies something greater than deliverance from bodily affliction, namely, the redemption of the whole man from sin and death; and Peter declares that it is only through faith in Christ that this salvation can be enjoyed. This is a truth, which, although opposed with virulence by the Jews, is believed by Christians upon satisfactory evidence. Disputes have arisen among us with respect to the extent of redemption, that is, with respect to the situation and character of the persons to whom its benefits are applied; but no doubt remains with those, who, in forming their opinions, are determined by the express authority of Scripture, that the future happiness of men must, in one way or other, be attributed to his mediation. His name gives hope and joy to the guilty. It is in his blood that we see the price of our pardon; in his grace, the means of our restoration to the divine image; in his promises, the sure ground on which we expect immortality. The gospel exhibits him alone as the object of our faith; and no other was pointed out by the Prophets.

Let us consider the effect of Peter's speech upon the council. The most furious passions, we may well believe, boiled in their

---

* Origen. contra Celsum, lib. i. 18—20. iv. 183, 184. v. 261, 262.

breasts; but such was the force of truth, that they were confounded and silenced. " Now when they saw the boldness of Peter and John, and perceived that they were unlearned and ignorant men, they marvelled, and they took knowledge of them that they had been with Jesus. And beholding the man which was healed standing with them, they could say nothing against it." The men, whom our Saviour chose to be the preachers of his religion, and the advocates of his cause, seemed, from their want of natural and acquired qualifications, to be altogether unfit for so important an office. They were acquainted with the subtilties of logic, and the arts of eloquence. They could not compose discourses, in which the artful disposition of the arguments, the plausible representation of facts, and the beauties of style, should steal upon the hearers, and, ere they were aware, disarm their resentment, and conciliate their good will. The utmost of which publicans and fishermen were capable, was to speak a few sentences, probably not well connected, and expressed in homely and inaccurate language. They had never addressed magistrates and priests; they had conversed only with their equals; and in the presence of persons celebrated for their sanctity and learning, it should not have surprised us, if they had been abashed and embarrassed, and had experienced a total suspension of their powers. But our Lord promised "to give them a mouth and wisdom, which all their adversaries should not be able to gainsay nor resist." He would supply, by the gifts of the Spirit, their want of talents and education; he would inspire the ignorant with knowledge, and enable " the tongue of the stammerer to speak plainly." In the present case, we see this promise performed. Peter and John now stood before the supreme council of the nation, in which were present the high-priest with his attendants, the principal persons in authority, and the scribes, well versed in the law, and practised in the arts of perplexing an antagonist. Yet they retained perfect composure of mind, and pleaded the cause of their master with such precision, and energy, and boldness, that their judges were astonished.

It was evident that the Apostles were "unlearned and ignorant men," not only from their appearance, which discovered the meanness of their condition, but likewise from their speech; for although our Lord promised to enable his disciples to plead his cause with irresistible efficacy, yet he did not promise to qualify them to speak their native language, or that of any foreign country, with propriety and elegance. Accordingly, their writings are not models of purity of style, and, in not a few instances, must have offended the fastidious ears of a Greek. It was not by the wisdom of words that the gospel was to be propagated. Their eloquence was the eloquence of truth, delivered with authority and earnestness, but without the decorations of art.

We are told, that "they took knowledge of them that they had been with Jesus." This remark has been understood to mean, that the rulers of the Jews recognized them to be his disciples, or remembered to have seen them in company with him; for some of the priests and great men occasionally attended our Saviour as spies upon his conduct, and with a design to perplex and ensnare him. I apprehend that something different is intended, namely, that they perceived a resemblance between their manner and that of their Master; the same intrepidity of spirit, the same dignity and energy of address. And when they saw, at the same time, the lame man standing before them, they were confounded. Not one in all the assembly could find any thing to reply. A sullen silence reigned throughout the court; and the proud doctors of Jerusalem felt their inferiority in the presence of two fishermen of Galilee.

What was to be done in these humiliating circumstances? To confess before the Apostles that they were vanquished, would have been mortifying in the extreme; and to sit and say nothing, would have subjected them to contempt and derision. They commanded the prisoners, therefore, to retire, that without restraint they might consult together about some expedient for extricating themselves from their present embarrassment. "But when they had commanded them to go aside out of the council, they conferred among themselves, saying, What shall we do to these men? for that a notable miracle hath been done by them, is manifest to all them that dwell at Jerusalem, and we cannot deny it. But, that it spread no further among the people, let us straitly threaten them, that they speak henceforth to no man in this name." Here, my brethren, a very extraordinary scene is presented to our view. We see an assembly of men, professors of the true religion, high in office in the Church, and pretending to be animated with fervent zeal for the glory of God, deliberating not how they shall prevail upon their countrymen to embrace Christianity, of the divine origin of which they had before them undeniable evidence, but what would be the most effectual measure to hinder its reception. They do not startle at their own impiety; they do not blush to reveal to one another their atrocious purpose. Not a single voice is raised in behalf of the truth; there is not a Nicodemus to speak a word, or even to suggest a doubt, in favour of the Messiah. Where was conscience during this consultation? Was it silenced by the clamours of passion? It was impossible that they should not have been conscious of the wickedness of their design, and have experienced uneasiness from the remonstrances of the inward monitor; but their example shows us the unhappy and dangerous situation of men, who have openly and decidedly embarked in a bad cause. Their passions are all interested in its success. Their pride is engaged to go on; and they cannot recede without incurring the reproach of inconsistence, and exposing themselves to the scorn and persecution of the associates whom they have abandoned.

The resolution adopted by the council was to charge the Apostles, with threatenings, "to speak henceforth no more to any man in this name." "And they called them, and commanded them not to speak at all, nor teach in the name of Jesus." Foolish men! How could they persuade themselves, that they should be able to stop the progress of the new religion which was patronised by God himself? Could their devices baffle his wisdom? or their authority prevail against his power? Upon the supposition that Peter and John had been terrified into silence, was there no other disciple of a more undaunted spirit, who would raise his voice in behalf of his Master? Although these men had altogether held their peace, surely in such a cause "the very stones would have cried out." But the specimen which the council had already seen of the character of the Apostles, afforded no reasonable hope that they would pay any regard to their menaces. When they first came into the presence of the Sanhedrim, they appeared to be superior to fear, and dared to publish the truth in a manner the most offensive. It was vain to expect that their courage would fail, after they had witnessed the confusion of their judges; and that they would be intimidated by a command, which could be considered in no other light, than as an ebullition of impotent rage, an expression of obstinate but dismayed hostility.

Accordingly, when they were again brought into court, their behaviour was such as might have been looked for, in these circumstances, from men firm to their purpose. "But Peter and John answered, and said unto them, Whether it be right in the sight of

God, to hearken unto you, more than unto God, judge ye. For we cannot but speak the things which we have seen and heard." This is an explicit declaration that they would not obey them; and in justification of this refusal, they appeal to their judges themselves. God is the supreme lawgiver, the King of kings, and the Lord of lords, by delegation from whom earthly rulers hold that authority which they lawfully exercise over their subjects. There can be no power, therefore, against the truth, but for the truth. In the empire of the universe, as in the kingdoms of men, a deputy has no right to repeal the laws of the sovereign, and to call upon the people to engage in acts of rebellion and treason. From that moment conscience ceases to recognise him as a representative of the monarch, and can regard him only as an usurper. We perceive, therefore, the limits of the obedience which we owe to our superiors in Church and State. In those cases which are agreeable to the laws of heaven, made known by the light of nature, and by revelation, or which, at least, are not inconsistent with those laws, we are bound; but in every other case we are free. God has a prior claim to our obedience, which no human interference, no relation which may be formed between us and others, no promise or contract can invalidate. Those, therefore, who refuse to comply with the unlawful orders of their superiors, are not disobedient subjects. In such cases they are not subject. Their refusal may indeed be stigmatized as criminal, and punished by tyrants and wicked rulers, who can brook no opposition to their imperious mandates; but God approves of it, and it will be applauded by good men as a noble stand for the rights of truth and conscience.

The principle which we are now considering is so obviously just, that we may submit to the most partial judges, whether it ought not to be steadily acted upon, on all occasions, in which the authority of God and that of man interfere. It is a principle, which the light of nature teaches; and we find Socrates declaring to his judges, that he would not, to save his life, desist from fulfilling the will of God, by teaching philosophy. "O Athenians, I will obey God rather than you."[*] It may indeed be alleged in defence of the most irregular and unjustifiable actions. Enthusiasm may fancy, and hypocrisy may pretend, a divine commission for the wildest excesses. The clearest and most valuable principles are liable to be

---

[*] Socrat. Apolog. xi.

abused. But in the present case, the Jewish rulers themselves could not question the application of it. What had the Apostles done? They had not taught a set of notions calculated to excite tumult and insurrection among the people; nor promulgated a system of impious and extravagant doctrines, for which they could produce no satisfactory evidence. They had spoken "the things which they had seen and heard." Fully assured of the truth of the religion which they preached, they could give indubitable proof of it, and had given such proof, by the miracle performed upon the impotent man. To be silent, therefore, would have been to offer violence to their convictions, to conceal from others what they were interested to know, and to betray the trust reposed in them, when they were appointed to the Apostolical office.

This bold answer, which must have been regarded by the council as an open contempt of their authority, was sufficient to have roused their anger to fury, and to have prompted them to adopt violent measures. For the present, however, they contented themselves with renewing their threatenings, not from real moderation, or an aversion to proceed to extremities, but because they were apprehensive, that a more severe exercise of their authority would be attended with danger. The truth of the miracle performed upon the lame man was manifest beyond contradiction. He had passed his fortieth year, when the disorder in his joints, although it could have been remedied at an earlier period, was become incurable by human means. The people glorified God, by acknowledging the cure to be an immediate effect of his power; and regarded with reverence and affection, the Apostles, as his favourites and ministers. At this crisis it would have been hazardous to punish them. The populace, capable of being easily inflamed, and hurried on to the most dreadful outrages, might have forgotten their usual respect for their rulers, and have sacrificed them in a paroxysm of rage. For this reason, the council dismissed Peter and John, although they knew that they would return to their former employment, and preach, through Jesus, the resurrection from the dead with redoubled zeal and courage. "So when they had further threatened them, they let them go, finding nothing how they might punish them, because of the people; for all men glorified God for that which was done. For the man was above forty years old, on whom this miracle of healing was showed."

Thus did our Saviour deliver his faithful servants out of the hands of their enemies, and preserve them for the important purposes which they had yet to fulfil.

To this illustration of the passage I shall subjoin the following observations.

First, When God is carrying on any design for the manifestation of his glory, great opposition will be made to it. Satan, his implacable adversary will not remain a quiet spectator; and the men, over whom his influence extends, will be stirred up to his assistance. In this combination, it should not surprise us, to find, not only persons of profane principles and wicked lives, but some, who, in consequence of their apparent attachment to religion, might have been expected to range themselves on the opposite side. When God was setting his Son upon his holy hill of Zion, not only did the "Heathen" rage, who were ignorant of prophecy, and had not seen the miracles of Jesus, but the "people" imagined a vain thing; the favoured people to whom the oracles of God were committed, and among whom the Messiah had appeared. Both said "Let us break their bands asunder, and cast away their cords from us."

In the second place, God may expose his people to much discouragement, when they are walking in his own way, and when the undertaking, in which they are engaged, is patronised by himself. The Apostles preached Christ in consequence of an express commission from heaven; and upon their success depended the accomplishment of the divine purposes relative to the establishment of the Church, and the conversion of the world. Yet in the outset they were opposed by the supreme authority in the nation. In the course of their ministry, they were subjected to many dangers and grievous sufferings; and most of them lost their lives in the cause. Superficial reasoners may conclude, that God is at variance with himself, embarrassing and retarding the execution of his own plans; and may complain, that, instead of rewarding, he punishes men for their zeal and fidelity. "But the foolishness of God is wiser than men." By such dispensations, he exercises the faith of his servants, and makes known the power of his arm, in carrying on his designs in spite of the utmost efforts of his adversaries; while, in the conduct of his people, such examples of courage, patience, and disinterested love are exhibited, as afford no slight testimony to the truth of religion. Thus he makes "the wrath of man praise him; and the remainder of it he restrains." Converts are made by the sufferings of the saints as well as by their doctrine. It was a saying among the Christians of antiquity, founded in experience, that "the blood of the martyrs was the seed of the Church."

In the third place, Jesus Christ requires no service from his disciples, for which he does not furnish them with necessary assistance. He is not a hard task master. "His yoke is easy, and his burden is light;" for as his commandments are reasonable, so by his grace we are enabled to obey them. When Peter and John were called to plead his cause before the Jewish council, they were "filled with the Holy Ghost." Hence cowardly fishermen became undaunted Apostles; simple and uneducated men have put learning to silence; and delicate women have endured, with unshaken firmness, cruel tortures, and death in its most terrible forms. "As thy days, so shall thy strength be."

In the fourth place, Great is the truth, and it shall prevail. It confounded and silenced the Jewish council; it made foolish the wisdom of the world, vanquishing its vain philosophy and sophistical eloquence by the plain doctrine of the cross; it will, in like manner triumph over the petulant and malignant opposition of infidelity; and a future age shall see superstition in all its modifications, delusions of every kind, enthusiasm, heresy, error, and licentiousness, vanish before it, as the shade of night before the sun. From what it has already done, we may calculate the effects which are yet to be expected from it. "When the Lord shall send the rod of his strength out of Zion, the people shall be willing in the day of his power; and he shall rule in the midst of his enemies."

Lastly, Let us be careful to maintain a good conscience in our religious profession. This was the constant study of the Apostles, who considered not what was honourable in the eyes of the world, and advantageous, and safe, but solely what was right. It was God alone whom they had resolved to obey; and they minded not the contrary commands and the threatenings of men. You will not enjoy peace of mind, nor act uprightly and consistently, till you have learned to regulate your conduct by the fixed standard of truth and rectitude, and not by the shifting opinions and fancies of men. There is one thing, in particular, of which you should beware; the vain attempt to serve two Masters, God and the world, conscience and inclination. The result of such an attempt will be, that you shall serve neither of them fully, and shall lose the reward promised by both. Choose your side, and be honest and uniform in adhering to it. "If the Lord be God, follow him; but if Baal, then follow him." Know neither father nor mother, neither sister nor brother, in your choice of religion. "Hearken, O daughter, and consider, and incline thine ear: forget also thine own people, and thy father's house." This should be the language of our lips and our hearts. "Speak, Lord, for thy servants hear. We renounce our own will; we desire only to know thine; and through thy grace we will do it, without startling at the consequences. Our souls and our bodies are thy property, for thou hast redeemed them; and we therefore dedicate them to thy service. O Lord our God, other lords besides thee have had dominion over us; but by thee only will we make mention of thy name."

LECTURE VI.

ANANIAS AND SAPPHIRA.

Chap. v. 1—11.

We have seen the success of the Apostles in persuading many of the Jews to acknowledge Jesus of Nazareth, to whose crucifixion they had lately consented, to be the Messiah promised to their fathers. These converts were formed into a new society, different from other societies, not only in its external aspect, and the design of its institution, but likewise in the principle by which its component parts were united. In associations for political or commercial purposes, all the individuals retain a regard to their private interest in its full strength, and concur in measures for the general good, because they will contribute to their personal advantage. But the first Christians were animated by a nobler spirit. Pure disinterested love was the soul of the rising Church, and gave birth to such expressions of benevolence, as have been rarely equalled in succeeding ages.

Among those who in the beginning embraced Christianity, it may be supposed that there were many persons in indigent circumstances. Few of the rich and great are, at any time, attracted by the humble and spiritual religion of Jesus Christ; and a profession of it was less likely to be adopted by many of that description, when the Church was not established by law, and neither honours nor emoluments were attached to the faith. It appears, however, that the primitive believers were not all in the lower ranks of life. Some of them, as we learn from the preceding chapter, had possessions of lands and houses, which, with generosity hitherto unexampled, they devoted to the supply of their brethren in need. "They sold them, and brought the prices of the things, that were sold, and laid them down at the Apostles' feet," that a common stock might be formed, out of which distribution should be made to the widow, the fatherless, and the orphan. Thus the new religion infused its best spirit into the breasts of the Jewish converts. Among its earliest effects, we see it prevailing over selfishness and want of feeling, the baneful influence of which often poisons the comfort of our social relations. It did not, however, operate in this manner upon every person who joined himself to the Apostles. The passage now read presents an instance, in which base passions were detected under the mask of pretended piety, and the semblance of disinterested goodness.

"But a certain man, named Ananias, with Sapphira his wife, sold a possession, and kept back part of the price, his wife also being privy to it, and brought a certain part, and laid it at the Apostles' feet." It is evident, that Ananias and Sapphira were numbered among the disciples; and there is no reason to doubt, that they were admitted to enjoy all the external privileges of the Church. As their conduct shows them not to have been sincere, we are led to inquire, by what motive they were induced to connect themselves with a society, which held out no allurement to the worldly passions; and the inquiry may be extended to many others, who, without experiencing the saving power of the truth, have since assumed the Christian profession, and even affected, on some occasions, no common zeal for religion. The same account may be given of all such cases. There are different motives, which may be conceived to operate upon different minds, yet all terminating in the same result; such a conviction of the truth as commands the assent of the understanding, and overawes conscience, but does not subdue the aversion of the heart; a general persuasion of the necessity of some religion, in consequence of which we embrace that which is best recommended; the example of others, which we implicitly follow; the authority and solicitations of friends; and sometimes a design to conceal, under a show of piety, the moral defects of the character.

It will be granted, perhaps, that these causes operate with great force in ordinary cases; but it will be objected, that their efficacy could not be the same in the days of Ananias and Sapphira, when contempt and persecution were the portion of the disciples of Jesus. This representation is not perfectly accurate. The rulers, the priests, and the scribes, looked upon the Apostles, and their adherents, with detestation and scorn; but the people at large entertained more favourable sentiments. Luke informs us, that "they were in favour with all the people; and that the people magnified them." The Apostles had been lately summoned before the council, but they were dismissed without punishment; and as yet, through the care of providence, the Church had sustained no rude assault from its enemies. The religion of the gospel, it must be acknowledged, was new, was contrary to the inveterate prejudices of the Jews, and was discountenanced by the persons of the highest authority and learning in the nation. But to these disadvantages, under which it laboured, were opposed the discourses of the Apostles, which were earnest and impressive, and the miracles which they performed in confirmation of their doctrine. It is no just ground of surprise, that in such circumstances some were induced to associate with them, whose minds had not been "brought into captivity to Christ," by the converting power of the truth. We learn from the history of the following ages, when Christians held their property and their lives at the caprice of every tyrant who swayed the Roman sceptre, and were exposed to frequent persecution, that many intruded themselves into the Church, whose conduct betrayed the baseness of the motives in which their profession was founded.

Ananias, with the consent of his wife, sold his possession. This was the common practice among the believers. It was the fashion of the time; and this couple could not but comply with it. Had they done otherwise, their character might have been suspected; and although the Apostles would not have called them to an account, because the sale of possessions was entirely voluntary, there being no law which obliged to it, there was a probability that their reputation would suffer in the public estimation. They would not be behind the most distinguished of the disciples; they would imitate Barnabas himself. Example has a powerful influence upon hypocrites, not, indeed, to excite them to the sincere practice of the holiness which they see in the saints, but to produce a studied imitation of their most distinguished actions, that tinsel may pass for gold. To the rivalship of excellence, to the love of praise, must be attributed many of those deeds which have a fine show of goodness and generosity; the zeal of religionists, the charities of the ostentatiously liberal, the grimace and fervour of the devotee.

But Ananias and Sapphira, when they sold their possession, did not, after the example of the other disciples, bring the whole of the price to the Apostles. Had they been influenced by a sincere faith, and by that generous love which animated their brethren, they would have made the same sacrifice to the public good, and have made it with the same promptitude and cheerfulness. But the absence of pure principle in this transaction, left room for opposite passions to contend in their breasts. A regard to reputation required the sale of their possession; but avarice considered it as too valuable to be exchanged for fame. Between the two passions, the dexterity of hypocrisy suggested a compromise. Avarice was contented with the retention of a part; and vanity was gratified by the surrender of the rest, under the pretext that it was the whole. In this manner, I think their conduct should be explained. They had two purposes in view; and in endeavouring to accomplish both, they were engaged in a train of meanness, deceit, and impiety, which merited the severe reprehension of Peter, and the dreadful punishment which divine justice inflicted.

Ananias and Sapphira, never doubting that the plan, which they had concerted, and executed with so much privacy, was secure from detection, expected to be welcomed by the Apostles with high commendations of their zeal and liberality. How much, then, must the unhappy man, who came alone with the unhallowed offering, have been dismayed, when Peter saluted him with these terrible words! "Ananias, why hath Satan filled thine heart to lie to the Holy Ghost, and to keep back part of the price of the land?" His crime is traced to the instigation of Satan, who had filled his heart with vanity, covetousness, dissimulation, and an impious disregard for the omniscience and justice of heaven. This is not to be understood as a figurative expression, denoting the turpitude and atrocity of his conduct; but as a true account of the secret influence by which he was impelled to commit so daring an action. The human heart is itself sufficiently wicked to contrive and perpetrate very aggravated crimes; but some sins are so heinous in their nature, and are marked with such characters of audacity and profligacy, that they seem to have been suggested by a spirit more completely depraved even than man. It is a fact ascertained by the Scriptures, that Satan does tempt the children of men, or that he excites their corrupt principles to action, by stimulating the imagination and the senses, and by perverting the reasoning faculty, although it is impossible to explain the mode of his agency. He is the "spirit, who works in the children of disobedience."

The sin, to which Satan had successfully solicited Ananias, consisted "in lying to the Holy Ghost, and keeping back part of the price." Some have represented it as the sin of sacrilege, which is the diverting of a consecrated thing from the service of God, the reservation of what had been previously dedicated to him for our own use, or the application of it to a secular purpose. This seems to be a mistake, as there is not a hint in the narrative that Ananias and Sapphira had devoted their possession to God; and Peter expressly says, that after, as well as before, it was sold, it was in their power to do with it what they pleased. The nature of the sin is distinctly pointed out as a lie to the Holy Ghost. As the construction of the original language is here different from that in the end of the fourth verse, where he is said, "not to have lied to men, but to God," some choose to read the words thus; "Why hath Satan filled thine heart to belie the Holy Ghost?" "Why hast thou pretended to be moved by the Spirit of God, to express sincere and generous love to the brethren, by giving the whole price of the possession for their use; while it appears, from the keeping back of a part of it, that thou art influenced solely by vanity and covetousness?" But I see no reason for altering our translation, as according to the one construction of the words as well as the other, they may be translated "to lie to the Holy Ghost."

That the charge brought by Peter against Ananias may appear to be well founded, it is necessary to recollect, that he and his colleagues acted under the direction, and by the assistance, of the divine Spirit, who not only instructed them in the mysteries of religion, but besides other extraordinary gifts, endowed them with the power of discerning spirits; that is, with the occasional knowledge of the thoughts, purposes, motives, and spiritual condition of certain individuals, for the regulation of their conduct in particular emergencies. When Ananias laid down part of the price at the feet of the Apostles, saying, by this action, which was meant to be understood according to the general practice, that he laid down the whole of it, he unquestionably told a falsehood; and although his intention went no farther than to deceive the Apostles, yet the lie was ultimately told to the Holy Ghost, who resided in them. As they were his ministers and agents, what was done to them was virtually and interpretatively done to him. Those who rejected their doctrine, rejected the Holy Ghost; those who lied to them, lied to the Holy Ghost.

Of this sin there were two aggravations. First, it was a sin of choice, committed with perfect freedom of will, and not under the influence of compulsion, or the terror of punishment. "Whiles it remained, was it not thine own? and after it was sold, was it not in thine own power? why hast thou conceived this thing in thine heart?" Ananias could have avoided this sin in different ways. He might not have sold his possession; he might have retained the price; or he might have contributed to the public stock any portion of it, great or small, provided that he had stated the amount of the donation, and had not attempted to make a part pass for the whole. So far is the example of the Christians of Jerusalem, in selling their possessions, from being obligatory upon succeeding generations, that it was not binding in their own age. Every man was then, as much as at present, absolute master of his property; and the only positive obligation, to which the Jewish converts were subject, is common to the disciples of Christ to the end of the world; namely, to devote a just proportion of their substance to the use of the poor, and the service of the Church. It is evident, from the words of Peter, that the extraordinary offerings then made were entirely voluntary. No law was enacted upon the subject by the Apostles; nor do we find in the New Testament any traces of the practice beyond the time to which this history refers. It was a spontaneous expression of charity, occasioned, we may suppose, by peculiar circumstances of the primitive Church, with which we are not acquainted. There was nothing, therefore, to alleviate the guilt of Ananias. He could plead no external motive of such force as to constitute what is called an irresistible temptation. It was his own wicked heart to which the whole blame was imputable. He sinned with a willing mind.

The conduct of Ananias was farther aggravated by the dignity of the person against whom it was an offence. "Thou hast not lied unto men, but unto God." He had, indeed, lied to men, in attempting to deceive the Apostles; but Peter means that he had not lied to them alone. It is observable, that whereas he affirms, in the preceding verse, that Ananias had lied to the Holy Ghost, he now charges him with having lied to God. It follows, that the Holy Ghost is not a creature, nor a rhetorical name for a divine operation or influence, but a person possessed of proper divinity. It is to no purpose to object to this inference, that an equivalent phrase is used, where it is manifest that the same conclusion cannot be drawn from it. When the Israelites murmured for want of flesh against Moses and Aaron, they are said to have murmured against God.

The instances are not parallel. In the latter case, the Israelites were guilty of murmuring against God, because they complained of Moses and Aaron his ministers; but in the former, Ananias is said not only to have lied to the Holy Ghost, because he lied to the Apostles, who were inspired by him, but to have lied to God in lying to the Holy Ghost; a charge, which would not have been true, unless both designations had belonged to the same person. In this, then, consisted the greatness of his sin, that it was an insult offered to the Spirit of truth and holiness, speaking and acting in the ambassadors of Christ. Every lie which is told to man is an offence against God, of whose law it is an express violation; but the proper object of this lie was the Holy Ghost, who was present with the Apostles in a manner totally different from the mode of his presence with any other person.

The expostulation of Peter with Ananias was terrible, because every word was re-echoed by his conscience; but still more terrible was the event which immediately followed. "Ananias, hearing these words, fell down and gave up the ghost; and great fear came on all them that heard these things." The suddenness of his death is not to be attributed to the violent agitation of his mind, as instant dissolution has been known to be the effect of paroxysms of joy and grief. The stroke was inflicted by the hand of God, who was pleased, for reasons which will be afterwards mentioned, to give this example of his holiness and severity. In this case, we see a specimen of those visible and alarming judgments, which, contrary to his usual procedure, he sometimes executes upon distinguished transgressors. In general, "no man knoweth love or hatred by all that is before him. All things come alike to all: there is one event to the righteous and to the wicked; to the good, and to the clean, and to the unclean." But on certain occasions, God steps aside from his ordinary course, when, by such deviation, some great end of his moral government will be gained. As it discovers rashness and presumption to construe common calamities as proofs of the peculiar guilt and demerit of the sufferers; so not to observe the clear tokens of the divine displeasure against individuals, which appear in the nature and circumstances of their punishment, indicates a high degree of stupidity, a temper approaching to atheism, under whatever pretences of caution and charity it may be disguised. There is a particular providence; and, consequently, there are particular interpositions of wrath as well as of mercy.

Let it not be supposed, that the severity of Peter, on this occasion, was ill suited to the mild genius of the gospel, and to the character of an ambassador of peace. He rebuked Ananias for his crime with the severity which it deserved; but it was not he who inflicted the punishment, nor is there any evidence that he knew that it would immediately follow. When he afterwards denounced the same judgment upon Sapphira, he might be directed by a supernatural suggestion, or he might infer it from the doom of her husband. Whether he was apprized, or not, of the event, Ananias died by the visitation of heaven; and Peter is vindicated from the suspicion of having carried his zeal and resentment to excess.

The next verse relates the burial of Ananias. "And the young men arose, wound him up, and carried him out, and buried him." I have no remarks to make upon these words; and shall not take up your time with inquiring who the young men were, by whom the last office was performed to this unhappy man, as I could only amuse you with conjectures, and the subject is of no importance. Let us proceed to the sequel of the story.

"And it was about the space of three hours after, when his wife, not knowing what was done, came in." For what reason she did not come with her husband, we are not told; but as three hours had passed since he left her, she had leisure to reflect upon her conduct, and there was a favourable opportunity for conscience to remonstrate. It has sometimes happened, that solitude, by leaving a person to his own thoughts, and leading him to review his purposes, with their aggravations and probable consequences, has made him startle at the projects of guilt which he had concerted with others, and tremble to execute what in company he had cordially approved. The presence of associates, the courage which they assume, the arguments which they employ, and the flattering hopes which they hold out, conspire to keep fear and remorse at a distance. It is not commonly till sinners have become hardened in iniquity by repeated acts, or by long indulging it in their hearts, that they are able to bear their own reflections. Sapphira, however, in the absence of her husband, continued steady to her purpose; and having received no intelligence of his fate, came, as soon as her affairs permitted her, to the place where the Apostles were assembled. Supposing, no doubt, that Ananias was already enjoying the reward of their pretended generosity, she made haste to share in the admiration and applause, bestowed by the bystanders upon a pair, so distinguished by their zeal and charity. But their dissimulation was detected and exposed; and nothing awaited her but stern reproof and exemplary punishment.

"And Peter answered unto her, Tell me whether ye sold the land for so much. And she said, Yea, for so much." This question might have suggested to her, that a suspicion was entertained of something unfair in the transaction, as it is not probable that she had ever heard any of the disciples interrogated in the same manner. Peter does not abruptly charge her with dishonesty and impiety, as he had done in the case of her husband. He simply inquires, whether they had sold the land for the sum presented as the full price. The unexpected question would have disconcerted an ordinary transgressor, who finding his plan discovered, would have been overwhelmed with confusion, and have either confessed his crime, or stood speechless. A guilty mind is naturally timid; the utmost precaution cannot render it perfectly secure and quiet; a look, a whisper, a casual expression, which seems to glance at the purpose of which it is conscious, will awaken its fears. Happy would it have been for this woman, if the question had staggered her ill-founded courage, and had led her, with unfeigned repentance, to acknowledge her wickedness. We have no authority to say, that her sin was unpardonable. She might not, indeed, have escaped the temporal judgment which was executed upon her husband, for God sometimes takes vengeance upon the inventions of those whom he pardons; but she would have died, like Achan, glorifying God by making confession. She affords an awful example of obduracy in sin. Still ignorant of the miserable end of her husband, experiencing no uneasiness from conscience, and intent upon consummating the base design in which they were engaged, this audacious woman was determined to brave the Apostle to his face. With a composed countenance, and an unfaltering tongue, she answered, "Yea, for so much;" aggravating her dissimulation by a deliberate and resolute falsehood.

"Then Peter said unto her, How is it that ye have agreed together, to tempt the Spirit of the Lord?" To tempt is commonly used in a bad sense for soliciting a person to evil. "But God cannot be tempted with evil; neither tempteth he any man." The word has sometimes a different meaning in Scripture, signifying to make trial of a person. Thus, when God "tempted" Abraham, he did not entice him to sin, but proposed a difficult act of obedience, and, in this manner, tried the strength of his faith and love. Concerning the Israelites in the wilderness, we are informed that they tempted the Lord; and we learn from their own words what was the nature of their crime. "They tempted the Lord, saying, Is the Lord among us, or not?" Notwithstanding the evidences which they had already seen of the presence of God, they presumptuously demanded a new proof of it. When Peter, therefore, charges Sapphira with having dared, in concert with her husband, "to tempt the Spirit of the Lord," the meaning obviously is, that their sin was a bold experiment, whether the Holy Ghost, by whom the Apostles were inspired with the gifts of tongues and of miracles, was a discerner of spirits, or could know the thoughts and intentions of the heart. As the Israelites called in question the power of God when they said, "Can he furnish a table in the wilderness?" so did they call in question the omniscience of the Spirit, by their attempt to impose upon his ministers. They ventured to make the trial, and flattered themselves that they should escape with impunity. The plan was the result of mutual counsel; and it was no small aggravation of it, that they had abused the intimacy and confidence of the conjugal relation, to stimulate one another to so nefarious a deed.

Then follows the sentence pronounced upon the unhappy woman, which divine justice immediately executed. "Behold, the feet of them which have buried thy husband are at the door, and shall carry thee out. Then fell she down straightway at his feet, and yielded up the ghost: and the young men came in, and found her dead; and, carrying her forth, buried her by her husband." Both were alike guilty. Whoever suggested the plan, the other party heartily concurred in it. The superior prudence and caution of the husband did not check the forwardness of the wife; nor did the wife, from the timidity natural to her sex, oppose any obstacle to the boldness of her husband. The same unhallowed love of reputation, the same base hypocrisy, the same disregard for the all-seeing eye of heaven, influenced both. They were hateful in their lives, and in their death they were not divided. They perished by the same doom; and their end ministers a solemn warning to others, that they may hear, and fear, and do no more wickedly.

This was the design of the signal vengeance executed upon those sinners, and was the effect which it actually produced. "And great fear came upon all the Church, and upon as many as heard these things." The first and great end of miracles, is to attest the divine commission of the person, by whose ministry they are performed. Nicodemus expressed the dictate of sound reason, when he said to our Saviour, "Rabbi, we know that thou art a teacher come from God: for no man can do these miracles that thou dost, except God be with him." But, besides this general end, they may be subservient to other purposes, and be employed as symbols or representations of spiritual things, and as characteristic of a particular dispensation. The Mosaic economy, which was dark and awful, "the way into the holiest of all being not yet made manifest," was ushered in by terrible displays of the divine power. The gospel was confirmed by miracles of mercy well fitted to express its gracious nature. Yet, as all the miracles of the old dispensation were not of the terrific kind, so those of Christ and his Apostles were not all gentle and beneficent. Some of them were indications of the just severity of God against sinners. In this mixture, we observe a contrivance of divine wisdom, for correcting the natural propensity of men to take encouragement from mild and lenient proceedings, to venture upon acts of disobedience. By occasional manifestations of the holiness and justice of God, sinners are intimidated, and saints are inspired with salutary fear. The fate of Ananias and Sapphira was a solemn admonition to the disciples of Christ, to take heed to themselves, lest they also should provoke the Spirit of the Lord; and to others, to beware of entering into the Church, unless their conviction of the truth was sincere, and their motives were upright. One design of divine punishments in this life, is the good of those who see them, or hear of them; what other purpose, besides satisfaction to incensed justice, they will serve in the world to come, we have no means of knowing. To thoughtless and secure sinners they say, "Except ye repent, ye shall all likewise perish;" and upon believers they inculcate the exhortation of Paul, "Let us have grace, whereby we may serve God acceptably, with reverence and godly fear. For our God is a consuming fire."

I shall conclude with the following reflections upon the passage.

It is vain to expect, that in this world the Church shall ever be perfectly pure. I mean, not only that imperfections will always adhere to the members of the Church, because "there is not a just man upon earth, that doeth good, and sinneth not;" but farther, that hypocrites will be found intermixed with the saints. The wheat and the chaff lie together upon the barn-floor. No percautions, however strict, can prevent their admission; no discipline, however vigorous, no doctrine, however faithful, will be able to expel them. There were an Ananias and a Sapphira in the society over which the Apostles presided.

We should guard against the predominance of every sinful passion, whether it be avarice, ambition, sensuality, envy, pride, or any other lust of the flesh or of the spirit. As "one sinner destroys much good," so one sin reigning in the heart, counteracts the efficacy of the best means, and may carry us to a very great length in depravity. If the restraints of providence are removed, and a strong temptation is presented in favourable circumstances, it will precipitate us into such excesses, as shall dishonour us in the eyes of men, and provoke God to pour out upon us the fury of his wrath. You see the dreadful effects of vanity and covetousness, in the conduct of Ananias and Sapphira.

Impenitent sinners are always in danger of perishing by the vengeance of heaven. Judgment, indeed, is God's "strange work;" but it is a work, which a regard to his glory sometimes calls upon him to perform. And when one victim falls, it is impossible to tell who shall be the next. A sentence of death is passed upon all unbelievers, and execution of which is delayed only by the long-suffering and patience of God. Let not men presume upon his patience; for, although divine, it has its limits, beyond which it will not extend. "Let sinners in Zion be afraid; let fearfulness surprise the hypocrites: who among us shall dwell with the devouring fire? Who among us shall dwell with everlasting burnings?" Such is the God with whom you have to do. He is a fire to consume the workers of iniquity; it flames around you, and is ready to kindle upon you; and there is no possibility of escaping from it, but by calling for help to Him who rescued the three Jewish confessors from the king of Babylon's furnace.

Let us, above all things, study to be sincere in religion. What will hypocrisy avail? Can our artifice impose upon God? Are we able to conceal from him, under a mask of piety and goodness, the real features of our character? Do not "his eye see, and his eye-lids try, the children of men?" "There is not any creature that is not manifest in his sight; but all things are naked and opened unto the eyes of him with whom we have to do." In vain did Ananias and Sapphira secretly concert their plan, and assume the confidence of conscious integrity to quash any suspicion of their baseness. A good name, the esteem and friendly offices of Christians, and even worldly advantages, may be the recompense of dissimulation in this world; but what awaits in the next? "What is the hope of the hypocrite, though he hath gained, when God taketh away his soul?" One faint spark of genuine religion is more acceptable to God than the ardent flames with which he offers up his devotions. Let it then be your constant and earnest prayer, that through grace you may be what you profess. "Let integrity and uprightness preserve me; for I wait on thee." The time will come, when, stript of every disguise, men shall appear in their real character; and, the false-hearted shall be exposed to the scorn of those, whose admiration they are now so eager to obtain. But then undissembled goodness shall be brought to light. Often concealed by modesty, by indigence, by reproach, and by obscurity of station, it shall be displayed at the tribunal of God, to the praise of his grace which inspired it, and to the honour of the possessor. "Thy Father, O Christian, who seeth thee in secret, will reward thee openly."

LECTURE VII

THE COUNSEL OF GAMALIEL.

Chap. v. 34—42.

It pleased God, as we read in this chapter, to enable the Apostles to work many miracles in confirmation of the gospel. But the stronger the light is, it is the more offensive to a diseased eye. The high priest and his adherents were filled with indignation against the men, who presumed, in defiance of their express prohibition, to preach Jesus of Nazareth as the promised Messiah; and by the wonders which they performed, were gradually undermining the authority of the rulers, in the opinion and affections of the people. They belonged to the sect of the Sadducees, who being a species of free-thinkers, and holding principles subversive of all religion, might have been supposed to view with indifference and contempt contests about articles of faith, and modes of worship. But the experience of late years has convinced us, by the scenes transacted in a neighbouring country, that infidelity and bigotry may be closely allied; and that the persecuting fury of the philosopher was never surpassed by the intolerant zeal of the most sanguinary religionist. There was, indeed, a particular cause for the violence of those impious men, the opposition made to their favourite doctrine, that there was no resurrection of the body; for the great theme of the Apostles' discourses was the illustrious manifestation of divine power in bringing Jesus from the grave, to establish the truth of his religion, and to give his followers the hope of a triumph over death. The pride of authority, and the pride of wisdom, could ill brook an insult so public, offered, too, by men, in their eyes, of despicable talents and character. "They laid hands, therefore, on the Apostles, and put them in the common prison."

At this crisis, God miraculously interposed in favour of his servants, to encourage them to persist in their duty, and to convince their persecutors, that vain were their endeavours to arrest the progress of the rising religion. "The angel of the Lord opened the prison doors, and brought them forth, and said, Go, stand and speak in the temple to the people, all the words of this life." But the rulers of the Jews were not diverted from their purpose by this unequivocal declaration of heaven against them. Having received information where the Apostles should be found, they brought them again before the council, and asked, why they presumed still to preach, and to persuade the people, that their priests and magistrates were guilty of innocent blood. The answer was firm and manly, and discovered a spirit which should animate every Christian minister, and every Christian man; a supreme regard to the authority of God. "We ought to obey God rather than men." Not content with having disclaimed the jurisdiction of the Sanhedrim, they proceeded without fear of the consequences, to repeat the charge which had given so much offence, "to bring this man's blood upon them," to accuse them to their faces of having put to death the Messiah; and, at the same time, to affirm, that "God had exalted him with his right hand to be a Prince and a Saviour." It is not easy to conceive the feelings of those haughty rulers, when they were addressed with such boldness by some vulgar men, who should have been overawed by their presence, and should have received their mandates with reverence. Luke expressively says, that they were "cut to the heart." In this state of mind they were purposing to proceed to violence, when the rising tempest was calmed by the wise and moderate counsel of one man, who remained cool and temperate amidst the general fermentation.

"Then stood there up one in the council, a Pharisee, named Gamaliel, a doctor of law, had in reputation among all the people, and commanded to put the Apostles forth a little space." This man has acquired reputation among Christians also, by his prudent and rational counsel at this conjuncture, and in consequence of the relation in which he once stood to the great Apostle of the Gentiles. Paul was brought up at the feet of Gamaliel. He is said to have been the son of that venerable old man, "to whom it was revealed by the Holy Ghost, that he should not see death before he had seen the Lord's Christ;" and who took up the infant Saviour in his arms, and said, "Lord, now lettest thou thy servant depart in peace, according to thy word: for mine eyes have seen thy salvation." By profession he was a doctor of law, that is, one of those who expounded the law of Moses to the people, and, according to the fashion of the times, carefully instructed them in the traditions of the elders, as the best commentary on his writings. We may remark, by the way, what was the nature of the learning which Paul acquired under this master, and which has been greatly overrated. It is sufficient to observe that it was Jewish learning, to convince those who are acquainted with the history of that age, that as it could not recommend him to the Gentiles, so it was of very little value in itself, consisting chiefly in the knowledge of the superstitious notions and idle dreams of men, forsaken by sound reason, and the Spirit of God. The sect, to which he was attached, was that of the Pharisees, which was distinguished by the overstrained strictness of its precepts, and its minute attention to religious ceremonies. Intolerance was natural to such a sect. But Gamaliel was an honourable exception. History occasionally points out individuals who have been preserved from the narrow, violent spirit of their party, by mildness of temper, a strong feeling of humanity, and the suggestions of a well regulated judgment. In the bosom of a persecuting Church, and among the proud domineering members of an establishment, gentle measures sometimes find an advocate, and dissenters, an apologist and patron. We perceive, then, on what account Gamaliel was held in reputation by the people. His station, his learning, and his piety, recommended him to their esteem, and must have given weight to the advice which he now offered to the Sanhedrim.

We are not able to point out with certainty the motive, which induced him to stand up in behalf of the Apostles. It has indeed been affirmed, that he secretly favoured the new religion, and afterwards openly professed it. He has been represented as a second Nicodemus, who, when the rulers were taking counsel against Jesus, ventured to say, "Doth our law judge any man before it hear him, and know what he doth?" But this is one among many instances, in which men have permitted their wishes and hopes to supply the place of evidence. There can be no better foundation for this opinion, if we give credit to the Jews, who show in their liturgy, a prayer said to have been composed by him, imprecating divine vengance upon the heretics, by whom are meant the followers of Jesus. Others have attributed his interference, not to any generous principle, but to the spirit of party. As those, who persecuted the Apostles, were Sadducees, this Pharisee felt himself engaged by interest and rivalship to support them. We do indeed meet with a case, which gives some plausibility to this conjecture. When Paul was brought before the Sanhedrim, and avowed his hope of the resurrection of the dead, the Pharisees arranged themselves on his side, and used nearly the same language, which was employed on this occasion by Gamaliel. It is possible, however, that this advice was dictated by a mind, which, although not free from prejudice against the truth, disapproved of compulsion in matters of conscience, and was willing that the new religion should be allowed a fair trial. It seems, indeed, to express a doubt, whether the cause of Christianity might not be the cause of God; but notwithstanding the cautious nature of his language, Gamaliel might be persuaded that it was an imposture, and would soon come to nothing. He might think that force was unnecessary, where the intrinsic weakness of the cause would speedily prove its ruin; or, as we have already hinted, he might, from principle, be adverse to employ it in the determination of controversies, which should be submitted to the decision of reason and Scripture. Upon this supposition, the Pharisee was more enlightened than some, who profess a religion which breathes a more liberal spirit. But our business is not with his motives, but with his counsel.

Having ordered the Apostles to be removed for a short time, he addressed the council in the following words. " Ye men of Israel, take heed to yourselves what ye intend to do as touching these men. For before these days rose up Theudas, boasting himself to be somebody, to whom a number of men, about four hundred, joined themselves: who was slain, and all, as many as obeyed him, were scattered and brought to nought. After this man rose up Judas of Galilee, in the days of the taxing, and drew away much people after him: he also perished, and all, even as many as obeyed him, were dispersed." The opinion of Gamaliel with respect to the present case was not hastily formed, but was the fruit of mature thought, and was founded in the wisdom of experience. Accordingly, he quotes in support of it two cases, recorded in the annals of the nation, with which all who heard him must have been acquainted. I shall not trouble you with the chronological difficulties in this passage. Josephus, in his Jewish antiquities, mentions one Theudas, who was the ringleader of an insurrection, and perished by the arms of the Romans, some years after the meeting of the council. This Theudas, of whom he takes no notice, is said to have appeared before it. There is no reason to suspect that Luke was mistaken, and consequently that it is a forged speech which he has put into the mouth of Gamaliel. As Theudas was a common name among the Jews, it might easily happen to belong to more seditious leaders than one. The silence of Josephus should no more invalidate the testimony of Luke, than the silence of Luke would invalidate the authority of Josephus. It must have been about thirty or forty years before this time, that the Theudas, of whom Gamaliel speaks, was at the head of a party; for Judas rose up after him, "in the days of the taxing," which probably means the taxing or assessment made by Cyrenius, governor of Syria, several years after the birth of our Saviour, when Archelaus, the son of Herod, was deposed, and Judea was reduced into the form of a province.

The Jews, who were a turbulent people, submitted with great impatience to the Roman yoke. They were indignant at the thought, that the chosen people, who hoped under the Messiah to possess the dominion of the world, should be enslaved and oppressed by foreigners and idolaters. Hence demagogues arose in frequent succession, and erecting the standard of liberty and religion, collected a number of followers, inflamed with rage, and animated with the prospect of glory and independence. Of this description were Theudas and Judas. The former "boasted himself to be somebody;" pretended to be the Messiah, or a Prophet sent by God, for the deliverance of his people. As the latter rose up "in the days of the taxing," he probably assumed no higher character than that of a patriot, who wished to emancipate his country from an ignominious and cruel subjection to strangers. But these, and all similar attempts, terminated in the destruction of those who were engaged in them. The wrath of God pursued the unbelieving, impenitent people. Their doom was fixed; and their repeated efforts, to withdraw themselves from the domination of their conquerors, only served to bring down upon them the full weight of their vengeance, by which both Church and state were overwhelmed.

Upon these instances of unsuccessful insurrection and imposture, Gamaliel founds the following advice. "And now I say unto you, Refrain from these men; and let them alone: for if this counsel or this work be of men, it will come to nought; but if it be of God, ye cannot overthrow it; lest haply ye be found even to fight against God." He dissuades them from violent measures, as impious or superfluous. If the new religion was from God, its progress could not be arrested by their opposition, which would involve them in the guilt and ruinous consequences of a contest with heaven; if it was a human contrivance, it would fall through its own weakness. Such is the counsel of Gamaliel; but justice is not done to it, if it be considered as a general rule, applicable to every case which may arise. Neither Scripture nor experience will warrant us to affirm, that a work or imposture of man will always come speedily to nought, or that a work of God will always prosper, whatever obstacles are opposed to it; for although there is no want of power to remove those obstacles, yet reasons, unknown to us, may induce him not to exert it. Christianity itself has, in some instances, been overthrown by the united activity of error and force. I appeal for proof to those countries, in which there was once many flourishing Churches, but Mahometanism is now the established religion. The reformation from popery is regarded by every protestant as a work of God; but it was successfully resisted in some nations of Europe, in which it had met with a favourable reception, and promised ultimately to prevail. On the other hand, we can produce works undoubtedly not of God, of which the success has been extensive and permanent. The reign of Antichrist, the adversary of God and his Son, the patron of error, idolatry, and wickedness, once extended over a great part of Europe, and is to last, according to prophecy, during twelve hundred and sixty years. The religion of Mahomet was contrived by the impostor himself, who at first persuaded, with some difficulty, his own relations to embrace it; but having been disseminated, by various means, among the neighbouring tribes, it passed the limits of Arabia, and, spreading over the eastern countries with the rapidity of lightning, is now established throughout the whole extent of the Greek empire, the former set of Christianity. It has already subsisted during the long period of twelve hundred years.

From these incontrovertible facts, it is evident, that the observation of Gamaliel cannot be adopted as a maxim which will hold universally, but must be received with certain limitations, which, indeed, are suggested by himself. By attending to his words, you will find that he does not lay down a general rule, but strictly confines himself to the present subject of discussion. " If *this* counsel or *this* work be of men, it will come to nought." And however rash and presumptuous it would be to pronounce, in this decisive manner, concerning every system of religion which may arise, the judgment of Gamaliel was well founded with respect to the religion preached by the Apostles. On the one hand, if this work was divine; if Jesus was the Messiah, and the gospel was his law sent out of Zion, Gamaliel was authorised, by the express declarations of Scriptures, to predict, that all the opposition of the Jewish rulers, and the combined efforts of earth and hell to obstruct it, should prove abortive. God had promised "to set the hand of his first born in the sea, and his right hand in the rivers; to beat down his foes before his face, and plague them that hate him; and to give him dominion, and glory, and a kingdom, that all people, nations, and languages, should serve him." On the other hand, if this work or counsel was from men, it required neither the spirit of prophecy, nor uncommon sagacity, to foresee, that its duration would be transient. Let us for a moment suppose, that Christianity was merely a contrivance of the Apostles; and then let us inquire, whether every thing pertaining to it was not calculated to hinder its success.

The doctrines which the Apostles preached were ill fitted to attract the attention, and to conciliate the approbation, of mankind. To tell the Jews, that the Messiah was of mean parentage, lived in poverty and affliction, died upon a cross, had now returned to heaven, without achieving the deliverance of his country from the power of the Romans, and had promised nothing to his followers but happiness beyond the grave, was to offend their pride, to disappoint their carnal expectations, to dissipate their dreams of glory and pleasure on the earth. To proclaim him to the Gentiles, was to speak upon a subject of which they had no idea, to recommend a person totally unknown, and whom they must have despised, both as a malefactor and a Jew. His resurrection, to which the Apostles referred as the decisive proof of his divine mission, was calculated to excite their derision, because they considered the resurrection of the body as neither credible nor desirable. To the Gentiles, acquainted only with their vain philosophy, and attached to its erroneous dogmas, the gospel must have seemed to be the wildest, most uncouth, and most unintelligible system, which ever insulted the human understanding.

The duties which this religion enjoined, were repugnant to the preconceived notions, and the corrupt passions of all classes of men.

Faith in Christ for justification, was a subject of which a Gentile could form no conception, and which, if he had understood it, must have provoked his ridicule, educated, as he was, in a proud dependence upon his own virtue as the only means of recommending him to God. Nothing could give more offence to a Jew, than to be told, that he must renounce his own righteousness, account his painful and scrupulous obedience to the law mere loss, and expect salvation from a person, whom the supreme court in the nation had put to death as an impostor and blasphemer. Precepts of humility, self-denial, chastity, temperance, justice, love to our enemies, and the forgiveness of injuries, will not be generally relished at any time; and were particularly ill-suited to the luxurious and licentious age in which the gospel was promulgated. Above all, the command to take up the cross, to forego worldly enjoyments, and to submit to sufferings for the sake of Christ and a good conscience, had a direct tendency to deter men from becoming his disciples. We may be persuaded to assent to speculative principles, and may even be prevailed upon, through indolence, inattention, and sophistry, to acquiesce in speculative absurdities; but the heart revolts when practical lessons are inculcated; when we are called upon to perform difficult duties, and to part with favourite gratifications.

Christianity avowed an intention to overthrow all the religions of the earth, and had therefore to contend with the strong attachment, which men generally entertain, to the religion in which they have been educated. Of the zeal of the Jews for their religion, we have abundant proof from Scripture. They gloried in the law of Moses, believed that it would be perpetual, and rested their hope of the divine favour upon the observance of it. The regard of the Gentiles to their superstitions was equally strong. Besides being handed down to them from their remote ancestors, whose authority commanded profound respect, and being considered as intimately connected with private and public prosperity, they allured the senses and the passions, by splendid spectacles, by licentious festivals, by the charms of the fine arts, and by the unbounded toleration of the corrupt propensities of the heart. Christianity came to set aside those religions. It had nothing of the accommodating spirit of paganism, which easily adopted the Gods and rites of other nations; it claimed to be the only true religion, and commanded its own institutions to be exclusively observed.

Lastly, The preachers of this unsocial religion were not fitted to diminish the prejudices of mankind against it. They were not illustrious by their birth, distinguished by their talents, celebrated for their wisdom and learning, and able to overawe and persuade others by their authority and eloquence. Upon the hypothesis that this work was of men, which is the foundation of our present reasoning, they were destitute of every qualification, natural and supernatural, for the undertaking in which they were embarked. Not having received the Holy Ghost, they could speak no language but their own, and that, too, in a clumsy, inaccurate manner; they could work no miracles; they could compose no regular discourses; they could only render themselves and their system contemptible, by their confusion and vulgarity. They were Jews, and on this account were held in contempt by the Gentiles, who looked down upon the whole nation as a superstitious, bigoted, unlearned, and unphilosophical people. It was sufficient to injure the reputation of any set of opinions, that it had originated in a country, the supposed seat of ignorance and barbarism.

Such were the improbabilities, that this religion, if it were a human contrivance, should succeed; or rather they were sure grounds, on which any man might have predicted, as Gamaliel did, that it would not succeed. It could hardly have maintained itself for any length of time in Judea; it could not have made its way at all into heathen countries. We know, however, that it did prevail in Judea, and gained over thousands and myriads of the inhabitants; that it spread over the whole extent of the Roman conquests, and found access to regions which their arms had never reached; that it humbled the proud philosopher, purified the slave of vice, tamed the fierce barbarian, and established the empire of truth and holiness over the fairest portion of the earth. "There is not a nation," says one of the Fathers in the second century, "whether of Greeks or of barbarians, in which prayers and thanksgivings are not offered up to the Father and Maker of all things, in the name of the crucified Jesus."* "We are but of yesterday," says another, addressing himself to the magistrates of the empire, "and we have filled every place, your cities, islands, garrisons, free towns, camp, senate, and forum; we have left nothing empty but your temples."† What, then, is the inference, which sound reason authorizes us to draw? Is it not, that the religion of Jesus Christ, which, in the circumstances

---

* Justin. Mart. Dialog. cum Tryph. † Tertul. Apol.

now detailed, was published with incredible success, was from God, and not from man? Infidels may torture their invention to account, on natural principles, for this strange fact, this moral phenomenon, the establishment of a religion so ungainly, so repugnant to the ideas, feelings, interests, and favourite pursuits of mankind, by the diligence and exertions of such weak instruments, upon the ruins of all the systems of philosophy and superstition which then existed; but their abortive malignity can only excite the pity, or the scorn, of every enlightened mind.

Thus far the reasoning has proceeded upon the supposition, that the Sanhedrim had adopted the counsel of Gamaliel, and that the gospel had been suffered to work its own way in the world. But, although the rulers of the Jews listened at this time to the voice of reason and moderation, yet it was not long till they recurred to violence, and began a furious persecution of the Christians. Their example was followed by the Gentiles; and for nearly three centuries, the disciples of Jesus were subjected to severe hardships, and cruel sufferings on account of their religion. Every motive of prudence and policy conspired to make men decline assuming the Christian name. The Heathens exhibited no portion of that tolerating spirit towards the new religion, which was exercised towards their different forms of idolatry; it was proscribed as a pestilent superstition, hateful to the Gods, and hostile to the peace and prosperity of the empire. If the seasons proved cold and barren; if fire consumed any of their cities; if earthquakes desolated the provinces; the Christians were accused as the cause of those calamities, and their punishment was demanded by the clamours of the people. The unresisting victims were driven into exile, doomed to perish amidst the unwholesome labours of the mines, exposed in the amphitheatres to be torn in pieces by wild beasts, that the eyes of their savage persecutors might be feasted with the spectacle, consumed at stakes, executed upon scaffolds, or put to death by slow tortures, in devising which, human barbarity, exasperated by hell, exhausted its ingenuity. Emperors and magistrates, forgetting the dignity of their character, philosophers their boasted moderation, relatives the sentiments of nature, and men their feelings of humanity, continued for ages to embrue their hands in the blood of the inoffensive and patient martyrs of Jesus. They hoped to subdue their courage, or to exterminate them from the earth. But all their efforts were baffled. Like the Israelites in Egypt, the more the Christians were afflicted, the more they grew. The blood of the martyrs was the seed of the Church. The places of those who fell were speedily supplied. The example of their virtues, and the power of the truth, induced many to become followers of their faith, at the hazard of all that was dear to them in the world. Hence, at the close of a long period of trial, when the Church might have been expected to exist only in the records of its enemies, the number of its members was so great, that Constantine found his interest united with his duty, when he declared himself its protector. The banner of the cross was displayed on the Capitol of Rome; and the religion of one, who had died the death of a slave, in a distant province, was embraced by the mighty conquerors of the earth. "The work was of God, and men could not overthrow it." Its enemies were found to fight against God; and they perished in the impious and unequal contest.

This event is totally different from the success of the Antichristian and Mahometan religions. These systems arose in a dark and ignorant age; were dexterously accommodated to the prejudices, the superstitious temper, and the licentious inclinations of men; and were propagated by the artifice of imposture, and the terror of the sword. In the success of Mahomet, there is nothing more extraordinary than that of any other conqueror, who flies, from province to province, at the head of a victorious army, and compels the subjugated, terrified inhabitants, to submit to his law. Christianity made its appearance in an age of science and literature, and professed an open hostility to all the sinful passions of men; but although unaided and unfriended, calumniated and opposed by the whole force of the Roman empire, it went forward in its course, like the sun, who sometimes eclipsed, and sometimes darkened with clouds, steadily advances to his meridian altitude, from which he pours a full tide of light and glory on the earth.

Thus I have considered, at some length, the celebrated counsel of Gamaliel. We have seen, that if the powers of this world had let the new religion alone, it was of such a nature, that, had it originated from man, it could not have succeeded. Its success, therefore, would, in these circumstances, have been a clear proof of its divinity. But since the rulers of the earth did not let it alone, the evidence acquires new strength from the formidable opposition against which it prevailed. Here we perceive the finger of God; and no man, who listens to the suggestions of reason, can refrain from saying, " Behold this hath the Lord wrought."

We learn from the following verses, that the rulers of the Jews complied so far with the counsel of Gamaliel, as to desist from their intention to put the Apostles to death. They contented themselves with scourging them, and dismissed them with a command, not " to speak in the name of Jesus." To this command they paid no regard; and the punishment inflicted upon them, instead of depressing their courage, served to animate their zeal. " And they departed from the presence of the council, rejoicing that they were counted worthy to suffer shame for his name. And daily in the temple and in every house, they ceased not to teach and preach Jesus Christ."

I conclude with the three following reflections.

First, It was no easy task in which the Apostles engaged, when they went forth to preach among the nations the gospel of the kingdom. Their situation was very different from that of the old philosophers, who delivered lectures at their ease, to an admiring audience; and from that of ministers of the gospel in the present time, who enjoy the protection of the laws. They were men, " who hazarded their lives," who rose superior to fear, and shame, and pain, who looked for nothing in this world but sufferings and death. How high does their character rise ? It may be compared with that of the most distinguished patriots, and eminent benefactors of mankind. Who could have expected to find such philanthropy, such noble and disinterested sentiments, in persons taken from the lowest ranks of society, and bred to the meanest occupations ? To what respect and gratitude is their memory entitled ; respect for their illustrious virtues, and gratitude for their generous exertions to promote the best interests of the human race ? How should we admire the grace of God, who called them to the arduous work, inspired them with the love, and zeal, and patience, and fidelity with which they performed it, supported them under manifold difficulties, and crowned their labours with success !

Secondly, God can always find the means of preserving his servants in the discharge of their duty. He can make their deliverance come from an unexpected quarter. He saved the Apostles, on this occasion, by the interposition of Gamaliel, a Pharisee, and an enemy to the gospel. History furnishes many instances of persons, who have favoured and forwarded the cause of religion from motives of worldly policy, in pursuit of their schemes of ambition, love, avarice, and rivalship; and we cannot but admire the wisdom and power of God, in " restraining the remainder of the wrath of the wicked," by the wrath or some other passion, of men as wicked as themselves. He makes the earth help the woman. He has the hearts of kings and of all men in his hands, and turns them " as the rivers of water."

In the last place, from the success of the gospel in past times, we may confidently hope for the fulfilment of the predictions relative to its diffusion and establishment throughout the earth. After its rapid progress under the Apostles and their successors, in the first ages, Christianity began to decline. Several countries, in which it was professed, were subdued by the Mahometan arms; and its light was almost extinguished in Europe, and the eastern church, by a dark cloud of superstition and idolatry. At the Reformation, it shone forth again; but how small a part of the civilized world enjoys the benefit of its salutary rays! And if we look to other regions of the earth, "behold darkness and sorrow, and the light is darkened in the heavens thereof." The success of Christian missions has not equalled the examples of former times, and the eager hopes of those who projected them. A few converts, collected, after long labour, out of many thousands, give no animating prospect of the speedy triumph of our religion. If the husbandman should gather two or three straggling stalks of corn, who would call this a harvest? But let us not despond. Jesus Christ lives, and "the residue of the Spirit" is with him. The gospel has nothing more formidable to encounter than the opposition which it has already subdued. When we see the mighty empire of Rome prostrate at the feet of Jesus Christ, and presenting homage to him as its sovereign Lord, we cannot despair, that the time will come, when India and China, and the islands of the sea, shall be added to the trophies of the cross. Let us " remember the years of the right hand of the Most High;" and let us pray, that he would again " make bare his holy arm, and openly show his salvation in the sight of the Heathen." " Then shall all the ends of the earth see the salvation of our God."

LECTURE VIII.

THE INSTITUTION OF DEACONS, AND THE HISTORY OF STEPHEN.

Chap. vi.

"YE have the poor always with you, but me ye have not always.' These words were spoken by our Lord in vindication of a woman who had poured a box of precious ointment upon his head, and was accused by the disciples of having profusely wasted what might have been devoted to a charitable use. They might well bear with this occasional testimony of respect for their Master, of whose presence they were soon to be deprived, since, the poor, for whose interests they seemed to be so zealous, should always remain with them. To the poor the gospel was preached. Our Saviour did not address himself exclusively to persons in the higher ranks, whose names would reflect honour on their teacher, and whose munificence would reward him ; but he selected, as the particular objects of his gracious instructions, those who were suffering the inconveniences and hardships of life. "God has chosen the poor of this world to be rich in faith, and heirs to the kingdom." In this choice, we see an instance, not only of the sovereignty of God, who in distributing his favours, disregards those distinctions which are so much valued among men, but also of wise provision for the trial and improvement of his people. If they were all rich and prosperous, few occasions would occur for performing the offices of charity; whereas, while some possess, and others want, the comforts and often the necessaries of life, there are constant calls to the exercise of condescension, sympathy, and beneficence. Thus a strong bond of union is formed between the giver and the receiver; and the Church "makes increase unto the edifying of itself in love."

Among those who first turned to the Lord in Jerusalem, there seem to have been many in necessitous circumstances. But large as was the demand for the relief of so numerous a class, it was cheerfully and liberally supplied, by a forward zeal and unbounded charity, of the more wealthy believers, who "sold their possessions, and laid the price at the Apostles' feet, that distribution might be made to every man, according as he had need." In a society so distinguished by the love which prevailed among its members, we should have expected, that the utmost harmony would reign, and that jealousy and discontent would be unknown. It is, therefore, with surprise, that we find this chapter opening with an account of the same complaints, which we are accustomed to hear among persons, whose principles are not so pure and disinterested.

" And in those days, when the number of the disciples was mulplied, there arose a murmuring of the Grecians against the Hebrews, because their widows were neglected in the daily ministration." Those Grecians were not Greeks, but Jews born in foreign countries, who used the Greek language in common conversation, and in the service of the synagogue. Having taken up their residence in Jerusalem in consequence of their conversion, or for other reasons, they composed a part of the Church in that city. They are distinguished, in this passage, not from Jews, for under this appellation both they and the inhabitants of Judea were comprehended, but from Hebrews, by whom are meant such Jews as spoke the Hebrew language, or the mixed dialect, which went under that name. These were accused by the Grecians of neglecting their widows, "in the daily ministration," while they seem to have attended to their own. The distribution of the public charity, it was alleged, was not made on fair and equitable terms. How weak a being is man! How apt to be turned aside from the path of rectitude and honour! Instead of acting on grand and liberal principles, he often permits selfishness to cramp the best affections of his heart, and draws around himself a narrow circle, of which he is the centre. Whatever is in any way connected with himself, acquires importance in his eyes; whatever is distinct or detached, is undervalued. The comparatively insignificant circumstances of being born in the same country, speaking the same language, and descending from the same remote ancestors, shall recommend a person more to our good will and friendly assistance, than the best qualities of the heart, and the strongest claims of necessity, in an absolute stranger. Thus, in the primitive Church, some widows were overlooked, because they spoke Greek, and others were punctually supplied because they spoke Hebrew; or, to give a more accurate statement, the former were neglected, because they were the widows of strangers; and the latter were attended to, because they were the widows of fellow-citizens and acquaintance. The administration was in the hands of the Hebrews, who allowed this low consideration to bias them in the management of their trust.

But how could any just ground for this complaint exist under the ministry of the Apostles, to whose care the contributions of the faithful were committed? Were not the wisdom, the piety, the zeal, the independence of mind, for which they were so eminent, sufficient to preserve them from the influence of local and vulgar prepossessions? If we admit, that they were chargeable with partiality in this matter, how does it appear, that they were worthy of their office, or proper persons to be employed in promulgating a religion, intended to abolish national distinctions, and to make of Jews and Greeks, bond and free, "one new man in Christ?" In answer to these questions, I observe that there is no evidence, that, at this time, the Apostles did manage the affairs of the poor. It is probable, that having found the time and attention which this business required to be more than could be spared from the immediate duties of their office, they had devolved it upon others; and it is to these deputies that the blame of partiality attaches.

This conclusion is supported, I think, by the second verse. Having called the disciples together, to propose an expedient for terminating the present dissension, and preventing any future cause of complaint, the Apostles begin with observing, that it was not reasonable, "that they should leave the word of God, and serve tables." The expression, "to serve tables," is of the same import with ministering to the necessities of the poor. Their tables were to be supplied with food convenient for them; such things as they wanted, were to be provided; and it would have been neither right nor becoming, that the Apostles should be so much engaged in this service, as to omit the more important duties of their office. Jesus Christ had sent them to preach the gospel; and no inferior design, however useful and urgent, should interfere with the great object of their commission. The words of the Apostles have much the appearance of a reference to a complaint, that if they had cared for the poor as they ought to have done, the widows of the Grecians would not have been neglected; or to a suggestion, that if they would now take them under their inspection, the evil would be redressed. To this complaint or suggestion, they reply, that as their past conduct was justifiable upon the principles of reason and duty, so they were determined still to confine themselves to their appropriate work, the dispensation of the word. They at once vindicate themselves from the charge of criminal neglect, and state the ground, on which they would not even now become stewards of the property of the Church. If this view of their words is just, it follows, that as they did not distribute the public stock, they could not be blamed for the mismanagement, which had occasioned the murmuring of the Grecians.

The remedy for the present disorder, which was proposed by the Apostles, and adopted by the multitude, was the institution of a new order of office-bearers, who should make the care of the poor the sole object of their attention. "Wherefore, brethren, look ye out among you seven men of honest report, full of the Holy Ghost and wisdom, whom we may appoint over this business. But we will give ourselves continually to prayer, and to the ministry of the word." The institution accords with the compassionate, benevolent spirit of the religion of Christ. We find nothing similar to it in the superstitions which prevailed in the Heathen world; no peculiar provision for the poor; no order of men appointed to relieve the fatherless, widows, and orphans. These unhappy persons, the religions of Greece and Rome left to perish, or to drag out an uncomfortable existence upon the precarious bounty of those, whom nature had inspired with some sentiments of humanity. It is the amiable character of the Messiah, that, in a temporal as well as in a spiritual sense, "he delivered the needy when he cried, the poor, also, and him that had no helper." The charitable spirit of the gospel excited the wonder and the envy of the Gentiles; and Julian, the mortal foe of Christianity, reluctantly confessed its unrivalled excellence, when he attempted to graft upon the decayed, sapless trunk of Paganism, it fairest fruits of love and beneficence.*

The design of creating the new office-bearers, who are known by the appellation of deacons, was to distribute to the necessities of the indigent members of the Church. To preach the gospel was no part of their duty. The Apostles say, that they would appoint the

---

* Jul. Epist. ad Arsacium apud Soc. lib. v. cap. 15.

persons whom the people should choose, " over this business." If Philip, one of the deacons, afterwards preached, it was in consequence of his being raised to the office of an Evangelist. Stephen did not preach, but only disputed with the enemies of the faith, as any private member of the Church might have done. The office was instituted, because the preaching of the gospel, and the requisite attention to the poor, were found to be incompatible.

As the trust, implied in this office, was important, and the peace of the Church, as well as the private good of not a few of its members, would depend upon the manner in which it was executed, the qualifications of those to whom it should be committed, were pointed out by the Apostles. The choice of the people was confined to such persons among them, as were of " honest report, full of the Holy Ghost and wisdom." They must be men of " honest report," of tried integrity and blameless reputation, that the members of the Church might place full confidence in them, and enemies might find no occasion of reproach. They must be " full of the Holy Ghost;" an expression which imports, that they should be richly furnished with his sanctifying influences, as Christians in general are exhorted to be " filled with the Spirit;" or that they should possess his extraordinary gifts, agreeably to the meaning which the phrase bears, in other passages of this book. Both senses may be admitted. The sanctifying grace of the Spirit was necessary to inspire them with the love, the fidelity, the zeal, the activity, which their office required ; and his extraordinary gifts, although not indispensable, might be considered as highly expedient in men, who sustaining a public character, would have frequent opportunities to demonstrate the truth of the gospel by signs and miracles. In the last place, they must be " full of wisdom," to distinguish real, from pretended, cases of necessity, to judge of the proportion, and the manner in which the public charity should be distributed, and to administer consolation and seasonable advice to the needy and af flicted. Such were the qualifications required in the first deacons, which rendered them worthy substitutes of the Apostles, in the superintence of the poor. To them they could safely entrust the whole charge, and consequently give themselves continually to prayer, and to the ministry of the word."

There are two particulars which deserve attention, in the appointment of these men to their office. The choice of them was committed to the people. "Look ye out among you seven men."

Thus the right of the people to elect the office-bearers in the Church was recognised. It is a right founded in the positive institution of Jesus Christ, made known, on this occasion, by the Apostles, and agreeable to the dictates of reason. To choose their own teachers and rulers was for many ages, regarded as a sacred privilege of Christians; and there are on record decrees of bishops, and councils, and popes, confirming it, and declaring the invalidity of such ordinations as had taken place in violation of it. It was in the progress of corruption, that this right began to be questioned, and was at length set aside. The advantages resulting from it are a proof of the wise care of Jesus Christ for his Church, and call upon Christians to maintain it against the usurpations of men. On the one hand, the choice which the people have made of their pastors and governors; the consideration that they have freely and deliberately committed themselves to their inspection, is calculated to keep alive an attachment to their persons, and to ensure respect to their instructions and reproofs. On the other hand, the esteem, which the people have expressed for them, by voluntarily placing themselves under their care, obviously tends to conciliate the affection of their spiritual guides, and to stimulate them to active exertions for the good of their charge. Thus a foundation is laid for that harmony and mutual good-will, without which the interests of religion cannot be expected to prosper. When pastors are set over the Church without its consent, both parties will regard each other with the indifference of strangers; or, what is worse, the people will hate the teacher, as an unhallowed intruder, and he will hate them, as insurgents against what he deems lawful authority.

But the right of the people extended no farther than the election of the deacons. They had no power to exercise in their appointment to office. Their separation to it, their investiture with authority to perform its duties, was the province of the Apostles. "Look ye out seven men,—whom we may appoint over this business." It is the ordinance of Christ, that to those who sustain any office in the Church, authority shall be transmitted from himself, its original source, by the medium of its ministers and rulers. The exclusion of the private members from any share in the transmission is clearly marked in the passage before us. The limits are distinctly drawn. The people elected, and the Apostles appointed. We never read in the Scriptures, that there is a power lodged in the Church at large, to preach the gospel, administer the sacraments, and govern itself.

This power was committed to Apostles, Prophets, Evangelists, Pastors, and Teachers, whom Jesus Christ has given to the Church, as an absolute sovereign delegates his authority to certain persons, bearing such titles, and exercising such functions as he is pleased to confer upon them. When a voluntary society is to be formed, the members first meet, and determine what shall be the form of government, and who shall be the governors. But in the case of the Church, the governors were before the society. The Christian Church did not exist when the Apostles received their commission; and those who at present bear rule in it, are their successors in every thing pertaining to their office, which was not extraordinary. It is manifest, therefore, that their power does not flow from the people, unless an express law can be produced, altering the original constitution, and ordaining, that, although the Apostles received the "keys of the kingdom" immediately from Christ, and the first office-bearers derived their power from the Apostles, it should be afterwards communicated by the Church in its collective capacity.

The measure proposed by the Apostles was unanimously approved, and was executed without delay. "And the saying pleased the whole multitude; and they chose Stephen, a man full of faith and of the Holy Ghost, and Philip, and Prochorus, and Nicanor, and Timon, and Parmenas, and Nicolas, a proselyte of Antioch: whom they set before the Apostles; and when they had prayed, they laid their hands on them." The imposition of hands was a rite used on different occasions; in blessing a person, in curing diseases, in imparting spiritual gifts, in setting one apart to an office. For the last of these purposes, it may still be practised, although miraculous communications have ceased. Prayer, which preceded the imposition of hands, was offered up for the divine blessing upon the new institution, and the persons elected, that they might be enabled to perform their duty with fidelity, and to the satisfaction of the Church.

The names of the seven deacons being Greek, it has been thought, that, with the exception of Nicolas, a proselyte of Antioch, a Gentile formerly converted to Judaism, they were all Grecians, or Jews of the dispersion, who spoke the Greek language. No persons were so likely to quiet the jealousies and murmurs of the Grecians, because, being of their own number, they would not be suspected of neglecting their widows. How noble was the conduct of the Hebrews, who, with a view to remove every ground of discontent on the part of their foreign brethren, were willing that the entire management of the funds of the Church should be confided to some of themselves! And how high must have been the character of the deacons for integrity, when, although they were all of one party, the Hebrews were under no apprehension of partiality in their conduct, and cheerfully entrusted them with the care of their poor?

We are informed, in the next verse, that "the word of God increased; and the number of the disciples multiplied in Jerusalem greatly; and a great company of the priests were obedient to the faith." Without stopping to make any remarks upon this verse, although the conversion of so many priests, who were engaged in opposition to the gospel, by their prejudices, and pride, and secular interests, might be illustrated as an evidence of its wonderful efficacy, I proceed to consider the history of Stephen.

In the fifth verse, he is described as a man "full of faith and of the Holy Ghost;" a firm believer of the gospel, and possessed not only of the graces, but likewise of the extraordinary gifts, of the Spirit. Accordingly, it is said in the eighth verse, that "full of faith and power, he did great wonders and miracles among the people." By these he established those who already believed, and presented evidence to others, by which some were undoubtedly gained over to the gospel. A person so eminent and active, would not long remain unnoticed by the adversaries of the Church. "There arose certain of the synagogue, which is called the synagogue of the Libertines, and Cyrenians, and Alexandrians, and of them of Cilicia, and of Asia, disputing with Stephen." They challenged him to a public disputation about the new religion, of which he was so zealous a partisan, in the hope that they should be able to confute his arguments, or at least, to draw from him some unguarded words, for which they might accuse him to the rulers. But "they were not able to resist the wisdom and the spirit by which he spake." We have no ground to think, that Stephen was a learned man, instructed in the arts of reasoning, and practised in controversy; and his eloquence was of the same kind with that of the Apostles, simple and unadorned. But he was endowed with heavenly wisdom, which sophistry could not withstand, and assisted by the suggestions of the Divine Spirit, who can overwhelm the proud polemic with irresistible conviction. When Stephen spoke, his antagonists were confounded. In vain did they torture their invention to devise objections to the gospel; they were instantly repelled. In vain did they attempt to reply to his arguments; to his reasoning from prophecy and miracles they could find nothing to oppose. Their ingenuity was exhausted; and they stood abashed and silent in his presence. A mortifying situation for men who had provoked the contest, and had entered upon it, in the full confidence of victory!

But, when arguments failed, their malice furnished an inexhaustible resource. "Then they suborned men, which said, We have heard him speak blasphemous words against Moses, and against God." They hired witnesses, and instructed them what to swear; not scrupling to make use of any means, however dishonourable and unjust, of effecting their purpose; and contriving, perhaps, to conceal the baseness of their conduct even from their own consciences, by the pretext of zeal for the glory of God. The charge, which the witnesses were directed to bring against Stephen, was, that "they had heard him speak blasphemous words against Moses, and against God." Blasphemy strictly signifies any thing spoken with a design to vilify the character of God, or to injure him in the opinion of others, by creating unfavourable thoughts of his attributes, his commands, or his dispensations. It conveys, therefore, the idea of the most atrocious and daring sin of which a creature can be guilty. The term has an odious sound, and awakens our abhorrence of the crime, and of the criminal. Hence it has been frequently employed, by religious controvertists, with great address, and with much latitude of application, to stigmatize the opinions and character of their opponents. Honest indignation may have sometimes had recourse to it, to brand those impious tenets, which subvert the foundations of our faith; but in not a few cases, it has served insidious malignity as an admirable expedient for discrediting a particular doctrine, and exciting clamour and persecution against its author and abettors. It was evidently with this intention, that the charge of blasphemy was now advanced against Stephen; and it had all the success which his enemies wished. The people, the elders, and the scribes, were alarmed; and hastening, with common consent, to bring to condign punishment the man, who had dared to revile the God of Israel, and Moses, his illustrious minister, they apprehended, and arraigned him before the council. This was the Sanhedrim, which had authority to take cognizance of cases of blasphemy.

In the following verses, and in the next chapter, we have an account of his trial, which commenced with perjury, was abruptly terminated by the impatient zeal of his accusers and judges, and was succeeded by the cruel murder of this righteous man. It was begun with perjury; for the witnesses, being suborned, accused him, upon oath, of a crime, of which, for aught that they knew, he was innocent. "They set up false witnesses, which said, this man ceaseth not to speak blasphemous words against this holy place, and the law." It was his constant practice to speak, in threatening and disrespectful terms of Jerusalem, the holy city, and of the temple, the habitation of God, and of Moses, the most eminent of his servants. On this account, he was guilty of blasphemy, according to the loose sense, in which that crime was then understood. No accusation could have been contrived, which would more certainly rouse the indignation of his judges; for notwithstanding their extreme degeneracy, the Jews still pretended to feel, and actually felt, an ardent zeal for the glory of God, and the religion which they professed. In support of this charge, it was farther affirmed by the witnesses, that they had heard him say, "that Jesus of Nazareth would destroy that place, and change the customs which Moses delivered them." Such assertions were shocking to a Jew, who believed that Jerusalem would be the capital of the Messiah's kingdom on the earth; that the temple would always be the place for offering victims and incense; and that the institutions of Moses would retain their authority and sanctity through all generations.

Upon the supposition, however, that Stephen did say what the witnesses testified against him, as perhaps he had done on the authority of Christ and the Prophets, what crime had he committed? In what did the alleged blasphemy consist? Had not Shiloh, where the tabernacle once stood, been laid desolate? Was not the first temple destroyed by the Chaldeans? Why, then, should the second temple be permitted to stand, if it was turned into a "den of robbers;" and especially, if the Messiah was come, and had made the "sacrifice and oblation to cease," by offering himself upon the cross? With respect to the law, it was indeed framed by the wisdom, and enacted by the authority, of God; but it was subservient to a better dispensation, and was no longer useful when that dispensation was introduced. Why should the shadow be retained, when the substance was enjoyed? Of what value was the image to those, who possessed the original? In the sacred writings of the Jews, there were many intimations, that the religion of the Messiah should be universal; and nothing more was necessary than dispassionate consideration, to convince any man, that its universality was incompatable with the perpetuity of the law. The temple of Jerusalem could not be a sanctuary to the whole earth; nor could the solemn feasts, which were celebrated thrice a-year, and at which all the males were commanded to be present, be observed by persons living in distant continents and islands. But these reflections never occurred to the Jews. They could not conceive, and they had no wish to enjoy, a more perfect system of worship than their own. As they had long been the peculiar people, the idea of abolishing the distinction between them and other nations, and placing them all on a level in respect of spiritual privileges, was so mortifying to their pride, that they could not hear it mentioned without impatience and rage. "It is blasphemy," they exclaimed, "against the holy place and the law. The fall of our temple, and the abrogation of our ritual, would be a failure of God's promises, and the utter ruin of religion."

Under the charge of having expressed sentiments so offensive and impious, Stephen had every thing to fear from the furious zeal of his judges. Nothing but his blood could atone for a crime of such magnitude. Yet his confidence did not forsake him, nor was his tranquillity disturbed. Conscious innocence, firm faith in his Saviour, and the hope of immortality, supported and cheered his mind in this trying hour. "All that sat in the council, looking steadfastly on him, saw his face as it had been the face of an angel." The precise meaning of these words cannot perhaps be ascertained. They seem to signify, that on this occasion there was something preternatural in his countenance, a divine splendour similar to that on the face of Moses when he came down from the mount, and which was a manifest token of the presence and approbation of God; or that there was such a mixture of majesty and mildness in his looks as may be imagined in the face of an angel, if he should become visible to men, and indicated the perfect composure of his mind, and the magnanimity with which he disregarded the malice and rage of his adversaries. He was as a rock in the midst of the ocean, upon which the tempests blow, and the waves dash in vain.

The remainder of this interesting history will be the subject of the next Lecture. In the mean time, I conclude with a few observations.

First, All the institutions of the Gospel bear a relation to the exigencies of the Church. There is nothing superfluous, nothing intended merely for show, nothing which could have been left out without inconvenience and detriment. In the kingdoms of men, we observe offices which serve no purpose but to augment the splendour of the sovereign, to increase his influence, and to provide honours and emoluments for his favourites. In corrupt Churches, superstition has introduced an expensive and useless appendage of bishops, archbishops, patriarchs, cardinals, and popes. But in the Church modelled after the Scriptural plan, we see no office without its appropriate duties, of which the beneficial tendency is obvious. There are pastors to " feed the people with knowledge and understanding ; there are elders to rule over them with vigilance and love ; there are deacons to supply the necessities, and sooth the sorrows, of the poor. Every thing has evidently proceeded from him, " who is wonderful in counsel, and excellent in working."

I observe, in the second place, that the best method to promote the glory of God, and the public good, is for every man to attend to his peculiar duties. " Let every man abide in his calling, and study to do his own business." This is the sphere in which providence has appointed him to move. To grasp at something farther, "to stretch ourselves beyond our measure," is to violate the order which God has established, and to forget the limited nature of our faculties, which are distracted and embarrassed by a multiplicity of objects. The care of the poor would have been a specious apology for interfering with the management of their affairs ; it had the appearance of great diligence, and great humanity. Yet, the Apostles declared, that it would have been unreasonable and incongruous in them to have neglected for this service, the proper duties of their office. Men never go out of their way without going wrong. They either mismanage the affairs, with which their inconsiderate zeal has incited them to intermeddle, or, when engaged in them, they forget the business of their own station. " As we have many members in one body, and all members have not the same office ; so we being many, are one body in Christ, and every one members one of another." On this ground, the Apostle addresses the following exhortation to Christians. "Having then gifts, differing according to the grace that is given to us, whether prophecy, let us prophesy, ac cording to the proportion of faith; or ministry, let us wait on our ministering; or he that teacheth, on teaching; or he that exhorteth, on exhortation; he that giveth, let him do it with simplicity; he that ruleth, with diligence; he that showeth mercy, with cheerfulness."

In the last place, We are admonished by the conduct of the enemies of Stephen, to examine, with care, the nature and motives of our religious zeal. It may be an unhallowed fire, kindled by hell, or by our own passions; not a pure flame, proceeding from love to God and man. "It is good to be zealously affected always in a good thing;" but zeal in a bad cause is the worse, the keener and more vehement it is. "The Jews had a zeal for God, but it was not according to knowledge;" and it hurried them on to the most dreadful excesses; to crucify the Lord of glory, to blaspheme his religion, to murder his servants, to add crime to crime, till, in the righteous judgment of God, they perished in their rage. How little are we acquainted with the spirit by which we are actuated! How apt are we to mistake error for truth, to be misled by fair appearances in ourselves as well as in others, to fancy that our hearts glow with ardour for the glory of God, when it is pride, or self-love, or party affection, which is stirring within us! We may be certain that our zeal is false, when it is excited by matters of less, but is indifferent to such as are of greater, moment; when it is violent against the sins of strangers, but indulgent to those of our friends; when it extinguishes love to the persons against whose opinions or practices it is directed; when it takes pleasure in exaggerating their faults, in expatiating on their blemishes, in holding them up to public detestation; when it is disposed to curse rather than to bless, not to save, but to destroy. May the Spirit of gentleness and love descend into our hearts! The man, in whose bosom he resides, is not the sport of the selfish and malignant passions. He only is a man of disinterested benevolence. He loves the persons whom duty commands him to oppose; his heart melts with tenderness, while he reproves and admonishes them; and the only triumph which he seeks, is the triumph of truth and grace in the salvation of their souls.

LECTURE IX.

THE MARTYRDOM OF STEPHEN.

Chap. vii. 54—60.

In the last Lecture, I entered upon the history of Stephen. We have seen, that, rendered conspicuous by his office, his gifts, and his activity, he was regarded with a jealous eye by the unbelieving Jews; that their hostility was exasperated by the ill success of the disputation to which they had challenged him; and that, with the revenge natural to base and little minds, they were impatient to destroy by violence, the man whom they could not vanquish by argument. I shall pass over his speech before the Sanhedrim, recorded in the preceding part of the chapter, because, being an abridged narrative of the history of the Jews, it does not fall within the limits of this course of Lectures, which is intended to illustrate the principal events connected with the rise and progress of the Christian Church. There is one observation, which must occur to every reader, namely, that the speech is incomplete. He sets out with a detail of the divine dispensations towards the patriarchs and their seed, and goes on, in regular order, till he come down to the days of Solomon, when he suddenly breaks off, and addresses his audience in the language of accusation and reproach. It is probable that his hearers gave signs of impatience; and Stephen, perceiving that they were about to interrupt him, seized the moments which remained, to tell them a few unwelcome truths, which, if they did not arrest them in their headlong career, would serve as his dying testimony against the incorrigible enemies of his Saviour. From the strain in which he speaks of the temple towards the close of his discourse, we may collect, that he would have proceeded to show that that magnificent structure was a typical temporary building; that there was no blasphemy in affirming that it should be destroyed; and that its fall might now be expected, as, by the incarnation and death of the Messiah, the end of its erection was accomplished. His audience seem to have perceived his design; their zeal was roused to fury at the most remote hint, which appeared disrespectful to their sacred institutions.

"When they heard these things, they were cut to the heart, and they gnashed upon him with their teeth." The word rendered, "to cut," has been chosen to express, in the strongest manner, the effect of the speech upon his accusers and judges. It signifies to saw asunder, and alludes to that cruel mode of putting criminals to death. The men, in whose presence Stephen now stood, entertained lofty ideas of their own character, and were fully persuaded that they were the favourites and devoted servants of heaven. With what indignation must they have heard, from one whom they so much hated, that they were "uncircumcised in heart," hypocrites, who had the seal of the covenant in their flesh, but wanted all the qualities of which it was a sign; that they "always resisted the Holy Ghost," by whom they believed themselves to be moved; and that they had now filled up the measure of the iniquity of their fathers, by betraying and murdering the Messiah? Such accusations inflicted a wound upon their pride, the pain of which goaded them on to madness. When a good man is unjustly reproached, he will feel the injury, and vindicate himself with the dignity of virtue; but he will, at the same time, commit himself, with all meekness, to him "that judgeth righteously." But when a bad man is charged with his crimes, wanting the support of a good conscience, and that steady confidence in heaven, which is the reward only of innocence, he frets and rages against those who have insulted his honour, and dissipated the pleasing illusions of self-love. Perhaps, his heart, for a moment, misgives him; a sudden ray of conviction, darting into his mind, discovers the hollowness of his pretences, and the baseness of his motives; stung by transient remorse, he is impatient of the anguish; his passions become ungovernable; and he bursts into fury, which torments himself, while it seeks to destroy the disturbers of his peace. Such were the feelings, and such was the behaviour of the enemies of Stephen. "They were cut to the heart, and they gnashed on him with their teeth;" expressing at once the torture which they suffered, and the ferocity of their temper. They resembled beasts of prey, eager to devour the man who has dared to attack them.

The situation of Stephen was critical. Every look and gesture of those who surrounded him menaced him with death; and had he betrayed symptoms of perturbation and alarm, we must have pitied the weakness of humanity thus severely tried, and have condemned him with a sigh. Trembling for his life, an ordinary man would have had resource to tears and supplications to melt the hearts of his persecutors; or, pale with fear, and stupified with despair, he would have sullenly submitted to his fate. How different was the conduct of the saint! With that calm dignity which religion inspires, he observed the rage of his enemies; and turning away from a scene, which exhibited the malignant passions in all their horrors, he lifted his eyes to heaven, in testimony of his resignation and his hope. In the moment of danger, and in the agony of distress nature itself teaches man to appeal to his Maker. The first cry which he utters is a prayer; and his eyes are directed to the sanctuary on high, from which God beholds the children of men. But it is the Christian alone, who feels that confidence of protection, who is cheered with that hope of sympathy and aid, with which a son runs to shelter himself in the arms of his father.

How transporting was the prospect which was presented to Stephen! In this world, good men walk by faith; and are supported amidst their sufferings, by a well-founded assurance of the invisible glories and joys of eternity. They see nothing more than others; they only believe more, and believe on better grounds. By an extraordinary dispensation, the evidence of sense was, in the present case, superadded to the evidence of faith. He, who was first called to seal the truth of the gospel with his blood, was favoured with a particular testimony of the divine approbation, to encourage others to follow him in the same arduous service. The interest which Jesus Christ takes in his faithful servants, who, for his sake, love not their own lives, was made manifest, to assure them in every age, that although they may not see him, as Stephen did, yet he looks on, while they are suffering in his cause, and opens his arms to receive their spirits, as they rise from the scaffold and the stake. "But he being full of the Holy Ghost, looked up steadfastly into heaven, and saw the glory of God, and Jesus standing on the right hand of God."

The whole of this dispensation was miraculous. Stephen was probably in the hall in which the Sanhedrim was assembled, and his natural sight was bounded by the roof. Even in the open air, the human eye, which perceives the sun and stars at the distance of many millions of miles, could not, in its ordinary state, have discerned the throne of God, placed beyond the limits of the visible creation. But, as we read in the next verse, "the heavens were opened." Shall we say, that by divine power, a representation of the celestial glory was made to his senses, in the same manner as objects, not really present, were shown to the Prophets in vision; or that his eyes were supernaturally strengthened to penetrate through the immense space which separates heaven from earth, and the veil which conceals the mansions of the blessed? To form conjectures upon a subject, of which we are completely ignorant, is idle; let us, therefore, content ourselves with the simple statement of Luke. He saw "the glory of God," God himself is invisible. "No man hath seen him;" and it is physically impossible that any man should see him, because eyes of flesh are capable of perceiving only material objects. The glory of God must therefore signify some symbol of his presence, perhaps a brightness surpassing that of the sun, which pointed out the place where he reveals himself to angels and saints, who contemplate with admiration his infinite perfections, and, at the uncreated source itself, imbibe the delicious draught of immortality and joy. Such a view of heaven revives the spirits of a dying saint; and he would willingly pass through a sea of blood to participate of its bliss.

But this was not the only sight which gladdened the last moments of the martyr. He saw "Jesus standing on the right hand of God." The Saviour ascended to heaven in our nature, which he will wear for ever, and in which the righteous will behold and admire the perfection of beauty; and he sits at the right hand of the Father, invested with the highest honours, and exercising sovereign authority. But on this occasion Stephen saw him standing. And why does he appear in this unusual posture? One of the Apostles, with a design to demonstrate his superiority to the Levitical priests, remarks that they "stood" when they ministered; but that he, having offered his sacrifice for sin, "for ever sat down on the right hand of God." A saint was surrounded with enemies thirsting for his blood, and in a few moments was to fall a victim to their rage. Jesus Christ rose up from his throne to observe the courage, the patience, and the faith of his disciple; to meet and welcome his spirit as soon as it had escaped into the peaceful asylum of heaven; and to introduce him into the presence of his Father, that he might receive from his hands the crown of glory. "When the heathen rage, and the people imagine a vain thing, he sits still and laughs at them." Their wild uproar does not disturb his tranquillity. But when a poor saint, despised and outraged by the world, is dying under its murderous hands, he rises; his heart is interested; his compassion is excited; he makes haste to succour the forlorn sufferer, and waits to embrace, and to solace him in his arms. How comfortable to Stephen was the sight of Jesus, standing on the right hand of God! How it elevated his soul! how it animated his resolution! how it inflamed his love! how it stript death of its terrors! "Let the flesh," he could say, "feel a few short pangs, and then I shall be with my Saviour, whose hand will wipe away all my tears."

In such a state of mind, Stephen could not be silent. Pleasurable emotions of the lighter or gentler kind may be suppressed, as pride or prudence shall direct; but when the heart is strongly affected, and overcome by sudden and excessive joy, it breaks through all restraints, and gives unequivocal signs of its sensations. "Behold," exclaims the martyr, "I see the heavens opened, and the Son of Man standing on the right hand of God." Although none were near him who feared God, yet he could not forbear to declare "what God had done for his soul." But his words are not to be considered merely as expressive of his triumph. They were a new testimony to the truth of the religion for which he was to lay down his life, and to the glory of his Saviour; and in this view, they were fitly spoken in the presence of his enemies. "It is no cunningly devised fable which I follow, when I believe, that Jesus of Nazareth is the Messiah, and that he has ascended from the cross to the throne. It is no longer the subject of my faith. I see it with my eyes; I behold him reigning with his Father, far above all principality, and power, and might, and dominion. The sentence which you dared pronounce upon him as a blasphemer is reversed. There stands the Son of Man, whom you persecuted under that humble title, placed, as he foretold to you, on the right hand of power. Over me it will be easy to prevail; but know that you are contending with him, who can dash his enemies in pieces as a potter's vessel."

The passions of his audience, already wound up to the highest pitch, now burst forth with ungovernable fury. "They cried out with a loud voice," to drown the voice of the blasphemer, and "stopped their ears," lest they should hear more of his words; and disregarding the solemnity of the place, and the gravity and deliberation, with which all judicial proceedings should be conducted, they "ran upon him with one accord," and "cast him out of the city," which his presence profaned, and "stoned him." Yet notwithstanding the excess of their rage, they could so far command themselves as to observe some of the forms of law. They did not murder Stephen with the first weapons which they could find, but stoned him, as God had commanded the blasphemer to be punished. "He that blasphemeth the name of the Lord, he shall surely be put to death, and all the congregation shall certainly stone him." They did not execute this sentence upon him in the streets of Jerusalem, but first dragged him out of the city, because God had said concerning the son of an Israelitish woman, who blasphemed in the wilderness, "Bring forth him that hath cursed without the camp." Although they were all eager to testify their zeal, by taking a part in his death, yet they waited till the witnesses had thrown the first stones; for the law required, that "the hands of the witnesses should first be upon him to put him to death, and afterward the hands of all the people." It seems, therefore, that amidst the disorder with which the trial was conducted, the council had regularly pronounced sentence upon him. But the observance of legal forms could not atone for the neglect of material justice in condemning him on false evidence, and interrupting his defence. Alas! this is not the only instance, in which law has been perverted to the destruction of the innocent, and the most nefarious deeds have been coloured over with an appearance of respect for order and equity.

"And the witnesses laid down their clothes at a young man's feet, whose name was Saul." Saul was neither a witness nor a judge; but his furious zeal had brought him to the place, and he expressed his approbation, we may presume, by gestures and words. I see him standing, with the rage of bigotry depicted on his countenance, encouraging the witnesses to avenge the honour of Moses upon the wretch who had dared to revile him, himself hurling a stone at his head, and relaxing into a vindictive smile, when the blessed martyr fell lifeless to the ground. In the school of Gamaliel, he had imbibed no portion of the moderate spirit of his teacher. The fire of youth, blown up into a flame by religious prejudice, could not be repressed by the calm lessons of reason and humanity. A career which commenced with such unfavourable symptoms, promised to be marked, in its progress, with violence and blood. A young man, who could thrust himself forward as an accomplice in such a transaction, seemed to discover a mind too arrogant and overbearing to be convinced, and a heart too callous to relent. The fervour of his passions might abate as he advanced in years, but the same dispositions would continue; and the impetuosity of zeal would be exchanged for more deliberate and systematic cruelty. Who could have recognised in this man "a vessel of mercy?" Who could have supposed, that ere long his zeal would be transferred to the service of Jesus of Nazareth; that it would glow with equal ardour, but with a purer flame, for the advancement of that religion, which it now sought to consume; that the persecutor would become an Apostle; and that he who joined in the murder of a disciple, would, in the same cause, willingly submit his neck to the stroke of the executioner's sword?

Let us return to Stephen, whom we left in the midst of his enemies. His courage was unshaken, and his mind was calm. "And they stoned Stephen, calling upon God, and saying, Lord Jesus, receive my spirit." God is a supplement, which would have been better omitted; and the verse should have been rendered thus. "They stoned Stephen, calling upon Jesus, and saying," &c. Whether we adopt the one translation or the other, the verse furnishes an example of religious worship, offered to Jesus Christ by one of the primitive disciples, standing on the verge of the eternal world, and under the inspiration of the Holy Ghost. There is not a higher exercise of faith, nor a more solemn act of religion, than to commit our departing spirits to the care of Him whom we address. This is the last and most important step; and the consequences of a mistake would be irretrievable. And to whom should this homage be paid, but to our faithful Creator? In whose hands can we safely entrust our souls, but in those of him who made them? Here, then, is a proof that our Lord Jesus Christ is a divine person, entitled to the same worship with the Father, unless Stephen died an idolater, and the Holy Ghost had suddenly abandoned him; a proof, which the adversaries of his Deity cannot evade, except by such pitiful shifts, as are sure indications of a desperate cause.

"Lord Jesus receive my spirit." His earthly tabernacle was battered and broken, and ready to fall down into the dust. But Jesus had taught his disciples, "not to be afraid of them that kill the body, and after that have no more that they can do." The immortal spirit cannot be pierced with the sword, nor consumed by the flames. It eludes the rage of persecutors; it escapes from the murdered body, and rises to heaven. Of the soul, as a substance distinct from the body, the light of nature gives some notices; and hence the celebrated saying of the philosopher Anaxarchus, when he was condemned by the tyrant of Cyprus, to be brayed to death in a mortar, "Beat the case of Anaxarchus; but thou dost not strike Anaxarchus himself."* But surer are the hopes of the Christian who knows, by infallible evidence, that although his body claims no higher origin than the dust, and in its frailty resembles the dust, which every wind may scatter; yet his spirit is a vital spark, kindled by the breath of the Almighty, and destined to glow for ever in the pure and serene atmosphere of heaven. The soul of Stephen was about to leave this world, and to pass into eternity. How dark and doubtful is the passage to those, who have nothing to guide their steps but the uncertain twilight of reason! "Whither art thou going? Into what region shalt thou enter? Art thou doomed to sink into insensibility and non-existence, or to wander for ever in darkness and sorrow?" A bright ray, piercing through the gloom, shines upon the dying saint, and leads his eye to those glorious mansions, in which he shall enjoy eternal repose beyond the reach of calamity and death. He beholds by faith what Stephen saw with his bodily eyes, "Jesus standing at the right hand of God," and expires with this prayer upon his lips, "Lord Jesus receive my spirit." "Lord," said the holy martyr, "I am dying for the honour of thy name. I willingly part with this mortal life at thy command. Now, while I yield up my body to be bruised and mangled by these men, take my soul to thyself, in whose presence it will speedily forget its sorrows." With the same language of faith and hope did Jesus himself close his agonies upon the cross. "Father, into thy hands I commend my spirit." And thus after having received, during the course of his life, many pleasing testimonies of the favour and guardian care of heaven, does a good man, supported by the consolations of religion, pass without fear into another world, where the same protection will be continued, and the same love will bestow its blessings in greater abundance.

The few moments of life which remained, Stephen spent in prayers for his murderers. Calm amidst their fury, full of charity,

---

* Diog. Laert. in vita Anaxarch.

while they breathed revenge and blood, "he kneeled down, and cried with a loud voice, Lord, lay not this sin to their charge." Human nature, in such circumstances, is apt to harbour very different sentiments. To be persecuted without a cause, to be loaded with foul imputations which we do not deserve, to be deprived of life by the hand of injustice, and, instead of being pitied under our sufferings, to be insulted; these are wrongs too irritating to be borne by an ordinary measure of patience. The victim exclaims against the unrelenting cruelty of his enemies. Finding no redress upon earth, he appeals to the tribunal of heaven, and dies invoking its vengeance. Our natural feelings concur in the appeal, and approve of the prayer; for, is it not right that the cry of blood should be heard, and that the violence of the wicked should recoil upon their own heads? How much nobler are the sentiments which religion inspires? It teaches us "to render blessing for cursing," and to seek the good of those who are inflicting upon us the greatest evils. Christian heroism is not of a stern and unrelenting character; it is associated with the milder virtues; the same bosom, which is fortified by invincible courage, cherishes all the tender affections; and while the saint encounters danger with the firmness of a philosopher, he melts with compassion towards his persecutors, upon whom the wrath of heaven is ready to fall. "Lord," cries exasperated nature, "let their sin be remembered, and do thou reward them according to their deeds." "Lord," says the heaven-born soul, "lay not this sin to their charge."

Such language, indeed, is now so common, in consequence of the example exhibited by Stephen, and by our Lord upon the cross, and of the general strain of the doctrines and precepts of our holy religion, that we hear it without much admiration. Almost every profligate, who is brought to the scaffold for his crime, professes to forgive his enemies, and to die in peace with all the world. But the difference is great between the unmeaning cant of virtue, and the real practice of it. It is no vulgar attainment to love the man who hates us; to divest ourselves of a wish to retaliate upon him who has poured bitterness into our cup; sincerely to desire the salvation of those, who, if their power were equal to their malice, would consign us to the flames of hell. Such benevolence never lodged in a soul, whose ideas and affections the Spirit of love had not first purified and elevated.

"Lord, lay not this sin to their charge." Stephen was fully apprized of the atrocious nature of the conduct of his persecutors, which implied the complicated guilt of murder and impiety; and of the dreadful punishment which was prepared for them by the justice of the insulted Saviour. Yet to that Saviour he made intercession in their behalf. The words must be understood as a prayer, that they might receive repentance unto life, and be pardoned through that blood, which they now despised as a common thing.

The melting charity of this prayer was sufficient to have softened the hearts of savages. Yet, it did not suspend the rage of the murderers of this holy man; but as he closed it, the mortal blow was inflicted, which filled up the measure of their guilt, and dismissed the saint to everlasting rest. "And when he had said this, he fell asleep." Nature had suffered violence; but the struggle was over, and its convulsive agitation was succeeded by a calm. "He fell asleep." The word is happily chosen, to express the peaceful nature of the death of the righteous, who, worn out with labour, and exhausted with sorrow, sink down upon the bed of dust to enjoy sweet repose. There let the blessed martyr rest, till the dawn of the last morning, when, awaked by the voice of his Saviour, he shall rise to receive an unfading crown, and to participate in the triumph of truth, which, by patience, and meekness, and blood, shall have overcome the rage of the world, and the malice of hell.

To this Lecture I subjoin the following improvement.

First, None are more violent and implacable enemies of the truth, than those who live in an insincere profession of religion. They have peculiar reasons for disliking it. It detects their hypocrisy, reproves their backslidings, condemns their innovations and corruptions, and disturbs their proud confidence and presumptuous hopes. With what indignation and fury do they rise up against such ungrateful doctrine? They hate it, because "it never speaks good concerning them, but evil." We have a pertinent example in the conduct of the Jews towards Stephen. The apostate Church of Rome has faithfully trodden in their steps. The most ferocious savages never exercised greater cruelty upon their deadly foes, than the genuine disciples of Jesus have suffered from the followers of Antichrist. And what evil had the victims of their barbarity done. Had they blasphemed the God of heaven; or committed crimes against the peace of society? No; but the Scriptures informs us, that they "tormented them who dwelt on the earth," not by fires, and racks, and other infernal engines, but by "prophesying," or by publishing truths, which exposed and condemned their errors and corruptions. This is the true history of persecution. It is the war of the seed of the serpent against the seed of the woman; the effect of that hatred which holiness excites in the unregenerate heart.

In the second place, Jesus Christ will not be wanted to his servants under those sufferings which they endure for his sake. He is too much pleased with their zeal in offering themselves as a sacrifice to his glory, to leave them unpitied and unfriended in distress. Does any man afflict a poor helpless saint, who passes for a mere cipher in the world's arithmetic? He says, "Thou hast touched the apple of mine eye. I feel the pain, and will avenge the injury." Are his disciples reproached, tortured, and put to death, by the wanton cruelty of the wicked? A voice cries to them from heaven. "Why persecute you me?" Our exalted Redeemer has a fellow-feeling with his people; and his hand is always ready to obey the suggestion of his sympathizing heart. Invisible to mortal eyes, he stands in the heavenly sanctuary, praying for grace to help them in time of need. Hence human nature has often been so powerfully supported as to astonish the spectators. It has not startled at the sight of death in its most horrible forms; it has shed no tears, and uttered no groans, when it was slowly consumed by fire, and torn in pieces by instruments of iron. Delicate women and children have tired their persecutors by their patience under tortures; and it was only when nature could hold out no longer against the approaches of death, that they yielded with a smile. "My grace is sufficient for thee; for my strength is made perfect in weakness."

In the third place, In whatever form death may befall a Christian, his latter end is peace. What! is it peace, if he should expire in agony, in indigence, and in solitude, without a friend to watch his bed, or a physician to administer cordials; or should die by the hands of the public executioner? Even in those cases my brethren, it is peace, because he dies in the Lord, and falls asleep in the hope of a resurrection to life. He may be carried away by a whirlwind; but it will convey him, like Elijah, to heaven. Do you think rather of the rich and honourable man, who is stretched upon a bed of down, surrounded with weeping relatives, and attended by men of skill, who exhaust their art to alleviate his pain? Ah! you do not consider, that perhaps remorse embitters his last hours; he shudders at the approach of death, and quits life in horror and despair. How much happier was Stephen, although bruised, and broken, and aching in every limb? The joy of hope refreshed his soul. Looking up to heaven, he beheld his Saviour waiting to receive him; and he committed his spirit to the care of this faithful and affectionate friend.

Who, then, will not say, "Let me die the death of the righteous; and let my last end be like his?" Who would not wish to leave the world with the same inward peace, and the same animating prospect? Remember that this shall be the privilege of those alone, who resemble Stephen in faith and holiness. It is faith in the atonement and intercession of Jesus, and the testimony of conscience to the sincerity of faith, which will cheer the evening of our days, and make the grave appear under the image of a place of rest; a blessed refuge from the malice of men, and the calamities of life.

the Apostles; but we must have recourse to it, if we understand the passage to mean, that the persecution was so violent as to cause the flight of all the disciples.

Whoever attentively considers what has now been advanced, will, I trust, be convinced, that the words of Luke do not refer to the whole body of the people. At the same time, the universal term which he employs, points out some class of persons, to which it should be applied. And whom can we so reasonably presume to be meant as those who were associated with the Apostles in preaching the gospel, and dispensing the ordinances of religion, Evangelists, Pastors, and Teachers? This idea, I am disposed to think, would occur to a careful reader from the words themselves. "They were all scattered abroad except the Apostles." Why are the Apostles excepted, if not with a design to intimate that the rest were of the same description, persons, who, as well as they, laboured in word and doctrine? How the Apostles could remain in the city, while others found it necessary to flee, I am not able to say. In a narrative so concise, the omission of several circumstances renders it impossible to explain every particular. Perhaps, they had more courage than their brethren; or, being willing to expose themselves to all the danger, they advised the other ministers of the word to retire, for a season, to those places in which they could freely employ themselves to the advantage of the common cause.

It is not a mere conjecture, that those who were scattered abroad were authorised preachers of the gospel. The supposition is confirmed by two facts afterwards recorded. The first among the dispersed disciples, who is said to have preached, was not a layman, to employ a term of ancient use in the Church, not a self-created teacher, who judged himself qualified, and therefore, called, to commence a public instructor. The preacher, as we shall soon see, was Philip, an Evangelist, that is, an extraordinary office-bearer, inferior only to the Apostles. The next of whom we have any account, were men of Cyprus and Cyrene, who having gone to Antioch, preached to the Grecians. We are not informed, on this occasion, whether they held any office in the Church; but, when Antioch is again mentioned, we read, that there were Prophets and Teachers in that city, among whom, we find Lucius, a man of Cyrene. It is highly probable, that he was one of those Cyrenians by whom the Church of Antioch was founded; and it is a natural inference, from his being a Prophet or Teacher, that the rest were likewise

Prophets, or persons invested with some ecclesiastical office. It may be presumed from these facts, that all those, who went every where preaching the word, were possessed of the same authority.

These remarks will at least show, that the argument for lay-preaching, which has been deduced from this passage, is not so clear as to justify the confidence with which it has been advanced. It is an instance, in which, by a mistake of the sound of Scripture for the sense, an opinion has been adopted, which is contrary to its explicit declarations in other passages. He who shall consider, that it was not to the Church at large, but to the Apostles, that Jesus gave the keys of the kingdom of heaven; that they, and not all the disciples, of whom there were more than five hundred, received a commission to go into all the world, and preach the gospel to every creature; that, when they planted Churches, they ordained elders in every city to instruct and govern them; that there is not, in the New Testament, a single case fairly made out, of a person who preached without authority, nor in the history of the Church, during the first century, as one, profoundly learned in Christian antiquity, and unbiassed by any particular interest, has assured us;[*] that Timothy was directed to commit the preaching of the gospel to faithful men, who should be able to teach others, and, consequently, that those, to whom it was not committed, had no right to teach; and, not to multiply particulars, that an Apostle expressly affirms that men cannot preach, that is, have no authority to preach, except they be sent: he who shall seriously and dispassionately consider these things, will reject as unscriptural the notion, however confidently and plausibly maintained, that every man who is qualified, or, in other words, judges himself qualified, may commence a preacher of the gospel; a notion manifestly calculated to foster vanity, ambition, and enthusiasm, and, when acted upon, to diffuse among the people ignorance, error, contempt for a regular ministry, and all the wild and pernicious effects of unenlightened zeal. Those who are unacquainted with the history of religion in this island, have no need to be told to what disorders it gave rise in the century before the last; and it is vain to expect that we shall ever "gather grapes of thorns, or figs of thistles."

We proceed to the account of the labours of Philip the Evange-

---

[*] Mosheim. de rebus Christian. ante Constantin. p. 151. 152.

list, in Samaria. "Then Philip went down to the city of Samaria, and preached Christ unto them."

Samaria was the ancient capital of the ten tribes, who revolted from the family of David; but was now inhabited by the descendants of the mixed people, whom the king of Assyria, when he carried those tribes into captivity, planted in their room. At their first settlement, those foreigners practised the idolatry of the countries from which they respectively came; but afterwards, in consequence of the instructions of an Israelitish priest, who was sent to teach them "the manners of the God of the land;" they associated with their own rites the worship of Jehovah. It was probably from his hands that they received the five books of Moses; and these, corrupted in several places, were the only books of Scripture which they acknowledged. They built a temple on mount Gerizzim, in which they offered sacrifices; and they observed the Jewish festivals, practised circumcision, and expected the Messiah. Of their system of religion, as it existed in the days of our Saviour, it is difficult to obtain a distinct and satisfactory account, because the implacable enmity of the Jews led them to represent it in the most unfavourable light. From the words of Jesus to the Samaritan woman, it appears to have been extremely corrupt. "Ye worship ye know not what." Yet, as they professed the same religion with the Jews, how much soever they differed in some material points, they are classed with them in the style of the New Testament, and are not reckoned among the Gentiles. The honour of having begun the conversion of the Gentiles, is not ascribed to Philip, who preached with success to the Samaritans, but to Peter, by whose ministry Cornelius, a Roman centurion, was brought to the knowledge of the truth.

From this imperfect view of the religious state of the Samaritans, it is evident, that they were not better disposed than their rivals the Jews, to embrace the doctrine of Christ. Their system was more erroneous, their prejudices were equally great, and their knowledge was less. When Philip visited them, there was less hope than ever that they would lend a favourable ear to the gospel, because their attention and affections were pre-engaged by one of those impostors, who, in all ages, have sported with the credulity of mankind. "There was a certain man called Simon, which before-time in the same city used sorcery, and bewitched the people of Samaria, giving out that himself was some great one: to whom they all gave heed, from the least to the greatest, saying, This man is the great power of God." Magic, which he professed, was held in high estimation by the Chaldeans, Egyptians, and other eastern nations. It was an imaginary science, founded in a supposed intercourse with demons, a sort of intermediate beings between the Gods and men, who were believed to possess great influence over human affairs. Magicians pretended to be able, by their aid, to cure or to inflict diseases, and to perform many other wonderful works. In most cases, their miracles were undoubtedly of the same kind with the juggling tricks of professed conjurors among ourselves. In some instances, they may have been effected by means of an acquaintance with the secret powers of nature. By a dexterous use of such knowledge, it was easy for an unprincipled man to raise the wonder of the ignorant, and to make himself pass for a superior being, or a person who was favoured with the immediate assistance of heaven. The opinion that magicians were assisted by evil spirits, although it could not perhaps be proved to involve any absurdity, is clogged with too many difficulties to be hastily admitted. The belief of such assistance has been generally entertained from certain principles in the human mind, which have given encouragement to the whole race of magicians, conjurors, necromancers, and fortunetellers; the credulity of a great part of men in both the higher and lower ranks, their love of the marvellous, their desire to penetrate into the secrets of futurity, their hope of protection from dangers and calamities, and of such success in their schemes of ambition, wealth, and pleasure, as it was vain to expect from their own prudence and ability.

To this class of deceivers Simon belonged. He "used sorcery" in Samaria, or, as the word signifies, exercised the magical art; and he "bewitched" the people, or astonished them. In the usual style of such impostors, he gave himself out to be "some great one." We are not told what character he assumed. Perhaps, he avoided any specific claim, and asserted his dignity in general and mysterious terms, calculated, by their indefinite nature, to work upon the imagination of the crowd, and to raise their admiration to the utmost height of extravagance. The Samaritans, the dupes of his artifice, exclaimed, "This man is the great power of God." They were at a loss by what title to distinguish him; but they regarded him, with reverence and awe, as a messenger from the God of heaven and earth, whom he had invested with his own almighty power.

Notwithstanding, however, the veneration in which Simon was held by the Samaritans, no sooner did the Evangelist appear, than the mimic wonders of magic shrunk before the genuine works of omnipotence. "What is the chaff to the wheat? saith the Lord." Magic, with its spells and incantations, its mystic rites and vaunted powers, could not bear to be compared with that splendid train of miracles, by which the gospel was confirmed. Unclean spirits, the pretended agents in this diabolical art, crying out with terror, fled from the bodies of the possessed; the limbs of those who were afflicted with palsy in a moment recovered their vigour; and the lame, throwing away their crutches, or rising from their beds, leaped for joy. By these real wonders, the charm which attached the Samaritans to Simon was broken; their attention was turned to the Evangelist; and they were prepared to give his doctrine a patient and favourable hearing. They believed him to be an ambassador from God, whose instructions they were bound to receive. "And the people with one accord gave heed unto these things which Philip spake, hearing and seeing the miracles which he did."

The labours of Philip were attended with great success. "The power of the Lord was present, to heal the Samaritans," to enlighten their minds, and to render them obedient to the faith. Their conversion must be ascribed to the influence of divine grace upon their souls, and not to the external evidence of miracles addressed to their senses, or to the arguments and eloquence of the preacher. "Neither is he that planteth any thing, neither he that watereth; but God that giveth the increase." "The light shineth in darkness, and the darkness comprehendeth it not, till God, who commanded the light to shine out of darkness, shine in our hearts, to give the light of the knowledge of the glory of God, in the face of Jesus Christ." "The Samaritans believed Philip preaching the things concerning the kingdom of God, and the name of Jesus Christ, and were baptized both men and women." How did Simon behave on this occasion? He also believed and was baptized, wondering at the miracles of Philip, which so much surpassed the feats that the art of magic had enabled him to perform. As it is manifest, however, from his subsequent conduct, that he was not a partaker of the grace of God, from which he should have never fallen, it is necessary to remark, that it is not always in the same sense that men are said, in the

New Testament, to believe. Sometimes the meaning is, that, under the influence of the divine Spirit, they unfeignedly received the testimony of God concerning his Son; and at other times, faith implies no more than such an assent to the gospel upon external evidence, as we give to propositions in philosophy, or to historical facts, of which we perceive satisfactory proof. Of this nature was the faith of Simon. It is excessive refinement, therefore, or rather a pitiful quibble, to maintain that none can be said to believe the gospel, but those who have been savingly illuminated. It is right to study the greatest accuracy in our expressions upon the subject of religion; but when it is strained beyond the standard of Scripture, and impeaches the language of inspiration, we must be excused for neither adopting nor admiring it, and shall be content to blunder on with an Apostle or an Evangelist.

Simon was admitted to baptism, because he made a credible profession of faith, and Philip perhaps did not suspect his sincerity. He might have long continued to sustain the character of a believer, had not an event taken place, which presented a temptation too strong to be resisted. "Now when the Apostles, which were at Jerusalem, heard that Samaria had received the word of God, they sent unto them Peter and John. Who, when they were come down, prayed for them, that they might receive the Holy Ghost. (For as yet he was fallen upon none of them: only they were baptized in the name of the Lord Jesus.) Then laid they their hands on them, and they received the Holy Ghost." The design of their mission was to assist Philip in his labours, to confirm those who believed, and, in particular, to impart spiritual gifts. Philip, it would seem, did not possess the power of communicating them, which appears to have been exclusively granted to the Apostles, to distinguish them as the immediate ambassadors of Christ, and the first ministers in his kingdom. "As yet the Holy Ghost was fallen upon none of them;" that is, his extraordinary gifts had not yet been conferred upon the Samaritans. They had already received his regenerating influences, for they already believed, and faith is one of the fruits of the Spirit. Peter and John therefore prayed, that God would bestow upon them the same supernatural endowments, which had been so liberally distributed to the Jewish converts; and then "laid their hands on them." This solemn rite, as we observed in a former Lecture, was used in the primitive Church, both in setting apart a person to a spiritual office, and in conveying miraculous powers.

In the present case, and in all others of the same nature, it was merely a sign, with which the thing signified was connected, not by the authority of the Apostles, but by the will of the Spirit.

It is not necessary to suppose, that the Holy Ghost, in the sense already explained, was given to all the Samaritans who believed, and were baptized. It does not appear, that, even in the Church of Jerusalem, which we may conceive to have been at least as highly favoured in this respect as any other, there was an indiscriminate distribution of his extraordinary gifts. When an election was to be made of persons to take care of the poor, the Apostles commanded the multitude to look out among them men " full of the Holy Ghost ;" and the command obviously imports, that every man was not so qualified. In that age, when the Spirit was poured out upon all flesh, upon persons of all ranks and conditions, it is certain that in some cases he was imparted to private members of the Church ; but it is probable, that the communication was more commonly made to those who sustained a public character. " To one was given the working of miracles ; to another prophecy ; to another discerning of spirits ; to another divers kinds of tongues ; to another the interpretation of tongues. But all these wrought that one and the self same Spirit, dividing to every man severally as he willed." In this manner, provision was made for the edification of the Church, as well as for the conviction of unbelievers. The first Christians were, for the most part, unlearned ; and the pastors were on a level, in this respect, with their flocks. But the want was amply supplied, when " to one was given, by the Spirit, the word of wisdom ; to another, the word of knowledge by the same Spirit." Were any person still in the Church, who could confer the Holy Ghost by the imposition of hands, he might dispense with a regular education for the ministry, and employ missionaries recently taken, like Matthew, from the receipt of custom, and Peter, from the trade of a fisherman. It is a surprising mistake to neglect the ordinary means of preparation as unnecessary, when those of an extraordinary nature have ceased. But to preach the gospel seems now to be accounted by some men an undertaking so easy, that almost any person may engage in it.

The character of the Apostles never appears more august, than when we view them as possessed of the power which was exercised, at this time, by Peter and John. It seems to exalt them above the standard of human nature, and to throw around them some degree of the lustre of divinity. To see men, who could control the laws of nature by a word, or a sign, and were able to transfer a portion of their authority to others, excites our veneration for them, as beings raised above all that wealth and grandeur can bestow. How insignificant is the philosopher with his boasted science, the statesman with his political wisdom, or the monarch with his sceptre, which he sways over a hundred provinces, when compared with men, whose command could change the established order of the universe! Here ambition might have beheld an object which would gratify its most extravagant wishes. By being endowed with the same power which the Apostles enjoyed, the possessor would be raised far above all his competitors for fame; or, if avarice were his predominant passion, would find an easy way to the acquisition of riches. Simon was unable to withstand the temptation. His pretended wonders were eclipsed by the real miracles which the Apostles performed; and, if he could prevail upon them to invest him with their power, and, above all, to enable him to communicate it to others, he flattered himself that he had discovered a certain road to distinction. He therefore offered them money, saying, "Give me also this power, that on whomsoever I lay hands, he may receive the Holy Ghost." It was the proposal of a base and impious mind, which supposed that spiritual gifts might be bartered for gold, and that others were governed by the same low motives, of which itself was conscious.

Simon was speedily undeceived with respect to the character of Peter and John. With what confusion and dismay must he have heard this answer! "Thy money perish with thee, because thou hast thought that the gift of God may be purchased with money." It is not to be understood as an imprecation of divine vengeance upon Simon. Notwithstanding the form of the words, which seem to contain a prayer or a wish, they amount to no more than a strong expression of abhorrence. "Let thy money perish as thou shalt, unless God give thee repentance." It is the indignant language of religious principle, resisting a nefarious attempt to corrupt it. It is a zeal for God kindled into a flame, at the avowed wickedness of a man, who sought to prostitute the most sacred things in the service of his passions. Peter proceeded to reprove and admonish him in very solemn and alarming terms. "Thou hast neither part nor lot in this matter: for thy heart is not right in the sight of God." He had thrown off the mask, and discovered his character in its genuine features. It was no violation of charity, but the judgment of truth, to pronounce him, notwithstanding his late profession, to be still in an unregenerate state. Yet Peter did not consider him as guilty of an unpardonable sin; and as the grace of God is rich and free, and is often exercised towards notorious transgressors, he concluded with the following exhortation. "Repent, therefore, of this thy wickedness, and pray God, if perhaps the thought of thy heart may be forgiven thee. For I perceive that thou art in the gall of bitterness, and in the bond of iniquity."

The spirit of Simon was appalled at the terrible words of the Apostle; and for a moment he trembled in the view of his danger. Hence he entreated Peter and John "to pray to the Lord for him, that none of these things which they had spoken should come upon him." But the favourable symptoms were not of long duration; for we are assured, by the testimony of ancient writers, that he afterwards apostatized from the Christian religion, and openly opposed the Apostles. I shall conclude the account of him, by laying before you a summary of the blasphemous and licentious doctrines which he is said to have propagated, extracted from Irenæus, who, in the second century, composed a learned work against heresies. "This man," he says, speaking of Simon, "was honoured by many as a God, and taught that it was he who had appeared among the Jews, as the Son, among the Samaritans, as the Father, and among other nations, as the Holy Ghost; and that he was the most sublime virtue, or the Father of all, by whatever name he was known among men. Having brought from the city of Tyre an infamous woman called Helena, he carried her about with him, affirming that she was the first conception of his mind, the mother of all beings, by whom in the beginning he formed angels and archangels. He persuaded those who believed in him and this woman, that they might live as they pleased, because men were saved by his grace, and not by good works; and that works are not good by nature, but by accident;" or, in other words, that virtue and vice are arbitrary and unfounded distinctions. The same Father goes on to inform us, "that his followers led flagitious lives, that they practised magic, and that they adored the images of Simon and Helena."* It is plain from this account, that it is inaccurate in ecclesiastical writers to call Simon the first heretic, and the father of heresy; for

---

* Iren. contra Hæres. lib. '. cap. xx.

f a heretic signifies a person who corrupts, while he professes and teaches, the Christian religion, the appellation does not properly belong to a man who explicitly abandoned it, and endeavoured to establish an impious system of his own. It is farther related, by some of the Fathers, that a statue was erected to him at Rome with this inscription, " To Simon, the holy God ;" and that an encounter having taken place in that city, between him and Peter, when the magician by demoniacal aid had ascended into the air, the prayers of the Apostle made him fall to the ground.* But these stories are, with good reason, now exploded as fabulous.

The example of Simon admonishes us not to be hasty in the conclusions which we draw from the impression made upon the hearers of the gospel. We must not, like some persons of easy belief, reckon every man, who seems to be awakened, a convert, and account a few tears, shed in a moment of compunction, an evidence of genuine repentance. In this way a long list might be speedily drawn up; but a short time would compel us to make many erasures. Let us never forget, that a profligate sorcerer, when he heard the gospel preached by Philip, renounced the magical art, came forward to confess his sins and to be baptized, and for a time was numbered among the disciples of Christ. The conscience of a very hardened sinner may be disturbed with temporary terror; and the passions of the most careless may, by peculiar circumstances, be interested and agitated. But the emotion subsides; the world again prevails by its allurements; sin regains the empire of the heart; and it happens to them according to the true proverb, " The dog is turned to his own vomit again; and the sow that was washed, to her wallowing in the mire."

Let those, who, like Simon, have disappointed the good hopes which were once entertained of them, by turning away from the truth, beware lest " their hearts be hardened through the deceitfulness of sin." Having suppressed their convictions, violated the fidelity which they had solemnly pledged to Jesus Christ, renounced the friendship, and forfeited the esteem, of good men, they are placed in very perilous circumstances. Conscience has sustained an injury by which it may be rendered insensible; God is provoked

---

* Justin. Martyr. Apolog. ii. Euseb. lib. ii. cap. 14. Constit. Apostol. lib. vi cap. 9.

to give them up to themselves; and pride, shame, habits of depravity, and the counsels of their wicked companions, are obstacles in the way of their return. How rarely are such persons reclaimed! How often do they proceed, by a slower or more rapid progress, till the devout penitent become an outrageous transgressor, and with the infidel or the atheist, "set his mouth against the heavens!" Stop, thou who hast strayed from the path of righteousness. Whither art thou going? Is not destruction before thee? Dost thou not see, at every step, the melancholy wrecks of those who have fallen and perished? And wilt thou, although forewarned of thy fate, press onward to ruin? Hear the voice of mercy, which calls to thee. "Return, O backslider, and I will heal thy backslidings." "Repent of this thy wickedness, and pray God, if perhaps thy sins may be forgiven thee." The Saviour, whom thou hast forsaken, prayed for his murderers; and why shouldst thou despair? His blood, which thou hast slighted, cleanses from all sin. Prodigal! hasten back to thy Father's house, which thou shouldst have done well not to have abandoned. Thou shalt find him, although offended, not inexorable. He is gracious and compassionate; he will run to meet thee and to embrace thee in his arms; and "there shall be joy in heaven over one sinner that repenteth."

LECTURE XI.

THE CONVERSION OF THE ETHIOPIAN EUNUCH.

Chap. viii. 26—40.

The preceding part of the chapter contains an account of the labours of Philip in Samaria, where he triumphed over the arts of magic, and prevailed upon the infatuated followers of a specious impostor to become the disciples of Jesus Christ. The passage now read presents him in a different scene, which, although much more contracted than the former, is not less worthy of attention, from the extraordinary means by which he was conducted to it, the distinguished rank of the person whose conversion was the result, and the remarkable display of the power of divine grace in that event.

It is evident, from the history of the Acts, that the Apostles were not left to the conduct of their own zeal and prudence in the choice of places for preaching the gospel. We are certain, that they were, at all times, under the special guidance of Providence; and several instances are recorded of immediate interpositions of heaven for their direction. The spirit hindered them from going to some places, which they were purposing to visit, and pointed out others, which were not comprehended in their plan. In the case before us, "the angel of the Lord spake unto Philip, saying, Arise, and go toward the south, unto the way that goeth down from Jerusalem unto Gaza, which is desert." The wisdom only of the Author of the gospel was competent to determine what spots were the most favourable for first sowing the seeds of divine truth; and to him the book of the decrees of heaven was unfolded, in which are written the names of those who are predestinated to eternal life, and the order in which each is to be called to the enjoyment of it.

The person, for whose sake the Evangelist was sent on the mission, is thus described. "Behold, a man of Ethiopia, an eunuch of great authority under Candace, queen of the Ethiopians, who had the charge of all her treasure, and had come to Jerusalem for to worship, was returning, and, sitting in his chariot, read Esaias the Prophet." In ancient times, there were two countries known by the name of Ethiopia; the one lying south-east from Jerusalem, and the other situated in Africa, beyond Egypt and Nubia. That it was the latter of which this devout eunuch was a native, is manifest, both from constant tradition, and from the name of his mistress; for the queens of the African Ethiopia, now called Abyssinia, were distinguished by the name of Candace, as the kings of Egypt, during a long succession, were denominated Pharaoh. This man was a proselyte to the Jewish religion. It is evident that he was not considered as one of the Gentiles, because, notwithstanding his conversion, they are not said to have been called, till Peter afterwards preached the gospel to Cornelius.

It may excite your surprise, that a person, born and residing in a country so distant from Judea as Ethiopia was, should have enjoyed opportunities of gaining such an acquaintance with the law of Moses, and the proofs of its divine authority, as had prevailed upon him to submit to it. But, at that time, the Jews were dispersed among all nations; and many thousands of them resided in Egypt, to which they had been attracted by the privileges conferred upon them by Alexander the Great, and his successors, to whose government it was subject. From Egypt some of them might have passed into Ethiopia, and communicated their religion to the inhabitants. According to the account of the Abyssinians themselves, the queen of Sheba, who came to see the glory of Solomon, reigned in their country. Having embraced the religion of that illustrious monarch, she introduced it into her own dominions; and it continued to be professed, till the nation was converted to Christianity. The prevalence of Jewish customs among that people at present, gives some countenance to this relation; and certainly proves, that from whatever cause, the religion of Moses was once generally adopted by them.

The Ethiopian eunuch was a person of distinguished zeal and devotion. Notwithstanding the multiplicity of business attached to his office, and the high rank which he held as a treasurer of the queen, circumstances which generally divert the minds of the great from religion, and make them regard its institutions with indifference or contempt, he had travelled many hundred miles through sandy deserts, to worship God in the temple of Jerusalem. At the passover, pentecost, and the feast of tabernacles, all the males in Israel were commanded to appear before the Lord, in the place which he had chosen. Obedience to this command was not practicable, except within the limits of a small country such as Judea. Yet, some of the Jews and proselytes, in distant regions, who were zealous for the law, and were permitted by their circumstances, occasionally visited the holy city at those stated times, to join with their brethren in the celebration of the festivals, and to offer sacrifices of atonement and thanksgiving. In the gospel of John, we read of Greeks who had come to worship at the feast; on the day of Pentecost, there were assembled devout men " out of every nation under heaven ;" and it was with the same design that this man had come from the kingdom of Ethiopia.

The manner in which he was employed in his return is a farther proof of his piety. " Sitting in his chariot he read the Prophet Esaias." It is not commonly by this expedient that men of rank relieve the tediousness of their journies. They amuse themselves with the shifting scene before their eyes, or with meditating schemes of ambition and pleasure, or with perusing some flimsy production, the offspring of a superficial understanding and corrupt imagination, which mingles poison with the entertainment, and while it stimulates the passions, silently undermines the fortresses of virtue. The Bible is proscribed, as too grave and too precise, to be the companion of those who wish to enjoy life as it passes away. `Yet it is the best enlivener of solitude, the most faithful guide in perplexity, the fortifier of every good principle, a never-failing auxiliary in temptation, the monitor of youth, the comforter of old age, the light of life, and the only surviving hope in death. The sentiments which it inspires ennoble the mind, give dignity to the character, and conduct to true happiness in this world and the next. The fulness of Scripture presents a pleasing variety; and the events which it records are better fitted to awaken the great and tender emotions of the soul, than the transactions of human society, or even the contemplation of the scenery of nature. To a mind capable of perceiving and relishing its excellence, the word of God will be a subject of meditation night and day. In the intervals of business, it will recur to this favourite study with eagerness; and imbibing its instructions and consolations, will forget the cares and troubles of the world.

While the eunuch was reading Esaias the Prophet, "the Spirit said unto Philip, Go near, and join thyself to this chariot. And Philip ran thither to him, and heard him read the prophet Esaias, and said, Understandest thou what thou readest?" In our age, when the pride of rank exacts from inferiors distant respect, and repels every attempt to approach nearer as an insult, such a question would be considered as rude and impertinent, and would be answered with a frown, or contemptuously disregarded. But, in ancient times, there was a more familiar intercourse among the different classes of men; and the great were addressed in a style of freedom very remote from modern manners. The passions of mankind are at all times the same; but the artificial forms of society are perpetually changing. It was owing to the simplicity of manners, which still prevails among eastern nations, that this blunt question, proposed to a courtier riding in his chariot, by a stranger walking on foot, and probably appearing by his dress to be a common man, was heard without surprise, and was answered with mildness. "How can I," said the eunuch, " except some man should guide me?"

There is something very amiable in this answer. It indicates a mind humble and docile. By a proud man the question would have been resented as an impeachment of his understanding; for the great must be treated by others as their superiors in wisdom, as well as in rank and authority. The Ethiopian eunuch frankly acknowledged his ignorance; and instead of endeavoring to palliate it by the pretext that he had not considered the passage, confessed his inability to discover its meaning without assistance. A mind thus conscious of its infirmity was not disposed, like the self-conceited Pharisees and Scribes, to cavil at the doctrines of the gospel, but would receive instruction, as the thirsty earth drinks in the rain. The same unassuming temper must be formed in us all, before we will receive the law from the mouth of Jesus as obedient disciples. " Verily I say unto you, Except ye be converted, and become as little children, ye shall not enter into the kingdom of heaven."

It is not uncommon to meet with persons, who aim at gratifying their pride by an appearance of humility, and make a show of ignorance, that the rapidity with which they seem to learn, may excite admiration. That the ignorance of the Ethiopian eunuch was not affected, is evident from his question in the thirty-fourth verse. "I pray thee, of whom speaketh the Prophet this? of himself, or of some other man?" With a view to evade the argument from this prophecy for the sufferings of the Messiah, the Jews have laboured to wrest its meaning; and have applied it sometimes to one person, and sometimes to another. I am ignorant, whether any comments of this nature were then current among them, and will not therefore affirm, that the eunuch had learned from them to speak in this doubtful manner of the prophecy. There is no reason to suspect, that he was influenced by prejudice against Christ Perhaps, he was unacquainted with his history and his name. In the companies which a man of his station may be supposed to have frequented in Jerusalem, the subject would not be often introduced, especially as Christianity was not now a new thing. But from whatever cause his ignorance proceeded, it must excite the surprise of every reader. It seems strange and unaccountable, that a passage, which describes with such minuteness the humiliation and sorrows of our Saviour, should have been so unintelligible to a devout professor of the Jewish religion, that he could form no conjecture respecting the person to whom the writer referred. We should reflect, that prophecies, which are perfectly plain after they are fulfilled, may have been attended with a considerable degree of obscurity prior to their accomplishment. While the event has not taken place, we see the prediction only by its own light, which exhibits the object, but so indistinctly, as not to show its exact shape and features. Besides, it should be considered, that the Jews, resting too much upon the figurative language of the Prophets, had conceived erroneous ideas of the Messiah as a temporal prince, and of his kingdom as a worldly state. They never dreamed of his sufferings, and the passages which foretold them they could not understand. When our Lord informed his disciples, that he should be delivered into the hands of men, " they understood not that saying, and it was hid from them that they perceived it not." And when, on another occasion, they discovered his meaning, they were offended. " Then Peter took him, and began to rebuke him, saying, Be it far from thee, Lord; this shall not be unto thee." It is no wonder that this proselyte could not perceive the sense of the prediction, since the disciples were equally ignorant of the general subject, till they were instructed by their Master, and by the event.

The passage which he was reading when Philip joined him, was the most proper which could have been found in the Old Testament, for explaining to him the character and the religion of Christ. It is impossible to believe that he lighted upon it by accident; he was secretly directed to it by that invisible hand, which was stretched out for his salvation. He might have opened the sacred volume at another place; and perhaps he was not conscious of any motive for choosing this prophecy in particular. But what men call accidents, are firm links in the chain of providence. There is no such thing as contingence in the world; chance is only a name for our ignorance of the process by which effects are produced. The series of events proceeds according to the plan settled in the counsels of heaven. The lot tossed in the lap, and drawn at a venture, assigns to us that portion which God has appointed; an arrow shot at random pierces the bosom which he has destined to death; the sparrow killed by the thoughtless cruelty of children, does not fall to the ground unnoticed by his eye; nor can a hair of our heads perish without his permission. If his interference extends to matters so minute, can we think it had no concern in the selection of the portion of Scripture which the eunuch was reading? Certainly it was God who pointed out the text, as it was he who provided a preacher to explain it.

The place of the Scripture which he read was this: "He was led as a sheep to the slaughter, and like a lamb, dumb before his shearer, so opened he not his mouth: in his humiliation his judgment was taken away: and who shall declare his generation? for his life is taken from the earth." There is some difference between the quotation and the original passage in Isaiah, owing, it is probable, to the former being taken from the Greek version of the Old Testament. The design of this Lecture does not require a particular explanation of it. It may suffice to observe, that it describes the sufferings of the Messiah, which he endured with meekness and resignation, like a sheep quietly following the person who leads it to death, or a lamb submitting in silence to be robbed of its fleece; and declares, that he was condemned through the injustice of men, and by violence was deprived of his life.

Such was the passage which the eunuch was reading; and the chapter in which it is contained, is one of the clearest and most affecting prophecies of the sorrows and death of our Redeemer. An occasion so favourable, and so evidently provided by heaven itself, the Evangelist could not permit to pass unimproved. "Then Philip," who at the desire of the eunuch had ascended his chariot "opened his mouth, and began at the same Scripture, and preached unto him Jesus." The sermon was worthy of the text, fraught with heavenly wisdom, and recommended by simple, but pathetic eloquence. It was dictated by a mind enlightened, and a heart animated, by the Spirit of truth and love. It was the effusion of a soul descanting upon its favourite theme, and desirous to excite in another the same sentiments of affection to the Saviour, which were so strongly felt by itself. He showed, that the Prophet speaks neither of himself nor of another man, but of the Messiah; that although his reign was described in splendid imagery, he was to suffer before he entered into his glory; and that the prophecies were fulfilled in Jesus of Nazareth, who having died upon the cross for the salvation of men, rose from the grave, and was now exalted "as a Prince and a Saviour, to give repentance to Israel, and forgiveness of sins." These we may conceive to have been the principal topics of discourse; and the preacher was not more interested in them than the hearer. With what earnestness did he listen to these new and surprising truths! How did he wonder at his former ignorance, and rejoice in the light which now shone into his mind! We read of no doubts, of no objections, of no unseasonable questions; but with silent acquiescence he hears and believes. The spirit of God was working in his heart. The courtier receives, with devout humility, the instructions of the Evangelist. He hears his voice as the voice of an angel, and blesses the day which had brought them together.

The effect produced by the discourse of Philip, is evident from the words of the eunuch. "And as they went on their way, they came to a certain water; and the eunuch said, See, here is water; what doth hinder me to be baptized?" The Evangelist had given a full detail of the religion of Christ, comprehending its institutions as well as its doctrines. Hence the new convert was acquainted with baptism. The preacher was wise, the hearer was prompt to learn, and the Holy Spirit, by illuminating his mind, and affecting his heart, enabled him to make rapid advances in knowledge. To every person in similar circumstances, baptism will recommend itself on several accounts. It is the rite by which we publicly recognise Jesus Christ as our Saviour, and dedicate ourselves to his service. It is the sign of our admission into the society of his disciples, in consequence of which we visibly become "fellow-citizens with the saints, and members of the household of God." It is a seal of the covenant of grace, a confirmation of its promises, by which those who receive it in faith are assured of the remission of their sins, and of their right to all the blessings which it signifies. The man, therefore, who has experienced the power of the truth, will set a high value upon this ordinance, from a regard to the authority which enjoins it, and to the important purposes which it is intended to serve. He will come forward with alacrity to profess that faith, which is the source of his peace and comfort, and to devote himself to the Saviour, who redeemed him with his blood. He will esteem it a high honour to be numbered with the children of God, and to be admitted to communion with the excellent ones of the earth. He will thankfully accept of this token of divine love, this support of his faith, of which he may afterwards experience the benefit, amidst the temptations of Satan, and the misgivings of his own mind. By such considerations was the Ethiopian eunuch influenced, when he said to Philip, "See, here is water: what doth hinder me to be baptized?" There is a becoming modesty in his manner of soliciting baptism. He does not demand it as his right; but while the question is expressive of earnest desire, he leaves the Evangelist to determine, whether he was worthy of so high a privilege.

"Philip said, If thou believest with all thine heart, thou mayest." Faith is the qualification for baptism prescribed by our Saviour. 'He that believeth, and is baptized, shall be saved." To adult persons, this ordinance should not be administered, till they are instructed in the principles of the Christian religion, and solemnly profess that they believe them. It is only faith unfeigned which gives any man a right to the ordinance in the sight of God. It is incumbent, therefore, upon those to whom the administration of it is committed, to act with much caution, lest they should be imposed upon by the arts of hypocrisy, to compare the profession of faith with the practice, the only criterion by which we can judge of its nature, and never to proceed without satisfactory evidence of the sincerity of the candidate. Of the prudence which ought to be exercised to preserve the fellowship of the Church in purity, and to guard the institutions of the gospel against profanation, we have an example in the conduct of Philip. "If thou believest with all thine heart, thou mayest." This was an appeal to his conscience, as there was not leisure to ascertain the genuineness of his faith in any other way.

The eunuch replied, "I believe that Jesus Christ is the Son of

God." This confession of faith is short, but comprehensive. It may be resolved into two propositions; that Jesus is the Messiah, and that he is the Son of God. The first is implied in his calling our Saviour Christ, which is of the same import with Messiah; for although that word has been since used as a proper name, it was then always employed as a title of office. The ancient Church believed in the Messiah, expecting salvation through a person whom God would send in his own time, to redeem them from sin and death. This general faith was no longer sufficient. The promised Redeemer had come into the world; and a particular acknowledgment of him, to the exclusion of every other, was required from all to whom the gospel was published. The second proposition is delivered in express terms, "Jesus Christ is the Son of God." The divinity of the Messiah is a fundamental doctrine in the religion of Christians, and was an article of faith under the former dispensation. The blood of a man could not have washed away the sins of the world; the wisdom of a man could not have enlightened the Church; the power of a man could not have rescued us from the yoke of our enemies, and defended us against their assaults. This truth, so important in itself, and so intimately connected with the other truths of the gospel, is now denied and blasphemed by the Jews; and there is evidence in the New Testament, that, so early as the time of our Saviour, they were beginning to abandon it. Manhood and divinity seemed to them to be incompatible. The faith of this new convert, with respect to the person of the Messiah, was sound. He believed the Son of Mary to be the Son of God, a partaker of the divine nature, as well as of the human; and assented to the creed of the ancient Church, expressed in the following terms of joy and triumph. "Lo! this is our God, we have waited for him, and he will save us: this is the Lord, we have waited for him, we will be glad, and rejoice in his salvation."

The confession of faith made by the Ethiopian eunuch is remarkable for its simplicity. The articles are few, and are expressed without circumlocution, or variety of phrase. It would have been well for the Church, if her creed could have remained equally plain and unembarrassed. But the introduction of heresies has rendered it necessary to state the opposite truths with precision; and the dishonest arts of heretics have compelled their antagonists to counteract their attempts to corrupt and disturb the Church, by a full and guarded exposition of the faith. They who are loudest in exclaiming against creeds and confessions, as encumbered with unnecessary articles, and as a restraint upon freedom of inquiry, are the very persons who have caused the evil of which they complain. We must lengthen our line as that of the enemy is extended, that we may encounter him on equal terms, and wrest the victory out of his hands.

The confession now made being satisfactory, "they went down both into the water, both Philip and the eunuch; and he baptized him." Those who understand the original language need not to be told, that the phrase, translated "to go down into the water," does not import that they waded into it, for the purpose of baptizing the eunuch by immersion. It necessarily implies no more than that they went close to it. With whatever confidence some affirm, that immersion was the primitive mode of baptizing, there is no evidence in the New Testament in favour of that practice. Cases are mentioned, in which it seems incredible that the body was dipped in water, as when thousands were baptized in the midst of a city, and families were baptized in their own houses at midnight. This, however, is not the only instance in which some men readily believe that things might have been done long ago, which they would not hesitate to pronounce impracticable in the present times. The water in baptism is intended to be a sign of the Spirit. Now, among all the passages which describe, in metaphorical terms, the communication of the Spirit, there is not one which alludes to immersion. The language of the Scripture uniformly refers to that mode of applying water which is practised in our Churches. The Holy Ghost is said "to fall upon men," "to be poured out upon them," "to be shed upon them," "to be sprinkled upon them." These expressions God has selected as the most proper to signify the communication of his influences. Is it not then strange to imagine, that a religious rite, and the language of Scripture, although both intended to give information upon the same subject, bear no resemblance to each other, and convey quite different ideas? According to the practice of sprinkling, Scripture and the symbolical action, harmonize; according to the practice of immersion, Scripture suggests one idea, and the action, another perfectly opposite. Such discordance should not be hastily imputed to him, who is "wonderful in counsel, and excellent in working." With relation to the present case, tradition and modern travellers inform us, that the water, to which Philip and the eunuch went down, was a spring or well, at which baptism could be administered only by sprinkling.

It would have been natural for so young a disciple, to wish that his spiritual teacher should remain with him, to instruct him more fully in the doctrines of the gospel, and to fortify his mind against temptations to abandon the faith. A person just initiated, seemed too inexperienced to be trusted alone. But the wisdom of Jesus Christ had otherwise determined. He was able, without the ministry of Philip, to carry on and to perfect the good work which he had begun. The eunuch was now possessed of that faith, which, terminating upon the Saviour himself, maintains an intercourse with him, by which the life of the soul is preserved and cherished. "When they were come up out of the water, the Spirit of the Lord caught away Philip, that the eunuch saw him no more." We are not able, perhaps, to assign the reason of this sudden separation; but the event served to establish the faith of the Ethiopian, to which, at the first view, it seems not to have been favourable. As a miracle, it added the sanction of heaven to the doctrine of Philip, and exhibited ocular demonstration of the truth of all that he had said relative to the miracles of Christ, and the extraordinary powers conferred upon the Apostles and Evangelists.

Accordingly, the faith of the new convert was not shaken, nor was his mind in any degree disquieted, by the unexpected loss of the company of Philip. We are informed, that "he went on his way rejoicing." And surely no man ever had better reason to be happy. He had found the Messiah, the desire of all nations; he had been admitted to partake of the blessings of salvation; his soul was full of the consolations of God, and of the hope of immortality. No doubts now perplexed his mind. The Scriptures were unveiled; and the wonders of redemption, which were unfolded to his view, transported him with admiration and gratitude. His lips, we may believe, gave utterance to the feelings of his heart; and the desert, through which he passed, was enlivened with the songs of salvation. In this happy frame, "he went on his way," hastening back to his own country, to impart the joyful tidings to his friends, and to recommend his new faith by the practice of every virtue. Had he returned to Jerusalem, he would have enjoyed the society of the Apostles and disciples; but Ethiopia was the theatre on which Providence had appointed him to act; and no man can so effectually prove the sincerity of his conversion, and so successfully promote the cause of religion, as by acquitting himself, in his proper station, with the spirit and temper of a Christian. "Let every man abide in the same calling wherein he is called. Brethren, let every man wherein he is called, therein abide with God."

I conclude with the following observations.

First, The Lord knows "them that are his," and will in due time call them to the enjoyment of salvation. Whatever obstacles are opposed to their salvation, and however far they have wandered from God, his grace will overtake them, and accomplish its designs. This observation is illustrated by the history before us. It does not appear, that in Jerusalem the Ethiopian eunuch had heard any thing about Christ. He had now left that city, and had advanced so far in his journey, that he was entering into countries where the good news of salvation had not been published. He was passing the boundary which separated light from darkness, and returning without the knowledge of the Saviour, to his own land, where he could not have obtained it by ordinary means. At this critical moment, a minister of Jesus was sent, by the special direction of the Spirit, to speak words by which his soul should be saved. "The election shall obtain, although the rest be blinded." God will either cause the gospel to be preached in the places where his elect reside, or he will bring them into a new situation, in which they shall enjoy the dispensation of it.

The second observation suggested by this passage, relates to the irresistible efficacy with which the word of God, accompanied with the influences of the Spirit, operates upon the soul. "It is quick and powerful." It may be compared to the lightning, which, in the twinkling of an eye, flies from the one end of heaven to the other. Sudden conversions, indeed, should be carefully examined, lest they be only deceitful appearances; but they should not be considered as impossible. In every case, the transition from death to life is instantaneous, although in some there may be a long preparatory process. This moment, the man of Ethiopia is so ignorant, that he cannot determine whether Isaiah, in one of the clearest passages of his writings, speaks of himself or of some other person. The next, he perceives the prophecy to be a description of the Messiah fulfilled in the sorrows and death of Jesus of Nazareth, whom he therefore acknowledges, with faith and joy, as his Saviour. The works of God do not, like those of man, require time to bring them to perfection. His almighty word creates, or makes something start out of nothing. "He speaketh, and it is done; he commandeth, and it standeth fast."

In the last place, the saving knowledge of Jesus Christ will dispose those who are possessed of it to submit to his authority. No sooner was the Ethiopian eunuch enlightened, than he professed a desire to dedicate himself in baptism to the service of his Redeemer. You believe that Jesus is the Christ. You therefore believe, that he is not only a Priest to die for your sins, but a Prophet to teach you the way of God, and a Lord to govern you. In all these offices you will acknowledge him, if your faith is sincere. But if there is any of them with which you are dissatisfied; if you would disjoin one from another, seeking, for example, to be saved from wrath by his blood, while you have no desire to be delivered from the dominion of sin by his power, know that Christ is not divided, and that the impious attempt betrays ignorance or hatred of his character. He who comes to Jesus, must resolve "to take his yoke upon him;" and if any of you say in your hearts, or in your conduct, "We will not have this man to reign over us," beware of the vengeance with which he will vindicate his insulted authority. "Those mine enemies, which would not that I should reign over them, bring hither, and slay them before me."

LECTURE XII.

THE CONVERSION OF PAUL.

Chap ix. 1—22.

The man, whose conversion is the subject of the present Lecture, has been already mentioned in this history; and the incidental hints respecting his sentiments and conduct, give a very unfavourable idea of his character. Young in years, he discovered no symptom of that generous spirit, and that tenderness of feeling, which are expected before the heart is narrowed and hardened by commerce with the world; but with an insensibility, which is the ordinary result of confirmed prejudices, and repeated crimes against humanity, he beheld, with approbation, the cruel death of a righteous man. His zeal hurried him on to take an active part in the persecution of the Church; and "entering into every house, and haling men and women, he committed them to prison." From this specimen, what could the disciples prognosticate but hostility protracted during life, and augmenting in fury, as its objects multiplied, and its sanguine hopes of success were disappointed? The most perspicacious eye could perceive no trait in his character, from which a change might be predicted. It could still less have been foreseen, that this man should ere long be a preacher of the faith, which he was so eager to destroy. But in the plastic hands of the Almighty, the powers of mind, and the qualities of matter, are passive and pliant. With the rudest and most untoward materials, he can rear a fabric, admirable in its contrivance, beautiful in its construction, and accommodated to the most valuable purposes. It is his glory still to call a magnificent world out of chaos; it is his pleasure to display the sovereignty and power of his grace, upon the most unlikely and forbidding subjects.

When we read, in the beginning of this chapter, that "Saul, yet breathing out threatenings and slaughter against the disciples of the Lord, went unto the high-priest, and desired of him letters to Damascus to the synagogues, that if he found any of this way, whether they were men or women, he might bring them bound unto Jerusalem;" we recognise the same spirit which had cordially consented to the murder of Stephen. The expression used by Luke is descriptive and animated. "He breathed out threatenings and slaughter." The persecution of the inoffensive disciples was the continual subject of his thoughts; his conversation was filled with invectives and menaces against them; and to harass and destroy them was the chief pleasure of his life. Jerusalem, populous as it was, furnished too narrow a range for his impatient and indefatigable zeal. The havock which he had already made, served only to whet his eagerness; and he longed for an opportunity of more extensive mischief, that he might diffuse the fame of his implacable hatred to the religion of Christ.

In Damascus, the capital of Syria, it appears that the gospel had made considerable progress. There the disciples multiplied under the protection of the laws, or, at least, not disturbed by the civil authority. It must have been the flourishing state of Christianity in Damascus, which attracted the notice of Saul to a place so remote. He applied to the high-priest for letters to the synagogues, empowering him to demand the surrender of such Jews as, by embracing the new doctrine, had incurred the guilt of apostasy from the religion of Moses. Damascus was in a foreign country, and under a different government; but the high-priest claimed a jurisdiction over all persons belonging to the Jewish Church, wherever they resided, and seems to have been permitted to exercise it, by Aretas the king. The offenders Saul was to bring to Jerusalem, because there only it was competent to the high-priest to punish them, or because it was necessary that they should be tried by the Sanhedrim, and the example, it was hoped, would terrify those at Jerusalem, who yet remained obstinate heretics.

Having procured such letters as he wished, Saul set out on his journey, and, we may be certain, suffered neither curiosity nor indolence to detain him on the road. His heart was too deeply interested in his commission to admit of any delay in executing it. Already he had approached near to Damascus, and perhaps within sight of its walls, when, in a very unexpected manner, his progress was arrested. God often permits the wicked to carry on their designs till they are on the eve of being accomplished, when he suddenly interposes to defeat them, in judgment or in mercy. He either overwhelms the builder under the ruins of his edifice, or makes him abandon his impious project, and consecrate his time and talents to the service of the sanctuary.

Before we consider the account of the conversion of Saul, it will be proper to make a few observations upon the extraordinary means by which it was effected. Jesus Christ did not call him by the ministry of any Apostle or Evangelist; and he called him, when, instead of attending upon the ordinances of religion, he was engaged in a scheme of persecution. The laws of nature and of grace are nothing but the order, according to which God exerts his power in the production of physical, moral, and spiritual effects. Creatures are obliged to conform to that order; but the Creator may step aside from it, when any end, worthy of his wisdom, is to be gained. Miracles are deviations from the laws of nature; and such conversions as that of Saul, are deviations from the laws of grace. When the world was created, the power of God was necessarily exercised in a different manner from that in which it is exercised in the ordinary government of it. It is not surprising, therefore, that when the Christian Church, which is represented in the Old Testament as a new and more glorious creation, was founded, divine grace should have adopted some unusual methods of accomplishing its designs. But as no man of a sound mind will infer from miracles, that he may safely disregard the established order of nature, and expect, for example, to be cured of an inveterate disease by a word, or to be fed with manna from heaven; so the history before us gives no encouragement to hope, that while men are neglecting and despising the instituted means of salvation, God will employ visions and revelations to awaken and convert them. The case of Saul affords no precedent, except as it shows the freeness of divine grace, to preserve the convinced sinner from despair. This is the only use which we are directed to make of it. "Howbeit, for this cause I obtained mercy, that in me first, Jesus Christ might show forth all long-suffering, for a pattern to them which should hereafter believe on him to life everlasting."

"And as he journeyed, he came near Damascus; and suddenly there shined round about him a light from heaven." The light was instantaneous; not like that of the sun, for the full splendour of which we are prepared by the gradual illumination of the atmosphere, as he approaches the horizon, but like the lightning which, bursting from the clouds amidst the darkness of the night, dazzles and confounds us. Its brightness was unusual, as Paul himself informs us in his speech to Agrippa. "At mid-day, O king, I saw in the way a light from heaven, above the brightness of the sun, shining round about me, and them that journeyed with me." It must have been different from any light with which we are acquainted; for when the sun is in the meridian, and shining in a cloudless sky, lightning itself would scarcely be perceptible. It was a signal of the approach of the Son of God, "who looketh on the sun, and it shineth not, and sealeth up the stars."

Paul tells us, in one of his Epistles, that "last of all, Christ was seen of him also, as of one born out of due time;" and asks, in another place, "Have I not seen Jesus Christ our Lord?" In the seventeenth verse of this chapter, Ananias says, that "Jesus appeared unto him in the way as he came." From these passages we conclude, that it was on this occasion that he was favoured with a sight of the human nature of our Saviour, by which he was qualified to be a witness, with the other Apostles, of his resurrection and exaltation. We are ignorant of the means by which Saul was enabled to see him.

Such was the effect of this vision, or of the dazzling brightness with which he was surrounded, that he fell to the earth. The shock was too violent for his bodily frame, and his mind was seized with terror. A flash of lightning strikes awe into the stoutest heart. Man is alarmed at any occurrence which reminds him of a power superior to his own, that could crush his puny strength; he looks with dismay at those appearances, which, being out of the ordinary course of nature, seem to portend the interference of the Deity, to inflict vengeance upon the guilty. Thus we see the proud and unrelenting persecutor lying prostrate on the earth. What now can we expect, but that a sentence of perdition shall be issued against him, and executed upon the spot? But mercy had cast him down, that it might raise him up again. We hear, therefore, only the language of expostulation. "Saul, Saul, why persecutest thou me?" How much must he have been surprised and confounded at this address! Never could he have suspected, in the pride of self-righteousness, that a voice from heaven would accuse him of an atrocious crime, or that his present conduct, which was applauded as a proof of ardent zeal for the glory of God, would subject him to the charge of impiety.

Saul was guilty of persecuting Jesus, because he defamed his name, and made every effort to extirpate his religion. We say that a man is persecuted after his death, when his memory is loaded with reproaches, and his friends are subjected to ill-usage on his account. Malignity sometimes continues, in the blindness of its fury, to pursue those who have escaped beyond its reach, and cannot be disturbed by it in the sanctuary of the grave. But something more is implied in the charge against Saul. Between Jesus and his people there subsists an intimate union. They are one body and one spirit. Their interests are mutual; their joys and afflictions are common. What is done to them, he accounts to be done to himself, whether it be an act of beneficence or of malice. The contempt and cruelty, of which they are the objects, he considers as a personal insult. "He that toucheth you, toucheth the apple of his eye." His love to them makes him feel the injury; and the head complains, when any man treads upon the foot. "Saul, Saul, why persecutest thou me?"

While Jesus accuses Saul as his persecutor, he deigns to expostulate with him. "Why persecutest thou me? Whence this furious zeal? What have I done to provoke such determined hostility?" "Lord! why didst thou condescend to reason with this man? It was with the same gracious intention, which induces thee still to reason with us, whom thou mightest overwhelm at once with confusion and ruin; to make the guilty reflect upon their conduct, and to excite them, from the fear of thy justice, to supplicate that mercy which thou art willing to exercise."

Saul heard the voice, but did not know from whom it proceeded. He therefore said, "Who art thou, Lord?" It was a question not of curiosity, but of anxiety and terror. "Who art thou whom I have offended?" It could not be the God of Israel, for whose law he was zealous even above his countrymen; who then was this person whom he was accused of persecuting? The voice answered, "I am Jesus whom thou persecutest." Never did information more unexpected and alarming burst upon the startled ear. Jesus, whom the Jews had crucified as the vilest of malefactors, without the gates of their city; Jesus, whom Saul believed to be an impostor, and whose name he had never mentioned but in terms of execration; Jesus, whose helpless followers he had, on all occasions, treated with the utmost indignity and cruelty; this Jesus now appeared in heavenly glory, and was recognised by his furious persecutor, in the act of going to Damascus to plague and destroy his disciples, as the Son of God, and the exalted Messiah.

His own mind would immediately suggest the dangerous and hopeless nature of his undertaking, which is pointed out in the following words. "It is hard for thee to kick against the pricks." This is a proverbial expression, signifying, that the design in which a person is engaged will prove abortive, and will terminate in his ruin. There is an allusion to a fierce ungovernable animal, which kicks at sharp spikes of iron, and while it vents its impotent rage, destroys itself. What has been the result of the frequent persecutions to which the Church of Christ has been exposed? Hypocrites have apostatised; some faithful men have fallen by the hands of their enemies; others have been grievously harassed, and compelled to leave their country and their kindred; but the immortal race of believers remains, and will continue, in defiance of the utmost exertions of the world. What has been the fate of their persecutors? They have fallen and perished, and left their names for a proverb and a curse. "God is known in her palaces for a refuge. For lo, the kings were assembled, they passed by together. They saw it, and so they marvelled; they were troubled, and hasted away. Fear took hold upon them there, and pain, as of a woman in travail." Had Saul been permitted to go on in his career, the disciples in Damascus would have been imprisoned, spoiled of their goods, banished, and murdered; but Christianity would have maintained itself against him, and his confederates. He would have been foiled in the unequal contest; and, sinking into eternal perdition, should have felt how vain it is to contend with superior power.

Astonished at the unexpected discovery, and trembling from a consciousness of his crime against the glorified Saviour, Saul said, "Lord what wilt thou have me to do?" Where is now the fierceness of the persecutor? Where his haughty defiance of Jesus of Nazareth? These sentiments are exchanged for profound submission. The disarmed foe lies at the feet of his omnipotent antagonist, and throws himself upon his mercy. He bows to his sovereign authority. Any thing which the supreme arbiter of his destiny shall command, he is ready to do; any thing which will atone for his past unprovoked opposition. All his strong holds are cast down;

all his lofty imaginations are abased. Formerly he believed, that he was contending with the followers of an impostor, who had paid the forfeit of his crimes with his life; but he finds that he was fighting against that almighty Lord, to whom men must submit or perish. "The Lord said unto him, Arise, and go into the city, and it shall be told thee what thou must do." Perhaps, in the present state of his mind, he could not have given attention to the instructions of the Saviour; and his situation on a public road, and in the midst of his unconverted companions, was unfavourable. It was in the calm and leisure of privacy, that he was to be prepared for the important services, in which Jesus purposed to employ him.

In the mean time, "the men which journeyed with him stood speechless, hearing a voice, but seeing no man." There seems to be a contradiction between this account, and that which is given by Paul himself in the twenty-second chapter; for he there says, that "they that were with him saw indeed the light, and were afraid; but they heard not the voice of him that spake to him." The accounts are easily reconciled, by supposing the one to mean, that they heard the sound of the voice, and the other, that they did not distinguish the words.* This circumstance amazed them, particularly because while they heard a voice, they "saw no man;" and they were speechless with astonishment. It appears from the twenty-sixth chapter, that they, too, fell to the ground; but they recovered more speedily than Saul, upon whom a stronger impression was made by the words which were addressed to him.

"And Saul arose from the earth; and when his eyes were opened, he saw no man: but they led him by the hand and brought him into Damascus. And he was three days without sight, and neither did eat nor drink." Had this blindness been the natural effect of the dazzling light, his fellow-travellers would have been affected in the same manner. It was a temporary punishment, inflicted by the power of Christ, which showed how easily he could have struck him dead upon the spot, and cast his guilty soul into hell; and taught him to admire and praise the gracious Redeemer, who, in the midst of wrath, remembered mercy to the worst of his enemies. Shut up to his own reflections, under this blindness, he

---

* The passages may be reconciled in a different way. The voice which they heard, was the voice of Paul; but they did not see the person whom he addressed. The voice which they did not hear, was the voice of our Saviour. Buxtorfii Catalecta. CL.

was engaged in exercises so solemn and interesting, that he had neither inclination nor leisure to attend to the concerns of his body. It was during this period, that that process of conviction was carried on, which he has described in one of his Epistles. "I was alive without the law once; but when the commandment came, sin revived, and I died. And the commandment, which was ordained to life, I found to be unto death. For sin, taking occasion by the commandment, deceived me, and by it slew me." When he compared his former life with the holy law of God, which he now, for the first time, understood, sins past reckoning rose to his view; he discovered the most frightful depravity in his heart; and his Pharisaical notions, his proud confidence in his own righteousness, perished as a dream. Full of remorse, and shame, and fear, he cried with the penitent publican, "God, be merciful unto me a sinner." It was during this period, that it pleased God "to reveal his Son in him" as the Messiah, who had brought in an everlasting righteousness, by which he obtained, through faith, that peace of mind which he ever afterwards enjoyed. It was during this period, that he was instructed in the knowledge of the gospel immediately by Christ, and was qualified in the same extraordinary manner, in which he had been called, to be an Apostle. "But I certify you, brethren, that the gospel which was preached of me is not after man. For I neither received it of man, neither was I taught it, but by the revelation of Jesus Christ." Amidst such distress and such joy; amidst such new and astonishing views as presented themselves to his opening mind, Saul forgot the necessities of the body. All this time was spent in tears, and prayers, and thanksgivings.

The following verses relate the cure of his blindness, his admission into the fellowship of the disciples by baptism, and the zeal and courage which he displayed in the service of Christ.

"And there was a certain disciple at Damascus, named Ananias, and to him said the Lord in a vision, Ananias. And he said, Behold, I am here, Lord." This is the language of a faithful disciple, who only waits for the commands of his Master, that he may obey them. "And the Lord said unto him, Arise, and go into the street which is called Straight, and inquire in the house of Judas, for one called Saul of Tarsus: for behold he prayeth." He no longer breathed out threatenings and slaughter against the disciples; nothing proceeded from his lips but earnest supplications for mercy.

This circumstance is mentioned to encourage Ananias to visit him. However wicked a man may have formerly been, we may presume that he is changed, as soon as we learn that he is frequent and fervent in prayer. The spirit of devotion cannot reside in the same bosom with the spirit of pride, dissimulation, injustice, and cruelty. The one will expel the other. "He hath seen in a vision a man named Ananias, coming in, and putting his hands on him, that he might receive his sight." This vision was intended not only to comfort Saul in his distress, but to prepare him to receive Ananias, as a messenger of Christ.

Ananias, when first addressed by our Saviour, answered, "I am here," signifying the utmost readiness to execute his orders; but he hesitates when he hears his commission. "Lord, I have heard by many of this man, how much evil he hath done to thy saints at Jerusalem: and here he hath authority from the chief priests to bind all that call on thy name." "Is it to Saul that thou sendest me? Is it thy will, that I should go and deliver myself into his hands?" The good man does not refuse to obey, but humbly expresses his apprehensions, which were too well justified by the past conduct of Saul. Ananias appears not to have known what had befallen him in the way.

"But the Lord said unto him, Go thy way: for he is a chosen vessel unto me, to bear my name before the Gentiles, and kings, and the children of Israel. For I will show him how great things he must suffer for my name's sake." "Lord! how unsearchable are thy judgments, and thy ways past finding out!" There were Pharisees in Jerusalem, who were not guilty of such crimes as Saul; men who disbelieved thy religion, but did not persecute thy followers; who were restrained by a sense of justice and humanity from injuring their persons, although they detested their error. These thou didst pass by, and leave to perish in ignorance; while to this man, compared with whom they were innocent, a man who impiously waged war with thyself, and would have rejoiced in the utter ruin of thy cause, thou wast pleased to exercise pardoning mercy. We adore the sovereignty of thy grace. Thou makest of the same lump one vessel to honour, and another to dishonour. Thou choosest the very worst of mankind as the fittest objects upon whom to display thy goodness, that the disappointed, confounded pride of man, may never more dare to stand forth as the rival of thy glory. What art thou not able to do, who couldst transform one of the most active agents of Satan into a zealous and successful minister of thy kingdom; and couldst make the lips which blasphemed thee, become the eloquent heralds of thy praise? Never shall we despair of any man, however far advanced in the career of impiety, after we have seen this example of the wonders which thy grace can perform."

This information removed the doubts of Ananias, who hastened with a joyful heart, to execute his commission. "And Ananias went his way, and entered into the house; and putting his hands on him, said, Brother Saul, the Lord (even Jesus that appeared unto thee in the way as thou camest,) hath sent me, that thou mightest receive thy sight and be filled with the Holy Ghost." Grace makes a man soon forget injurious treatment; and most willingly does a Christian pardon those whom his Lord has forgiven. The blasphemies and cruelties of Saul are remembered no more. Ananias sees in him, not the murderer of the saints, but "a new creature, created in Christ Jesus to good works; and he salutes him by the compellation of brother, bidding him welcome to the privileges of the heaven-born family. By the imposition of his hands, Saul recovered his sight, and received the gifts of the Spirit, which were necessary to qualify him for the Apostolical office. "And immediately there fell from his eyes as it had been scales; and he received sight forthwith, and arose, and was baptized." Thus he was received into the communion of the Church, and dedicated to the service of Christ.

Saul immediately joined himself to the disciples, and openly appeared as the friend and champion of the truth. "And straightway he preached Christ in the synagogues, that he is the Son of God;" in the same synagogues to which he had carried letters from the high priest, requiring them to deliver up to punishment those by whom this truth was avowed. So powerful were his arguments, that the Jews were confounded. With their objections, he was well acquainted, for they had been often urged by himself; but he was now able to point out their futility. A change so sudden and so great was beheld with astonishment. "All that heard him were amazed, and said, "Is not this he that destroyed them which called on this name in Jerusalem, and came hither for that intent, that he might bring them bound unto the chief priests!" Some would be content to wonder; others were stimulated, by offended pride and disappointed bigotry, to revenge; but a few, we may believe, carefully inquiring into the cause of an event so extraordinary, perceived in his conversion such evidence in favour of the gospel, as prevailed upon them to imitate his example.

The conversion of Paul, considered in all its circumstances, presents an argument of great strength for the truth of Christianity. About the fact itself there can be no dispute; and the only question between us and the enemies of revelation respects the conclusion to be deduced from it. I acknowledge, that a change from one system to other does not, in every case, afford evidence against the first, and in favour of the second, because the change is often the effect of fickleness, of passion, of self-interest, or of vanity. But when a man forsakes a religion, which he has long and zealously supported, and goes over to a religion which he has long and zealously opposed; when every motive of honour, profit, and personal safety, is on the side of the former, and all those motives operate against the latter; and when his character is such, as to obviate any suspicion that he was deceived by others, or imposed upon by his own imagination; the presumption is strong, that the evidence in favour of the religion which he has adopted, is at least probable, and deserves to be carefully examined. The zeal of Paul for the law of Moses was equalled only by his antipathy to the gospel. Yet, we find him suddenly changing sides, commencing one of the boldest and most active propagators of the gospel, and employing his powers of reasoning to prove, that the obligation of the law of Moses was annulled, and that no man could be saved by the observance of it. How shall we account for this revolution in his sentiments and conduct? It cannot be explained by any of the ordinary principles which influence the determinations of men. The reasons for continuing in the Jewish religion were various and weighty. It was the religion of his fathers, which they had received from God himself; it was the religion of his country, of the rulers and great men, of his companions and friends; it was the religion which opened to him the only path to reputation and preferment; it was the religion in which he had made great proficiency, and on which were founded his hopes of acceptance with God; it was the religion to which he had, in the most decided manner, given the preference, and which he could not renounce without acknowledging himself to have been in an error, and incurring the censures and reproaches of the world. Christianity was contrary to his Jewish and Pharisaical prejudices with respect to the character of the Messiah, the nature of his kingdom, and the plan by which a sinner is justified; was embraced chiefly by persons in the lower ranks, and was taught by illiterate men; was proscribed by the laws, and persecuted, so that whoever professed it must give up all hope of living quietly and safely, and reckon upon ill-usage of every sort, and probably in the issue, a violent death; and would be the cause of peculiar trouble and danger to him, whom the Jews would unite to persecute as an apostate and a traitor.

In a worldly point of view, the change from Judaism to Christianity was highly imprudent, or rather would have been a certain indication of madness. But Paul was not mad; he laboured under no disorder of mind, which might have led him to extravagance of conduct; he was not a visionary, who is the sport of the illusions of fancy, nor a weak man, who is the dupe of the artifice of others. All his writings, and all his actions subsequent to his conversion, show him to have been a man of sound judgment, of strong intellectual powers, of consummate prudence, and of steady principles. He was not one of those inconstant, restless beings, who run through every form of religion. He never made but one change, and he persevered in it amidst the severest trials. At the time when he was converted, his mind was not in a state which disposed it to receive strange and unaccountable impressions. He was not troubled with remorse for any crime; he was not apprehensive of danger; he was not labouring under bodily infirmity; he was not in solitude. He was on a journey, in the midst of his friends, and in open day; he was confident of the goodness of his cause; his disbelief of Christianity, and his determination to oppose it, were never more decided. At this moment his views of the gospel underwent a total change. His hostility to it ceased. He acknowledged Jesus Christ to be the Son of God, devoted himself to his service, accepted of one of the highest and most dangerous offices in his Church, and commenced an avowed and indefatigable advocate of his cause.

It is impossible, I think, when all the circumstances are considered, to account for this conversion, except on such grounds as shall fully establish the truth of the gospel. Nothing could have effected a change so great, so sudden, so much opposed by all the feelings of human nature, but evidence, which the mind of Paul was unable to resist. Had the gospel not been true, it would not have counted Saul of Tarsus among its friends. Not only does his conversion demonstrate the truth of Christianity, but it gives a high degree of credibility to this particular history. Such a conversion evidently required such an extraordinary interposition. Paul was out of the reach of ordinary means. He would have disdained to hear an Apostle; he would not have listened with patience to any arguments in favour of the gospel; and we cannot suppose that he would have carefully and dispassionately investigated the subject by himself. It was almost necessary to employ miraculous means to bring this man to the acknowledgment of the truth; and if we believe his conversion to have been sudden, we must also believe that it was accomplished in the manner described in this chapter.

The case of Paul deserves the serious consideration of infidels, who should either give a satisfactory solution of it, in consistency with their own principles, or admit the force of the argument which it affords in behalf of the gospel. It is an instance of an unbeliever, a man of some learning, and considerable abilities, who yielding to the conviction, publicly adopted our religion after having virulently and pertinaciously opposed it. Their refusal to imitate his example, must proceed from their not having considered the evidence, or from their having found it defective. Among those who have examined the subject, there can be no doubt to which of these causes their conduct should be ascribed. Christianity will stand the test of the strictest inquiry. We have nothing to fear from fair discussion. Unbelief is not the consequence of just reasoning, but of sophistry, prejudice, presumptous ignorance, and licentious dispositions. Infidels sometimes maintain, that God ought to work miracles in every age for the confirmation of the gospel; and, on this ground, may insinuate, that they have the same right as Paul to have their doubts removed by a supernatural interposition. But the demand is not reasonable. If the ordinary evidence is sufficient to satisfy those who will candidly attend to it, God is not obliged, at the request of every caviller, to break in upon the established order of providence. Let them first show, that it is impossible at present to know the gospel to be true without a new revelation; and it will then be time to examine, whether such a revelation should be granted.

To the friends of Christianity, the conversion of Paul is fraught with instruction. It confirms their faith by a new proof of the divinity of the gospel. It illustrates the power and grace of their Redeemer. It shows them, that his religion is safe amidst the most vigorous and best directed attacks of its enemies, since he is able to change them into friends, or to crush them and their designs. The conversion of such persons as Paul is indeed extremely rare. Infidels commonly die as they lived, especially when they have signalized themselves by their unhallowed zeal. None of the most noted characters of this description, in our times, has glorified God by a recantation of his error. Christianity does not need their aid. It would have succeeded in the beginning, although Paul had continued to persecute it; it will go on without them, and in spite of their exertions. Jesus Christ rules "in the midst of his enemies." But divine grace could subdue the proudest and most determined unbeliever; and instances are not wanting, in which its power has been displayed in opening the blind eyes, and turning them from darkness to light. Let us rejoice that the truth shall be ultimately victorious; and let us conclude with this prayer of the Church to her almighty Redeemer. " Gird thy sword upon thy thigh, O most mighty; with thy glory and thy majesty. And in thy majesty ride prosperously, because of truth, and meekness, and righteousness; and thy right hand shall teach thee terrible things. Thine arrows are sharp in the hearts of the king's enemies; whereby the people fall under thee."

LECTURE XIII.

THE CONVERSION OF CORNELIUS.

CHAP. X.

The conversion of Cornelius, who was the first-fruits of the Gentiles, is supposed to have taken place about seven or eight years after the ascension of our Saviour. Yet, before he left his disciples, he gave them a commission to go "into all the world, and preach the gospel to every creature." The terms in which it was expressed were perspicuous; and as there could be no dispute about their duty, so there ought to have been no delay in performing it. During all this time, however, the Apostles confined their labours to their own countrymen, and to the Samaritans. If they did not understand their commission, we see a remarkable instance of the power of prejudice in preventing the mind from perceiving what is perfectly obvious; if they understood, but did not execute it, their conduct shows with what difficulty inveterate opinions and habits are renounced. To whatever cause we impute the delay, it is manifest, that although we should venerate the Apostles as ambassadors of Christ, and gratefully remember their pious labours, the benefit of which we at this moment experience, yet we are not indebted to their liberality for the interest which we possess in the new dispensation. The comprehensive scheme, which associated the Gentiles with the Jews in the enjoyment of the divine favour and the blessings of redemption, was not suggested by their enlightened benevolence.

But the prejudices and the reluctance of men cannot defeat the purposes of heaven. The gospel had now been fully preached to the Jews, and the foundation of the Church had been laid among the children of the covenant. The time was come, when the designs of mercy to those who were "aliens from the commonwealth of Israel," should be accomplished. To ensure the execution of the plan, extraordinary measures were adopted. By a new revelation, that Apostle, who was chosen to break down "the middle wall of partition," was prepared for the service; and all the circumstances were disposed in such a manner as to remove the scruples which he felt, in consequence of his national and religious habits.

Of the person, whom divine grace selected to be the first among the Gentiles who should receive the knowledge of the truth, the following account is given in the beginning of the chapter. "There was a certain man in Cesarea, called Cornelius, a centurion of the band, called the Italian band, a devout man, and one that feared God with all his house, which gave much alms to the people, and prayed to God alway." By birth he was probably a Roman; by profession he was a soldier; and he resided in Cesarea, with the part of the army under his command. Among military men, examples of piety are rare. They are too commonly distinguished by their irreligion and profligacy. The precariousness of life, amidst the dangers of war instead of exciting them to prepare for eternity, is grasped at as an argument to justify a course of dissipation. "Let us eat and drink: for to-morrow we die." Too thoughtless to reflect upon any serious subject, and too much the slaves of their passions to submit to the discipline of virtue, they acknowledge no law but the law of honour, which does not refrain from baseness, but resents even to blood the imputation of it; permits without reproach the seduction of the innocent, the desolation of families, and the murder of a friend, who, in an unguarded moment, has offended them; prescribes the exterior forms of politeness, and leaves the heart polluted and degraded by the most odious vices.

Cornelius was an honourable exception; for "he was a devout man, and one that feared God." He appears from this account to have been a proselyte of the gate, which was the designation bestowed by the Jews upon a heathen living among them, who acknowledged and worshipped the God of Israel, but did not submit to circumcision. Such proselytes were still Gentiles in the estimation of the Jews; whereas proselytes of righteousness who were circumcised, and kept the whole law, were incorporated with the nation. The character of a devout man, given to Cornelius, is illustrated and confirmed by several particulars. "He feared God with all his house." The pious sentiments which he entertained towards Jehovah, he was successful in inculcating upon his family. Although not a descendant of Abraham, he imitated his example, which God so highly commends. "I know him, that he will command his children and his household after him, and they shall keep the way of the Lord, to do justice and judgment." The personal religion of that man may be justly suspected, who suffers his children and domestics to live in ignorance and vice, without using his best endeavours to instruct and reform them. "He gave much alms to the people." This circumstance is the more decisive in favour of his character, as he was by birth and education, a Gentile, and consequently had not been trained to sentiments of kindness and compassion. Among the ancient heathens, the claims of the indigent and afflicted were little regarded. Corrupt nature had hardened the heart and a vain philosophy could not soften it. The charities, which are now so common in Christian countries, that they scarcely excite any admiration, result directly, or indirectly, from that principle of love to man, which revealed religion alone inculcates and inspires. "He prayed to God alway." It is almost unnecessary to remark, that nothing more is meant than he prayed frequently, or at the stated hours of the Jews, who offered up their supplications and thanksgivings, in the morning, at mid-day, and in the evening. Thus Daniel "prayed and gave thanks before his God three times a day;" and the Psalmist says, "Evening, and morning, and at noon, will I pray, and cry aloud: and he shall hear my voice."

One of the hours of prayer was the ninth hour, or three o'clock in the afternoon, when the evening sacrifice was offered. At this time the piety of Cornelius was rewarded with a divine communication, by which we are encouraged to imitate his example, in the hope of enjoying fellowship with God. "He saw in a vision evidently about the ninth hour of the day, an angel of God coming in to him, and saying unto him, Cornelius." Some of the visions recorded in Scripture, were representations made to the mind in sleep, but with such characters of their celestial origin, as easily distinguished them from the wild creations of fancy. When Cornelius saw this vision, he was awake. The objects which he beheld, had a real existence, and the words which he heard, were actually pronounced. The minister of the divine will was an angel, who entering into the place where the good man was pouring out his soul before God, saluted him by his name. The suddenness of his appearance, his majestic form, and that consciousness of inferiority and guilt, which man is apt to feel when any event takes place out of the ordinary course, agitated and alarmed him. " When he looked on him, he was afraid, and said, What is it, Lord ?" The question proceeded from reverence and fear. " Have I offended ? or hast thou any command to deliver ? Here I am, ready to obey." The angel immediately relieved his anxiety, by saying, " Thy prayers and thine alms are come up for a memorial before God." In the Levitical law, the incense burnt before the Lord, and the handful of fine flour for a sin-offering, which the priest threw into the fire of the altar, are both termed a memorial. By applying the same designation to the prayers and alms of Cornelius, the angel signified that they were spiritual sacrifices, with which God was well-pleased. Cornelius was not a Jew, nor even a proselyte of righteousness ; but he believed in the true God, and this faith rendered his religious services acceptable.

But if the prayers and alms of the devout centurion ascended as incense, what more did he want ? Was there any defect to be supplied in his religion, by which he already enjoyed the divine favour ? It cannot be doubted, that Cornelius was at present in a state of salvation, and that, if he had resided in Rome, or in some other distant place, where the gospel was not published, he might have lived and died in peace and safety, without ever knowing that Jesus Christ had come into the world. His faith in the Messiah was sincere. But he was now in the country, which had been the scene of the incarnation, miracles, death, and resurrection of the Son of God ; and it was not fitting, that, in this situation, any good man, who was waiting for his manifestation, should have remained ignorant of that important event. An angel, therefore, descended from heaven, as on another occasion a star had appeared, to conduct this pious Gentile to Christ. Besides, by the knowledge of the Saviour, his views would be enlarged, and his spiritual joy would be increased ; and this stranger, who, although a fearer of God, was excluded by uncircumcision from the communion of the Jewish Church, would be admitted by baptism to be a fellow-citizen of the saints. The angel therefore gave the following direction. " And now send men to Joppa, and call for one Simon, whose surname is Peter. He lodgeth with one Simon a tanner, whose house is by the seaside ; he shall tell thee what thou oughtest to do." Cornelius might have received this information from one of the disciples, whom providence could have introduced to his acquaintance ; or an Apostle might have been sent to Cesarea, to preach the gospel to the centurion. But the case required an unusual procedure. It was a new era in the history of the Church. No longer bounded by the circumscribed limits of a small country, it was to extend "from sea to sea, and from the river unto the ends of the earth." To this change, which could not be accomplished without the abrogation of the ancient law, even the believing Jews would with difficulty be reconciled. An angel, therefore, was employed to direct Cornelius to send for one of the Apostles, that he might, with full confidence, engage in his new and unprecedented mission, and that others might be prevented from objecting to his conduct, which God himself had expressly authorised.

It is worthy of observation, that, although God was pleased, for wise purposes, to deviate from his ordinary plan, in order to warn Cornelius of his duty; yet he was, at the same time, careful to maintain the authority and honour of his own institution for the conversion of sinners. The angel did not preach the gospel to Cornelius, but informed him where he should find a person who would preach it. God has not employed as the messengers of his mercy, superior beings whose greatness would have made us afraid, and to the charms of whose eloquence the success of his word might have been ascribed. "He hath put the treasure in earthen vessels, that the excellency of the power may be of God, and not of men." We are addressed by mortals like ourselves, to whom we can listen without terror, and who being sinful, weak, and imperfectly enlightened, can be considered only as instruments of the divine operations. This contrivance, so admirably calculated to secure glory to God in the salvation of men, no dispensation proceeding from himself, will ever disparage. Angels may sometimes summon sinners to hear the joyful tidings, but they will be proclaimed by one of themselves. The expectation of immediate revelations to awaken the careless, is not justified by any promise of Scripture, or any recorded example; and it could not be realized without weakening the authority, and diminishing the importance, of the ministry of reconciliation.

As soon as the vision was past, Cornelius called two of his servants, and a devout soldier, who waited upon him continually; and having related the message of the angel, in which they were all interested, he despatched them to Joppa. Let us observe in what manner Peter was prepared to comply with the invitation of Cornelius.

"On the morrow, as they went on their journey, and drew nigh unto the city, Peter went up upon the house-top to pray, about the sixth hour. And he became very hungry, and would have eaten: but while they made ready, he fell into a trance." In the eastern countries, the roofs of houses are flat; and this is a circumstance necessary to be known, in order to understand several passages of Scripture. They afforded a convenient place for prayer, being removed from the noise and interruption of the family. At the sixth hour, or noon, which was one of the hours of prayer among the Jews, Peter having retired to the house top, and being hungry, while they made ready some food for him, fell into a trance. A trance, or ecstacy, signifies a state of mind, in which a person is so much engaged with a particular subject, that the exercise of his senses is suspended, and he is insensible to every thing which is passing around him. Whether the objects which Peter saw had any real existence, or were merely represented to his mind, it is impossible to determine. We are certain, that the vision was not the offspring of imagination, but an effect of the power of God, and an authentic revelation of his will. He beheld " heaven opened," or an appearance as if the heavens had parted asunder, and a vessel, " like a great sheet," let down, which contained all sorts of quadrupeds, tame and wild, and reptiles and birds. At the same time, he heard a voice saying, " Rise, Peter; kill, and eat." As many of the animals were such as were forbidden by the law of Moses, he objected to the command, saying, Not so, Lord; for I have never eaten any thing that is common or unclean." He probably considered it, not as authorising him to transgress the ceremonial law, but as a trial of his respect for it; for it does not appear, that at this time, either he, or any of the Apostles, expected a change of that law. " But the voice spake unto him again the second time, What God hath cleansed, that call not thou common." The prohibited animals were not unclean from any natural impurity, but in virtue of a positive institution, in consequence of which an Israelite could not use them for food without contracting defilement. They were cleansed when the institution was revoked; and might henceforth be eaten without any other scruple than what arose from a regard to health, or to taste. " This was done thrice," for the same reason that the dream of Pharaoh was doubled, " because the thing was established by God, and God would shortly bring it to pass."

That we may understand the import of this vision, it is necessary to reflect, that the Jews were a holy people, separated from the nations of the world, and consecrated to the service of God. The separation was in part effected by circumcision, which was a token of the covenant of God with the seed of Abraham; but the same rite was practised by the Arabians, the descendants of Ishmael, and adopted from them, or from the Jews, by some other tribes. A more complete distinction was made by the laws respecting meats, and is, in fact, assigned as the intention of those laws. "I am the Lord your God, which have separated you from other people. Ye shall therefore put difference between clean beasts and unclean, and between unclean fowls and clean; and ye shall not make your souls abominable by beast, or by fowl, or by any manner of living thing that creepeth on the ground, which I have separated from you as unclean. And ye shall be holy unto me: for I the Lord am holy, and have severed you from other people, that ye should be mine." In consequence of this injunction, it was impossible for a Jew to mingle on familiar terms with the Gentiles, without contracting pollution, because at their tables he would meet with some kinds of food, which his religion taught him to hold in abhorrence. While Jews and Gentiles retained their peculiar usages, they were objects of mutual aversion and contempt. The voice from heaven declared, that the distinction of meats into clean and unclean was abolished; that every animal proper for food might be used with a good conscience; and, consequently, that the principal ground of separation between Jews and Gentiles was removed. For it is evident, that the intention of the vision was not merely to declare, that under the new dispensation the precepts concerning meats had ceased to be obligatory, but to show, that these being repealed, the separation, which was the ultimate end of them, was also repealed, and the Jews might now freely associate with the Gentiles. Hence Peter says in the twenty-eighth verse, "Ye know, how that it is unlawful for a man that is a Jew, to keep company, or to come unto one of another nation: but God hath showed me, that I should not call any man common or unclean." The vision was admirably contrived, in all its circumstances, by divine wisdom. Occasion was taken from the hunger of Peter to represent to him an assemblage of all sorts of animals which might be used for food; and the command to eat any of them at pleasure implied such a change of system, as allowed the Jews to keep company with the Gentiles, of whose entertainments they might now partake without any danger of impurity.

The literal meaning of the vision was obvious. How much soever Peter was surprised, he must have understood it to be the will of God, that the precepts with regard to things, clean and unclean, should be abrogated; and that the disciples of Jesus should not be burdened with a yoke, which had been so uneasy to the disciples of Moses. But the ultimate design of it would not so readily occur to his mind. To a Jew it was not a natural thought, that the Gentiles should no more be considered and treated as impure. It was therefore necessary, that the Apostle should be farther enlightened on this new and important subject; and this was done by the arrival of the messengers of Cornelius, and by a suggestion of the Spirit. "While Peter doubted in himself, what this vision which he had seen should mean," messengers came to invite him to visit a Gentile, and instruct him in religion, and "while he thought on the vision, the Spirit said unto him, Behold, three men seek thee. Arise, therefore, and get thee down, and go with them, doubting nothing: for I have sent thee." Thus he learned, that what God had cleansed, no man should call common, whether the subject were an animal or a man. The Gentiles were cleansed by the repeal of those laws, which distinguished them from the people of God, and excluded them from the communion of the Church.

The scruples of the Apostles being in this manner removed, he descended from the roof of the house, and welcomed the messengers of Cornelius, although it is probable, that they also were uncircumcised. On the morrow, he set out with them for Cesarea, where the centurion waited for him, having assembled his kinsmen and friends, to hear the good news of salvation. "And as Peter was coming in, Cornelius met him, and fell down at his feet, and worshipped him. But Peter took him up, saying, Stand up; I myself also am a man." From the simple relation of this fact, it cannot be determined, whether Cornelius intended to offer religious worship, or civil homage, to Peter, because among some nations, both were expressed by kneeling, or by prostrating one's self upon the ground. He seems to have been overpowered by a strong sentiment of veneration for the Apostle; and was unable, in this state of mind, to fix with precision the boundaries of respect. It is evident that he was guilty of some excess; and, although we can nardly conceive him to have honoured Peter as a God, because this

Gentile was not a polytheist, but a worshipper of Jehovah, yet the reverence which he felt for him was greater than was due to a mere man.

There is one feature in the character of all the Apostles, which must attract the notice of every attentive reader of their history, namely, their disinterestedness. We discover, on no occasion, any symptoms of selfishness. Advantages they undoubtedly enjoyed, in the admiration and zealous attachment of their followers, for personal aggrandizement; but they never yielded to the solicitations of ambition. The glory of their Master, and the salvation of souls, were the great objects which they steadily pursued. They were content to be overlooked and forgotten; and if they sometimes magnified their office, their sole purpose was to promote the ends of their ministry. Instead of encouraging, they immediately checked, a disposition in others, to fix upon them that admiration which was due to Jesus Christ, from whom their miraculous powers, and all their talents, were derived. How marked is the difference between them and their pretended successors at Rome, who, by a long train of artifice and hyprocrisy, rose to a proud domination over the Christian world; or Mahomet, whose imposture rewarded him with an empire? Their disinterestedness is an evidence that they were sincerely persuaded of the truth of the gospel, and the gospel must therefore be true; for as the circumstances in which they are placed, rendered it impossible that they should themselves have been deceived, so it is manifest, that they could have no intention to deceive others.

After this seasonable admonition to Cornelius, Peter conversed with him in a friendly manner, and went into the house, where he found a large company assembled. He was aware that the Gentiles would be surprised at his conduct, which was so different from that of his countrymen, and was forbidden by the Jewish religion. He informed them, therefore, that God himself had abolished the distinction between the Jews and other nations. "Therefore," he says, "came I unto you, without gainsaying, as soon as I was sent for: I ask, therefore, for what intent ye have sent for me." In return to this question, Cornelius related his vision; and concluded by declaring to the Apostle, that they were met to receive, with enentire submission, the word of God from his lips.

"Then Peter opened his mouth, and said, Of a truth I perceive that God is no respecter of persons; but in every nation, he that feareth him, and worketh righteousness, is accepted with him." These words have been grossly perverted. They have been represented as a declaration, by the highest authority, that men may be saved without revelation, if they worship the true God, the Maker of heaven and earth, and practise virtue according to the dictates of conscience. It is manifestly supposed, we are told, that persons fearing God, and working righteousness, may be found in every nation. For the refutation of this pernicious comment, we need go no farther in quest of arguments, than the passage itself, viewed in connexion with the preceeding verses. Cornelius, we have seen, was directed by a vision to send for Peter, who would tell him "what he ought to do." Can we believe, that the first words that the Apostle speaks, are, in fact, a declaration, that the gospel, which God had interposed in a miraculous manner to make known to the centurion, was not necessary to him because there were other means, by which the divine favour might be obtained? Surely, there never was so imprudent a missionary as this man, who, with his first breath, disappoints the expectation of his audience, by informing them, that the great end of religion may be accomplished without his instructions. Besides, Peter evidently refers to the case of Cornelius, who was not a heathen, left to the conduct of the light of nature, but one, who living in Judea, and having access to the Scriptures, had learned from them "to fear God, and work righteousness." Before the words can be applied to mere heathens, it must be proved, that a person, by unassisted reason, may acquire the knowledge of the true God, and, without the aid of supernatural grace, may perform such works as the unerring Judge, "by whom actions are weighed," will accept. He who should prove this, would overturn the whole scheme of Christianity.

The true meaning of the passage is so obvious, that it is not easy to conceive how any person could have missed it. To respect persons, is to be influenced in our treatment of them, by partial considerations, and not by a fair and equitable view of their case; showing favour to one on account of his nation, his parentage, his rank, or his relation to us, and rejecting another equally worthy, because his circumstances are different. "I perceive," says Peter, " that in this sense God is not a respecter of persons; for although he chose the Jews to be his peculiar people, yet if any man be found among the Gentiles, who fears him, and works righteousness, he is accepted. Piety and holiness are equally pleasing to God in the uncircumcised as in the circumcised." Of this impartiality the case of Cornelius was a proof. He was not one of the seed of Abraham; but his prayers and his alms went up as a memorial before God. The Most High did not reject his offerings, because he could not boast of a descent from the patriarchs. His Gentile extraction was no obstacle to the success of his religious services, since they proceeded from a pure heart, which alone God regards. There is not a single word spoken with respect to the acceptance of virtuous Gentiles, who have not enjoyed the advantages of revelation. This question was not at present before the Apostle. The only subject of inquiry was, whether the gospel might be preached to the Gentiles, and they might be received, without circumcision, into the fellowship of the Church. God himself had given a decision, by approving of Cornelius in an uncircumcised state, and sending Peter to instruct him in the way of salvation.

After this introduction, the Apostle proceeds to give a summary of the gospel, which it does not fall within the design of this Lecture to consider. I shall therefore pass on to the last part of the chapter, which records another miraculous interposition, the manifest intention of which was to obviate all objections to the admission of the Gentiles to a full participation of the privileges of the new covenant.

In the first age of Christianity, the extraordinary gifts of the Spirit were frequently bestowed upon the disciples of Jesus; and they were usually imparted, after baptism, by the ministry of the Apostles. In the present case, the order and the mode were changed; for the Holy Ghost fell upon Cornelius and his company before they were baptized, and without the imposition of hands. "While Peter yet spake these words, the Holy Ghost fell on all them which heard the word." We cannot tell, whether this new event was necessary to remove some remaining doubts in the mind of Peter himself; but we may presume, that if he had proceeded, without this interposition, to baptize and lay his hands upon the Gentiles, the Jews who accompanied him would have remonstrated; and their brethren in Jerusalem, who afterwards called him to an account, would not have been so easily satisfied. So unexpected was the event, and so contrary to their narrow notions, that "they of the circumcision which believed, were astonished, as many as came with Peter, because that on the Gentiles also was poured out the gift of the Holy Ghost. For they heard them speak with tongues, and magnify

God." As the case now stood, all objections were precluded. God himself had baptized the Gentiles with the Holy Ghost; and who, then, could hesitate to admit them to the baptism of water? The question of Peter must have carried conviction to the most prejudiced Jew who was present. "Can any man forbid water, that these should not be baptized, which have received the Holy Ghost as well as we?" "Shall the sign be denied to those, to whom the thing signified has been already granted? Shall any of us dare to exclude from our communion, persons between whom and us God has made no difference, by imparting to us all the same spiritual gifts?" The acquiescence of the Jews was testified by their silence; and Peter commanded Cornelius and his company to be baptized in the name of the Lord. "And thus by revelation God made known the mystery, which in other ages was not made known unto the sons of men, as it was now revealed unto his holy Apostles and Prophets by the Spirit; that the Gentiles should be fellow-heirs, and of the same body, and partakers of his promise in Christ, by the gospel."

How happy was the change which now took place in the condition of the Gentiles! Their own writings contain many melancholy proofs of the ignorance and profligacy into which they had fallen. In genius and taste they may be allowed to have excelled; but a peasant, in a Christian country, is more enlightened, upon the subject of religion, than the wisest of their philosophers, and any illiterate man who sincerely believes the gospel, surpasses them all in the knowledge and practice of virtue. Nothing can be conceived more childish and corrupt than their superstitions; nothing more abandoned than their manners; nothing more cold and unprofitable than their most refined speculations. In this situation, "the day spring from on high visited the heathen world, to give light to them that sat in darkness, and in the shadow of death." The altars of idolatry were overthrown; the hopes of the guilty were revived by the revelation of a Saviour; the prospect of immortal happiness beyond the grave was opened; the soul was purified by faith; and, in the beautiful language of the prophecy, "the wilderness and the solitary place was made glad, and the desert rejoiced, and blossomed as the rose." We should never think of the call of the Gentiles, without the most lively gratitude. God hath remembered us in our low estate: for his mercy endureth for ever."

Let us Gentiles be careful to improve the privileges which have been transferred to us from the Jews. " The kingdom of God was taken from them, and given to a nation bringing forth the fruits thereof." In these words it is intimated, that God intended to form a people, who should make a better return for his favours than the Jews; and we know with what faith and joy the gospel was received by the Gentiles. But, if they shall prove as perverse as the Jews, is there any reason to expect that they shall be treated with greater lenity than the seed of the patriarchs? We are certain, indeed, that they shall never be cast off in a body; but there is no promise ensuring the continuance of the gospel in any particular nation. Remember the once flourishing Churches of Asia and Africa, which are now extinct, or retain a faint existence amidst ignorance and superstition, under the dominion of their Mahometan oppressors. Our privileges infer an awful responsibility. An account will be demanded by him, who is " no respecter of persons, " and will not suffer his grace to be despised with impunity. Let these words sink down into your ears. " Thou wilt say, then, The branches were broken off, that I might be graffed in. Well; because of unbelief they were broken off, and thou standest by faith. Be not high-minded, but fear; for if God spared not the natural branches, take heed lest he also spare not thee. Behold, therefore, the goodness and severity of God: on them which fell, severity; but towards thee, goodness, if thou continue in his goodness; otherwise thou shalt be cut off."

LECTURE XIV.

HEROD AND PETER.

Chap. xii.

After the persecution, which arose upon the death of Stephen, the disciples enjoyed an interval of repose. The rage of their enemies was exhausted, or suspended by some cause, of which this history does not inform us.* Perhaps, the conversion of Saul had some influence, by disarming a furious adversary, who stimulated the zeal and activity of others. But the Church was destined, in the early stages of its existence, to pass through scenes of sorrow and blood, with a design to illustrate, by its effects in sustaining the sufferers, and ultimately prevailing against the most formidable opposition, the divine origin of our religion, and the almighty power of its Author. It was impossible that the Christians, living among the men who had crucified their Master, and professing a system of doctrine which was abhorred as an impious attempt to set aside the institutions of Moses, should long remain unmolested. During the restraint which Providence sometimes imposes upon the wicked, they may seem to be favourably disposed towards religion, and may treat good men with apparent respect and kindness; but the enmity of their hearts to truth and holiness is not diminished, and waits only for a favourable opportunity to discover itself. For a short time, the sun may shine, and the sky may wear the aspect of serenity, but the clouds will return, and the storm will again beat upon the heads of the righteous.

The Chapter now read records a second persecution to which the rising Church was exposed. "Now about that time, Herod the

---

* According to Dr. Lardner, it was at this time that the Emperor Caligula proposed to erect his statue in the temple; and it was owing to the consternation into which the Jews were thrown, that the persecution was suspended.. Vol. I. 121—125, 2d edition.

king stretched forth his hands to vex certain of the Church." The persecutor was grandson of Herod the Great, who attempted to destroy our Saviour in his infancy, and nephew of that Herod, by whose command the Baptist was beheaded. Notwithstanding the praises lavished on him by Josephus, for his munificence and the mildness of his dispositions, he appears, from this account, to have inherited a portion of the cruelty, as well as the honours and dominions, of his grandfather and uncle; and he has transmitted his name to posterity, as one of those bloody tyrants, who have abused their power for the oppression of innocence and truth. After the death of the first Herod, the royal title of the family expired; but it was restored in the person of this man, whom the Roman emperor appointed king of Judea. Having been educated in the religion of Moses, he is represented by the Jewish historian as so zealous for the law, that hardly a day passed in which he did not offer sacrifices. He might be prompted, therefore, by his own bigotry, to persecute the disciples of Jesus; and in his court, which would be frequented by the priests and rulers, there were not wanting enemies to the Christians, who improved the royal favour, to gratify their private resentment, or their religious intolerance. "He stretched forth his hands to vex certain of the Church."

The first sufferers were persons of less note than the Apostles, probably some of the private members of the Church, who were distinguished by their station in society, or their activity; and as Herod is said only to have vexed them, it would seem that they were not put to death, but subjected to some lighter punishment. A nobler sacrifice was necessary to appease the rage of the king, and to satisfy the demands of his sanguinary counsellors. "He therefore killed James, the brother of John, with the sword." James is called the brother of John, to distinguish him from another James, the son of Cleophas, who is styled the brother of our Lord, because his mother was sister to the Virgin. When the two sons of Zebedee came to our Saviour, soliciting seats in his kingdom, on his right and left hand, he refused their request, but told them that "they should drink of his cup, and be baptized with his baptism." We see the prediction fulfilled with respect to the elder brother, who tasted the bitter cup of affliction, and was baptized with a baptism of blood, when he suffered a violent death.

The Apostolical office was the highest and most honourable in the Church; but it held out no prize to tempt the ambition of worldly men. In their eyes, it was the pre-eminence of shame; and in consequence of the situation of the Church, it was the post of danger. The Apostles were hated above the other Christians as the ringleaders of the apostasy, the men who had kept alive the memory of Jesus, and had prevailed upon many thousands to become his disciples. What courage, what resolution, what disregard of life, what superiority to those terrors, which operate with so much force upon common minds, were requisite as qualifications for so dangerous a station! Those who actually filled it, were men of low birth and no education, and, as some parts of their conduct indicate, of a timid and cowardly temper. Yet, they displayed a spirit of heroism, which was never surpassed. "They jeoparded their lives unto the death, in the high places of the field." We venerate their memory; but let us not forget to admire the grace of God, which "gave power to the faint, and to them who had no might, increased strength."

The death of this righteous man involved the Church in deep affliction; but it was highly gratifying to the blood-thirsty Jews. "Ye shall weep and lament, but the world shall rejoice." They exulted in the just punishment of an irreclaimable heretic; they flattered themselves, that the example would terrify others into a recantation of their error; and they hoped, that the sword would not be returned to its scabbard, till it had executed justice upon all the leading men in the Church. These sentiments were openly expressed; and Herod, eager to ingratiate himself still more with the people, readily complied with their wishes. "And, because he saw it pleased the Jews, he proceeded further, to take Peter also." From whatever motive the persecution was begun, it was continued from policy. This indeed is the principle, which has commonly directed the exercise of that power, which civil governments claim, to interfere in matters of religion. It is not truth, but expediency, which, in most cases, has regulated its operations. Hence forms of religion, not merely differing in some particulars of inferior importance, but directly opposed to each other, have been successively patronised by the same legislature, and even established, at the same time, in different provinces; plainly because nothing was thought of but to secure the authority and influence of government, by gratifying the wishes and prejudices of the people. The alliance between Church and State is conceived to be so close, that if the one fall, the other cannot long be supported. The Church, therefore, is upheld for the sake of the State; and in defence of the former, some men display the most furious zeal, who give evidence, by their general profaneness and profligacy, that they hold religion, considered in itself, in absolute contempt. Non-conformity is accounted a certain indication of disaffection, as if no man could be a good subject, who presumed to exercise his own judgment, and refused to be controlled by the opinion of others neither wiser nor better than himself, in a matter infinitely more important than all temporal concerns, and the design of which is utterly lost, if it do not proceed upon examination and choice. Every loyal man should embrace that faith, to which the state has given its sanction; and the state has preferred it to any other, because it serves better as an engine of political influence. The appeal is never made to the Scriptures, by which alone all questions of this nature should be decided. Force is an easier and more compendious method of silencing the objections of dissenters. It is acknowledged, that persecution has often originated in sincere but mistaken zeal for what was conceived to be the truth; but in many cases, and especially with persons in power, religion is merely a pretext, and the real causes are to be found in the jealousy of governments, the avarice, ambition, and resentment of ministers, or the machinations of a corrupt, interested priesthood, exerting themselves to maintain that craft by which they have their gain. Such is the history of a power, which has been represented as the gift of God to the rulers of nations, and contended for with as great vehemence of argument, and bitterness of zeal, as if Christianity itself, deprived of its protection, would speedily perish from the earth!

" Then were the days of unleavened bread." The Israelites were commanded to eat unleavened bread for seven days at the time of the passover. The season is mentioned, to assign the reason why the king did not immediately put Peter to death. He was more scrupulous than the priests, at the time of our Saviour's crucifixion, and would not profane the feast by a public execution; or he was afraid, lest the friends of Peter should excite the people, to make use of their right to demand the release of a prisoner, for obtaining his pardon.

"When he had apprehended Peter, therefore, he put him in prison, and delivered him to four quarternions of soldiers," that is, to sixteen soldiers, four of whom guarded him by turns; "intending after Easter to bring him forth to the people." The term,

Easter, denotes, in this country, the day observed by many Churches, in memory of our Saviour's resurrection, But the Greek word signifies the passover, and should have been exactly translated, because the historian is speaking not of a Christian, but of a Jewish festival. With the execution of Peter, Herod purposed to close the solemnity. The time was come, when they who killed the disciples of Jesus, thought "that they did God service." By the infatuated Jews, the murder of this righteous man would be deemed a sacrifice not less acceptable to him than that of the paschal lamb.

"Peter, therefore, was kept in prison;" and while he was so strictly watched, there was no prospect of his escape. "But prayer was made, without ceasing, of the Church unto God for him." The danger of Peter must have excited particular interest, as his services had been so valuable, and his loss would be severely felt. But hope is the life of prayer, for who would ask what he knew to be unattainable? and, in the present case, hope seemed to have no rational foundation. The death of the Apostle was fixed for the next day; and, during the short interval, what could occur to prevent it? The first Christians were persuaded that nothing is impossible to him who believes, because nothing is impossible to God. Daniel was preserved in a den of lions, and the three Jewish confessors, in the midst of a fiery furnace. God could bend the heart of the tyrant to mercy, or defeat his purpose by his sudden death, or incline the people to intercede for the life of his servant, or deliver him by a miracle. They did not limit the Holy One of Israel, and say, "How can this thing be!" Reflecting on his power, they overlooked the obstacles to the answer of their prayers, and "being strong in faith gave glory to God."

The event showed, that the prayer of faith is effectual, and encourages us to trust in God, in seasons of the greatest perplexity. "And when Herod would have brought him forth, the same night Peter was sleeping between two soldiers, bound with two chains; and the keepers before the door kept the prison." How happy is the man who is at peace with God! Assured of his favour, and resigning himself to the disposal of infinite wisdom and goodness, he enjoys an inward calm amidst the fiercest storms of adversity. It was the last night of Peter's imprisonment, and on the morrow he was to suffer a violent death; yet he sleeps more soundly, perhaps, than Herod in his palace, not because nature was exhausted by anxiety and long watching, but because he felt no fear. To him death, although styled the king of terrors, was not terrible. He had learned from his Saviour " not to be afraid of them that kill the body, and after that have no more that they can do." Death is but a sharp pain, past in a moment; and why then should it alarm a Christian? It is probable, that he has suffered more in some acute disease; and if the conflict were more dreadful, it will instantly be forgotten amidst the joys of heaven. Give a man the testimony of a good conscience, and the lively hope of immortality, and you transform him into "a hero, who will smile on the rack, and triumph in the flames. Peter was sleeping between two soldiers, bound with two chains, which were fastened to his hands, and to the right and left hand of the soldiers, according to the manner in which prisoners were secured. The keepers stood before the door, so that his escape was impossible, by any human means.

In the account of his deliverance, there is little which requires illustration. The minister of providence was an angel, to whom the gates and guards presented no obstruction. As soon as he entered, a light shone in the prison, which showed him to be a heavenly messenger, and assisted Peter to find his way without difficulty. When he awoke the Apostle, and commanded him to rise, the chains fell from his hands, and the words of the Psalmist were literally fulfilled, " The Lord looseth the prisoners." He then ordered him to gird himself, and bind on his sandals, and cast his garment about him. These things would be wanted, when he had left the prison. There were two wards to be passed, at which guards were stationed; but there they met with no opposition. All the soldiers were cast into a deep sleep. It is evident from the stir among them in the morning, that they were ignorant of the transactions of the night. The iron-gate, which led into the city, was opened by an invisible hand. The angel and Peter went out, and both walked together through one street, when the angel departed. The miraculous interposition terminated, where ordinary means were sufficient. The presence of the angel was no farther necessary to Peter, who could easily find a place of safety from the pursuit of his enemies.

The age of miracles is past. Angels do not now come, in a visible manner, to perform services to the saints; but their agency is as real and beneficent as ever. " They are all ministering spirits, sent forth to minister for them, who shall be heirs of salvation." They defend the people of God against the incursions of their spiritual adversaries, and preserve them from dangers which are often unperceived. "The angel of the Lord encampeth round about them that fear him, and delivereth them." These glorious creatures do not disdain to minister to man, who was made a little lower than they. His nature, united to the Son of God, reigns above all principalities and powers on the throne of the universe; and every believer can call the Lord of angels his friend and brother. Perhaps, those remarkable events, which sometimes occur in the history of the saints, and for which it is difficult to assign any satisfactory cause; those wonderful escapes, those inexplicable impressions on the mind, those unexpected revolutions in their favour, the sudden and unlooked for patronage of the wicked, the unaccountable failure of the designs of their enemies, the surprising accomplishment of their hopes, when the ordinary means had been tried in vain, and every appearance seemed to justify despair, may be referred to the secret operations of their powerful and vigilant guardians.

Peter was suddenly awaked out of a sound sleep; his eyes were dazzled with the light which shone in the prison; the deliverance was altogether unexpected; and the mode of effecting it was miraculous. These circumstances conspired to agitate his mind, and to render him incapable of calm and regular thought. Hence, " he wist not that it was true which was done by the angel: but thought he saw a vision." But when he was left alone, " he came to himself," or recovered from his surprise; and finding himself freed from his chains, and in one of the streets of the city, he said, " Now I know of a surety, that the Lord hath sent his angel, and delivered me out of the hand of Herod, and from all the expectation of the people of the Jews." His grateful heart would send up ejaculations of praise to the Saviour, and be inspired with new ardour to serve so gracious a Master.

He then reflected upon the course which it would be proper to pursue, both for his own safety, as a strict search would be made for him, and for the relief of the anxiety of his friends; " and when he had considered the thing, he came to the house of Mary, the mother of John, whose surname was Mark, where many were gathered together praying." In those days there were no Churches, or buildings appropriated to religious worship. The disciples met in private houses, and frequently, in times of persecution, in less convenient places. This assembly was convened in the night, principally because the next day was fixed for the execution of Peter, but partly from fear of the Jews. In the first ages, the Christians often held their meetings in the night; and from this precaution, which was necessary to avoid the danger of discovery, their enemies ungenerously stigmatized them as persons who fled from the light, and chose the veil of darkness to cover the abominable crimes, which were committed in their conventicles.* If they appeared in open day, they were assaulted, and dragged to prison and to death; if they sought concealment, they were loaded with the foulest imputations. In the house of Mary, prayers were offered up for the deliverance of Peter. Even at this late hour, his friends did not despair. God was able to disappoint the designs of Herod, and the hopes of the Jews, on the eve of accomplishment.

At this moment, "Peter knocked at the gate; and a damsel came to hearken, named Rhoda. And when she knew Peter's voice, she opened not the gate for gladness, but ran in, and told how Peter stood before the gate." The description of this young woman, forgetting, in a tumult of joy, to open the gate to admit him, although this was the first step which cool reflection would have dictated for his safety, is perfectly natural, and would be injured, instead of being improved, by a commentary. "They said unto her, Thou art mad." So much did the answer of their prayers exceed their hopes, that they could not believe it; and the person who told them of their success, appeared to be out of her senses. " But she constantly affirmed that it was even so. Then said they, It is his angel." As the word, translated angel, is used also for an ordinary messenger, some have thought, that they supposed the person at the gate to be a messenger come with intelligence from Peter. But Rhoda knew him by his voice; and from this circumstance they must have concluded that it was either Peter himself, or some being who could personate him. The Jews believed, that every good man was attended by a particular angel, to whose care he was entrusted. Judging it impossible that it was Peter himself, the disciples assembled in the house of Mary said, " It is his angel;" imagining that the angel, who constantly waited upon the Apostle, was come to give notice of him to his friends. But, although the

---

* Minucius Felix, ix.

notion of guardian angels seems to have been adopted, at least by some persons in the primitive Church, it does not follow that it is true; for their private opinions are not the standard of our faith, any more than the private opinions of good men in the present times. It is not confirmed by the authority of our Saviour, or of the Apostles.

"But Peter continued knocking: and when they had opened the door, and saw him, they were astonished. But he, beckoning unto them with the hand to hold their peace, declared unto them how the Lord had brought him out of prison." The joy of the disciples must have been great, to see their beloved brother snatched by divine power from impending death, and their prayers answered in so surprising and seasonable a manner. "And he said, Go show these things unto James, and to the brethren," that they also might admire the goodness of the Saviour, and turn their prayers into praises. "And he departed, and went into another place" of greater security. Having been delivered by a miracle, he was to save himself from the pursuit of his enemies by the exercise of his prudence.

The two following verses give an account of the consternation and bustle of the soldiers, when they found, the next day, that the prisoner was gone. Neither their search, nor the diligence of Herod, could find him. Disappointed in his design against the life of the Apostles, and mortified at not being able to gratify the expectation of the people, he wreaked his vengeance upon the soldiers, who were guilty, in his eyes, of an unpardonable offence. And, indeed, as they could give no account of the matter, he would naturally suspect, either that they had slept upon guard, a crime not to be forgiven, or that they had connived at the escape of the prisoner.

After these events, Herod went to Cesarea, to celebrate games in honour of Cesar. The death of James was forgotten; or if he remembered it, it was with regret, that he had been prevented from sacrificing this other victim to his bigotry or his policy. He was supported by the approbation of the people; and there was no earthly tribunal to which he was amenable. But there was a God in heaven, who makes inquiry after blood, and whom the death of a righteous man, how much soever undervalued by the world, interests more than the fall of a mighty monarch. His justice sometimes pursues the guilty with a quick pace; and forces to their lips the cup which they have given to others, mixed up with the bitter ingredients of his wrath.

Tyre and Sidon were maritime cities, in the vicinity of the dominions of Herod. The inhabitants, being employed in trade, had perhaps neglected agriculture; and their territories were too small to yield what was sufficient for the annual consumption. With the profits of trade, or with the wares which they manufactured and imported, they purchased corn and cattle in Judea, or in some of the provinces belonging to the king. Hence, when by some cause not mentioned, they had incurred the displeasure of Herod, they were anxious to pacify him. They dreaded his resentment, which they were unable to resist, and by which they might be deprived of the necessary supplies. To ensure the success of their embassy, they had made Blastus, the chamberlain, their friend. Kings, who are regarded as independent sovereigns, the arbiters of nations, are often mere pageants, moved by persons of inferior rank behind the curtain. When war and peace are traced to their sources, they are found, in many cases, to proceed, not so much from the ambition and caprice of the ostensible lords of the world, as from the passions of their ministers, and the secret influence of women and favourites. The springs and wheels, which move the mighty machine, are not seldom constructed of the vilest and most contemptible materials.

The favour of the king being gained by the mediation of his chamberlain, Herod, on the second day of the games, as Josephus informs us, sat upon his throne, arrayed in royal apparel, curiously wrought with silver, which being struck by the beams of the rising sun, emitted a dazzling lustre, that filled the spectators with awe. The oration, which he delivered to the ambassadors of Tyre and Sidon, might be worthy of admiration for its eloquence and wisdom; but the applause of the people is an equivocal proof. Truth seldom reaches the ears of kings. They are addressed in the smooth language of flattery, which exaggerates, with unrestrained license, any good qualities of which they are possessed, and blushes not to adorn the most stupid and worthless, with the highest endowments of intellect, and the noblest attributes of virtue. The grossest adulation is eagerly received by men, whom power and splendour have intoxicated. "The people gave a shout, saying, It is the voice of a God, and not of a man." Such extravagant flattery, to which the heathens were accustomed, was altogether unprecedented among the Jews. Perhaps, they were heathens who joined in this idolatrous exclamation. It might seem incredible, that beings possessed of common sense should ever have been so completely blinded and degraded, as to exalt into a God a man like themselves; but this folly was not greater than the Gentiles had already committed, in worshipping stocks and stones, the works of their own hands, or in taking a tree, as the Prophet says, in a style of bitter irony, and making a fire of the one part of it, and a God of the other. We, at this late period of the world, have our belief in the wildest excesses of polytheism confirmed by facts, which have passed before our eyes, and have fixed an indelible stain upon the age, and upon human nature. Amidst the light of revelation, and the improvements of philosophy, have we not heard one of the most unprincipled and sanguinary adventurers, who was ever raised up by Providence to be a scourge of the human race, addressed by his detested slaves, in language sacred to the Divinity, and hailed as another Messiah, sent by Heaven to emancipate mankind? It is still more unaccountable, that any man in his senses, and conscious of his infirmities, should have quietly suffered a compliment so manifestly excessive and ridiculous, that it might have been justly resented as an insult. Did not Herod feel that he was a man, and nothing more? He needed food and rest as well as other men; his head ached; his pulse beat with feverish quickness; his heart quaked at the thought of death, which would lay his honours in the dust. How then could he fancy himself a God!

In the fulness of his pride, he overlooked these monuments of his frailty. No reprimand, or frown, checked the madness of the people. Elevated upon his throne, the puny wretch snuffed up, with self-complacency, the incense offered by his worshippers. "But he was a man, and no God in the hand of him that slew him." "Immediately the angel of the Lord smote him, because he gave not God the glory: and he was eaten of worms, and gave up the ghost." The angels are always ready to execute the orders of their Lord, and fly with equal speed to confer benefits upon the righteous, and to inflict punishment upon the wicked. Herod did not give glory to God, by checking the idolatrous flattery of his subjects, and referring to him all his power and greatness. The measure of his iniquity was full. To injustice and cruelty he now added blasphemous pride. The divine honour, thus openly insulted, demanded his destruction. In the midst of the acclamations of the multitude, and the impious triumph of the king, he was seized with a loathsome and mortal distemper, and expired in a few days, a signal monument of the righteous judgment of God, and a solemn lesson of humility to the great men of the earth, whom the Almighty can dash in pieces as a potter's vessel. Josephus, whose account exactly agrees with that of the inspired historian, represents him as acknowledging amidst his torments, the justice of his doom, and exclaiming to his friends who surrounded him, "Behold, I, your God, am commanded to surrender my life. My fate convicts you of falsehood. I, whom you styled immortal, am hurried to death. I must submit to the sentence of God."

Thus perished this impious persecutor; and the hand of God has since been visibly displayed in the destruction of others, who had distinguished themselves as the enemies of his Church. "No weapon that is formed against thee shall prosper; and every tongue that shall rise against thee in judgment thou shalt condemn. This is the heritage of the servants of the Lord, and their righteousness is of me, saith the Lord."

I conclude with a few reflections suggested by this passage.

First, Self-denial and courage are qualities, which enter into the composition of the Christian character. Self-denial is necessary, because there are many privations to which the follower of Jesus must submit, many acts of mortification which he must perform, many hardships, unpleasant to human nature, which he must undergo. Without courage, he could not face the formidable obstacles which lie before him in the path of obedience, nor endure the trials of his faith and patience. Neither a selfish nor a timid man is fit to be a Christian. He alone is worthy of this character, who, entirely devoted to his Saviour, is willing to sacrifice every personal consideration for his glory, and is resolved that nothing shall stop him in the course of his duty. Such were the Christians of the Apostolic age. Such was James, who laid down his life for the gospel; and such was Peter, who cheerfully consented to follow his Lord to prison and to death. Our circumstances, indeed, through the goodness of Providence, are different from theirs; we enjoy peace and security in the profession of religion. But in the most tranquil season, we must bear the world's scorn, and resist the world's solicitations; and the hour of temptation may come suddenly upon the Church, that they who are approved, may be made manifest. The following words of Christ are applicable to every period. "If any man will come after me, let him deny himself, and take up his cross and follow me."

In the second place, When we reflect upon the terrible sufferings of the primitive Christians, and of the faithful in succeeding ages, let us submit, without repining, to the comparatively slight inconveniences, which we may incur in the cause of religion. Perhaps, we have been compelled by conscience to adopt a form of religion which is not fashionable, and, on this account, are deprived of some advantages which we should enjoy by conforming to the established faith. We may be a proverb of reproach among fools, and among pretenders to wisdom. It may occasionally be our lot to encounter the sneer of contempt, and to be the butt of ridicule, and wit embittered by malignity. Our familiar friends forsake us; and by the companions of our former folly, we may be branded as hypocrites or madmen, because we will no longer run to the same excess of riot. These, it must be owned, are trials which will be keenly felt by every honest and delicate mind. But we have not yet "resisted unto blood, striving against sin." Our lives have not been endangered; our property has not been confiscated; nor have we been compelled to exchange the sweets of liberty for the gloom of a prison. With the history of the martyrs before our eyes, shall we not be ashamed to complain? Surely, if we escape thus, let us be thankful that our passage to heaven is so easy, while to others it has been difficult and boisterous.

In the third place, Let us proceed with confidence in the performance of our duty, since we are assured, "that the Lord knows how to deliver the godly out of temptation." The case of Peter shows, that no earthly power can prevent their deliverance. God can restrain the fury of their enemies, or, permitting it to operate, can afford protection to its intended victims. "Why art thou afraid of a man that shall die, and of the son of man, that shall be made as grass?" Is he not in the hands of the Lord? And if the breath of the Almighty blow upon him, shall not his goodness wither, and his power and glory be laid in the dust? Know, Christian, that thou art safe in the path of duty; but that, when thou hast left it, thou hast no promise of divine protection. The wisest and most comfortable plan, is to commit ourselves to God, to resign the management of our affairs to his unerring wisdom, to confide in his power, and to believe, that, in obeying the dictates of reason and religion, it shall ultimately be well with us.

In the last place, All the impenitent enemies of the Church shall perish. Defended by omnipotence, she is invincible. Assaulted by the mightiest potentates of the earth, she remains, while they have fallen and not a vestige can be traced of their kingdoms and empires. "In that day will I make Jerusalem a burdensome stone for all people; all that burden themselves with it shall be cut in pieces, though all the people of the earth be gathered together against it." An eloquent Father of the Church has left a treatise on the deaths of persecutors, which records many instances of the miserable end of those who had distinguished themselves by their opposition to the gospel.* Since his time, other examples of divine vengeance have appeared, from which we are led to say, " Verily, there is a reward for the righteous: verily he is a God that judgeth in the earth." "Upon this rock, I will build my Church: and the gates of hell shall not prevail against it." In this attempt even the power and policy of the spirits of darkness shall be baffled. Let not the hearts of Christians despond, when the ungodly prosper, and the earth is filled with violence. While God permits them to pursue their career, they are fulfilling his designs, and shall not be able to accomplish their own. The Assyrian may be the rod of his anger for the correction of his people; but when this purpose is effected, the rod shall be broken, and thrown into the fire. "God is in the midst of her; she shall not be moved: God shall help her, and that right early. The heathen raged, the kingdoms were moved; he uttered his voice, the earth melted. The Lord of hosts is with us, the God of Jacob is our refuge."

---

* Lactan. de mortibus persecutorum.

LECTURE XV.

PAUL AND BARNABAS IN LYSTRA.

Chap. xiv. 8—18.

Antioch of Syria was the first city, in which the gospel was publicly preached to the Gentiles. "The hand of the Lord was with his ministers: and a great number believed, and turned unto the Lord." In the same city, the disciples received the appellation of Christians, by which they have ever since been distinguished. By these remarkable events, Antioch has acquired celebrity in the annals of the Church; and it appears to have been chosen by Providence as a central spot, from which the rays of divine truth should be diffused throughout the heathen world. In the beginning of the thirteenth chapter, there is an account of the separation of Barnabas and Paul, to the work of preaching to the Gentiles, in consequence of a command of the Spirit, addressed to the Prophets and Teachers in Antioch. The opposition which they encountered in the course of their mission was not strange, as their doctrine was new, and adverse to the opinions and corrupt passions of mankind; but it seems to have chiefly proceeded from the Jews. That incorrigible race discovered in every country the same hostile spirit to Christianity and its Author. Justin Martyr affirms, that they not only did not repent of their wickedness in crucifying the Messiah, but sent chosen messengers from Jerusalem to all nations, to inflame the minds of men against his religion.* It is related, in the preceding chapter, that the Jews in Antioch of Pisidia, not content with contradicting and blaspheming the things which were spoken by Paul, "stirred up the devout and honourable women, and the chief men of that city, and raised persecution against him and Barnabas, and expelled them out of their coasts." The same part

---
* Dialog. cum Tryph.

was acted by the Jews of Iconium, who "stirred up the Gentiles, and made their minds evil-affected against the brethren. And when there was an assault made both of the Gentiles, and of the Jews, with their rulers, to use them despitefully, and to stone them, they were aware of it, and fled unto Lystra and Derbe, cities of Lycaonia, and unto the region that lieth round about: and there they preached the gospel."

The passage which I have read, begins with the account of a miracle, performed in the first of those cities. "And there sat a certain man at Lystra, impotent in his feet, being a cripple from his mother's womb, who never had walked." His case resembles that of the man who was cured by Peter and John at the gate of the temple; and a particular statement of it is given, to show the reality, and the greatness of the miracle. It was not an incidental, but a radical infirmity, which was removed. He was impotent in his feet; he had been lame from his birth; and the disorder was such, that at no period of his life had he been able to walk. His situation rendered him the proper object of a miracle. No person of humanity could look upon him without pity; and his cure would appear to all to be the effect, not of superior skill, but of supernatural power. Thus, the design of the miracle would be gained, which was not only to relieve the patient, but to demonstrate to the inhabitants of Lystra, that God was present with Paul and Barnabas, and consequently that their doctrine was true.

Miracles are a sign to "them that believe not." They are not merely prodigies, or strange sights, intended to raise the wonder of the spectators, and to draw their attention to the person who performs them, but tokens, or proofs, of the divine approbation of him, and of the religion which he teaches. To the Jews, the argument from prophecy was sufficient to prove that Jesus was the Christ; and accordingly, we find the Apostles insisting much upon it, in their discourses to that people. But to the Gentiles, it would not have been addressed with propriety, or any hope of success, because they were not acquainted with the prophecies, and had no evidence, that the books containing them, were written prior to the event. Miracles were an obvious and easy species of evidence. It required no investigation or discussion; it pressed upon the senses; and the right inference could be drawn by the plainest understanding. "Rabbi, we know, that thou art a teacher come from God; for no man can do these miracles that thou dost, except God be with him." The purpose for which the Apostles were furnished with the power of working miracles, was to prove to the ignorant, the illiterate, and the unthinking, who are the great majority of mankind, the divine authority of the gospel.

Paul perceived that the lame man had "faith to be healed." This faith seems to signify either a general belief of the power of Barnabas and Paul, or rather of Jesus Christ, whose ministers they were, to heal infirmities and diseases; or a persuasion, that a cure would be performed upon himself in particular. In the former case, his faith was founded on the account which he had heard of the character and miracles of Christ, and of the extraordinary gifts which he had bestowed upon his followers; in the latter, it was the effect of a supernatural impression upon his mind. This faith Paul perceived by the power of discerning spirits, or the power with which the Apostles were occasionally endowed, of discovering the thoughts and dispositions of men. "If thou canst believe," said our Lord to a father deeply afflicted by the sufferings of his son; "if thou canst believe, all things are possible to him that believeth." The expectation which the promises of God, or the suggestions of his Spirit have excited, shall not make him ashamed. "Paul therefore, steadfastly beholding this man, said with a loud voice, Stand up right on thy feet. And he leaped and walked." The cure immediately followed the command. The disorder in his joints was removed; his limbs recovered strength, and with the fondness so natural to a man who has recently acquired a new power, which he had long and earnestly desired, but despaired of ever possessing, he tried it in every way, leaping and walking.

Paul said, "with a loud voice," Stand up right on thy feet. The miracle was wrought for the sake of the inhabitants of Lystra, as well as of the impotent man; and for this reason it was publicly announced. The circumstances in which the miracles of the gospel were performed, leave no room for suspecting, that they were dexterous impositions upon the credulity of mankind. That they were real miracles is evident from this important fact, that they were not done in a corner, but in the chief places of concourse; in the streets of cities, in the midst of assembled multitudes, in the presence of enemies as well as of friends. The miracles of false religions were performed, or are said to have been performed, in distant ages, of which we have only fabulous accounts; in remote countries, where any thing may be feigned to have taken place, without the risk of detection; in temples under the command of priests, who could securely practise there the arts of deceit; or in some obscure retreat, sheltered from every inquisitive eye, before witnesses, select, and favourably disposed. "If they shall say unto you, Behold he is in the desert, go not forth: behold, he is in the secret chambers, believe it not." Truth courts the light, that it may be made manifest. The juggling tricks of heathenism and popery require only a strict examination, to be rejected with contempt: whereas, the miracles of Christianity are displays of omnipotent power, which will be the more admired, the more closely they are considered.

The evidence of miracles is not irresistible, but may be counteracted by the power of prejudice. The Jews attributed the miracles of our Saviour to Satanical influence; the Gentiles believed, that those of the Apostles were operations of magic; and the inhabitants of Lystra were disposed to turn this miracle into an argument in favour of their own idolatrous religion. "And when the people saw what Paul had done, they lift up their voices, saying, in the speech of Lycaonia, The Gods are come down to us in the likeness of men." The Gentiles had corrupted the fundamental doctrine of the unity of God; and their various systems of religion were founded on the supposition of a plurality of Deities, male and female, differing in their rank, their attributes, and the provinces or functions assigned to them. These imaginary beings were conceived to superintend the affairs of the earth. There was, indeed, one sect of philosophers, the disciples of Epicurus, who, while they admitted their existence, denied that they governed the world; but they were justly suspected of atheism.* Other sects of philosophers, and the common people, believed, that men were objects of the attention and care of the Gods, who observed their conduct, and interfered in their transactions, and, for this purpose, descended, on some occasions, to the earth in a visible form. Their histories and poems are full of such appearances. When the inhabitants of Lystra, therefore, cried out, "The Gods are come down to us in the likeness of men;" they did not express surprise at the event as unusual, but rather joy because the Gods had deigned to honour their city with a visit. They have come down to us, "in the likeness of men."

---

* Cier. de natura Deor. i 43.

They were supposed to appear in the human form, which was believed to be their real shape; for the heathen Deities were clothed with bodies like ours, and differed from men only in the extent of their power, and the attribute of immortality.

As soon as the idea was adopted, that Paul and Barnabas were Gods, the people assigned to them their respective names. "They called Barnabas Jupiter, and Paul Mercurius, because he was the chief speaker." Jupiter was the Supreme Divinity of the heathens, whom they called the Father of Gods and men, and represented as swaying his sceptre over heaven and earth. Sometimes they speak of him in a style not unworthy of the true God, describing him as shaking heaven with his nod, and terrifying the world by his thunder; but, at other times, they degrade him below the dignity of a man, by portraying him with the basest passions, and foulest crimes, of a profligate. There is something mysterious and inexplicable in the creed of the Gentiles, affording a lamentable proof of the astonishing, and almost incredible, blindness and stupidity of the human mind. This Jupiter, whom they placed at the head of the universe, they believed to have been a man, who was born, reigned, and died, in the island of Crete. An inextricable confusion pervades the Pagan mythology; it is full of inconsistencies and absurdities, which, one should think, could not have been digested by the most barbarous nation, and still less by the learned Greeks and Romans; and there is no way of accounting for the fact, that they did give credit to the tales of their priests and poets, but by the information of Paul, "that because they did not like to retain God in their knowledge, God gave them over to a reprobate mind." Mercury was one of the sons of Jupiter. Among the various offices with which he was invested, it is necessary to mention only, that he was reputed the messenger of the Gods, and the interpreter of their will. Paul was called Mercury, because he most frequently addressed the people. If he was a God, there was none whose character so exactly suited him, as that of the Deity who conveyed the messages of Jupiter to mankind. Barnabas was supposed to be Jupiter, because he was older than Paul, or of a more dignified appearance.

If the Gods had condescended to visit the city of Lystra, religion required that they should be received with appropriate honours. "The priest of Jupiter, therefore, which was before their city," or had a temple without the walls, or in the suburbs, "brought oxen and garlands unto the gates, and would have done sacrifice with the people." Sacrifices were a distinguished part of the worship of the heathens; and in this general feature, their religion resembled that of the Jews. The practice was undoubtedly derived from traditionary accounts of the original institution of sacrifices; for the death of irrational animals would not have occurred to the uninstructed human mind, as a proper expedient for propitiating the Deity. The victims were generally crowned with garlands of flowers. The religion of the Gentiles was of a cheerful nature. The eye was captivated with magnificent spectacles; the ear was charmed with the sound of musical instruments, and the melody of songs; and, at some festivals, the grossest debauchery was permitted in honour of their licentious Divinities.

The intended sacrifice was prevented by the zeal of Barnabas and Paul. "Which, when the Apostles, Barnabas and Paul, heard of, they rent their clothes, and ran in among the people, crying out, and saying, Sirs, why do ye these things?" In the usual sense of the term, Barnabas was not an Apostle; but it literally signifies a person sent, a messenger, or missionary, and the title is probably given to him in reference to his mission from Antioch, to preach the gospel to the Gentiles. Paul, in one of his Epistles, speaks of certain brethren, who were "the messengers or Apostles of the Churches, and the glory of Christ." When Paul and Barnabas were informed of the intention of the people, they "rent their clothes." This was a custom of the Jews, at the death of their friends, in times of public calamity, and when they heard blasphemy, or witnessed any great transgression of the law. The Apostles therefore expressed, after the manner of their country, grief at the conduct of the people, and abhorrence of their idolatry. "They ran in among them, saying, Sirs, why do ye these things? We also are men of like passions with you." It has been remarked, that the word translated, "of like passions," properly signifies, subject to the same infirmities and sufferings, or fellow mortals. Their being of "like passions" with them would not have appeared to the Gentiles a good reason why Paul and Barnabas should not be worshipped; for Jupiter and Mercury, and all the Gods and Goddesses of Paganism, were supposed to be actuated by the same passions with men, and, if history might be credited, had given many shocking displays of wrath, revenge, envy, and lust. But, if they were fellow-mortals, beings subject, like others, to disease and death, it was evident that they were not Gods; for the heathen Deities were accounted immortal, and were chiefly distinguished by this privilege from their worshippers. Mortals, indeed, there have been, who demanded religious honours; and base flatterers have not been wanting to comply with the extravagant request. Some of the Roman emperors were deified during their lives. But, surely, the worshippers and the worshipped must have secretly regarded each other with mutual contempt; the former scorning the inflated worm, who dreamed of divinity, because accident had raised him to a throne; and the latter despising the abject slaves who courted his favour by such degrading homage. The remains of his reason must have nauseated their incense, while it gratified his vanity. "Sirs, why do ye these things." Jealous of the glory of the true God, the Apostles rejected, with abhorrence, any honour offered to them, which intrenched on his prerogative. "We are mere mortals like yourselves, and wish for no other token of respect, than that you should listen to us, while we call upon you to renounce your idolatry. We preach unto you, that ye should turn from these vanities unto the living God."

In the Old Testament, the heathen Gods are frequently styled vanities. It is a contemptuous title, which at the same time, is expressive of their nature. Of the Deities, whom the blinded nations adored, some had no existence, except in the imagination of their worshippers; and the rest were dead men and women, whom the gratitude and admiration of posterity had consecrated. Their images, in which a divine virtue was supposed to reside, were constructed of stone, and wood, and the precious metals; and were alike unworthy of religious honours, and incapable of doing either good or evil, as inanimate matter in any other shape. "They had eyes, but they saw not; and ears, but they heard not. They that made them were like unto them; so was every one that trusted in them." All was vanity. These pretended Gods, and their unprofitable service, the apostles called upon the men of Lystra to forsake, and henceforward to worship "the living God." The living God is Jehovah the self-existent being, who comprehends in himself the past, the present, and the future, and is the source of life to all who breathe and think. His existence alone is necessary and immutable; that of all other beings is contingent and fluctuating. He is here opposed to the Gods of the Gentiles, who were dead men, or imaginary beings, and whose lifeless images, enveloped in clouds of smoke, and adored with profound reverence, were as insensible of their unmerited honours, as the walls of their temples. "Choose now," said the Apostles, "whether you will serve the living or the dead." "None of the vanities of the Gentiles could give rain;" they had less power even than the men who implored their protection. "But the living God made heaven and earth, and the sea, and all things that are therein." The universe arose out of nothing at his command, was arranged by his wisdom, and is sustained by his power. It demonstrates his existence and attributes; and, in language understood in every nation, calls upon the spectators of his glory to adore and serve him.

But if the God, whom Paul and Barnabas preached, was the true God, the Creator of the world and its inhabitants, why was he so late in asserting his claim to their homage? Whence had he remained unknown for many ages, while other beings were suffered to usurp his place and his honours? To obviate this objection against the Christian doctrine as a novel system, which laboured under the great disadvantage of being opposed to the ancient established opinions of mankind, the Apostles subjoin the following remark. "Who in times past suffered all nations to walk in their own ways." The cause of the recent introduction of his worship, was, not that he was an upstart God, a Divinity of yesterday, but that, for wise and holy reasons, he had permitted the nations, during a long succession of ages, to apostatize from himself, and follow the suggestions of their vain imaginations. Although, as we shall afterwards see, he did not leave himself altogether without a witness, yet he laid no restraint upon them in their deviations from truth; and employed no extraordinary means to stem the torrent of apostasy. No Prophet arose among them to reprove their errors, and restore the knowledge and service of the Creator. "The times of this ignorance he winked at," seeming to take no notice of it, as a man closes his eyes, that he may not observe what is passing around him. Every nation was suffered to adopt whatever form of religion was most agreeable to its taste. Gods were multiplied by the creative power of superstition; temples rose in every city, and altars in every grove; so that the true God was banished from the greater part of his own world. The duration of this period of darkness and impiety is expressed by the indefinite phrase, "times past." Idolatry seems to have begun early after the flood. It was practised in the family of Abraham prior to his call.

But the true God continued to be known and worshipped long after, by individuals and families, amidst the general corruption. The covenant with Abraham and his posterity, by which they were constituted the peculiar people of God, did not operate to the exclusion of other nations, till about the time of the deliverance of the Israelites from Egypt. The oracles of heaven were then committed to his descendants, and the rest of mankind were abandoned to their own conduct.

Notwithstanding the rejection of the Gentiles, their idolatry was inexcusable, because " God did not leave himself without a witness, in that he did good, and gave them rain from heaven, and fruitful seasons, filling their hearts with food and gladness." Canaan was a land " flowing with milk and honey," and it is called "the glory of all the lands." But notwithstanding the high character bestowed upon it, in consequence of the divine blessing, which rendered it uncommonly fertile, the other regions of the earth were not deserts, yielding only briers and thorns. Some of the countries, which the Gentiles inhabited, abounded in the choicest productions of the vegetable kingdom. The rain fell upon their fields, and the year was crowned with the goodness of the Lord. There is not a more agreeable prospect than a country smiling under the influences of heaven, presenting to the eye vallies covered with corn, and mountains clothed with pasture, or shaded with forests. As such a scene charms us with its beauties and cheers our hearts with the hope of plenty, so it is fitted to raise our thoughts to the source of all good, the almighty, and beneficent Parent of the universe. A reflecting mind learns wisdom from trees, and flowers, and every thing.

No man, who consults his reason, can consider the productions of the earth as the result of chance, because chance signifies no cause of any kind, but merely expresses our ignorance. It is not less irrational to imagine, that vegetation is the effect of certain independent qualities, or powers of matter. Men may impose upon themselves by words and theories ; but it is impossible to conceive what is lifeless and inert to act, without being first acted upon by some external cause, or an unconscious substance to work according to a regular and uniform plan. Wherever we observe design, wherever we see an end aimed at, and a series of means employed to accomplish it, reason and experience point to an intelligent agent. It was never supposed by any man in his senses, that a watch was made by itself, or that a house was reared by the accidental meeting of wood, and stones, and mortar. The process, by which "our hearts are filled with food and gladness," consists of so many steps, all conducting to a specific termination, that no person can survey them, without an immediate conviction of the existence and providence of God. From the surface of the ocean, of rivers, and of lakes, and from every part of the earth, water is raised, in the form of vapour, to the sky. There it is condensed by cold, and falls down by the law of gravitation. The rain penetrating the soil, cherishes the seeds deposited in it, and entering the roots of vegetables, ascends by the stem or trunk, and is circulated through the branches and leaves. At the same time, plants imbibe nourishment from the air and the sun; and arriving at maturity, by slower or more rapid progress, according to their nature, present their fruits to man, as a gift of the bounty of his Creator.

This process is so often repeated, that it attracts little notice. Many a careless spectator of the varied scenes of spring, summer, and autumn, never extends his thoughts beyond the objects before his eyes. But the changes produced upon the face of the earth, by the vicissitudes of the seasons, are unquestionable proofs of divine wisdom and beneficence. The heathens, amidst their ignorance, were not so atheistical as some modern philosophers, who would confine the attention of others, as well as their own, to the operation of natural causes. They erred only in overlooking the true Author of their enjoyments, and returning thanks for their fruitful seasons to Jupiter, and Ceres, and Pomona, instead of acknowledging the various productions of the earth to be the work of one God, "from whom cometh down every good and perfect gift." The uniformity amidst variety, which is observable in the system of nature, the regularity of the seasons, the connexion and combination of the causes which contribute to the fertility of the earth, and the sameness of the result, afford evidence upon which we may safely rest this conclusion, that there is one First Cause, "who worketh all in all." Thus in the darkest times of heathenism, there were not wanting testimonies to the existence and perfections of God. "The invisible things of him were clearly seen from the creation and government of the world, even his eternal power and godhead; so that the Gentiles were without excuse." This is the important truth, which it was the intention of Paul and Barnabas to establish.

It was, however, with difficulty, that they prevailed upon the people to abstain from offering sacrifice to them. The men of Lystra were addicted to idolatry, in which they had been trained from their earliest years; and so fully were they persuaded of the divinity of the two Apostles, that their own testimony hardly sufficed to convince them of their error. It was with reluctance that they renounced the flattering idea, that their city had been honoured with a visit of the Gods.

We learn from this passage, that the contemplation of nature should be rendered subservient to the purposes of piety. God did not place so many glorious luminaries in the heavens, nor diversify the surface of the earth with mountains and vallies, nor collect the immense mass of water in the ocean, merely to furnish us with the pleasures of imagination. Man is delighted with the view of what is sublime and beautiful, and with the instances of curious contrivance, and exquisite workmanship; but the ultimate design of this delight, is to conduct him to the knowledge and love of its Author. All the objects around us bear witness to the existence of God. Philosophy will afford us much entertainment, by unfolding the secret operations of nature; but the pleasure of the unlettered Christian, who knows scarcely any thing about the laws of the material system, the structure of plants, and the mechanism of animals, is incomparably greater, when he traces, in the grand outlines of creation, the footsteps of his Father, and sees in its varying scenes, the wonders of his power, and the smiles of his goodness.

Let us give thanks to God for our deliverance from that gross idolatry, which once prevailed among all nations except the Jews. It is not to reason that we are indebted for this deliverance. We indeed find no difficulty in proving, that there is only one God, the exclusive object of religious worship; but to demonstrate a truth already known, is a much easier task than to discover a truth buried under the rubbish of prejudice and superstition. The wisest and greatest men of antiquity were polytheists. They adored, with the vulgar, the Gods of their country. The doctrine of the unity of God has never been publicly professed by any people, who had not been previously enlightened by revelation. The Mahometans have learned this fundamental truth from our Scriptures. Notwithstanding the ignorant declamations of infidels con cerning the powers of reason, and discoveries which may be made by its assistance, experience will justify us in affirming, that, without the gospel, we should have been as gross idolaters as our forefathers. Were Christianity banished from the earth, as some men earnestly wish, the absurd and exploded systems of Paganism would be restored; or some modification of folly not less extravagant would be substituted in their room. No sooner had the French nation, a few years ago, renounced the religion of Christ, than they began to revive the antiquated rites of Greece and Rome, and publicly adored a prostitute, under the title of the Goddess of Reason. It is the gospel which has turned us "from vanities, to serve the living God."

In a word, As we profess to be the servants of the living God, let us remember, that it is a pure and spiritual worship which he requires. He must not be treated as one of the idols of the Gentiles, to whom their votaries presented the empty homage of ceremonies and oblations. Then only do we serve him, in a manner worthy of his character and attributes, when we present to him the offering of our hearts; when we love him above all things, confide in his power and faithfulness, commit ourselves to the direction of his wisdom, submit to his authority, and regulate our thoughts and actions by his law. Then only do we acceptably serve him, when we offer up praises from a grateful heart, and prayers expressive of holy desires; and when we perform all our religious duties in the name of the great Mediator, the High-Priest of our profession. " For though there be that are called gods, whether in heaven or in earth (as there be gods many, and lords many,) but to us there is but one God, the Father, of whom are all things, and we in him; and one Lord Jesus Christ, by whom are all things, and we by him."

LECTURE XVI.

THE COUNCIL OF JERUSALEM.

Chap. xv. 1—31.

The important nature of the transaction, related in this passage, and the discussion into which we shall be unavoidably led, in consequence of the different systems which it has been brought forward to support, might draw out this discourse to an inconvenient length. I shall therefore consume no part of our time with any introductory remarks, and shall study the greatest possible brevity, while I endeavour to explain, as distinctly as I can, the three parts into which the chapter naturally divides itself; the dispute in Antioch, which was the occasion of a reference to the Apostles and elders at Jerusalem; their deliberations and decision upon the question; and the letter containing their decree, which was sent to the Churches of Syria and Cilicia.

The origin of the dispute is stated in the first verse. " And certain men, which came down from Judea, taught the brethren, and said, Except ye be circumcised after the manner of Moses, ye cannot be saved." It appears from the fifth verse, which I consider as referring to those teachers, and not to any abettors of their doctrine in Jerusalem, that, prior to their conversion, they were Pharisees; and they seem to have retained the peculiar opinions of their sect, with regard to the justification of a sinner. The law of Moses was virtually abolished by the death of Christ, in which its design was accomplished; but few among the Jewish believers were apprized of the expiration of its authority. The simple observance of its rites, however, was not yet unlawful, if it proceeded from a principle of conscience, mistaken, indeed, but revering what was still supposed to be obligatory; or from a charitable intention to avoid giving offence to the weak. But those men taught, that obedience to the law of Moses was indispensably necessary to salvation; or that circumcision, and the other duties, ceremonial and moral, which it enjoined, were the express condition of our acceptance with God. Hence, they urge it with the utmost rigour upon the Gentiles. As they professed Christianity, they must have assigned some efficacy to faith; and their system probably resembled that absurd and pernicious doctrine, which is still current in the Church, that our own good works, and the righteousness of Christ supplying their defects, are conjunct causes of justification; a doctrine which robs divine grace of its due honour, impeaches the merit of the Saviour as imperfect, and subverts the foundation of the gospel. We perceive, then, the reason that Paul, although he circumcised Timothy out of respect to the prejudices of the Jews, wrote to the Galatians in the following terms. "Behold, I Paul say unto you, that if ye be circumcised, Christ shall profit you nothing. For I testify again to every man that is circumcised, that he is a debtor to do the whole law. Christ is become of none effect unto you, whosoever of you are justified by the law; ye are fallen from grace." We discover, at the same time, the cause of the zeal, with which the men from Judea were opposed by Paul and Barnabas, whose regard to the truth of the gospel, and concern for the souls of the disciples, would not suffer a doctrine so dangerous to be quietly disseminated. "They had no small dissension and disputation with them." That their arguments were more powerful than those of their opponents, it is impossible to doubt; but controversies, both in religion and in politics, are not always determined by superior evidence, but are often prolonged by pride and obstinacy, by ignorance and prejudice.

Some, perhaps, are surprised that the men from Judea should have dared to contend with Paul and Barnabas, of whom the one was an Apostle, and the other a Prophet. Were any person now alive invested with the same authority, and endowed with the same extraordinary gifts, we are apt to think that we should willingly submit to the decision of this infallible judge. But we impose upon ourselves, by not attending to the difference of our circumstances. We look back to Barnabas and Paul with veneration, unabated by any personal quarrel, or by a near inspection of their frailties. We view them only at a distance, and in the august character of ambassadors of Christ. But were they living, and associating with us, we should be familiarized to their presence, and, amidst a conflict of opinions and interests, should be ready enough to forget the respect, to which, in our calm moments, we deemed them entitled. The opposition made to them on this occasion, is not a proof that their inspiration was not generally acknowledged by the Christians of their own age. The Israelites rebelled against Moses, whom they believed to be the minister of God. Under the influence of temptation, men often transgress the precepts of our religion, the divine authority of which they will not venture to dispute.

The controversy might have been determined in Antioch. The authority of Paul was as great as that of any other Apostle; Barnabas was a Prophet; and there were other inspired men in the city, as we are informed in the thirteenth chapter, as well as ordinary teachers, who had power to rebuke and exhort, and to reject heretics, after a first and a second admonition. But such was the violence of party, that a decision on the spot was not likely to terminate the difference; and it was expedient to refer the question to a higher assembly, in whose authority all would acquiesce. Besides, it was not a local, but a general question, which might be agitated in any other part of the world; so that it was necessary to obtain a final sentence, which should be alike respected in Antioch, and in all the cities of the Gentiles, " They determined, therefore, that Paul and Barnabas, and certain other of them, should go up to Jerusalem unto the Apostles and elders about this question."

Different opinions have been entertained with respect to the persons by whom this resolution was adopted. The supposition that Paul and Barnabas were commissioned by the false teachers, is, on many accounts, highly improbable. There is as little ground to think that the determination was made by the brethren, or private members of the Church, mentioned in the first verse. The structure of the passage does not give countenance to this idea. Zeal for the pretended authority of the Church in its collective capacity, is carried to excess, when an Apostle and a Prophet are represented as receiving and executing its commands. We know that there were in Antioch Prophets and Teachers, with whom Paul and Barnabas associated in their ordinary ministrations; and it is consonant to all our ideas of propriety and order, to conceive the determination to have been their deed. They alone were concerned, by the express command of the Spirit, in the separation of Paul and Barnabas to the work of preaching the gospel to the Gentiles; and no satisfactory reason can be given for supposing, that their authority was inadequate to the present purpose, or that it was suspended to make way for the interference of the people.

The history of this transaction is very short, and several particulars are undoubtedly omitted. It is by no means an improbable opinion, that as this controversy was not confined to Antioch, but had caused disturbance in the Churches of Syria and Cilicia, they concurred in this determination; and that their delegates were among the persons who accompanied Barnabas and Paul. This is not a mere assumption to serve the purpose of a party, by providing a sufficient number of members to render the assembly at Jerusalem a Council. It is supported by the following argument, that if they had no immediate concern in that assembly, if they made no reference to it, and had no delegates present in it, it is not easy to conceive on what principles they were bound by its decree, unless it should be affirmed, that the Apostles were representatives of the Catholic Church, and consequently of the Syrian and Cilician Churches. This answer, I acknowledge, would be satisfactory; but it should be observed, that upon this supposition we have here an example of a representative assembly of the Church, which authorises the holding of similar assemblies for deciding controversies, and deliberating on affairs of general concern. If to evade the consequence, this solution be rejected, I know not how we shall get rid of the difficulty, without admitting that the representatives of those Churches were present, and acted in their name. A decree of the Apostles, it must be allowed, would have been obligatory upon all Christians throughout the world; but the decree was also enacted by the elders; and what right the elders of Jerusalem had to make laws for other Churches, no man is able to tell. The abettors of Independency must be above all others perplexed to account for the fact; for they surely will reject the idea, that one Church may impose its decisions upon another, its equal in privileges and power. If any man should think that the sentence of the elders was obligatory upon other Churches, because it was conformable to the mind of the Spirit, he is requested to observe, that, upon this hypothesis, it was not at all binding as their decree; and that the Scriptural sentence of any man, or of a child, would have had the same obligation. But the transaction cannot be thus explained away, without manifest absurdity.

Whatever opinion is formed upon the subject, it is evident that the reference was made to the Apostles and elders. When the Apostles are considered as the immediate ambassadors of Christ, the highest office-bearers in his Church, they appear in a character peculiar to themselves, and exercise functions, in which no person could co-operate with them. But, on some occasions, we see them acting in a subordinate character, placing themselves on a level with the ordinary pastors and governors of the Church, assuming the designation of presbyters or elders, joining with them in setting persons apart to the ministry, and receiving from them commissions for particular services. That the reference was not made to them as inspired men, the infallible judges of controversies, is evident, because it was made at the same time to the elders; for the wisdom of the elders could not improve the dictates of inspiration, and there was no defect in the Apostolic power, which their concurrence could supply. But their public character remained; and as they stood in no peculiar relation to any particular Church, we must conceive them to have acted, not in a private capacity, but in the name of all the Churches upon earth. Although it is commonly presumed, yet it would be difficult to prove, that the elders, to whom the reference was made, were those alone who constantly resided in Jerusalem. That city is perhaps mentioned only as the place of meeting. Without, however, contesting this point, let us suppose that none but the elders of Jerusalem are meant. Had the Church of Antioch intended that the controversy should be decided by immediate revelation, or by Apostolical authority, there was no cause for sending so far, as Paul, who was not behind the chief of the Apostles, was among them; or if expediency required a deputation to Jerusalem, it would have been an affront to the Apostles, to consult, at the same time, the elders, who were not inspired. The purpose, therefore, of the Church of Antioch, seems to have been to submit the question to a larger assembly than could be collected in their own city; and we cannot imagine any reason why the Apostles admitted the elders to deliberate along with them, but to establish a precedent for calling Councils in cases of emergency. Let it be observed, that no reference was made to the Church of Jerusalem, or the brethren at large. Accordingly, they took no part in the discussion; and we shall afterwards see, that from them the decree derived no portion of its authority.

Some, with a view to prove that the present case does not furnish an example of a reference from an inferior to a superior court, assign as the sole cause of submitting the question to the elders, as well as the Apostles, that as the men from Judea pretended to have received authority from the elders, it was necessary to apply to them for the knowledge of the fact. But the truth could have been ascertained with much less trouble by a single messenger, and without a solemn and public consultation. Besides, when the Apostles and elders assembled, the subject of inquiry was not a question of fact, but of doctrine; not whether the men from Judea had authority to teach, but whether the observance of the law of Moses should be enjoined upon the Gentiles.

There are no remarks, connected with the main design of this Lecture, suggested by the two next verses, which indeed are so plain, as to require no illustration. In the fifth verse, we are informed, that "there arose up certain of the sect of the Pharisees which believed, saying, That it was needful to circumcise them, and to command them to keep the law of Moses." I am inclined to consider these words as a part of the speech of Paul and Barnabas, in which they relate the cause of their coming to Jerusalem, rather than as the statement of a new fact, that the doctrine, which had caused so much disturbance in Antioch, was espoused by some persons in the former city.

Let us now attend to the proceedings of the assembly which met to discuss the important question, upon which the peace and enlargement of the Gentile Churches depended. "And the Apostles and elders came together for to consider of this matter," to canvass the arguments on both sides, and to pass a final sentence. In the form of procedure, there was nothing different from what may be practised, and often is practised, in other assembles. No person rose and pronounced the dictates of inspiration, by which the rest were overawed; but Apostles and elders consulted together on equal terms, and the decree was the result of their united deliberations. It was founded upon a well-known fact, corroborated by other facts, which were brought forward in the course of the inquiry; and upon an argument drawn from the Scriptures.

It appears from the following verses, that there were other persons present, besides the Apostles and elders, and the commissioners from Antioch, who are called "the multitude," and "the whole Church." Nothing, however, can be plainer, than that they were present to hear, not to deliberate and judge; for, besides that the reference was not made to them, Luke expressly affirms, that none came together to consider this matter but "the Apostles and elders." As the question, however, was of the greatest importance, affecting the interests of the Gentile believers, and prescribing the terms of their admission to the privileges of the gospel, it could not but ex cite general attention. "The whole Church" can mean only the whole assembly present, not all the members of the Church in Jerusalem; for as we are certain that there were in that city many thousands who believed, it is utterly improbable that so great a multitude should have been permitted to meet in public, by a government ill-affected to them and their cause. Besides, as what would be impossible now, was equally impossible then, although some men seem to forget this very obvious truth, and to believe any thing to have been practicable, if it is said to have taken place at the distance of a sufficient number of centuries, all the disciples could not have met in one place, except the temple from which such a concourse of suspected persons would have been excluded, especially when their design was to set aside the institutions of Moses; or some square or market-place, in which it is absurd to suppose them to have assembled. To evade this objection to the idea, that this was a Church-meeting, some enter into calculations, by which the believers in Jerusalem are reduced to the smallest possible number. In the same spirit, we see an eagerness to show, that, in the Apostolical times there were not so many disciples in any city, as could not have conveniently met in one place of worship, from an apprehension, lest, if there should be found to have been several congregations in the same city, and these were all accounted one Church, it should follow, that Churches were not then independent, but were united, according to the Presbyterian or Episcopalian plan, under one general government. While every unprejudiced reader of the New Testament must be convinced, that this hypothesis is not true with respect to Jerusalem, and appears to be equally erroneous with regard to some other cities, there is one thing, of which these inconsiderate reasoners have need to be reminded, that the tendency of their calculations is to prove, that the success of Christianity, in the first ages, was by no means so great as we have been always taught to believe; and that, if the gospel, as they pretend, collected only scanty handfuls here and there among Jews and Gentiles, the argument for its divinity, founded on its rapid and extensive progress, is divested of its splendour, and loses much of its force. If, by the same means which support a party, the cause of religion is injured, the advantage is dearly purchased.

When the Apostles and elders came together to consider this matter, there was "much disputing;" not, we may presume, among the Apostles themselves, but among the other members of the Council, some of whom retained a strong predilection for their ancient institutions. I should not, however, willingly believe, that any of them went so far as to maintain the observance of the law of Moses to be necessary to justification; but, imagining it still to be in force, they contended, that obedience to its precepts should be required from the Gentiles as well as from the Jews. To terminate this dispute, which betrayed ignorance, and might generate strife, Peter rose, and addressed the assembly to the following purport: That, as they all knew, God had employed him, a considerable time before, to preach the gospel to the Gentiles; that He, to whom the state and dispositions of the heart are manifest, gave testimony to their sincerity in believing it, and his acceptance of them, by the descent of the Holy Ghost; and that, to those who were originally uncircumcised and unclean, he had imparted, by means of faith, that holiness of heart, of which circumcision and the legal purifications were typical. "Now, therefore," he adds, "why tempt ye God, to put a yoke upon the neck of the disciples, which neither our fathers nor we were able to bear?" To impose the law of Moses upon the Gentiles was to go contrary to the will of God, who, by receiving them, when uncircumcised, into his favour, had plainly declared, that they ought not to be subjected to it. Peter calls it, "a yoke, which neither their fathers nor they were able to bear," to admonish his brethren, not to lay a burden upon others, which they had experienced to be intolerable. The multiplied, expensive, and troublesome services of the law would justify this description of it; but its propriety will farther appear, if we consider, that the law "could not make him that did the service perfect, as pertaining to the conscience," by delivering him from a sense of guilt; that the repetition of its sacrifices reminded the worshippers of sin, and showed that they were insufficient to expiate it; and that its whole contexture was calculated to create and cherish a spirit of bondage and fear. There could be no good reason for wishing to retain, and to enforce upon others, so imperfect a system of religion. In the following words, the Apostle suggests another argument against imposing the law of Moses upon the Gentiles, namely, that it would be inconsistent to urge upon them as necessary to salvation, what was not the foundation of their own hope. "The Gentiles expect salvation without observing the law; we, who do observe it, trust not in our own works, but in the merit of the Saviour; and why should any man require that from another, upon which himself places no dependence?" "We believe that, through the grace of our Lord Jesus Christ, we shall be saved even as they."

When Peter had finished his speech, Barnabas and Paul successively rose to support it, by the relation of many similar facts; and they were heard with that profound attention which the novelty and importance of the detail naturally excited. "Then all the multitude kept silence, and gave audience to Barnabas and Paul, declaring what miracles and wonders God had wrought among the Gentiles by them."

The last person who delivered his sentiments upon the subject was James. Having recapitulated the speech of Peter, he adds, "And to this agree the words of the Prophet, as it is written, After this I will return, and will build again the tabernacle of David, which is fallen down; and I will build again the ruins thereof, and I will set it up: that the residue of men might seek after the Lord, and all the Gentiles, upon whom my name is called, saith the Lord, who doth all these things." I shall lay before you the original passage in the prophecies of Amos. "In that day will I raise up the tabernacle of David that is fallen, and close up the breaches thereof, and I will raise up his ruins, and I will build it as in the days of old: that they may possess the remnant of Edom, and of all the heathen which are called by my name, saith the Lord, that doth this." There is a considerable difference between the two passages; and to reconcile them has caused no small perplexity and labour to commentators. The translation of the seventy comes very near the words of James; but it is evident that it could not be cited at this time, when the Apostle was addressing an assembly of Jews in their own language. Some have recourse to the supposition, that the passage in Amos has been since corrupted by the Jews, who are accused, by the Fathers, of having vitiated other parts of Scripture, which most expressly militated against them. This, however, is an idea which should not be hastily admitted. Perhaps, we may account for the difference, by saying that James intended to give the sense, not the exact words, of the prophecy; and in respect of the sense, the two passages perfectly harmonize. In both, God promises "to raise up the fallen tabernacle of David;" or to raise his family, when sunk into obscurity, to greater glory than ever, by the birth of Jesus Christ, who should ascend the throne of that monarch, and enjoy everlasting dominion. What would be the consequence, or rather, what was the design of this dispensation? It is thus expressed by James; "That the residue of men might seek after the Lord, and all the Gentiles upon whom my name is called;" in which words, the conversion of the Gentiles is plainly foretold. It is thus expressed by the Prophet: "That they may possess the remnant of Edom, and of all the heathen which are called by my name;" that is, in consequence of its exaltation, the family of David shall "possess the remnant of Edom, and of all the heathen;" an event, which was accomplished, when, in the words of the Psalmist, "the heathen were given to Christ for his inheritance, and the uttermost parts of the earth for his possession," and being converted to the faith, they were called by the name of the Lord. The passages differ only in sound, and may be reconciled without the dangerous charge of corruption, and the desperate expedient of conjectural emendation. "Known unto God are all his works from the beginning of the world." The divine prescience accounts for the prediction of the conversion of the Gentiles so long before it took place. God acts according to a plan settled from eternity, and executed in the revolutions of time. In calling the Gentiles, he was doing only what his counsel had determined before to be done. The argument from the prophecy is plainly this, that since it appeared to have been the will of God, from the earliest ages, to admit the Gentiles into his Church, the believing Jews should beware of opposing it, by requiring their subjections to the law of Moses, to which they would not willingly submit.

"Wherefore my sentence is, that we trouble not them which from among the Gentiles are turned to God; but that we write unto them, that they abstain from all pollutions of idols, and from fornication, and from things strangled, and from blood." "Pollutions of idols," are explained, in the twenty-ninth verse, to be "meats offered to idols." The Gentiles believed, that, in partaking of sacrifices and other consecrated meats, they had fellowship with the Gods. On this account, meats offered to idols were an abomination to the Jews. With a view, therefore, not to shock the feelings of the Jews, and that the believing Gentiles might not symbolize with idolaters, and lay a stumbling block before their weak brethren, the use of such meats was forbidden, although it appears, from the reasonings of Paul on the subject, that in all cases it was not unlawful. "Fornication" was a crime, not only much practised among the Gentiles, but generally reputed to be harmless. It was connected, too, with their idolatrous worship; and prostitution in their temples and sacred groves, was a part of the homage which they paid to some of their execrable Deities. In writing to the Gentiles, it was necessary to take particular notice of a crime, to which the temptation was strong, from its frequency, and the opinion of its innocence. "Things strangled and blood" may be conjoined; the former signifying the bodies of animals, which have been put to death by suffocation, and in which the blood is retained; and the latter, blood taken from an animal, and separately used.

Whether this was a temporary prohibition, or was intended to be binding upon the Church in every age, is not a question connected with the religious principles of any party. Christians, in different communions, have been divided in their sentiments. It is affirmed by some, that " things strangled, and blood," were prohibited, because they were used by the Gentiles in their idolatrous sacrifices. The Psalmist speaks of their "drink-offerings of blood." According to this opinion, the prohibition must be considered as occasional and local. In a Christian country, where such idolatrous rites are not practised, the reason of it does not exist, because the use of blood gives no countenance to the worship of idols, and, consequently, cannot be a cause of offence. It is maintained by others, that the prohibition was not founded in any temporary cause, but has the same authority under the gospel which it had under the law, and even from the time of the deluge, when the command to abstain from the use of blood was given to Noah and his sons. No argument can be drawn in favour of this opinion, from its being introduced in the same decree with fornication, which is always unlawful, because duties ceremonial and moral are often mingled in the same general precept, without any distinction of their nature. It is not a proof of the perpetuity of the prohibition, that it was not peculiar to the Mosaic covenant, but was in force from the period of the flood. That there were ceremonial ordinances before the law was given from Sinai, is evident from the institution of sacrifices and circumcision, and from the distinction of animals into clean and unclean, which already existed when Noah went into the ark. As these rites, some of which were of a still more ancient date, are confessedly abolished, the antiquity of the precept concerning blood can throw no light upon the question respecting its duration. It is a groundless fancy, that there is a moral reason for abstinence from blood, or that it was originally enjoined in order to restrain men from shedding the blood of their brethren. Between these two things, there is no conceivable connexion. It is not from literal thirst for blood that murder is committed; and they who most plentifully use the blood of animals, are conscious of no greater propensity to kill their neighbours, than those who abhor it. Had men been forbidden to take away the life of the inferior animals, it might have been asserted with more plausibility, that the design of the Creator was to guard human life against violence. Under the law, blood was forbidden, because it made atonement for sin. It was then sacred; it was appropriated to the service of God. But now, when the consecration is at an end, and the legal sacrifices have ceased, blood is not more sacred than water, and may be used with as little risk of profanation.

It is surprising, if this precept was intended to continue in force to the end of the world, that there is no mention of it in any of the Epistles, nor so much as a distant allusion to it. Paul seems to teach a different doctrine, when he condemns those who command to abstain from meats, which "God hath created to be received with thanksgiving, of them which believe and know the truth." "For every creature of God;" that is, unquestionably, every creature fit for food, for of others he cannot be supposed to speak; "every creature of God is good, and nothing to be refused, if it be received with thanksgiving." If blood is excepted, why does the Apostle say "every creature?" Why does he not, to prevent mistake, rather say, every creature, "except such as God has reserved out of the general grant?" As he was warning Christians against the doctrine of those who should afterwards introduce a superstitious distinction of meats, we cannot but wonder that he has taken no notice of a distinction, which, if it exist at all, is an important part of religion. No accurate writer would lay down a general rule without stating the exceptions, especially when he was bringing forward the rule, in opposition to those who had subjected it to arbitrary limitations.

Let it not be objected, that, in the twenty-eighth verse, abstinence from blood is called "a necessary thing," as well as abstinence from fornication and pollutions of idols. Things are necessary on different accounts; some, because they are of moral obligation, and others, because they are enjoined by positive command; some, because they are always useful, and others, because they are useful for a season. If any thing is connected with a particular end, as an indispensable mean of accomplishing it, it is necessary to that end. The end which James proposed, in requiring the Gentiles to refrain from things strangled, and from blood, was to promote concord and peace between them and the Jews, who, when they saw the Gentiles, from respect to them, who held blood in abhorrence, denying themselves the use of it, would be the more easily reconciled to their exemption from the other precepts of the ceremonial law. This, I think, may be collected from the words which he immediately subjoins. "For Moses of old hath in every city them that preach him, being read in the synagogues every Sabbath day." They may be thus paraphrased. "The writings of Moses are read in the religious assemblies of the Jews, who are dispersed among the cities of the Gentiles. In this manner, they are well acquainted with the precepts of his law. Having been accustomed, from their earliest years, to regard those precepts as divine, they cannot at once be persuaded to renounce them. It is necessary, therefore, that the Gentiles, who are now united with them in the same society, should be required to concede a little to their prejudices; and that, while they abstain from fornication as a crime, and from pollutions of idols, as criminal in their nature or their consequences, they should likewise abstain from things strangled, and from blood, which are abominable to the disciples of Moses."

On these grounds, I consider the precept as a temporary expedient, adapted to a particular state of the Church. Its obligation has long since ceased; and "to him that esteemeth any kind of meat to be clean, to him it is clean." But let every man be fully persuaded in his own mind. "Let not him that eateth, despise him that eateth not; and let not him that eateth not, judge him that eateth."

It was the judgment of James, that the yoke of the ceremonial law should not be imposed upon the Gentiles; and that, with the exceptions already considered, they should enjoy perfect liberty. In this judgment the whole council acquiesced. "Then pleased it the Apostles and elders, with the whole Church, to send chosen men of their own company to Antioch, with Paul and Barnabas; namely Judas surnamed Barsabas, and Silas, chief men among the brethren: and wrote letters by them after this manner, The Apostles, and elders, and brethren, send greeting unto the brethren which are of the Gentiles in Antioch, and Syria, and Cilicia." It is observable, that the brethren are mentioned in the superscription of the letter; and that the whole Church or assembly concurred in the mission of Judas and Silas. From these facts it has been concluded, that the decree was enacted by the authority of the brethren, as well as by the Apostles and elders; and, therefore, that to exclude the brethren from all concern in the government of the Church, is a violation of their original and inalienable privileges. But let us not judge according to appearances. Let us remember, that the reference of the controversy was not made to the Church, but to the Apostles and elders; that the Apostles and elders alone came together to consider it; that we do not find a single member of the Church rising, in the course of the discussion, to deliver his sentiments; and that the sentence is called, in the next chapter, the decree that was ordained of the Apostles and elders, without any mention of the Church, or rather to the express exclusion of the brethren. These facts, I presume, are sufficient to convince a cool and dispassionate inquirer, that there is some other way of accounting for their interference, than the supposition that they exercised judicial authority; a supposition particularly perplexing to those who are most disposed to adopt it, the friends of Independency, because, while they maintain the equality of Churches, and their entire exemption from all subjection to any society or court upon earth, this would be an example of the members of one Church exercising jurisdiction over those of another. Upon their principles, therefore, as well as ours, nothing more can be implied in the concurrence of the brethren, than that they approved of the deed of the Apostles and elders; in the same manner as in the succeeding ages, the laity, although they had no concern in enacting the decrees of Councils and Synods, sometimes expressed their consent by subscribing them.* If, as we have already shown, this was only a partial assembly of the believers in Jerusalem, whatever was the power of the Church, a part had no right to exercise it; and the interference of the individuals who happened to be present, could not therefore be an act of authority, but was a simple testimony of approbation. The Apostles and elders might the more readily allow them this privilege, and perhaps request their concurrence, because, although their sentence stood in no need of confirmation by the suffrage of the people, it would, when accompanied

---

* Grotii Anotat. ad Acta Apostol. xv. 22.

with it, be more cordially received. The Gentiles would rejoice to learn, that the Jewish believers in Jerusalem were willing, that they should not be encumbered with the yoke of the ceremonial law; and the converted Jews of the dispersion would acquiesce with less reluctance when they found, that the exemption of the Gentiles was agreeable to their brethren in Judea. This explanation is satisfactory, because it is consistent; whereas the opposite opinion represents Luke as guilty of great inaccuracy and confusion, in first repeatedly defining the members of the Council, and then, at the close, abruptly introducing a new party, which he had before studiously excluded.

In the letter of the Council, there is scarcely any thing which has not been already considered; and I shall therefore pass it over with a few remarks. It contains a censure of the doctrine of the false teachers, who "troubled the Churches with words, subverting their souls." It denies that they had received authority from the Apostles and elders, as they appear to have pretended. "To whom we gave no such commandment." It mentions the names of the messengers sent by the Council, to deliver their decree, and more fully explain it. "It seemed good unto us, being assembled with one accord, to send chosen men unto you, with our beloved Barnabas and Paul; men that have hazarded their lives for the name of our Lord Jesus Christ. We have sent therefore Judas and Silas, who shall also tell you the same things by mouth." It declares the exemption of the Gentiles from the law of Moses, and points out the limitation, to which they were required to submit, in the exercise of their liberty. "For it seemed good to the Holy Ghost, and to us, to lay upon you no greater burden than these necessary things; that ye abstain from meats offered to idols, and from blood, and from things strangled, and from fornication." It recommends obedience to the decree as conducive to their personal holiness, and to the peace of the Church. "From which if ye keep yourselves, ye shall do well." Lastly, it concludes with a wish or prayer, for the welfare of the Churches. "Fare ye well."

The decree is announced with great solemnity. "It seemed good to us, and to the Holy Ghost;" that is, it seemed good to the Council, because it seemed good to the Holy Ghost. This ought not to be considered as a claim of inspiration, but as a simple assertion, that the sentence was not expressive of their private opinion, but of the mind of the Spirit, which they had collected from Scripture, and from his recent dispensations to the Gentiles. On this account they are warranted to assume the style of authority, and to demand obedience from the Churches. The sentence was not, as some wish to represent it, a mere advice, such as one Independent Church may give to another. That it was an act of jurisdiction, an authoritative deed, is evident from its being called in the next chapter a decree. The word is used, in other places of the New Testament, to signify the commands of princes, and the ordinances of the ceremonial law. and in its present application must bear a similar sense. Language so solemn ought to be cautiously adopted by other Councils; but I see no reason for asserting, that it would be arrogant to speak in the same style, unless they could refer to some miraculous operations by which their sentences were confirmed. If the Scriptures have not been given in vain, miracles are not now necessary to assure us of the truth. They are written with such plainness and perspicuity, as all Protestants acknowledge, that in matters relating to faith and practice, their meaning may be certainly known. The decree of a Council, which is clearly founded upon Scripture, undoubtedly seems good to the Holy Ghost; and what should hinder it from saying so, I confess myself unable to comprehend.

In the two following verses we are informed, that the messengers of the Apostles and elders repaired to Antioch, and delivered the Epistle to the multitude, who "rejoiced for the consolation." The controversy was satisfactorily terminated; and their privileges were established by such authority, as would preclude the danger of future disturbance.

From the preceding illustration it appears, that the Church in the Apostolic age, was not broken down into small parts, detached and independent, but was united, not only by love and a common profession, but by the external bond of a general government. The assembly which was held in Jerusalem, may, with propriety, be called a Council or Synod, between which words there is only this difference, that the one was used by the Latins, and the other by the Greeks. It was an assembly summoned to decide upon a cause, which affected itself not alone, but the whole Christian world. The members of whom it was composed, were the Apostles, the representatives of the Catholic Church, the elders, and the delegates from Antioch, among whom there probably were deputies from the Churches of Syria and Cilicia. A controversy, which could not be determined in the place where it originated, was submitted to their judgment; they proceeded in the ordinary way, by reasoning upon it; and finally pronounced a sentence, by which all parties were bound. This is the model of Presbyterian Synods, and the Scriptural warrant which we produce for holding such assemblies.

In all past ages, the meeting at Jerusalem has been considered as a Council. Modern Independents, indeed, generally object to this opinion, for obvious reasons; but it was adopted and maintained by some of their wiser and more enlightened predecessors. In this number was the celebrated Dr. Owen, whose distinguished piety, extensive learning, and profound knowledge of the Scriptures, have placed him in the first rank among Christian divines. I shall conclude their argument with the following quotation, which is worthy of particular attention. "No Church is so independent, as that it can always, and in all cases, observe the duties it owes unto the Lord Christ, and the Church Catholic, by all those powers which it is able to act in itself distinctly, without conjunction with others. And the Church that confines its duty unto *the acts of its own assemblies,* cuts itself off from the external communion of the Church Catholic; nor will it be safe for any man to commit the conduct of his soul to such a Church."*

We have arrived at a remarkable period in the history of the primitive Church. Its constitution, as arranged by the Council of Jerusalem, was to continue unaltered to the end of the world. From that time, Jews and Gentiles were to compose one holy people in the Lord. The law of Moses, which was abrogated by the death of Christ, was gradually forsaken by the believing Jews; and, after the destruction of Jerusalem, the observance of its rites was abandoned by all who professed Christianity, except a few obscure heretics, who were excluded from the communion of the Catholic Church.

Let us rejoice, that God has established a Church upon earth, enlightened by heavenly truth, governed by divine laws and institutions, invested with high privileges, and protected by his gracious providence; and that in consequence of the free access into it which has been conceded to the Gentiles, the prophecy is fulfilled, " Mine

---

* Owen's True Nature of a Gospel Church, chap. xi.

house shall be called an house of prayer for all people." While we are thankful, that we have been admitted into its external communion by baptism, let us remember, that the saints alone are its genuine members; and let it be our care to possess the spiritual qualifications, without which the Head of the Church will not acknowledge us. As the ceremonial law is repealed, and circumcision is not now necessary to constitute us the people of God, let us stand fast in the liberty, with which Christ has made us free; and beware of entangling ourselves with a new yoke of bondage, by subjecting our consciences to human authority in religion. Our Saviour redeemed us with his blood, that we should no longer be the servants of men; and all who profess to be his disciples, should recognise him as their only Teacher and Lawgiver. "This is my beloved Son, in whom I am well pleased: hear ye him."

LECTURE XVII.

THE MISSION OF PAUL AND SILAS TO MACEDONIA.

Chap. xvi. 1—18.

In the fifteenth chapter, we have an account of the proceedings of the first Christian Council, which was assembled to maintain the purity of the gospel against the attempts of some men to corrupt it, and to settle the terms on which Jews and Gentiles should unite in one holy society. It was unanimously determined, that obedience to the law of Moses was not necessary to justification; and that the Gentile converts should not be required to observe its rites, which were no longer obligatory, as the design of their institution had been accomplished by the sufferings and death of the Messiah. In accommodation to the present circumstances of the Church, two exceptions were made, of meats offered to idols, and of blood; partly to guard the believing Gentiles against a relapse into idolatry, but chiefly to concede a little to the prejudices of the Jews, that they might the more readily consent to the exemption of the Gentiles from the general system of ceremonies. We see, in the conduct of the Council, an example worthy to be imitated by the rulers of the Church, who should unite with their zeal for reform, attention to the most prudent measures for the preservation of peace and unity among the disciples of Christ.

This chapter begins with the relation of a fact, concerning the propriety of which doubts may be entertained, after the solemn decision of the Council, and the part which Paul had acted in procuring it. "Then came he to Derbe and Lystra: and behold a certain disciple was there, named Timotheus, the son of a certain woman, which was a Jewess, and believed; but his father was a Greek: which was well reported of by the brethren which were at Lystra and Iconium: him would Paul have to go forth with him, and took and circumcised him, because of the Jews which were in those quarters: for they all knew that his father was a Greek."

The same Apostle, who had no small dissension and disputation with those who asserted the necessity of circumcision, himself circumcised Timothy. It should be remembered, that as it was the circumcision of the Gentiles, which Paul so strenuously resisted, there is no direct inconsistency in his present conduct, as Timothy was of Jewish descent by his mother. It was the unhappy consequence of her marriage with a Gentile, that her son had not received the seal of God's covenant in his infancy; and this, as well as many other instances of the unfavourable influence of such ill-assorted connexions upon the religion of a family, should excite the attention of Christians to the exhortation, "not to be unequally yoked together with unbelievers." But the principal argument in vindication of the conduct of Paul is derived from the different lights in which circumcision might be viewed. The men of the sect of the Pharisees, who troubled the Church of Antioch, affirmed that it was absolutely necessary to salvation. Believing that a sinner is justified at least in part by his works, they considered circumcision and the other observances of the Mosaic law as duties, without which no person could obtain the divine approbation. Had Paul circumcised Timothy upon this principle, he would have been chargeable with renouncing the truth of the gospel. But circumcision might be practised, without any idea of its necessity or merit, out of respect to the Jews, who looked upon the uncircumcised as unclean persons, and avoided intercourse with them. If any man was willing to submit to it, with a view to conciliate their favour, and to gain opportunities of promoting their conversion, there was no law, which forbade him. It was precisely on this ground that Paul proceeded in the case before us. He took Timothy and circumcised him, "because of the Jews which were in those quarters." As he purposed to employ him in the ministry of the word, he was careful, in the first place, to remove an obstacle, which would have hindered his success among the Jews. In consequence of his circumcision, they would not refuse to associate with Timothy; and having no objection to his person, they would listen, with less prejudice, to his doctrine. When the conduct of the Apostle is examined with candour, we perceive nothing blame-worthy, or inconsistent with the spirit of the decree of the Council, but a prudent accommodation to circumstances, in order to accomplish an important end. This is one of the instances, in which "to the Jews Paul became a Jew, that he might gain the Jews."

It would be an abuse of this example, to infer from it, that we may comply with all the prejudices of others, and conform to all their customs, for their good. The limits, within which this liberty is permitted, are very circumscribed; and prudence, conscience, and the word of God, must determine them. In general, it should be regarded as a sacred and inviolable maxim, that we never should " do evil, that good may come." To adopt this licentious principle, would be to destroy the distinction between virtue and vice, and to pretend to serve God by trampling upon his laws.

Timothy being now associated with Paul and Silas, " they went through the cities, and delivered them the decrees for to keep, that were ordained of the Apostles and elders, which were at Jerusalem." The sentence of the Council is called a decree, to signify, that it was not merely an advice, or a simple declaration of their judgment, but an authoritative decision, to which the disciples were bound to submit, if they would remain in the fellowship of the Church. Although there was only one general decree embracing the several subjects of discussion, yet the historian speaks of it in the plural number, because it related to more points than one, declaring that circumcision and obedience to the law of Moses were not necessary to salvation, exempting the Gentiles from any obligation to observe it, and at the same time, prescribing some limitations to the exercise of their liberty. As the decree was delivered to the Churches in other countries as well as to those of Syria and Cilicia, who had sent deputies to Jerusalem, the Council which met there, must be considered as a general one, exercising jurisdiction over the Catholic Church.*

Of the happy consequences which resulted from the publication of the decree, we are informed in the fifth verse. " And so were the Churches established in the faith, and increased in number daily." They were confirmed in the belief of the truth, which the corrupt opinions lately disseminated had a tendency to overthrow. The doctrine of justification was placed upon its proper foundation; and Christians were taught to rest their hope of eternal life upon the grace of our Lord Jesus Christ, without the works of the law. The increase of the Church must be ultimately accounted for by that divine power, which accompanied the ministrations of the Apostles; but the decree of the Council was obviously calculated,

---

* Lect xvi.

as an external mean, to promote it. Circumcision, and the long train of rites enjoined by the law of Moses, were impediments to the conversion of the Gentiles, which it removed. Without subjecting themselves to that burdensome ceremonial, they were required only to embrace the gracious doctrines, and to submit to the gentle law, of Jesus Christ. The middle wall of partition was broken down; and they were admitted, upon the same terms with the Jews, to the favour of God and the privileges of the new dispensation. It is thus that God brings good out of evil. Although heresies and dissensions are immediately prejudicial to the Church, by disquieting the minds of men, and producing an alienation of affection, which is the usual effect of a difference of sentiment, yet they ultimately contribute to its purification and establishment. When controversies about doctrines arise, individuals may be seduced into error and apostacy by the plausible reasonings of false teachers; but in consequence of the closer attention which is given to the subject of discussion, it comes to be better understood than before, is expressed with greater accuracy of language, and is supported by arguments more judiciously selected, and more skilfully arranged. Those who are conversant with ecclesiastical history, will recollect more than one instance in proof of this observation. If it is of importance to know the will of our Maker, who certainly has not obtruded upon us useless speculations, the discussion which stimulates our inquiries, and increases our caution, which leads us to examine the evidence of doctrines with care, and to adopt them only in consequence of conviction, is an eventual benefit; and we should admire the wisdom of God, who renders the opposition of ignorance and prejudice subservient to the display and confirmation of the truth.

In the verses which are next in order, there is a concise account of the progress of Paul and Silas. " Now when they had gone t' roughout Phrygia, and the region of Galatia, and were forbidden of the Holy Ghost to preach the word in Asia, after they were come to Mysia, they assayed to go into Bithynia: but the Spirit suffered them not. And they passing by Mysia, came down to Troas." Asia does not signify, in this passage, the whole of Asia Minor, which comprehended Galatia, and Bithynia, and many other provinces; but that part of it which was distinguished by the name of proconsular Asia. In this region they were forbidden to preach by the Holy Ghost, who also hindered them from going into Bithynia. The reasons of these restrictions we cannot assign, nor are we informed of the manner in which they were communicated; but it left no doubt in the minds of Paul and Silas with respect to their duty. The Apostolic age was an age of miracles. God interposed by a series of supernatural operations, to introduce and establish the new dispensation. Although, however, his interference in succeeding ages, has not been so manifest, yet we know, that the course which the gospel has followed, coming to one nation, and departing from another, has been regulated by his Providence. The possession of the advantages of revelation, and the want of them, do not fall out by chance, nor proceed from the arbitrary determinations of men. The dispensation of the gospel affords a signal display of the divine sovereignty. By the command of Jesus Christ, it is to be preached to "every creature;" but he disposes the order, and appoints the seasons, of its propagation. To some nations, it has not yet been published; others, by whom it was once enjoyed, have lost it; and in our own days, we have seen it communicated to tribes, who had for many ages been involved in the thick darkness of ignorance and idolatry. Before the end of the world, the doctrine of salvation shall illuminate every region of the earth; the rays of the Sun of Righteousness shall be as widely diffused as those of the natural sun. In the mean time, it is obvious, that in granting the gospel to one nation, and withholding it from another, God is not chargeable with partiality and injustice. The objections which have been repeatedly urged upon this subject, and the difficulty which some have experienced in finding a satisfactory answer to them, proceed from inattention to these two facts; that man is a guilty creature, whom his Maker might have justly left to perish in his sins, and that the gospel is a pure effect of his grace. Surely, he is at liberty to select the objects of his favour; and he does no injury to one person who deserves nothing, when he bestows an unmerited blessing upon another. "Even so, Father, for it seemed good in thy sight."

It is proper to remark, that although the Holy Ghost now forbade Paul and Silas to preach the word in Asia and Bithynia, it was not his intention to exclude them for ever from the enjoyment of the gospel. It was afterwards published in those countries with success; and in Nice, the capital of Bithynia, a general Council was assembled, in the reign of Constantine, the first Christian emperor, to oppose the progress of the Arian heresy. But the time of visitation was not yet come. The Holy Ghost had other purposes to accomplish; and he hastened Paul and Silas to the place.

While they were in Troas, "a vision appeared to Paul in the night: There stood a man of Macedonia, and prayed him, saying, Come over into Macedonia, and help us." Among the various methods, by which God, in ancient times, revealed his will to the Prophets, one was by visions, which were representations of certain objects and transactions to the senses of a person when awake. In sleep, they were instructed by dreams, which among the heathens also, were considered as a medium of communication with the Gods. "If there be a Prophet among you, I the Lord will make myself known unto him in a vision, and will speak unto him in a dream." In the vision of Paul, "there stood a man of Macedonia," or the appearance of a man, whose country was known by his dress, as well as by his words; for "he prayed Paul, saying, Come over to Macedonia, and help us." The request was concise, but pressing. It represented the inhabitants of Macedonia as in circumstances of want or danger, from which they were unable to extricate themselves, and the gospel which Paul preached as the only mean of relief. Some of the heathen nations were celebrated for their skill in civil and military affairs, and had cultivated with great success, the fine arts of painting, poetry, music, architecture, and statuary.

These attainments, however, related merely to the accommodation and embellishment of this transitory life. They had applied, likewise, to the study of philosophy, and had displayed great ingenuity and subtilty in the various branches of geometry, logic, and ethics. But their researches into the nature of God, the sources and extent of virtue, and final destination of man, being conducted by the uncertain light of reason, had served only to bewilder them. "Professing themselves to be wise they became fools." Of the true method of propitiating the Deity they were utterly ignorant; and the plans which fancy had suggested, had multiplied crimes, and augmented the load of guilt, with which their consciences were already oppressed. The lapse of ages beheld them departing farther and farther from the truth. The corruption of morals kept pace with their errors in speculation. Their philosophers could give them no information respecting the true religion, which was unknown to themselves. They were idle theorists, and often impudent profligates, who extolled virtue, and practised the most odious vices.* The spiritual condition of the Gentiles was deplorable, and seemed to be hopeless. No human means could retrieve it; reason, which, in its best state, is an insufficient guide, was overwhelmed by an accumulated mass of superstition and licentiousness. It was the gospel only which could help them; that blessed revelation, which has dispelled the darkness of the human mind, pointed out an atonement in which the guilty may confide, disclosed the prospects of futurity, and brought down to earth those heavenly influences, by which our nature is restored to its original purity, and fitted to attain its supreme good in the enjoyment of its Creator.

Paul having inferred from the vision, that he was called to preach the gospel in Macedonia, set out, without delay, for that country, and, after a prosperous voyage, arrived at Philippi. "And after he had seen the vision, immediately we endeavoured to go into Macedonia, assuredly gathering that the Lord had called us for to preach the gospel unto them. Therefore, loosing from Troas, we came with a straight course to Samothracia, and the next day to Neapolis; and from thence to Philippi, which is the chief city of that part of Macedonia," or the first city, to which a person came, who was travelling from Neapolis; "and a colony," being inhabited by Roman settlers, and governed by the Roman laws. After an interval of some days, Paul and his commpanions went "on the Sabbath out of the city by a river side, where prayer was wont to be made." It is probable that this place of prayer was one of those oratories, which the Jews erected for the purposes of devotion; for we can hardly think, that prayer was wont to be made on the naked bank of the river, where the persons assembled would have been liable to be disturbed and insulted. These oratories were different from synagogues. The latter were houses, constructed like our Churches, for the reception of a congregation, in which all those parts of divine worship that were not peculiar to the temple, were performed; whereas the former were open above, commonly shaded with trees, and intended solely for prayer and meditation. They were usually built in retired places, on mountains, on the banks of rivers, and on the shore of the sea. It has been supposed, that it was to one of those sacred places to which our Saviour repaired, when " he went out into a mountain to pray, and continued

---

* Cic. Tuscul. Disput. Lib. ii. 4.

all night in prayer to God," or, as the passage might be rendered, " spent the night in an oratory."*

Paul addressed " the women, which resorted thither," declaring to them first the doctrine of salvation. Had any men been present, the historian, we presume, would have mentioned them, and the Apostle would not have confined his discourse to the women. There were undoubtedly men in Philippi, who professed the Jewish religion; but it has been remarked, to the honour of the female sex, that they often excel us in the punctuality with which they perform the duties of religious worship, and in the ardour of their devotion, in consequence, perhaps, of their being less distracted by the business and commerce of the world, or of the greater warmth of their affections. Women ministered to our Saviour during his humiliation upon earth; women first visited his sepulchre in the morning of his resurrection; women performed good offices to the Apostles, and assisted them in their labours; and a woman was the first in Philippi who embraced the Christian faith.

" And a certain woman named Lydia, a seller of purple, of the city of Thyatira, which worshipped God, heard us: whose heart the Lord opened, that she attended unto the things which were spoken of Paul." The opening of the heart is expressive of that operation of divine grace upon the soul of Lydia, which disposed her to give serious attention to the doctrine which Paul preached. The human heart is naturally shut against the truth by spiritual blindness, and the influence of sinful affections. The unregenerated man is incapable of perceiving its excellence, and dislikes it, because it aims at humbling his pride, and detaching him from the unhallowed objects of his love. External means are not sufficient to remove those obstacles to a cordial reception of the gospel. You may describe colours, in appropriate terms, and with glowing eloquence, to a blind man; but no distinct idea of them will be excited in his mind, while he is without the organ, by which only they are perceived. In what manner God acts upon the soul when he renews it, it is impossible to explain. The Scriptures inform us, that " he opens our eyes, enlightens our understandings, changes our hearts, makes us willing, and fulfils in us all the good pleasure of his goodness, and the work of faith with power." With these and similar declarations we should be satisfied. In the economy

---

* Mede's discourse on Josh. xxiv. 26.

of grace and of nature, we must be content with the knowledge of facts. There is a veil upon the mode of the divine operations, which presumption may attempt to remove, while humble piety will be employed in observing and admiring the effects. Happy is he who can say with the man, whom our Saviour cured, " One thing I know, that whereas I was blind, now I see." There is not a principle of our religion more clearly taught in the Scriptures, and which should be more steadfastly maintained, than that the conversion of a sinner is the effect of supernatural influence. It is a principle which is in unison with all the other parts of the system, and contributes, in concert with them, to promote its ultimate design, the glory of almighty and sovereign grace. To God is reserved the exclusive honour of our salvation; and the proper sentiments of man are humility and gratitude. " The Lord opened the heart of Lydia, that she attended unto the things which were spoken of Paul."

The sincerity of her faith was demonstrated by her immediate submission to the institutions of Christ, and by her kindness to Paul and his brethren. Nature teaches us to love our benefactors, and the grace of God will inspire a particular affection to those who have been the instruments of our spiritual good. Indifference to the persons and interests of the ministers of religion proceeds from indifference to religion itself, and may be justly considered as a proof, that those, in whom this temper prevails, have not experienced the peace and comfort, which the instructions and exhortations of the faithful servants of Jesus Christ communicate to believers. " And when she was baptized and her household, she besought us, saying, If ye have judged me to be faithful to the Lord, come into my house, and abide there. And she constrained us."

The gospel which was now preached for the first time in Philippi, was confirmed by a display of that miraculous power, which Jesus Christ had conferred upon the Apostles. " And it came to pass, as we went to prayer, a certain damsel, possessed with a spirit of divination, met us, which brought her masters much gain by soothsaying." Those who can consult the original, will find, that the spirit, who possessed this young woman, was the same, who was supposed to inspire the priestess of Apollo at Delphi, and to deliver oracles in the name of that pretended Deity. That this was a real possession might be proved by all the arguments, which apply to the cases of the same kind, that occur in the Gospels. The opinion, that the Evangelists, when relating possessions, do not express their own conviction, but accommodate their language to the vulgar belief of their age, is inconsistent with their acknowledged integrity and veracity, represents them as ascribing miracles to our Saviour which he did not perform, and is contradicted by a variety of circumstances, which clearly show the unhappy persons to have been under demoniacal influence. By representing this spirit as the same individual, or of the same character, with the spirit who actuated the Delphian priestess, Luke seems to favour the idea, that impure spirits were concerned in the heathen oracles, and that the prophets of paganism spoke by their inspiration. This opinion was commonly held by the Fathers; but by the more sceptical moderns, those prophets are generally believed to have been impostors, and the oracles to have been contrivances of the priests to impose upon the credulity of mankind. The truth, perhaps, lies between these extremes; and while much may be ascribed to the artifice of men, something should be allotted to the interference of the demons of darkness. Satan was the God of this world; he reigned among the Gentiles, during the ages of idolatry, without a rival; and he may have been permitted to exercise a power over his deluded votaries, which ceased when Christianity was fully introduced. "I beheld Satan, as lightning, fall from heaven." Our Lord refers to the overthrow of heathenism, which, in its frame and constitution, in its impious dogmas, its idolatry, its profane rites, and its oracles, as well as in the crimes which it tolerated and encouraged, was the work of the grand adversary of God and man.

The demon who resided in this woman, is called "a spirit of divination," agreeably to the import, although not to the literal sense, of the original term. To divine, is to disclose secrets, and foretel future events. It is easy to conceive Satan, if his preternatural agency upon the mind be admitted, to have enabled the subjects of his inspiration to reveal secrets, because deeds committed in darkness, and in the closest retirement, are open to the inspection of a spirit. He could farther have made them acquainted with distant transactions, the immediate knowledge of which it was impossible to have obtained by natural means. He might have given them some notices of futurity, by informing them of such things as he intended to do, or as were already in a certain train to be accomplished He undoubtedly can conjecture with much greater sagacity than we, what will be the result in a variety of cases, from the superior powers of his mind, his longer and more extensive experience, and is more perfect acquaintance with human nature in general, and the dispositions and circumstances of individuals. In every other respect, futurity is hidden from him as well as from us, by an impenetrable veil. A real prophecy, or the prediction of an event, which shall be produced by causes not yet in existence, or depends upon the free agency of men, we may safely pronounce him to be as incapable of delivering, as the most short-sighted of mortals. Prophecy would not constitute a proof of a divine revelation, or of a divine mission, unless it were a supernatural gift. It is the prerogative of God "to declare the end from the beginning." Yet with such scanty knowledge, Satan aped the oracles of Jehovah. As he had his temples, and altars, and priests, so he had likewise his prophets.

The possessed woman "brought her masters much gain by soothsaying," or prophesying. She acted the same part, we may presume, with our own fortune tellers, and amused the credulous multitude with liberal promises of future felicity. If her predictions happened to be fulfilled in one or two instances, her credit would be maintained, notwithstanding their failure in many. The eager desire of mankind to anticipate their future fortunes, prepares them to listen, with fond credulity, to the pretensions of impostors, and long maintains the delusion, in spite of the plainest admonitions of reason and experience. It is with inexpressible mortification, that they, at last, see the book of fate snatched from them, at the moment when they expected to break its seals, and peruse its mysterious contents.

The conduct of the damsel in reference to Paul and his brethren, is not so easily explained. "The same followed Paul and us, and cried, saying, These men are the servants of the most high God, which show unto us the way of salvation." This account of Paul and Silas was certainly just They were indeed the servants of God, who had come to Macedonia to declare to the inhabitants of that country the way of salvation from sin and death. But why did the unclean spirit bear so honourable a testimony to men, in whose success his destruction was involved? Shall we say, that he was compelled by the superior power of Jesus Christ, to publish, to his own confusion, what he would have willingly suppressed? or were the words spoken in derision of their character and pretensions? Was it the design of the cunning spirit to conciliate their favour by flattering compliments? or did he hope by the promptitude, with which he commended them, to make the Philippians believe, that he and they were acting in concert?

Whatever was the motive of this unexpected eulogium, "Paul was grieved." Religion stands in no need of commendation from the father of lies. He therefore "turned and said to the spirit, I command thee, in the name of Jesus Christ, to come out of her." In these words there was a virtue, which the demon, with all his pride and malignity, was unable to resist. "And he came out the same hour." The name of Jesus, whose voice made the spirits of darkness tremble, when he sojourned on the earth, was still terrible to them. The authority, which accompanied it, drove them from their strongholds, and wrested from their hands the unhappy captives, whose minds and bodies they had cruelly abused. This was a triumph gained over Satan in his own territories, and in the presence of his devoted subjects. By the dispossession of the demon, the superiority of Jesus whom Paul preached, was demonstrated. The tendency of the miracle was to persuade the Philippians to abandon their idols, of whose disgrace and defeat they had been witnesses; and we know, that to some of them, this evidence of the truth of Christianity was not presented in vain. Lydia was not the only convert in the city. There were some brethren, as we learn from the last verse of the chapter; and a Church was formed in Philippi, to which Paul afterwards addressed one of his Epistles. Of the tumult which ensued, and the sufferings which Paul and Silas endured, an account will be given in the next Lecture.

The passage which has now been explained, suggests the following remarks.

First, The sovereignty of God, displayed in sending the gospel to one nation in preference to another, lays those to whom it is granted, under a strong obligation to thankfulness. The value of the gift is enhanced by the discrimination which is exercised in conferring it. I would not be understood to insinuate, that common blessings should be lightly esteemed. Selfishness may wish to monopolize the goodness of heaven; but a generous heart feels its own happiness augmented by the happiness of others. This, at least, all must acknowledge, that our individual share of enjoyment is not impaired by the admission of our brethren to partake of the beneficence of our Creator. The light of the sun **gives** equal pleasure to the eye which beholds it, as if it were the only eye in the universe; the atmosphere furnishes the constant means of sustaining our life, although it is breathed by millions of our fellow-creatures. But when it pleases God, instead of extending his favour to all, to confine it to a few select objects, to bestow upon a part of his offspring the portion which all the members of the family equally need, what gratitude should they feel, who are distinguished from their brethren! We see how the pious Israelites were affected by the divine favour to their nation; and let us, in similar circumstances, beware of insensibility, the sure sign of a hard and reprobate heart. " He showeth his word unto Jacob, his statutes and his judgments unto Israel. He hath not dealt so with any nation : and as for his judgments they have not known them. Praise ye the Lord." Many of the human race are perishing for lack of knowledge, while to you, without any merit on your part, the instructions and consolations of religion are abundantly afforded. This is not an accidental distinction, but the result of the will of God; it is not a trifling benefit, but a blessing of greater magnitude than all the advantages of soil and climate, of civilization and good government; a blessing, of which the consequences will extend into eternity. This blessing God has granted to you, and withheld from others. " What shall I render unto the Lord for all his benefits towards me? I will take the cup of salvation, and call upon the name of the Lord."

Secondly, The consideration of divine grace as the sole cause of the success of the gospel, is not a speculative point, but a principle calculated to produce the best effects upon the heart. It has a direct tendency to encourage the spirit of devotion. It makes us look up to God as the source of all good, depend upon him for the salvation of our souls, and hope in his favour and assistance for all our advances in goodness and happiness. This is certainly the most becoming and pious state of mind; and that doctrine may be presumed to be from God, which promotes it. It gives no countenance to pride and self-conceit, which are fostered by the opinion, that the success of the gospel depends upon the sincerity and other good dispositions of the hearers. To teach sinful men, that their own will must finally decide, whether the grace of God shall be received or rejected, turns their attention to themselves, and cherishes a sentiment of self-estimation and self-confidence, which is inconsistent with the duty of "glorying only in the Lord." The Scriptural doctrine of grace as the efficient cause of conversion, takes away from every man every pretext for alienating himself from his Maker, who should be the constant and supreme object of his love, and trust, and gratitude. It annihilates his boasted dignity and excellence, and leaves nothing to be seen and admired but the divine goodness. This is true religion, for, in harmony with all the works of God, it terminates in the manifestation of his glory.

Thirdly, When the gospel comes to any nation, or to any individual, in the power and demonstration of the Holy Ghost, it destroys the works of the devil. We know no instance of possession in the present times; but the apostate spirit "still works in the children of disobedience." He has established his dominion in their hearts; and he maintains it by ignorance, unbelief, the love of the world, and the complicated system of corrupt affections. By the word of God, his authority is subverted, and his strongholds are overthrown. He is expelled from the souls, as, in former times, he was driven from the bodies, of men. The spiritual darkness, amidst which he reigned, vanishes when the light of truth enters the mind; the lofty imaginations, the proud self-sufficient thoughts, which he encouraged as the bulwarks of his kingdom, are laid low in the dust; the fascinating influence of sin is dissolved; and the soul now possessed of other views and principles of conduct, gladly returns to the service of its rightful sovereign. Although we have now no opportunity to observe the miraculous effects of our Saviour's name upon demons, yet his power in destroying their spiritual domination, strengthened as it is by the consent of their subjects, is daily exerted. Every convert feels it; every believer can bear testimony to it from his own success in resisting temptation. It is visible in the change which it produces upon those who are brought to the knowledge of the truth: for when he who was the slave of vice becomes the servant of God; when the pursuits of sensuality are abandoned for the duties of piety and holiness, it is manifest, that the person, who is thus transformed, has been delivered out of the snare of the devil.

LECTURE XVIII.

THE CONVERSION OF THE JAILOR OF PHILIPPI.

CHAP. xvi. 19—40.

I ENTERED, in the last Lecture, upon a review of the transactions of Paul and Silas in Philippi. Soon after his arrival, the Apostle repaired to a place without the city, where prayer was wont to be made, and addressed the women who were assembled there on the sabbath. We have seen him performing a miracle upon a young woman, who was possessed by a spirit of divination, which demonstrated, that Silas and he were truly "the servants of the most high God, which showed unto men the way of salvation."

It might have been expected, that the sudden and wonderful effect of a few words spoken in the name of Jesus, would have made a strong impression upon the witnesses, and that, if they were not persuaded to embrace Christianity, they would, at least, have been afraid openly to oppose it. Whatever were the sentiments and feelings of others, the masters of the young woman thought of nothing but revenge. "They saw, that the hope of their gains was gone." Delivered from the power of the demon, who had been permitted to use her as his instrument for deluding the people, she could no longer reveal secrets, and tell fortunes. The revenue which had flowed from the credulity of the multitude, was irrecoverably lost. Idle and profligate, as persons concerned in such affairs usually are, they foresaw, that instead of living at their ease upon the profits of imposture, they should be compelled to betake themselves to honest industry in order to procure a subsistence. With this prospect in their eye, they were not disposed to consider the miraculous nature of the event, to inquire into the power by which it was effected, and to examine the character of the religion, which it was intended to attest. About these subjects, persons of this description would have given themselves little trouble at any time. In the present state of their minds, they were impatient to avenge themselves upon the men who had wrested benefits from them, which they accounted far more valuable than truth.

They, therefore, "caught Paul and Silas and drew them into the market-place, unto the rulers, and brought them to the magistrates, saying, These men, being Jews, do exceedingly trouble our city." The masters of the young woman had probably little knowledge of the character of Paul and Silas. Christianity was new in Philippi, and such persons would be among the last who turned their attention to it. By calling the two preachers Jews, they seem to have supposed that they were propagating Judaism, or the peculiar tenets of some of its sects. Christianity was for some time, confounded with the Jewish religion, by the heathens, who viewed it at a distance, and with such contempt, as prevented a particular inquiry into its nature. Hence, Christ is carelessly represented by an ancient historian, as one of those seditious leaders, who frequently appeared among the Jews, and excited them to rebel against the Roman government.* Paul and Silas were charged by the accusers "with troubling the city, and teaching customs, which were not lawful for them to receive, neither to observe, being Romans." Philippi, I have already remarked, was a Roman colony. Now, there was a law of the Romans, which prohibited the worship of new Gods, or of the Gods of other nations, and commanded the people to adore those alone, who were acknowledged by the state. This law Paul and Silas had transgressed, by introducing the worship of Jehovah, the God of Israel, and exhorting the Philippians to renounce the service of their idols. In ancient, as well as in modern times, there was an established religion, to which the people were required to conform. Heathenism, indeed, exercised, on some occasions, a spirit of toleration. One country did not condemn the religion of another as false, but allowed its Gods to be true Divinities, and to be entitled to respect and homage, within the boundaries of the province or nation, over which they presided. Sometimes one nation adopted the Gods of another, and permitted the erection of temples and altars to them, and the public celebration of their rites. But it is unfair to represent this liberality as the constant character of heathenism, with an insidious design to throw a reflec-

---

* Suet. Claud. cap. 25.

tion upon Christianity, as having disturbed the peace of the world, by introducing bigotry and intolerance. Among the heathens, there were religious wars, carried on with as much rancour and fury as any one of those which have been waged, under the same pretext, among Christians. There were religious persecutions; and ancient history furnishes examples of the proscription of particular modes of superstition, and the infliction of punishment upon those who practised rites forbidden by the laws. The greatest philosopher of antiquity was a victim to religious fanaticism. The records of the Church for almost three hundred years, exhibit paganism in the shape of a ferocious and sanguinary monster, making havock of the harmless disciples of Jesus, because they refused to join in the idolatrous worship of their countrymen.

The masters of the young woman accused Paul and Silas of "troubling the city;" of introducing innovations, and exciting disputes, from which, unless they were speedily checked, no person could tell what serious consequences might ensue. We see that the charges commonly brought against those who promulgate opinions contrary to the established faith, are not of modern date. The same unmeaning outcry was raised in Philippi, which has been a thousand times repeated by the ignorant or the interested, against dissenters from the national creed. "These men are discontented and disloyal: they wish to become leaders of a faction; religious reform is merely a pretext; and so close is the alliance of Church and State, that the fall of the one, will involve the other in its ruin." It is thus, that the majority in Heathen and Christian countries, and among all denominations of Christians, Roman Catholics and Protestants, Episcopalians and Presbyterians, usually represent the few, who venture to exercise the right of private judgment in the choice of their religion. Who are foremost and loudest in advancing these accusations? Are they persons, who, after a deliberate and impartial investigation, are fully convinced of the truth of their own system? Are they in earnest about religion, and do they "tremble for the ark of God," lest, by controversies and novel opinions, the minds of men should be misled and unsettled? No; in their principles and motives, they, for the most part resemble the masters of the woman, from whom Paul expelled a spirit of divination, and like them are alarmed for their gain, or are influenced by some consideration not more honourable. They enjoy emoluments which might be lost, should the established system be changed; they suspect that, if the thoughts of men are once turned out of the beaten tract, they will begin to inquire into other subjects, and may discover abuses, which they are personally concerned to retain; or, if no immediate danger to their interests is apprehended, they must show their superiority, by a contemptuous treatment of those who differ from them, and recommend themselves to the higher powers, by a furious zeal against innovation. In ninety-nine cases in a hundred, a sincere regard for religion is as little connected with the declamations against dissenters, as it was in the case before us, when a clamour was raised about the dangerous consequences of permitting the gospel to be preached, by some men who gained their livelihood by supporting a fortune-teller.

Let us now observe what was the effect of the accusation upon the people and the magistrates. "And the multitude rose up together against them." The passions of the people are easily roused, and a rumour, or bold assertion, is sufficient to bring them together, and impel them to action. In heathen countries, they were generally more attached to their superstitions than the higher ranks; and in any country, they are ready, under the dexterous management of those who expect to profit by their excesses, to display a furious and destructive zeal for their religion. The magistrates seem to have been as intemperate as the people. Without waiting to make inquiry into the true state of the case, or allowing the accused to defend themselves, "they rent off their clothes, and commanded to beat them." A summary sentence was pronounced, and executed on the spot. And that Paul and Silas might be reserved for such other punishment as their conduct should be found to deserve, they were committed to prison; and the jailor inflamed with the same zeal against those blasphemers of the Gods, which his superiors displayed, treated them with great severity. "They cast them into prison, charging the jailor to keep them safely; who, having received such a charge, thrust them into the inner prison, and made their feet fast in the stocks." Paul and Silas might have saved themselves from punishment, by the declaration which they made next morning, that they were Roman citizens; but they did not choose to plead their privilege, when it might have been construed as a proof of unwillingness to suffer for the gospel. They submitted to stripes and imprisonment, because they were called to bear testimony to the truth, by their patience, as well as by their miracles. Their meekness and resignation might be rendered, through the blessing of God, the mean of drawing the attention of the spectators to a religion, which could give composure and fortitude to the mind in the most trying circumstances.

But however unjustifiable was the conduct of the magistrates in treating Paul and Silas as criminals, without any proof of their guilt, Providence over-ruled it for promoting the object of their mission to Philippi. Their prison proved a scene in which the power and grace of the Saviour were displayed. " And at midnight Paul and Silas prayed, and sang praises unto God: and the prisoners heard them." Prayer is the natural language of the soul, imploring, in its distress, divine assistance and consolation. It was therefore, an exercise suited to the present situation of these good men, to whom the grace of God was necessary, that they might bear the present trial with patience, and be prepared for the issue of it. But, why did they also sing praises to God? Is there any thing calculated to inspire cheerfulness in the condition of men, whose backs have been torn with a scourge, and whose feet are made fast in the stocks? Do songs accord with the gloom of a prison? A Christian has causes of joy and gratitude, independent upon external circumstances. Paul and Silas gave thanks to God for the high honour of being called " to suffer shame for the name of Christ ;" for the peace of mind which they enjoy amidst their outward troubles; for the certain knowledge of the love and care of their Redeemer; and for the hope of immortality which raised them above the fear of death. " God their Maker gave them songs in the night," which they sang with such devout fervour and animation, that the other prisoners heard them. At this moment, God was pleased to bear testimony, by a miracle, in favour of his suffering servants, and, by one of those extraordinary methods, which were sometimes employed in the commencement of Christianity, to save a " vessel of mercy." " And suddenly there was a great earthquake, so that the foundations of the prison were shaken; and immediately all the doors were opened, and every one's bands were loosed."

There is every reason to suppose, from the time when this earthquake happened, and the purpose which it served, that it was preternatural. Its effects were moderated by the power of God, so that the foundations of the prison were shaken, but it was not thrown down; and although the chains of the prisoners were loosed, none of them was permitted to escape. They were detained by their own fears, or by the secret restraints of providence, which intended to alarm the conscience of the jailor, without exposing him to any personal injury. Awaking from sleep, and naturally concluding that the prisoners had embraced the opportunity of regaining their liberty, he was filled with apprehensions for his own safety. He who suffered a criminal to escape from justice, was doomed by the law to undergo the same punishment which would have been inflicted upon him. The horrors of his situation rushed at once into his mind, and incited him to form a hasty and desperate resolution against his life. "And the keeper of the prison awaking out of sleep, and seeing the prison doors open, he drew his sword, and would have killed himself, supposing that the prisoners had been fled."

To this rash and impious deed, the mind of a heathen was familiarized. It was approved, in certain circumstances, by the different sects of philosophers; it was practised by some of their most eminent men; and no suspicion was entertained that it was offensive to the Gods. Nature, indeed, exclaims against it; but her voice is not heard amidst the tumult and uproar of passion. When a great and unexpected loss is sustained; when the proud spirits, overwhelmed by disgrace; when the mind is agitated by the prospect of some dreadful calamity; when the bright visions of honour and felicity, which enchanted the imagination, are dispelled, and hope seems to have fled for ever, the heart sickens at existence, and sees in its lengthened line, only the prolongation of its misery. Death appears to afford the sole means of relief. "Rather than be thus tormented," cries the impatient, desponding sufferer, "it is better to rid myself at once of all my sorrows, and either to take my chance of another state of being, or to sink into insensibility." This is the phrensy of the mind, during which the admonitions of reason and religion are disregarded. Could men summon up as much fortitude as to bear the first onset of calamity, its violence might gradually abate. The passion, which torments them, might at length lose its influence. Time lays its healing hand upon the wounds of the heart. To him who has resolved to live, some unforeseen deliverance may arise in the perpetual vicissitude of human affairs; but our hopes are sealed up in the grave. How can he expect a welcome in the other world, who rushes into it, stained with his own blood? Will the Father and Fountain of Life, show mercy to those who indignantly throw his own gift in his face?

The self-murderer, intent only upon escaping from his present agony, listens to none of these considerations. His furious spirit breaks from its confinement, and leaps into eternity.

The design of the jailor was prevented by Paul, who " cried with a loud voice, saying, Do thyself no harm; for we are all here." These seasonable words arrested his arm, already raised against himself. But although he was delivered from the dread of temporal punishment, his mind was not at ease. He was distracted with new terrors; he felt the anguish of an awakened conscience. The impression was sudden, and was undoubtedly produced by the power of the Spirit of God. Perhaps, the jailor had heard as much of the doctrine of Paul and Silas, from their own lips, or from the report of others, as was sufficient now, when he was led seriously to reflect upon it, to excite an anxious concern for the welfare of his soul. At any rate, although a heathen, he had such knowledge of good and evil, as would convince him, under the faithful admonitions of conscience, that he was a guilty creature, and was exposed to the wrath of his Maker. Although the Gentiles had not the written law, yet " the work of the law was written in their hearts, so that their thoughts sometimes accused, and sometimes excused them." These notices of duty, rendered clearer and more authoritative by the divine Spirit, darted a light into his mind, which showed him his character in all its deformity, and overwhelmed him with confusion and dismay. Hence, " he called for a light, and sprang in, and came trembling; and fell down before Paul and Silas; and brought them out, and said " Sirs, what must I do to be saved?"

It is not to be supposed, that the jailor had distinct ideas of the nature of the salvation which is revealed in the gospel. But he was convinced, that a creature fallen under the displeasure of God, is in most alarming circumstances; and that to be delivered from this condition, to escape the vengeance, and to be restored to the favour of the Almighty, is a blessing of greater value than any which the world can bestow. The first object of the desire of an awakened sinner, is pardon. His conscience pronounces a sentence of condemnation upon him, which the law of God confirms. While its awful threatenings sound in his ears, like the tremendous voice of the trumpet on Sinai, which made Moses fear and quake, he longs to hear the gentle and tranquillizing language of mercy. What would not this man give for peace with his offended Creator? In his present state he can find no rest. His mind is incessantly foreboding evil; he trembles on the brink of perdition, expecting every moment to fall into it; he suspects danger from every quarter, for there is not a creature which may not be made a minister of divine vengeance; the day is spent in anxiety, and the night in tears and groans. He turns successively to the various earthly sources of comfort, but finds them all empty. He tries, without success, every expedient to relieve himself. He is willing to perform any duty however painful, and to offer any sacrifice however costly, which shall extricate him from danger. He would listen with pleasure to any man, who could point out a refuge from the vengeance by which he is pursued. "What shall I do to be saved?" cried the jailor of Philippi, in the agony of his soul. A few hours before, he had rudely thrust Paul and Silas into the inner prison, and made them fast in the stocks; but now he applies to them for counsel in the most momentous of all concerns, and humbly prostrates himself at their feet. The demoniac had declared them to be "the servants of the most high God, who showed unto men the way of salvation." He remembered her words, which, when he first heard them, had probably excited his ridicule, and was willing implicitly to submit to their instructions. "Tell me what I should do?"

The answer of Paul and Silas is related in the next verse. "And they said, Believe on the Lord Jesus Christ, and thou shalt be saved, and thy house." This short sentence contains the substance of the gospel; but we can consider it as only a summary of what was spoken in reply to the question. It was necessary to inform the jailor, who Jesus Christ was, for he cannot be supposed to have known much more concerning him than his name, and what is that salvation, of which he is the author, as well as to explain the nature of faith which was recommended to him, as the mean of obtaining an interest in it. A heathen would have naturally thought of purifications and sacrifices, as expedients for rendering the Deity propitious. He had been accustomed to attach great importance and efficacy to these observances. So every man who is convinced of sin, his own heart suggests penitential tears, confession, acts of mortification, and amendment of life, as the only recommendations to the divine favour; for the idea of obedience or good works, as the condition of the blessings which we expect from our Creator, is interwoven with the frame and principles of our nature. Man, in a fallen state, fondly recurs to that constitution, which was adapted only to a state of innocence and perfection. But the gospel points out a shorter and surer way to salvation. Let the sinner believe in Jesus Christ, and he shall be saved. Conscious of guilt and moral impurity, and renouncing confidence in his imaginary virtue, let him rely upon the atonement and meritorious obedience of the Son of God, and he shall obtain the pardon of his offences, and a right to the forfeited inheritance of immortal felicity. As by the first man we were ruined, by the second man, who is the Lord from heaven, we are restored. Do you ask how this plan of justifying the ungodly, is consistent with the wisdom and justice of God? The answer is ready. As our guilt was transferred to Jesus Christ, that he might expiate it by his death upon the cross; so his merit is transferred to those who believe the record of the gospel, or cordially trust in him whom it reveals. By the sacrifice of our Redeemer, the demands of justice were satisfied; and it is, therefore, agreeable to justice, to exempt from punishment, those in whose room it was offered. "He hath made him to be sin for us, who knew no sin; that we might be made the righteousness of God in him." While this plan secures the honour of the divine perfections and government, it is most acceptable and consoling to a sinner, overwhelmed by a consciousness of crimes, and of spiritual impotence. The obedience which to him would be impracticable, has been already performed; and nothing is required from him but that he should consent to what his Saviour has done, "rejoicing in Christ Jesus, and having no confidence in the flesh."

The jailor was encouraged to believe, by the promise of salvation not to himself alone, but also to his house. "Thou shalt be saved, and all thy house." These words cannot signify, that through his faith, all the persons, old and young, belonging to his family, should be entitled to salvation; but that such of them as believed in Jesus Christ should be saved, as well as himself; and that his children should be admitted into the covenant of God, and to their seed after them." The children of believers enjoy great advantages from the prayers, the instructions, and the example of their parents, which are often followed, through the blessing of God, with happy effects. The actual salvation of them all, cannot, with any appearance of truth, be affirmed, because we observe too many instances of their forsaking the God of their fathers; but certainly there is ground of hope, with respect to such of them as die in early life. That there were other adult persons in the family, besides the jailor himself, is evident from the thirty-second verse, where we read, that

Paul and Silas "spake unto him the word of the Lord, and to all that were in his house." They did not speak in vain; for we are farther informed, that "he and all his were baptized straightway." The word of God is quick and powerful. It operates with rapid and irresistible energy, illuminating in a moment the darkened mind, as in the beginning, when God said, "Let there be light, there was light;" and effecting a complete revolution in the state of the heart. The human soul is originally like a dreary wilderness, the habitation of dragons and of every foul bird, and fertile only in briers and thorns. But by the command of God, the desert is converted into a fruitful field; it becomes the garden of the Lord, in which peace resides, and all the graces flourish. How surprising the change, which, in the course of a single night, was effected in the house of the jailor! It was turned into a sacred mansion of faith and devotion, where, instead of the language of profaneness, and the invocations of idolatry, were heard the songs of salvation.

How happy was this family! The new convert rejoiced, and so did all his house. "The voice of rejoicing and salvation is in the tabernacles of the righteous." There is no joy like that which flows from the belief of the gospel. It purifies, while it refreshes the soul; it gives a more elevated tone to the feelings than worldly pleasures can give; it contains no poisonous mixture, which afterwards corrodes the heart; it sheds a lustre upon every object, and cheers even the dark hours of adversity; and, in a word, it is permanent, going with us, whithersoever we go, accompanying us to death, and springing up within us, as "a well of living water," in the world to come.

Remark the great change which has taken place in the temper and manners of this man. The day before, he had treated Paul and Silas with cruelty, aggravating the unjust sentence of the magistrates, by the unfeeling harshness with which he executed it. But now he soothes and comforts them, not only from gratitude to the men, who had been the instruments of bringing salvation to his house, but from that humanity, which the grace of God never fails to inspire. "And he took them the same hour of the night, and washed their stripes. And when he had brought them into his house, he set meat before them." Do you wish to see a man of feeling? Look not for him in the stories of romance, nor among those affected sentimentalists whose tears flow at tales of fictitious distress, while their sensibility is not awakened by the real miseries of life. You will find him in the abodes of piety, and among the select few, whose hearts are softened by the love of God. They love others, "not in word, neither in tongue, but in deed and in truth." They watch the beds of the sick and dying; visit the receptacles of poverty, to wake up joy in the bosoms of the naked and hungry; pour consolation into the hearts of the widow and the fatherless; and go in quest of the sheep which have wandered into the wilderness, the outcasts, whom the proud virtue of the world has abandoned. They weep over an enemy when he has fallen; and like the good Samaritan, pour oil and wine into the wounds of a Jew. To alleviate sorrow, and diffuse happiness, is their sweetest enjoyment.

I shall pass over the remaining verses with a few remarks. "And when it was day, the magistrates sent the sergeants, saying, Let these men go. And the keeper of the prison told this saying to Paul. The magistrates have sent to let you go: now therefore depart, and go in peace." During the night, the passion of the rulers had subsided, and reflecting upon what they had done, they perceived that they had been guilty of an abuse of their authority, for which they might be called to account. They had punished and imprisoned two men, upon a simple accusation, without allowing them to defend themselves. They gave orders, therefore, to set the prisoners at liberty, not doubting that they would quickly withdraw from the city. But Paul and Silas now thought it proper to assert their rights. They were Roman citizens, whose persons and privileges were guarded by the laws with jealous care. To scourge a Roman was a crime, which subjected the offender to severe punishment; and it was an aggravation of the present case, that citizens had been scourged without any evidence of their guilt. "They have beaten us openly uncondemned, being Romans, and have cast us into prison, and now do they thrust us out privily? nay verily; but let them come themselves, and fetch us out." Had those ministers of Jesus Christ been governed by the same principles which usually influence men on similar occasions, they would have prosecuted the magistrates with the utmost rigour of law. They were satisfied, however, with alarming and humbling them, not to gratify their pride and resentment, but, in the most public manner, to vindicate their own character, for the credit of the gospel. It would add to its reputation in the eyes of the people, that its preachers were not vagrants, without a country or a name, but men under the protection of the laws, whom no person, however high in office, could wrong with impunity.

How submissive have those insolent magistrates suddenly become! Instead of resenting the answer of Paul and Silas, as disrespectful to their dignity, they go to the prison, implore the forgiveness of the men, whom they had treated so ignominiously, and request, for they would not now venture to compel them, to depart out of the city. Had they known the character of the persons whom they had injured, they would not have been so much afraid. From their resentment they had nothing to dread. Those meek disciples of Jesus were ready to pardon their worst enemies, and would, the next moment, have performed any office of kindness to them. Their Master had taught them "to love their enemies, to bless them that cursed them, to do good to them that hated them, and to pray for them which despitefully used them, and persecuted them." "For your hatred," said a bishop and a martyr, addressing himself to the heathens, "we render benevolence; and in return for the torments and punishments which are inflicted upon us, we show the way of salvation. Believe and live; and may you who persecute us in time, rejoice with us through eternity."*

We learn from the history which we have considered, what state of mind is necessary to prepare us for giving serious attention to the gospel. It was not, till the conscience of the jailor was alarmed, that he began to inquire what he should do to be saved. We know with what indifference we listen to a discourse which does not interest us. While it excites, perhaps, the liveliest emotions in others, it procures our attention with difficulty. Such is the nature of the gospel, that without a peculiar train of sentiments and affections, it must be the most insipid of all subjects. What pleasure can a person, whose thoughts are engrossed by the pursuits of the present life, and who is careless of his immortal soul; what pleasure can he derive from hearing of the love of God in giving his only begotten Son, and of Jesus Christ in dying upon the cross for our salvation; of the riches of divine grace in the justification of the ungodly; and of the sanctifying influences of the spirit? While the awakened sinner grasps at every word of consolation which the

---

* Cyprian. contra Demetrianum.

gospel speaks, the secure sinner, who stands in as much need of salvation as he, yawns and sleeps, or regards it merely as a tale of other times, and other men. It is the wounded heart which feels the virtue of the balsam of divine grace. "They that are whole have no need of the physician, but they that are sick." It is, therefore, the first concern of all to acquire the knowledge of their own character, which is the foundation of spiritual wisdom. Much may be learned by attention to their conduct, which often furnishes incontestable proofs of innate depravity, by listening to the testimony of conscience, and by consulting the word of God; but above all, they should earnestly implore the assistance of the Spirit of truth, who opened the eyes of the jailor of Philippi. Then, and not till then, will the gospel be to them "as cold water to a thirsty soul, or as good news from a far country."

The question, "What shall I do to be saved?" is the most important which can be proposed. It is a question in which all men are equally concerned. The reason that so few are earnest in the inquiry, is to be found in the insensibility of their hearts: but why are they so insensible? Why are they alive to all interests but those of their souls? Why are they eager in the pursuit of wealth, honour, and amusement, while the great salvation is neglected? If any awakened sinner is putting the question; if, under an apprehension of the wrath of God, he is desirous to know by what means he shall escape, we have no other answer to return than that of Paul and Silas, "Believe in the Lord Jesus Christ and thou shalt be saved." How thankful should we be, that we are not left to conjectures, where uncertainty is so distressing, and an error would be fatal! As conscience retains some degree of authority among the Gentiles, they must often feel a sense of sin, and be perplexed in their endeavours to find out the means of relief. "Wherewith shall I come before the Lord, and bow myself before the high God? Shall I come before him with burnt-offerings, with calves of a year old? Will the Lord be pleased with thousands of rams, or with ten thousands of rivers of oil! Shall I give my first-born for my transgression, the fruit of my body for the sin of my soul?" Disregarding the voice of revelation, men, in Christian countries, have suffered themselves to be misled by the suggestions of pride, and the dreams of superstition. We see the sinner labouring to conciliate the favour of his Maker, at one time, by vows, prayers, and penitence, and at another, by pilgrimages, austerities, and cere monial observances. But the doctrine preached by Paul and Silas is the truth, which has in every age, proved "the power of God unto salvation." Nothing else can give solid peace to the anxious, trembling soul. Let us embrace and hold it fast, if we would not be disappointed; and remember, that Jesus Christ is the only hope of the guilty. " God so loved the world that he gave his only begotten Son, that whosoever believeth in him should not perish, but have everlasting life." His blood ensures the pardon of our sins, however numerous and aggravated; his spirit is able to purify our souls; his merit will entitle us to heaven; and his power will preserve us, notwithstanding our weakness, and the temptations to which we are exposed, till our hope be crowned with the full fruition of eternal felicity.

LECTURE XIX.

PAUL AND SILAS IN THESSALONICA AND BEREA.

Chap. xvii. 1—12.

The treatment which Paul and Silas had met with in Philippi, gave them no encouragement to continue their labours in Macedonia. They had been accused of violating the laws, scourged in an ignominious manner, and committed to prison. From this specimen of the dispositions of the people and their rulers, they had cause to reckon upon persecution in every city; and had they consulted their personal safety, they would have speedily retired from a country, in which it was manifestly dangerous to remain. But Paul and Silas were men of bold and intrepid spirit. Their call to visit this region of the earth was express. They were certain, from their commission, as well as from their experience at Philippi, where some persons had been converted, that their exertions should not prove altogether vain; and they were willing to contribute to the glory of Jesus Christ, and the salvation of souls, at the hazard of their lives. Hence, upon leaving Philippi, they went forward to Thessalonica the capital of Macedonia.

"Now when they had passed through Amphipolis and Apollonia, they came to Thessalonica, where was a synagogue of the Jews." This verse has been supposed to throw light upon the account which Paul gives of his travels, in the Epistle to the Romans. "From Jerusalem and round about unto Illyricum, I have fully preached the gospel of Christ." Illyricum was a province, or rather the common name of several provinces, stretching along the Danube, from the Hadriatic gulph to the confines of Macedonia. It has been inquired at what time that country was visited by the Apostle, as there is no express mention of it, in the history of his peregrinations by Luke. His words now quoted, do not necessarily imply, that he actually preached in it, but only that in the course of his journey he approached its borders. This happened in his way to Thessalonica; for Apollonia stood in the vicinity of Illyricum, if it was not, as some have affirmed, one of its cities. The range of the labours of this zealous and indefatigable missionary, extended over a surface of many hundred miles in length, among nations of different languages and manners, some more, and others less advanced in civilization, but all, in consequence of their heathen prejudices, and the depravity of their hearts, disaffected to the gospel, and disposed to contemn and persecute its preachers. How pleasing is it to follow him in this tour of benevolence; to contemplate a man who has renounced the ease and comforts of home, not to amass wealth, or gratify curiosity, or acquire knowledge, which he may ostentatiously display on his return, but to perform the unsolicited offices of love to strangers; to impart to them the best of all gifts, the blessings of salvation; to do good to others, not only at the expense of time and labour, but at the risk of his life! It was thus that Paul, like his Master, "went about doing good."

In Thessalonica, Paul and Silas found a synagogue of the Jews. In all countries, into which that people were dispersed by the Babylonian captivity, and by subsequent events, they retained the faith of their fathers, and openly professed it, when they were permitted by the governments, to which they were subject. At a distance from Jerusalem, it was not lawful to offer sacrifices, because there was only one altar, which was erected by divine appointment in the temple; but they could assemble in any place to hear the law expounded, to join in prayers and thanksgivings to God, and to inflict censures on such of their brethren as were guilty of offences against religion. For these purposes, when there was a sufficient number of Jews in the city, they built a synagogue, which was fitted up like the Churches of Christians, for the performance of public worship.

"And Paul, as his manner was, went in unto them." It appears from these words, to have been the custom of Paul to go into the synagogues, and preach the gospel to the Jews. Although he calls himself the Apostle of the uncircumcision, signifying that the Gentiles were the chief objects of his ministrations, yet he did not consider himself as precluded from addressing the Jews; in the same manner as Peter, who was the Apostle of the circumcision, occasionally preached to the Gentiles, and was, indeed, the person first employed to make known to them the way of salvation. Within a few years, the Jews were to be rejected for their unbelief; but the hour of judgment and vengeance was not yet come. In the mean time, they were so far from being overlooked, that Paul, and the other Apostles, we may presume, adopted the same plan, when he found any of them in heathen countries, disclosed to them first the purpose of his mission. This preference was due to them as descendants of the patriarchs, the people whom God had long acknowledged as his own, to whom the promise of the Messiah was made, and who professed themselves ready to receive him, as soon as he should appear. Besides, there were many of the elect among them, who were to be separated, by means of the gospel, from their impenitent brethren, before the latter should be cast out of the pale of the Church. As our Lord had commanded the Apostles "to preach in his name repentance and remission of sins, among all nations, beginning at Jerusalem," they probably considered this order as an intimation, that they should, in every instance, offer salvation to their own countrymen, before they turned to the Gentiles.

In the synagogue of Thessalonica, " Paul reasoned with the Jews three sabbath days out of the Scriptures." The Jewish sabbath was now virtually abolished, and the Lord's day was substituted in its room. The Apostles might occasionally observe it from the same motive, which led them to comply with some of the ceremonial institutions; and, at the same time, it afforded them a favourable opportunity of preaching to their countrymen, who were assembled on that day to worship God according to the law. The subject upon Paul chiefly insisted, in his discourses to the Jews and to the Gentiles, was "Christ crucified." Although it was offensive to both, yet he made it his favourite theme. There was a particular reason for introducing it in an assembly of Jews. The death of the Messiah was the point at issue between them and the Apostles. The former objected to it as inconsistent with the design which, they supposed, the Messiah was to accomplish, and consequently as a proof, that the person, whom it had befallen, was a deceiver; the latter affirmed it to be the only mean of effecting what was the real object of his mission, the spiritual redemption of the people of God. The objections of the Jews arose from their own misconceptions. They were a carnal race, attached to the covenant which God made with their fathers, chiefly on account of the temporal advantages which it promised. Looking into the Scriptures, under the influence of this temper, they found predictions of the glory of the Messiah, the splendour of the Church under his reign, and the felicity of his subjects, expressed in language, borrowed from the pomp and transactions of worldly kingdoms. Of those prophecies they adopted a literal interpretation, and conceived the Messiah to be a temporal monarch, under whose dominion wealth and honours should abound. In this imaginary system, the sufferings and death of the principal actor could find no place. They deranged the whole scheme, and levelled with the dust the ambitious hopes, which it had been contrived to support.

The gospel could not be believed by the Jews, unless their erroneous ideas respecting the Messiah and his work were corrected. The method which Paul employed for this purpose, was to reason with them out of the Scriptures, " opening and alleging, that Christ must needs have suffered, and risen again from the dead; and that this Jesus whom I preach unto you, is Christ." In every controversy, it is necessary that there should be some common principle, in which both parties agree, because without such agreement, arguments may be multiplied, and the dispute may be prolonged, without end. The Scriptures of the Old Testament were received by the Jews as the oracles of God, the infallible standard, by which all opinions and practices in religion should be tried. Paul appealed to this standard, and showed, that the prevailing ideas of the character and office of the Messiah, were completely at variance with it. He pursued the same plan, which our Lord followed in his conversation with the two disciples on the road to Emmaus, proving from Moses and the Prophets, that the Christ must have suffered, before he could enter into his glory. The prophecies of Isaiah alone were sufficient for his purpose, as they contain descriptions of the humiliation and death of the Messiah, so minute and plain, that it is not easy to conceive how the Jews could overlook or misunderstand them. The necessity of the sufferings of our Redeemer was an obvious inference from the prophecies, because what God has expressly foretold must be accomplished; and this proof was all that was requisite for the conviction of his audience. But the Apostle would farther show that his sufferings were necessary, from the justice of God, which required the blood of our Saviour to be shed, as the meritorious cause of the remission of sins. They would have been necessary, although they had not been predicted; for the necessity of events does not properly arise from the prophecy which announces them, but from the nature of things, or the divine constitution. Prophecy is merely a declaration of what God has purposed to do.

The arguments which Paul deduced from the Scriptures, were intended to prove not only the death, but also the resurrection of Christ, which it was predicted with equal clearness, and was, with great propriety, submitted to the consideration of the Jews, to reconcile them to the idea of his death, as not inconsistent with the design of saving his people, nor fatal to their hopes, because he had been restored to life, and invested with supreme authority over heaven and earth. It was the decisive evidence that he was the true Messiah. It refuted the calumnies of the Jews, who charged him with imposture and blasphemy; and was the testimony of God himself, that he was his beloved Son.

From this general reasoning concerning the death and resurrection of the Messiah, the transition was easy to the particular proof, that "this Jesus, whom Paul preached, was Christ." The Apostle had only to show, that the prophecies, which he had cited, were fulfilled in Jesus of Nazareth.

The effect of his discourse is pointed out in the fourth verse. "And some of them believed, and consorted with Paul and Silas," leaving the synagogue, and forming a new religious society, which professed faith in Jesus Christ, and observed the ordinances of the gospel. It is plain, however, that all the Jews did not believe, although they all heard the reasoning of the Apostle. To what, then, should we attribute this difference? Not to the superior discernment of those who were convinced, nor to their greater candour and docility, but to the grace of God, from which the efficacy of the truth is derived. "I have planted, Apollos watered; but God gave the increase. So then, neither is he that planteth any thing, neither he that watereth: but God that giveth the increase." These Jews were not the only converts. "Of the devout Greeks a great multitude believed, and of the chief women not a few." The devout Greeks were those persons who are commonly called proselytes of the gate. The appellation is founded on the words of the law, "the stranger that is within thy gates," and was given, in the first instance, to Gentiles living among the Jews, who remained uncircumcised, but acknowledged and worshipped the God of Israel. It was afterwards extended to all the Gentiles, in whatever part of the world they resided, who renounced idolatry, and observed the moral precepts of the law.* Of these there were many in Thessalonica, for "a great multitude" is said to have believed, and there is no reason to suppose, that they were all obedient to the faith. "The chief women" were women of rank in the city. In the twelfth verse, females of the same class are called "honourable women." They were already proselytes, and they now became disciples of Jesus. In the most favourable seasons, when a profession of religion exposes to no danger, and demands no extraordinary sacrifice, it seldom succeeds in gaining the attention and sincere attachment of the great and opulent. It is therefore no inconsiderable proof of the divine power which accompanied the first publication of the gospel, that some of the higher orders were found in the number of converts, at a time, when Christianity was generally despised, and the probable consequence of openly embracing it, would be the forfeiture of worldly honours and enjoyments.

The success of Paul was contemplated by the unbelieving Jews, with great dissatisfaction. They were offended at the doctrine which he preached, and the more displeased, because it was favourably received by some of their own countrymen, and by many of the Greeks. With the zeal of religionists, therefore, and the jealousy of rivals, they bestirred themselves to arrest its progress. "But the Jews which believed not, moved with envy, took unto them certain lewd fellows of the baser sort, and gathered a company, and set all the city on an uproar, and assaulted the house of Jason, and sought to bring them out to the people." The associates of the Jews are described as "lewd fellows of the baser sort," or worthless persons of the lowest class, who sauntered about the market place, and other places of public resort, and having nothing to do, were prepared to assist in any kind of mischief. They were choice materials, of which to compose a mob, ready, at the instigation of its leaders, to commit violence upon persons and property. It is the complaint of one of the Fathers, that the most active enemies of the Christians, were the off-scouring of society, the vile rabble, the unjust, the impious, and the base, who were abhorred by the Gentiles themselves. With the assistance of such friends, he Jews assaulted the house of Jason, in which Paul and Silas

---

* Medes's discourse on Acts xvii. 4.

had taken up their residence; but, through the care of providence, they were not at home, or they must have fallen a sacrifice to the rage of the populace. A body so tumultuous, so susceptible of every casual impression, is not easily governed, and wants only a signal, or an accidental word, to hurry it into excesses far beyond its original intention.

Disappointed in their design against Paul and Silas, " they drew Jason and certain brethren unto the rulers of the city, saying, These men that have turned the world upside down, are come hither also, whom Jason hath received." The men of whom they complain, were Paul and Silas, whose doctrine, they affirm, had caused disturbance and disorder wherever it was preached, and would produce the same effects, if they were permitted to remain in Thessalonica. In a certain sense, it was true, that the Apostles "did turn the world upside down." The gospel professed an intention to change the face of human affairs; to overthrow all the religions which existed in the earth; to abolish idolatry, and withdraw the worshippers of the Gods from the temples; to put an end to barbarous shows and licentious festivals; to make the slaves of vice sober, chaste, just, and merciful; to call off the thoughts and affections of men from the vanities of time, and to raise them to eternal and invisible objects. This is the grand revolution which it proposed to accomplish, and which it did actually effect in many regions of the earth. Compared with the advantages resulting from it to mankind, as inhabitants of this world, and expectants of another, those which have arisen from the happiest political changes, are unworthy to be mentioned.

The accusation of the Jews, however, was of a different nature. "These all do contrary to the decrees of Cesar, saying, That there is another king, one Jesus." Paul and Silas had transgressed the law of the senate, and emperor of Rome, which enacted, that no person should assume the title of king without their permission. But this was not the whole of their crime. By calling Jesus of Nazareth a king, they set up a rival monarch, and persuaded the subjects of the emperor to transfer their allegiance to him. They proclaimed another king besides Cesar, whose authority was to be established upon the ruins of the existing government. Who is not shocked at the deliberate malice of these Jewish zealots? They knew well, that the royalty which the Christians ascribed to their Lord, did not interfere with the claims of earthly princes and magistrates; and it was chiefly on this account that they refused to acknowledge Jesus to be the Messiah. Had he, indeed, been such a king, as should have been a rival to Cesar; had he delivered his country from the Roman yoke, and ascended the throne of Judea, they would have welcomed him with acclamations of joy. But finding that his kingdom was not of this world, and that he offered to save them, without freeing their country from the domination of foreigners, and loading them with wealth and honours, they loudly demanded his punishment. "Crucify him, crucify him." Yet, when they wanted to awaken the jealousy of the Romans against his disciples, they took advantage of the ambiguous title of king, to assert that it rscognized in Jesus of Nazareth a right to reign, incompatible with the supreme authority of the emperor. It would have been easy to retort the accusation; for who did not know, that the Jews waited with impatience for the coming of the Messiah, to restore their national independence?

Religion is artfully loaded with false imputations, because it is only by this expedient that its adversaries can hope to expose it to hatred and contempt. Were it exhibited in its genuine character, it might not command the sincere esteem, and cheerful submission of all to its authority; but scarcely any man would be bold enough to avow opposition to it. In the first ages, Christianity was malignantly represented as an innovation, which threatened to subvert the whole system of human affairs, to overthrow civil establishments, and to propagate faction and rebellion. Insinuations, and public charges of the same nature, have since been advanced, not indeed against religion itself, of which even its worst enemies know how to speak with respect; but against every attempt to free it from corruptions, and restore it to its primitive purity. The exertions of reformers have been associated with the movements of sedition; and magistrates have been called upon to watch and to repress them, as dangerous to the peace of society. If, indeed, a false religion were so closely interwoven with a particular form of government, that they could not be separated without dissolving the complex system, the general reception of pure Christianity, and the fall of that government, would be connected as cause and effect. But such a revolution would be purely accidental. In other circumstances, the government would sustain no injury by the change. The gospel does not intermeddle with the constitution of states, but contents itself with enjoining obedience to lawful authority, as a sacred and indispensable duty. Nothing would afford such security to governments as the religion of their subjects; and the purer is the religion, the greater would be the security. Men would then quietly submit to their rulers, " not only for wrath, but also for conscience' sake." The laws would be obeyed, not from constraint but from principle. The fear of God operating upon the heart in every situation, and in all the occurrences of life, would prevent crimes, against which no human vigilance could guard, and which, under the shelter of secrecy, are committed in the hope of impunity. It is evident, therefore, that the introduction of Christianity into countries where it is unknown, and the correction of those abuses which have impaired its influence, and counteracted its spirit, among nations by whom it is professed, would be productive of the greatest advantages, in respect of their temporal welfare. Religion may be made the pretext for insubordination and rebellion, but it is only the pretext. It condemns such practices, and disowns those who are engaged in them.

The Jews, by their false accusation of Paul and Silas, " troubled the people and the rulers of the city," who were probably afraid of being punished for allowing another king to be proclaimed in Thessalonica. As the offenders themselves, however, could not be found, they were satisfied with taking security from Jason and the other brethren, that they would behave like good subjects, and exert themselves to preserve the peace of the city.

It being no longer safe for Paul and Silas to remain in Thessalonica, "the brethren immediately sent them away by night unto Berea; who coming thither, went into a synagogue of the Jews." " These," the historian adds, " were more noble than those in Thessalonica, in that they received the word with all readiness of mind, and searched the Scriptures daily, whether those things were so." He compares the Jews of the two cities, and gives the preference to those of Berea, whom he calls more noble than the others. He does not allude to their birth, or their rank in life, but to the qualities of their understandings and hearts. The Jews gloried in their extraction as noble, because they were descended from Abraham, a man illustrious among his contemporaries, and a distinguished favourite of Heaven. But the boast of ancestry is a vain thing; and true nobility consists, not in an honourable pedigree, but in integrity of heart, and the love of truth. The Jews of Berea were more noble, because they were not so prepossessed against every opinion contrary to their own, as to refuse to give it a candid examination. They were desirous of instruction, and willing to receive it, from whatever quarter it came. Hence, "they received the word with all readiness of mind, and searched the Scriptures daily whether those things were so." According to the arrangement of the sentence, it seems to be suggested, that they first received the word preached by Paul and Silas, and then searched the Scriptures of the Old Testament for the proof of it. But this, undoubtedly is not the idea which was meant to be conveyed; for it would discover no nobleness of mind to embrace a doctrine, and afterwards to inquire into its evidence. The order in which those Jews proceeded was exactly the reverse. When Paul and Silas affirmed that Jesus was the Christ, they turned to their sacred books; and finding that all the marks of the Messiah were united in his character, they immediately acknowledged him.

But why, it may be asked, did they adopt this procedure? If Paul was an inspired ambassador of Christ, was he not entitled to the same ready and undoubting assent as the Prophets? Whence, then, was it necessary for those whom he addressed, to compare his doctrine with theirs, before they should believe it? I answer, that to such as acknowledged the Apostolical authority of Paul, the comparison was not absolutely necessary, although even their faith must have been confirmed, by observing the exact correspondence between the gospel and the law. This correspondence would afford them, and it still affords us, a pleasing and satisfactory proof, that both have proceeded from the same author, "the Father of lights, with whom there is no variableness, neither shadow of turning." But, there is no evidence, that the divine commission of Paul was, at this time, recognised by the Jews of Berea. We are not told, that he had performed any miracles before them. As they could not, therefore, regard him in any other light than as a person, who delivered what he honestly conceived to be the truth, both prudence and piety required them to appeal to the Scriptures, and to bring his doctrine to the test of that infallible standard. It was by the argument from prophecy, that they were convinced of the divine authority of the gospel.

The conduct of the Berean Jews must be commended, and ought to be imitated, by us all. The clear and unequivocal declarations of Scripture demand our assent, without inquiry or hesitation.

But, the doctrines which men found upon Scripture, should be investigated with great care and caution, because they are only their inferences from it, in deducing which they may have erred through precipitance, inadvertence, or the influence of prejudice. "Prove all things, hold fast that which is good." To yield up our judgment in religious matters to any individual, or to any Church, is to invest that individual, or that Church, with the attribute of infallibility; and consequently, while we retain the character of Protestants, is practically to adopt one of the worst errors of popery. You can have no certainty, that any doctrine which you hold, is true, unless you have seen it, with your own eyes, in the Scriptures. The faith of those who submit to be guided by the sentiments of others, however learned, and wise, and holy, is downright presumption; a venture, in the most momentous of all concerns, upon the diligence, impartiality, and capacity of others, of which they can never be fully assured. Let them seriously consider, that, although their creed should happen to be right, its orthodoxy will not recommend them to God who perceives, in their undue respect for human authority, a criminal indifference to truth, and a virtual rejection of his testimony as the only foundation of faith.

The result of the inquiry instituted by those Jews, was the conversion of many of them; and, at the same time, the gospel was believed by a considerable number of the Greeks. The news of this success having reached Thessalonica, the Jews of that city came to Berea, and so inflamed the inhabitants against Paul, that he was compelled to withdraw to another place. Passing these events without farther notice, I conclude with the following reflections.

First, The difficulties which we may encounter in the course of our duty, will not justify us in abandoning it. When Paul and Silas found it necessary to leave Philippi, they repaired to Thessalonica; and upon meeting with opposition in Thessalonica, they went to Berea. Persecuted in one city, they fled to another, not to remain there in concealment and inactivity, but to persist in the perilous work of preaching the gospel. Christians are not, indeed, required to disregard the suggestions of prudence, and to expose themselves wantonly to danger; but in the way which Providence has clearly marked out to them, they should resolutely advance, without turning to the right hand or to the left. If we perform our duty when it is easy and safe, but neglect it, when accompanied with trouble and danger, it is manifest, that the principle of our obedience is wrong. Sincere love to God, and reverence for his authority, would operate with a steady influence upon our minds, in all the diversified situations and occurrences of life.

Secondly, The opposition which has been made, in past ages, to the gospel, reflects honour upon it. Its excellence may be inferred from the character of the men, by whom the opposition has been conducted. It has not proceeded from the sober, the humble, and the candid, from such as were in earnest about religion, and spent their days in piety and holiness: but from persons full of prejudice, and governed by interest, like the Jews; from "fellows of the baser sort," the gross vulgar, immersed in ignorance and low habits of vice; or from men conceited of their fancied wisdom, rioting in luxury, engaged in the pursuit of wealth and honours, and hostile to religion in any other view than as an engine of state. It is a strong presumption in favour of the gospel, that such men have condemned it. That religion, surely, has descended from heaven, which pride, sensuality, and covetousness, have united to oppose.

Thirdly, We should beware of forming our opinion of men, and parties, from the representations of enemies. Were we to judge of Christianity itself by this rule, we should conclude, that, instead of being worthy of all acceptation, it deserved to be rejected by the universal suffrage of mankind. The Jews affirmed, that it was calculated "to turn the world upside down." Prejudice is apt to misapprehend, and malice is disposed to misrepresent. Without being conscious of any unfair intention, we observe the character and conduct of our opponents with a partial eye; and too often, we allow ourselves to paint their actions with colours purposely shaded, to impute motives to them which charity would not suspect, and to condemn them with a degree of severity, which our consciences do not approve. By a person, therefore, of candour and prudence, the testimony of an adversary will not be received, unless it be favourable, or be supported by unquestionable evidence. We hear, almost every day, reports circulated to the disadvantage of sects and individuals, which we find, upon inquiry, to have no foundation, or to have taken their rise from circumstances wilfully exaggerated, or hastily misunderstood. Let us, on all occasions, strictly adhere to the rule which our Lord has prescribed. "Judge not according to the appearance, but judge righteous judgment."

In the last place, There is a perfect harmony between the law and the gospel, between the religion of Moses and that of Jesus Christ. The latter, indeed, is only a continuation of the former, with such alterations and improvements, as were adapted to the progress of events. The external form is different, but the substance is the same. In both, the object of worship, the foundation of hope, the spiritual promises, and the moral precepts, are the same; and they are chiefly distinguished by the degrees of light, and the measures of divine communication, under each. Christianity was not a new religion to those who understood the design of the institutions of Moses, and had given attention to the instructions of the Prophets. The Jews who examined their ancient Scriptures with discernment and impartiality, immediately embraced the gospel as the completion of the law. We have seen an instance in the conduct of those of Berea. From the beginning of the world, God has been carrying on one consistent scheme for the salvation of mankind by his Son Jesus Christ, who was first revealed in promises, types, and predictions, and was afterwards manifested in human nature, "to put away sin by the sacrifice of himself." There is but one Church under a diversity of administrations, composed of believers in every age; and, for this reason, the admission of the Gentiles into the Christian Church is described by their "sitting down with Abraham, and Isaac, and Jacob in the kingdom of heaven." The work of God in our redemption is great and wonderful, comprehending all time, embracing all events, which, in one way or another, are rendered subservient to it, and in its consequences stretching into eternity. It is worthy to be studied, and cannot be contemplated without admiration and praise. "Of him, and through him, and to him, are all things: to whom be glory, for ever. Amen."

LECTURE XX.

PAUL IN ATHENS.

Chap. xvii. 15—34.

The obstacles to the success of the gospel, when it was first published, were of too formidable a nature, to have been surmounted by human courage and prudence. It was encountered by the prejudices and bigotry of the Jews; by prejudices the more obstinate, as they were founded in reverence for the religion which their ancestors had received from God himself; by bigotry originating in the distinction which had long subsisted between them and the Gentiles, and anxious to secure the perpetual monopoly of the blessings of the covenant. But, it was not in the moral state of the Jews alone, that Christianity met with opposition, which no imposture, however dexterously managed, could have overcome. The age in which it appeared, was an age of learning and science. The boundaries of knowledge were extended; the human mind was highly cultivated; and the mythological tales of antiquity were despised, and openly derided. A new system of falsehood had no chance of eluding the test of severe examination, and could not have defended itself, against the arguments and the scorn of philosophical inquirers. We have already seen the gospel triumphing over the hostility of the Jews, many of whom embraced it as the completion of their law, and became the disciples of Him, whom their rulers had rejected and crucified. We are now to observe the issue of its conflicts with the philosophy of Greece. By some men, whose minds the pride of wisdom had elated, Paul was treated with great contempt; but even in Athens, the school of science and refinement, Christianity could boast of its success; and we know, that before three centuries had elapsed, it trampled in the dust the sophistry and eloquence of the heathen world.

The Apostle having been compelled, by the arts of the Jews, to leave Berea, was conducted to Athens, where he remained for some time expecting the arrival of Silas and Timotheus. Athens was the most celebrated city of Greece. Originally the capital of a small and barren principality, it rose to distinction, not only by the number of its inhabitants, and the magnificence of its buildings, but by the influence which it acquired over the counsels and affairs of the Greeks, by its extensive commerce, its numerous and flourishing colonies and dependencies, the wars in which it was engaged, and the exploits of its statesmen and generals; but, above all, by the unrivalled eminence which it attained, in the arts and sciences. In this city, genius, taste, and skill in the elegant and ornamental studies, seemed to be assembled, as in their favourite residence. Here, philosophy carried on its profound and subtle researches into the nature of man, and the constitution of the universe; here, eloquence rose to a degree of excellence, which has seldom been equalled, and never surpassed; here, architecture and statuary displayed those exquisite productions, the remains of which are beheld with admiration, and present the finest models to modern artists. But, while we fondly cherish the memory of the polite and ingenious Athenians, how mortifying is it to reflect, that when Paul visited the city, it was "wholly given to idolatry!" We perceive the strength of our faculties contrasted with their weakness; and the melancholy conviction is forced upon us, that the highest cultivation of reason, unassisted by revelation, is insufficient to preserve us from the utmost extravagance and folly in religion. The most enlightened city in the heathen world, was full of idols. It was crowded with images, and temples, and altars. The Athenians were more addicted to idolatry, and had multiplied the objects of it more than any of their neighbours. "In this city," says an ancient writer, "It is easier to find a God than a man." How just is the account given by Paul of the Gentile philosophers! "Professing themselves to be wise, they became fools: and changed the glory of the incorruptible God into an image made like to corruptible man, and to birds, and four-footed beasts, and creeping things."

"The spirit of Paul was stirred in him," by the idolatry of the Athenians. The indignity offered to the true God, by the worship of his unworthy rivals, roused his zeal, and he felt the most lively pity for a people, who, notwithstanding their distinguished attainments, were, in the language of the Scriptures, "sitting in dark ness, and in the region and shadow of death." "He therefore disputed in the synagogue with the Jews, and with the devout persons, and in the market daily, with them that met with him." In the synagogue, he had no occasion to dispute upon the subject of idolatry, because it was abhorred by the Jews, and the devout persons, or proselytes, had renounced it; but agreeably to his usual practice, he addressed himself first to his countrymen, proving that Jesus of Nazareth whom he preached, was the Messiah. His labours, however, were not confined to the synagogue. In the market, the place of public resort, he entered into conversation with the Gentiles; and although the subject is not particularly mentioned, yet it is evident, from what follows, that he endeavoured to convince them of the folly and impiety of their religion, and declared to them the living God, and his Son the only Mediator.

The attention of the Athenians was excited by this new system, so different from their own religion, and from all the modifications of polytheism, with which they were acquainted. The philosophers were surprised and displeased, that a barbarian, for such they accounted Paul, should presume to appear in Athens, and publish doctrines contrary both to the established faith, and to their peculiar dogmas. We are informed, that "certain philosophers of the Epicureans, and of the Stoics encountered him." It was natural that these should be the first to contend with him, because among all the sects of philosophy, there was none, to whose tenets Christianity was more adverse. The Epicureans were Atheists. According to them the world was formed by chance, out of materials which had existed from eternity. Acknowledging from complaisance, the Gods, who were publicly worshipped, they excluded them from any concern in human affairs, and affirmed, that regardless of the prayers and actions of men, they contented themselves with the enjoyment of indolent felicity. They pronounced pleasure to be the chief good, and the business of a wise man to consist, in devising the means of spending life in ease and tranquillity. All the genuine motives to the practice of virtue, and all just ideas of virtue itself, were banished from the philosophy of the Epicureans, which made self love the sole spring of our actions, and gave loose reins to the sensual appetites. The system of the Stoics was of a different character. They believed the existence of God, his government of the universe, and the subsistence of the soul after the death of the body. But they confounded the Deity with his own works, and supposed him to be the soul of the world. If on the subject of providence they expressed many just and sublime sentiments, they connected with it the doctrine of fate, or of an inexplicable necessity, the immutable decrees of which God, as well as man, was compelled to obey. Their notions respecting the soul were very different from the Christian doctrine of immortality; for they imagined, that in the future state it should lose all separate consciousness, and be resolved into the divine essence. Unlike the herd of Epicureans, they placed the happiness of man in the practice of virtue, and inculcated a comparatively pure and exalted morality; but the praise to which this part of their system entitled them, was forfeited by a spirit of pride, strained to the most audacious impiety. "Between God and the good man," they said, "there is only this difference, that the one lives longer than the other." They proceeded still farther, and dared to maintain, "that there was one respect in which the wise or good man excelled God; the latter was wise by nature, but the former, from choice." It is not easy to determine, whether the self-sufficient Stoics, or the profligate disciples of Epicurus, were less disposed to lend a favourable ear to the gospel. On the one hand, it commanded the lovers of pleasure to renounce the impure gratifications of sense, and to seek happiness in the favour of God and the cultivation of holiness; and, on the other, it humbled the proud moralists, by mortifying descriptions of human depravity, by referring them not to their own merit, but to the divine mercy, for the hope of immortality, and by the unwelcome information, that they must be indebted for true virtue, and should ascribe all the praise of it, to supernatural assistance.

"The Stoics and Epicureans, therefore, encountered him: and some said, what will this babbler say?" It is unnecessary to detail the criticisms of learned men upon the word rendered "babbler."* The term employed in our translation, probably conveys with sufficient accuracy the idea which was entertained of Paul, by those haughty philosophers. They considered him as a contemptible prating fool; a man who would speak, and at the same time, had nothing to bring forward, but the extravagant and incoherent fancies of an ignorant mind. To the learned Greeks, the doctrine of Christ crucified appeared to be foolishness. In Christian countries, where

---

* Wits. in vita Pauli. sect. vi.

better opportunities of perceiving its truth and excellence are enjoyed, the sentiments of the learned and the unlearned, prior to the supernatural illumination of their minds, are not more favourable, although, in consequence of their education and their habits, they may speak of it in terms of respect. In their eyes, it is folly, and those who preach it, are babblers. "The natural man receiveth not the things of the Spirit of God; for they are foolishness unto him: neither can he know them, because they are spiritually discerned." "Others said, He seemeth to be a setter forth of strange Gods: because he preached unto them Jesus, and the resurrection." When Paul affirmed that Jesus was the Son of God, and that having been exalted to the right hand of the Father, and invested with authority over all persons and things, he was entitled to the religious homage and obedience of mankind, he proclaimed a God, of whom the Athenians had never before heard even the name. The idea of a resurrection was not absolutely new to the Gentiles, but it was the object neither of their belief nor of their hopes. Some are of opinion, that those hearers of Paul were guilty of a gross mistake, and supposed, that the resurrection was the name of a person, or a female Divinity, to whom, in conjunction with Jesus Christ, religious honours should be paid. Paul seemed to them to be a setter forth of strange "Gods," of more than one new object of adoration. And, indeed, as some of the heathens had erected temples to Honour, Piety, Hope, and Concord, or to abstract ideas and qualities, which fancy had deified, we can conceive them to have imagined, that there might be a goddess called Resurrection. By the laws of the Athenians, and of other ancient nations, all attempts by private persons, to make any innovation in the religion of the state, were strictly prohibited. It was one of the charges against Socrates, "that he did not acknowledge the Gods whom the city acknowledged, and that he introduced new Gods."*

"And they took him, and brought him unto Areopagus." The Areopagus was a court of great authority, which derived its name from the place where its meetings were held, a hill in the city sacred to Mars. It was composed of a considerable number of judges, who were persons of experience, integrity, and blameless reputation, and had power to superintend the manners of the people, and to punish offences against religion and the state. Paul does not seem to have

---

* Xenoph. Apolog. Socrat.

been brought into this court in the character of a criminal, but for the purpose of explaining his doctrine in the presence of men, who were deemed capable to judge of it, and could publicly admit or reject the new religion which he published. The Athenians were influenced, on this occasion, more by curiosity, than by zeal for their own religion, or by a disposition candidly to examine the claims of Christianity. When Paul came before the court, they said, " May we know what this new doctrine, whereof thou speakest, is ?" They did not expect, and they were not disposed to receive, instruction from a person, whom they reputed a babbler; but they hoped to be entertained with his novel and extravagant opinions. Novelty, indeed, had irresistible charms in the eyes of that people, in whose character there seems to have been a mixture of lightness and fickleness. "For all the Athenians, and strangers which were there, spent their time in nothing else, but either to tell or to hear some new thing." This unfavourable account of the inhabitants of Athens, was not dictated by partiality, on the part of the sacred historian, or by resentment at their usage of Paul. The same account is given by other writers; and their celebrated orator, Demosthenes, has reproached them with idle curiosity at a time, when the danger which threatened their country, demanded serious deliberation, and active exertions for the public safety.*

Having been requested to explain the nature of his doctrine, Paul addressed the Court of Areopagus in a speech, which consisted of two parts, in one of which he exposed the folly of heathen idolatry, and, in the other, announced the most important articles of the Christian faith. " Then Paul stood in the midst of Mars hill," or Areopagus, "and said, Ye men of Athens, I perceive, that in all things ye are too superstitious." There is an inaccuracy in the translation of this verse. Superstition conveys the idea of something wrong in religion. It originates in misconceptions of the object of worship, which give rise to a multiplicity of arbitrary and fanciful observances, with a view to appease his anger, and conciliate his favour. The Apostle might have justly accused the Athenians of superstition, or rather of idolatry; but it may be doubted, whether, at this time, he intended to bring forward either the one charge or the other. To call a man too superstitious implies, that he might, without a fault, be superstitious in a moderate degree. It

---

* Demosth. Philip. I.

is not the thing itself, but its excess, which is blamed. But, in the opinion of Paul, the religious system of the Athenians was essentially erroneous. The Greek word rendered, superstitious, denotes a fearer or worshipper of demons, who were conceived to be a class of intermediate beings between the Gods and men, but sometimes in Scripture signify the Gods themselves, who were adored by the heathens. By the Athenians, it was used to describe a devout or religious person. It is probable, that it is employed by the Apostle in the same sense, and that this is his meaning; "I perceive, that in all things ye are more devout than the inhabitants of other cities." He gave them this character, because he had observed that their city was "wholly given to idolatry." The objects of worship were more numerous in Athens, than in any other place which he had visited; and the people displayed peculiar zeal and assiduity, in performing the rites of their religion.

In proof of their uncommon devotion, Paul appeals to an altar, which he had seen in the city, with this inscription, "To the unknown God;" and which afforded decisive evidence of the extraordinary piety of the Athenians. It discovered so anxious a desire to leave no Divine Being without his due honours, and to secure the favour of all who might have influence over human affairs, that rather than be guilty of an omission, they would pay homage to a Deity, with whose name and attributes they were not acquainted. Different accounts have been given of the occasion on which this altar was erected. We are told, that during a pestilence, which desolated the city, the Athenians having in vain applied for relief to their national Gods, were directed, by the philosopher Epimenides, to offer sacrifices to the unknown God, as alone able to remove the calamity.* There is another opinion, which is the more probable, because the words of Paul seem to import, that this altar was dedicated to the God of the Jews. In consequence of the dispersion of that people, the Gentiles had obtained some notices of him, but still he was to them an unknown God, because their information respecting him was very limited and indistinct. Among the Jews themselves, he dwelt in thick darkness, and was sometimes addressed as a God that "hid himself;" the symbols of his presence were confined to the recesses of the sanctuary, into which, none but the high-priest, once a year, was permitted to enter; and they carefully

---

* Diog. Laert. in vita Epimenidis.

concealed his name, Jehovah, from the Gentiles, and superstitiously avoided pronouncing it in common conversation. It was called the ineffable name. It is no wonder that a God, who withdrew from the sight of his own worshippers, should have been characterized by strangers as The Unknown. An obscure rumour of his divinity had reached the ears of the Athenians; and that devout people, dreading his power, and eager to gain his patronage, had consecrated an altar to his honour, and performed such rites as they supposed would be pleasing to him. But they worshipped him ignorantly, having no knowledge of his real character, nor of his sacred institutions. In answer to the question, "May we know what this new doctrine, whereof thou speakest, is?" Paul informed the Areopagites, that he had come to declare this unknown God, and to teach them to worship Him, in an intelligent and acceptable manner. "Whom ye ignorantly worship, him declare I unto you." This is the design of the subsequent part of his speech, in illustrating which, I shall point out the several particulars contained in it, without exactly attending to the order, in which they are delivered.

The Apostle begins with informing his audience, that the unknown God was the Creator of the world, and of all the orders of beings which inhabit it. "God made the world, and all things therein." In particular, he asserts that he was the Maker of man. "He hath made of one blood all nations of men, for to dwell on all the face of the earth." Concerning the origin of the universe, different opinions were entertained by the Gentile philosophers. The Epicureans taught, that it was formed by chance, or by a fortuitous concourse of atoms, and pretended to account for the production of men and other animals, without the interposition of the Gods, in a manner not more creditable to their understandings than to their piety. Others believed the world to be eternal; or holding the preexistence of matter, assigned to the Deity merely the office of giving it its present form and arrangement. By all the philosophers, the idea of a proper creation was rejected, as being contrary to their established maxim, that out of nothing, nothing could be made.* In opposition to this fundamental principle of Heathenism, Paul declared that God had called the heavens and the earth into existence by his almighty word.

---

* Ocell. Lucan. de Universi Natura, cap. i. Sallust. de Diis et Mundo, cap. xvii.

He proceeds to lay down, in the next place, the doctrine of providence. God who made the world is "the Lord of heaven and earth: He giveth to all life, and breath, and all things: He hath determined the times before appointed, and the bounds of our habitation." The Apostle adds, "In Him we live, and move, and have our being;" and quotes the saying of the poet Aratus, "For we are also his offspring." The doctrine of providence was not new to the Gentiles, like that of creation. It was, indeed, denied by the followers of Epicurus, who represented the Gods as indifferent spectators of what was passing on the earth, and the Stoics, notwithstanding their fine sayings on the subject, may be charged with having virtually overthrown it, by their notions of fate; but other philosophers, and the common people, believed, that the Divine government extended to this world, and regulated the affairs of individuals, and nations. Hence, the supplications, thanksgivings, and sacrifices, which were offered up on public and private occasions. Our views of providence have been enlarged and corrected by revelation, which informs us, that God is constantly present with his works; that he cares for all his creatures, and for the individual, as well as the species; that our situation in life, and the changes in our condition, are determined and disposed by his wisdom; and that the laws of nature are the operations of his power, by which the order of the universe is maintained. "All things," said a heathen poet, "are full of God." The enlightened eye perceives him, not only in that majestic orb of light, which blazes in the heavens, but in the meanest reptile, and in the humblest weed which springs from the earth. We feel him stirring within us. It is by his secret influence, that our blood circulates, our stomach digests its food, and our lungs perform their important functions; it is by him, that our spirit thinks, and wills, animates our bodies, and receives impressions from the organs of sense. The universal Parent sustains and nourishes every being, to whom he has imparted life, and exercises a particular care towards men, "for we are also his offspring."

From these principles Paul draws the following inferences.

First, God is not confined to a particular place. "Seeing that he is Lord of heaven and earth, he dwelleth not in temples made with hands." The Gentiles believed, that, by the performance of certain ceremonies, the Gods were induced to descend into the temples which had been erected to their honour, and that they resided in the images by which they were represented. Their deluded worshippers, therefore, resorted to the temples, in the persuasion, that their devotions would be more acceptable there than in any other place; and sometimes, they contended who should sit nearest the images, that their prayers might be better heard. In opposition to these gross conceptions, Paul declared, that the Most High is not a local Deity, but a great and incomprehensible Being, whose essence fills heaven and earth. Once, indeed, there was a temple, in which he dwelt by a glorious symbol, and received the oblations and prayers of the Israelites; but they were too well instructed to suppose, that Jehovah himself was confined within the walls of a house. The whole earth exhibited signs of his presence; and his gracious aid was obtained in every place, where his name was devoutly invocated.

Secondly, He is independent and self-sufficient. "Neither is he worshipped with men's hands, as though he needed any thing." Although the more enlightened Heathens were convinced, that the Gods were not in want of any thing, which it was in the power of men to bestow, yet the common people believed, that in presenting costly oblations, they conferred a favour upon them which they were bound to repay; and, hence, they reproached them with ingratitude, and treated them with indignity, when they were disappointed of the blessings which they expected to obtain. Some were even so gross as to imagine, that their Deities were gratified with the smell of the incense and the sacrifices which were burnt upon the altars.* But, to what want can he be subject, who "giveth to all life, and breath, and all things?" The bounty of his providence is a proof, that his stores are inexhaustible. He who sustains from day to day, and from year to year, millions of creatures, can stand in no need of foreign supply. It is the duty of men to adore him with reverence and gratitude, and by performing this reasonable and delightful service, their own happiness will be promoted; but the praises, the obedience, and the gifts of all orders of beings in the universe, would make no addition to his infinite and immutable felicity.

Thirdly, He is a spiritual and invisible being. "Forasmuch then, as we are the offspring of God, we ought not to think that the Godhead is like unto gold, or silver, or stone graven by art and man's device." The Heathen Deities were supposed, by their votaries, to

---

* Arnobii adv. Gentes. Lib. vii.

have bodies, which, although immortal, were, like ours, nourished with food and drink, might suffer weariness and pain, and needed to be refreshed by rest and sleep. The images which they formed of gold, silver, and stone, were conceived to be true representations of them. But, more exalted conceptions of the Father of their spirits, should have been entertained by his rational offspring. A corporeal being is necessarily limited in his essence, and in all his perfections. How could such a being, circumscribed in place and in power, have given existence to the immense system of creation; and how could he superintend its affairs! The living soul in man is the more excellent part of his compound nature; and the heathens themselves regarded the body as its prison. Why did they admit the thought, that what they felt to be an incumbrance, constituted a part of the nature of the Gods, who were so much exalted above them? Man, indeed, is prone to believe, that the object of his worship is such a one as himself. But, when we elevate our minds to the Greatest and Best of all beings, it is surely more consonant to reason, to remove from the idea of him all the imperfections of creatures; to attribute to him every possible excellence in the highest degree; to conceive of him as independent upon time and place, and comprehending in his mysterious existence all space, and all duration. This sublime conception accords only with a spiritual being. The pure spirituality of the divine essence, however, is a discovery which we owe solely to revelation. When our Saviour said, "God is a spirit," he expressed a truth, unknown to the wise men of the ancient world.

With these reasonings, Paul intermixes an observation upon the duty of men in reference to their Maker, the knowledge of whom they should have exerted the utmost diligence to acquire; for he had revealed himself in the works of creation and providence, with a design, "that they should seek the Lord, if haply they might feel after him, and find him, though he be not far from every one of us." Reason, the distinguishing attribute of man, finds its noblest employment, in tracing the power, and goodness, and wisdom of its Author, in the frame and constitution of the Universe. Before the eyes of all nations the book of nature is unfolded, in which the existence and attributes of God are written in legible characters. His works were the only means of knowing him, which the Gentiles possessed. The Apostle represents those means as not the most favourable to the success of their inquiries, because the information which they communicated was imperfect, and the conclusion to which they led was uncertain. He compares the Gentiles to a blind man, or to a person in the dark, groping for an object, which he does not well know where to find. The description is just and striking. How many have been their mistakes, and how gross their errors, in both ancient and modern times! Unable to determine, whether there is one God or a thousand, whether he governs the world, or neglects it, what is the nature of his government, what homage he demands from his creatures, and what expectations they should entertain in reference to a future state, do they not present the melancholy spectacle of men, whose spark of reason was insufficient to dispel the gloom, in which they were enveloped? The cause, however, of their ignorance is to be found, not so much in the obscurity of nature, as in the weakness and depravity of the human understanding. Our intellectual powers were enfeebled by the fall; our minds are perverted by prejudice, and misled by the imagination and the passions. The characters in the book of nature are as distinct as ever, but our mental sight is impaired, so that we read with difficulty, and commit many errors, till Jesus Christ, by the gospel, restore clearness and vigour to our eyes.

Although it was the will of God, that men should seek after him, yet the Gentiles had not found him. They had embraced the illusions of fancy for truth, and had adored the creature in the room of the Creator. God had left them to the wanderings of their vain minds, and had not interposed to check the progress of error. "The times of this ignorance he winked at." This is an allusion to a person who intending not to intermeddle with what is transacting around him, closes his eyes, that he may seem not to observe it. God gave no revelation of his will to the Gentiles; he sent no inspired messenger to reclaim them from idolatry. Does it appear strange, that he should have neglected so great a portion of his rational offspring, although he beheld them engaged in pernicious errors, and departing farther and farther from his ways? Let it be considered, that he was under no obligation to interpose in favour of persons, who had already disregarded the voice of nature, and had voluntarily permitted their reason to be warped and blinded by their passions. Besides, it seems to have been his intention in leaving men to multiply follies and crimes from age to age, till religion and virtue were utterly lost, to demonstrate the necessity of revelation, and to prepare the world for gratefully receiving that discovery of his will, which he purposed to make in the fullness of time. " For after that, in the wisdom of God, the world by wisdom knew not God, it pleased God by the foolishness of preaching to save them that believe."

But the season of dereliction was past. God had remembered his forlorn creatures, and mercifully provided means for reclaiming them from ignorance and impiety. " But now he commandeth all men every where to repent." These words do not imply, that the former idolatry of the Gentiles was innocent, and that now only it was their duty to forsake it; but they obviously signify, that the plan of the divine procedure towards them was changed. God had sent forth his ministers to convince them of their wickedness, in apostatising from their Maker and Benefactor, and to command them to return to his service. This command was enforced by one of the most awful doctrines of our religion, that of the future judgment, in its circumstances more solemn than the judgment which the Gentiles expected; not a private inquiry into the actions of each individual at his death, but a public trial of the human race, assembled together to hear the sentence, which will consign them to everlasting happiness, or misery. " Because he hath appointed a day in the which he will judge the world in righteousness, by that man whom he hath ordained; whereof he hath given assurance unto all men, in that he hath raised him from the dead." The mention of the judgment, led the Apostle, by a natural transition, to the grand subject of his mission. It does not appear, whether he was permitted to illustrate the topics, introduced in the conclusion of his speech; but it is not improbable that the Athenians, from curiosity, would listen for some time, to his account of Jesus and the resurrection.

The curiosity of a part of the audience was soon satisfied; and the doctrine of Paul seemed to them to be less deserving of patient attention, than of ridicule. " When they heard of the resurrection of the dead, some mocked." By the Gentiles, a resurrection was accounted neither credible nor desirable. They believed that at death, the body mingled for ever with its native earth; and that, if the soul was not extinguished with the breath, it subsisted in an unembodied state, or was clothed with a new and purer vehicle. They laughed, therefore, when Paul assured them, that, at some distant period, the dust lying in the grave should resume its original form, and be again endowed with life and sensation. "And others said, We will hear thee again of this matter." They were neither prepared to assent to what he had told them, nor disposed to reject it, without examination. Although strange, it might be true; and it was therefore entitled to another hearing. Their language indicated a state of mind, which, upon reflection, and more ample information, would probably terminate in conviction.

There were a few, however, to whom his doctrine seemed not only curious and probable, but true. Among these, were Dionysius, a member of the court of Areopagus, and a woman called Damaris, and some others, whose names are not mentioned. The number of converts was small, but they were the first-fruits of an abundant harvest. The philosophical pride of Athens ere long humbled itself before the cross of Christ; and Jehovah reigned alone, amidst its deserted temples, and its idols laid prostrate in the dust.

Let the boast of reason cease. Let infidels no longer dare to decry revelation as unnecessary, and to extol the powers of the human mind as a sufficient guide in religion. The strength of reason has been tried; and the experiment was made in the most favourable circumstances. You have not been hearing of barbarous tribes, among whom intellect had received no cultivation, and we perceive rather the instincts of the lower animals, than the nobler faculties of man. You have been introduced to the Athenians, the most enlightened and refined people of antiquity. And what were the achievements of reason, in the seat of elegance and philosophy? Did it discover the unity of God, and present to him a pure and rational worshp? Do we find in the writings of those polished Greeks, a complete system of natural religion? Alas! we see in Athens, not only the common idolatry of heathen cities, but its utmost extravagance, as if unassisted reason, the more it was improved, had served the more, by its false lights, to lead mankind astray. Let us learn from this memorable example, that we stand in need of a surer and a more perfect guide; let us rejoice, that the gospel, like "the day-spring from on high," has arisen upon us, to conduct us in the way of truth and peace. Infidels themselves are indebted to it, although they disdain to acknowledge the obligation. By its aid, they see farther and more distinctly than the greatest philosophers of ancient times, whom they do not surpass in intellectual vigour, nor equal in diligence of research. Yet, with base ingratitude, they turn the benefit which they have derived from revelation, into an argument against it; and exclaim, that the glorious luminary, from which they have stolen their light, is useless, and should be blotted out of the heavens.

Let us remember, that great privileges infer high responsibility. "The times of this ignorance God winked at; but now commandeth all men every where to repent." At no time, indeed, did he tolerate idolatry, for it was impossible, that he should have ever approved of those who worshipped and served the creature, instead of the Creator. In the Epistle to the Romans, Paul asserts, that the Gentiles were "without excuse." But, our Saviour has shown, that the punishment inflicted upon sinners in the future state, will bear an exact proportion to their means of information, and their excitements to duty.

Speaking of the city, by the inhabitants of which his Apostles should be rejected, he says, "It shall be more tolerable for the land of Sodom and Gomorrah in the day of judgment than for that city." He selects the worst of the heathens, and declares, that their doom shall be less severe than that of the despisers of the gospel. Our privileges are greater than even those of the hearers of Christ, during his ministry upon earth. Revelation is completed; it is confirmed by ample and luminous evidence; and the Holy Ghost is sent forth to enlighten our minds. If, after all, we remain ignorant of the true God, or form false and dishonourable conceptions of his attributes and dispensations; if we neglect to worship him, or content ourselves with offering to him only bodily service; if we give that obedience to the world and the flesh, to which he alone is entitled, what apology can we plead for our conduct? Are we not the most ungrateful and perverse of men? What then can we expect, but that in the day of retribution, our privileges, of which we vainly boast, shall each of them have a voice to accuse us, and shall demand our condemnation, for the glory of divine justice? Happy are they who live in a Christian land, if they only prize and improve their advantages. But as for those by whom they are neglected, it would have been better for them, that they had lived and died among heathens. They should have perished by a milder doom. "For this is the condemnation, that light is come into the world, and men loved darkness rather than light, because their deeds were evil."

LECTURE XXI.

PAUL IN CORINTH.

Chap. xviii. 1—17.

The commission of Jesus Christ to his Apostles, authorised them to preach the gospel, and to form Churches, in every region of the earth. As it was impossible for them literally to execute this commission, we must conceive it to have been delivered to them as the first in a long succession of preachers, whose progressive labours should ultimately diffuse the light of truth throughout the habitable world. Yet, no exertion was wanting on their part, to disseminate, as extensively as possible, the religion of their Master. With more enlightened views, and purer motives than the Pharisees, they compassed sea and land, to make proselytes to Christianity. The notion that some of the Apostles were bishops of particular cities, is inconsistent with the nature of their office. They were not sent to preside over the Church of Jerusalem, of Antioch, or of Rome. The whole world was their diocese, and the catholic society of believers was their flock. In general, they did not stay long in a place; but having sown the seeds of truth in one city, or country, they made haste to perform the same salutary work, in another. We have seen Paul preaching in several provinces of Asia, then passing over to Macedonia, and afterwards making Greece the scene of his labours. We have seen him in Athens, disputing with the philosophers; and we are now to see him in Corinth, conflicting with the obstinacy and furious zeal of the Jews.

Corinth was a city of Greece, which enjoyed, from its situation, uncommon advantages for commerce, being built upon a neck of land, which was washed on both sides by the sea. It was taken and destroyed by the Romans; but it soon rose from its ashes, and, at the time when Paul visited it, was in a very flourishing state.

Wealth was accompanied with luxury, its usual attendant, insomuch, that the Corinthians were infamous among the heathens for their profligate manners; and to live after the manner of the Corinthians, was a proverbial expression for leading a dissipated life. Venus, the goddess of licentiousness, was publicly worshipped in the city, and a thousand prostitutes were consecrated to her service. In a scene of so much depravity, the gospel was as unlikely to succeed, as in the refined city of Athens. If philosophy fosters that pride of understanding, which revolts at the humiliating lessons of faith, sensuality indisposes the heart for submitting to the holy discipline, which religion enjoins. Yet, in Corinth the gospel proved mighty "to cast down the strongholds of iniquity, and to bring the thoughts of men into captivity to Christ."

When Paul came to Corinth, " he found a certain Jew, named Aquila, born in Pontus, lately from Italy, with his wife Priscilla, (because that Claudius had commanded all Jews to depart from Rome,) and he came unto them." When the emperor Claudius ascended the throne, he made laws in favour of the Jews, who had been grievously harassed by his predecessor Caligula; but about the eighth or ninth year of his reign, he withdrew his protection from them, and published an edict banishing them from Italy. The historian Suetonius is supposed to refer to the event, which is here related by Luke, when he says in his life of Claudius, that " he expelled from Rome the Jews, who were constantly exciting tumults, at the instigation of Christ.*" It is not easy to determine what he intended by this accusation of our Saviour. The most probable account of it is, that having no knowledge of him but from the calumnious reports of the Jews, he concluded, that he was the ringleader of one of their sects; and was thus hastily induced to impute the seditious conduct of the men of that nation, who resided in Rome, to the influence of his doctrine. It is certain, that among those Jews there were some Christians, as Aquila and Priscilla, who would lead "quiet and peaceable lives in all godliness and honesty;" but the Romans had not yet learned to distinguish them from such as adhered to the religion of Moses; and being all confounded under one denomination, they were involved in the same charge, and subjected to the same punishment. " Aquila and Pris-

---

* Suet. Claud. cap. 25.

cilla had lately come from Italy, because that Claudius had commanded all Jews to depart from Rome.

Paul associated with them, as being, perhaps, the only Christians in the place; " and because he was of the same craft, he abode with them and wrought, for by their occupation they were tent-makers." The Apostle, who was a disciple of Gamaliel, had applied to the occupation of tent-making, not so much from necessity, we may presume, as in compliance with a national custom. Among the Jews, it was usual for persons of education to learn a trade, by which, if circumstances should require it, they might support themselves, without being burdensome to others. It is a saying of one of the Rabbis, "that he who does not teach his son some art or calling, acts no better than if he taught him to be a thief." No honest employment was accounted dishonourable. Paul engaged in work with Aquila and Priscilla, because there was yet no Church in Corinth, to which he could look for maintenance, according to this incontrovertible maxim, "The labourer is worthy of his hire." In certain cases, when there were Churches, he declined making a demand upon them, in consideration of their peculiar circumstances, or to prevent any from alleging or suspecting, that he was influenced by mercenary views, and to show by his disinterestedness, how fully he was convinced of the truth of the gospel, and how pure was his zeal for the salvation of souls. But his claim was unquestionable; and he did not fail to assert it in the most implicit terms, even when he waved the exercise of it, from prudence or generosity.

Concerning Aquila and Priscilla we may remark, that although they may seem to have been persons of an obscure condition, depending for subsistence upon their own labour, yet their names are recorded in Scripture, to be transmitted with honour to the latest posterity. Mention is made of them in several places of the New Testament. In the Epistle to the Romans, Paul speaks of them in the following terms; "Greet Priscilla and Aquila, my helpers in Christ Jesus: who have for my life laid down their own necks; unto whom not only I give thanks, but also all the Churches of the Gentiles." This example holds out an inducement to others in similar circumstances, to exert themselves in the service of religion. Their situation may preclude them from obtaining the celebrity which is attached to eminence in learning and science, and to splendid achievements; but by the faithful performance of Christian duties, by usefulness within the sphere of their influence, by helping the ministers of Christ, in imitation of Aquila and Priscilla, while they encourage them in their work, and second by example and private exhortations their public instructions, they shall acquire the esteem of good men, and what is infinitely more important, shall be honoured with the approbation of God. The fame which the world lavishes upon its favourites, is fleeting as the breath which bestows it; but "the righteous shall be in everlasting remembrance."

The business of tent-making did not hinder Paul from discharging, as he had opportunity, the duties of the Apostolical office. "He reasoned in the synagogue every sabbath, and persuaded the Jews and the Greeks." The gospel treats us as rational creatures, propounding arguments to convince our understandings, and motives to interest our hearts. When the heathens reproached the Christians, with demanding a blind assent to their religion, and saying to them, "Do not examine, but believe," they had forgotten, or they intentionally overlooked the evidences, which the gospel exhibited of its divine authority, and the means employed by the first preachers of Christianity, to prevail upon men to embrace it.* Paul, for example, did not require the Jews at Corinth to believe without proof, that Jesus was the Messiah; but he reasoned with them, demonstrating from the Scriptures, that he was the person foretold by the Prophets. It appears from the following verses, that his labours were not altogether unsuccessful; but when he is said to have "persuaded" the Jews and the Greeks, or such of the latter as being proselytes, frequented the synagogue, Luke refers rather to the tendency, than to the effect, of his discources. They were calculated to persuade. Such considerations were brought forward, as were well fitted to convince his hearers of the truth of the gospel.

"When Silas and Timotheus were come from Macedonia, Paul was pressed in spirit, and testified to the Jews, that Jesus was Christ." On the arrival of these friends and fellow-labourers, he felt an unusual earnestness for the conversion of his countrymen. His zeal was animated by their presence, or by the agency of the Spirit of God upon his mind. The word translated "pressed," is the same which is used, when our Lord says, that he had a baptism to be baptized with, and was "straitened" till it was accomplished;

---

* Orig. contra Celsum, Lib. i.

and when Paul informs us, that the love of Christ "constrained" him. It is expressive, in all those passages, of strong desire, and a deep sense of obligation, inciting a person to the performance of his duty. The perilous situation of the Jews presented itself with redoubled force and interest to his mind; and his heart glowed with ardent love to their souls, which would not permit him to rest, till he had used every endeavour to accomplish their salvation.

His labours were bestowed upon an ungrateful people. "They opposed themselves and blasphemed." They cavilled at his arguments, and treated his affectionate exhortations with contempt. Their furious bigotry broke out in reproaches, not only against Paul, as an apostate from the religion of his fathers, but against Jesus, whom they reviled as an impostor. Their violence would be the greater, because they felt themselves pressed by his reasonings. Men full of prejudice, can hardly be expected to listen calmly to those who would convince them of their error; and what is wanting in argument, they usually supply by vehemence and abuse. It is an expeditious and easy plan, to blacken the reputation of an antagonist, to whom they are unable to reply.

Finding it to be in vain to make any farther attempts for their conversion, the Apostle "shook his raiment, and said unto them, Your blood be upon your own heads; I am clean: from henceforth I will go unto the Gentiles." Our Lord commanded his Apostles, when the inhabitants of any city would not receive them, "to shake off the very dust from their feet, for a testimony against them." That dust would remain as a memorial, that the ministers of salvation had come to them, and had been despised; or the action was intended to signify, that those ministers should henceforth have no communication with such obstinate sinners. With the same design, Paul now shook his garment, or shook off the dust which adhered to his garment. Symbolical actions were frequent among the Prophets, and were probably so congenial to the manners of the Jews, as to be easily understood. "Your blood be upon your own heads; I am clean." "If you perish, it is by your own fault; I am free from blame." Although every man shall be finally condemned for his personal sins, yet others may be accessary to his ruin. They contribute to it, who tempt him to commit sin; who, in any way, encourage him to continue in it; who withhold that instruction, and those admonitions, by which he might have been preserved from falling, or restored; who neglect any thing, which they should have done, for the salvation of his soul. Happy is that minister of religion, who can say, with a pure conscience, to the infatuated sinners, who have resisted his endeavours for their good, " Your blood be upon your own heads; I am clean!" It is a consoling reflection, that he has been faithful to his fellow men, and to his Saviour. "His witness is in heaven; his record is on high." But the ministers of religion are not alone concerned to be thus pure. Parents, husbands, wives, friends, and acquaintance! beware, lest the objects of your most tender affections, the companions of your social hours, appear before the tribunal of God, and attribute their eternal perdition to the unworthy example which you set before them; to your imprudent indulgence; to your unwise counsels, and unseasonable complaisance; to your total disregard of their spiritual interests, amidst much solicitude for their temporal welfare. Let no person say with Cain, " Am I my brother's keeper?" If Providence has put it in the power of one man to excite another to do good, or to entice him to evil, he is his keeper, and shall be answerable for the abuse of his influence.

While the Apostle laid the guilt of their perdition upon the Jews themselves, he intimated, that they should be deprived of the means of salvation which they had contumaciously resisted. "From henceforth I will go unto the Gentiles." The gracious designs of Heaven were not to be disappointed by their rejection of the gospel. There were others, to whom the good news might be published, and by whom they would be joyfully received. " I will now preach to the Gentiles."

The opposition of the Jews did not discourage Paul from proceeding in his work. "He departed thence, and entered into a certain man's house, named Justus, one that worshipped God, whose house joined hard to the synagogue." These words do not mean, that leaving Aquila and Priscilla, he went to live with Justus; but that not finding it safe to resort any more to the synagogue, or being positively excluded from it, by a decree of the rulers, he accepted the offer made by this proselyte of his house, for holding religious assemblies. Some of the Jews were persuaded by the reasonings of Paul. Of this number was " Crispus, the chief ruler of the synagogue, who believed in the Lord with all his house. And many of the Corinthians hearing believed, and were baptized." These were not Jews alone, but natives of the place, who were converted by his discourses, especially after he had begun to preach in the house of Justus, where he was heard by a promiscuous audience.

"Then spake the Lord to Paul in the night by a vision, Be not afraid, but speak, and hold not thy peace. For I am with thee, and no man shall set on thee to hurt thee: For I have much people in this city." The Apostle was not a timid man. Of a firm and ardent temper, he engaged with earnestness in any enterprise, and was prepared to abide by his purpose, in the face of opposition. But the most courageous are but men, who may experience moments of weakness, and disappoint the expectations of others, by a cowardly flight from danger. Jesus Christ, therefore, appeared to his faithful servant, to assure him of his assistance and protection. There were other trials awaiting him, besides those which he had already undergone. "Speak, and hold not thy peace." The policy of worldly men is supple and accommodating. Keeping its own interest, the main spring of all its actions, continually in view, it consults the tastes and humours of others, and, with dexterous facility, adapts itself to the ever varying aspect of affairs. Its looks are studied; its words are carefully weighed. It seeks by flattery to gain the heart, and thus to make sure of the object of its arts, who will suffer himself to be led, in the chains of vanity and self-love, a captive at its pleasure. What is agreeable and soothing is readily told; but if any thing would wound the pride of others, or offend their prejudices, the salutary truth is buried in silence. The Apostles of Jesus Christ renounced the artifices of dishonesty. Their aim was not the praise of men, but their salvation, not their own private interests, but the honour of their Master; and to accomplish these important ends, they did not "hold their peace," although they foresaw, that their words should excite the ridicule or the indignation of their audience. In the present case, Paul was assured, not that his doctrine should be applauded, and his person held in admiration, nor that he should escape without reproach, and suffer no sort of molestation; but solely that "no man should set on him to hurt him." He might be persecuted, but he should not be destroyed. This promise did not fail, when the Jews laid hold of him, and led him to the tribunal of Gallio; for the deputy refused to hear their accusation, and dismissed the prisoner in peace. Almighty power controls the wrath of the wicked, and, when it rages as the sea in a storm, says to it, "Hitherto shalt thou come, and no farther."

The care of Providence was exercised towards Paul, that by his ministrations many of the Corinthians might be saved. "I have much people in this city." It is almost unnecessary to remark, that this declaration does not refer to the few, who were already converted, but to those who were yet to be called. They were all known to the Son of God, who sees the future as well as the past, and, by means of the gospel, carries into effect his eternal purpose of grace with respect to his elect. Some would persuade us, with a design to obscure the evidence arising from this passage in favour of the doctrine of election and sovereign grace, that nothing more is intended than that Jesus Christ "who searches the heart, and tries the reins of the children of men," perceived, that many of the Corinthians, who were yet in a state of heathenism, were disposed to believe. But when the Scripture accounts for the conversion of sinners, it does not ascribe it to their previous good dispositions, but to the mercy of God. "So then it is not of him that willeth, nor of him that runneth, but of God that showeth mercy." How the Corinthians, who were ignorant of the true God, and engaged in the errors and crimes of polytheism; who having lost all just ideas of religion, were either seduced by a proud and ostentatious philosophy, or immersed in the grossest sensuality, were prepared to receive the heavenly doctrines, and pure precepts of Christianity, we shall leave it to the authors and abetters of this absurd notion to explain. Let them show us, in what intelligible sense idolaters and profligates were disposed to become the disciples of Christ. His people in Corinth were such persons, as are elsewhere termed "the election," and "vessels of mercy;" or such as he had predestinated to salvation, and to faith and holiness, as the means of obtaining it. Those whom he has predestinated, he calls by the gospel, which his providence sends to the places where they reside, and continues there, till they are all converted. Of this class there are many in the city; and while the sovereignty of divine grace appears in the case of every individual, who is chosen to eternal life, it is displayed, in a very strong and impressive light, in the instance before us. There were many of the elect, in one of the most debauched cities of the heathen world. It is evident, therefore, that the purpose of God is not founded in the foresight of good qualities in the objects of his choice, but in the independent determination of his own will, acting under the direction of his wisdom. The notion of merit, or of virtuous dispositions, or of the most remote inclination to virtue, as the cause of the distinction, which God has made in favour of some, will be rejected as unscriptural and impious, by every man who has attentively read and considered the words of Paul, addressed to the same persons, to whom this passage relates. "Know ye not that the unrighteous shall not inherit the kingdom of God? Be not deceived: neither fornicators, nor idolators, nor adulterers, nor effeminate, nor abusers of themselves with mankind, nor thieves, nor covetous, nor drunkards, nor revilers, nor extortioners, shall inherit the kingdom of God. And such were some of you: but ye are washed, but ye are sanctified, but ye are justified in the name of the Lord Jesus, and by the Spirit of our God."

Encouraged by this promise not only of protection but of success, Paul, "continued in Corinth a year and six months, teaching the word of God among them." The Jews beheld the progress of the gospel with an evil eye; and at length, their zeal being unable to restrain itself, "they made insurrection with one accord against Paul, when Gallio was the deputy of Achaia, and brought him to the judgment-seat, saying, This fellow persuadeth men to worship God contrary to the law." This charge was founded not only upon his teaching that Jesus was the Messiah, but upon his doctrine with regard to the institutions of Moses, which, he maintained, were not to be imposed upon the believing Gentiles, and having received their completion in the gospel, were to be abolished. There was nothing in this doctrine hostile to the law; but the Jews did not understand the harmony between the two systems, and the subservience of the one to the other. He, therefore, who affirmed, that circumcision was not necessary, that sacrifices were no longer required, that there was no distinction of meats into clean and unclean, and that the Gentiles were admitted, through faith, to the possession of the same spiritual privileges with the Jews, seemed to teach men to worship God contrary to the law.

"When Paul was about to open his mouth," to reply to the accusation of the Jews, Gallio, without waiting to hear him, said, "If it were a matter of wrong, or wicked lewdness, O ye Jews, reason would that I should bear with you." "A matter of wrong or wicked lewdness," signifies any crime committed against the peace of society, any act of injustice, violence, or fraud. Society cannot subsist without laws defining and securing the rights of individuals; and it is the duty of persons in authority, to see those laws impartially executed. Magistrates are not appointed for their own honour and emolument, but for the public good, that the sober and peaceable part of the community may be protected, and the unruly and injurious may be restrained. Had Paul been accused of theft, robbery, murder, or sedition, Gallio would have considered himself as bound by his office to inquire into the charge. "But if it be a question of words, and names, and of your law, look ye to it; for I will be no judge of such matters." The proconsul, we may believe, did not well understand the subject of dispute between Paul and his adversaries. Having learned in general, that they contended among themselves, whether the title of Messiah should be given to Jesus of Nazareth, and the ceremonies enjoined by Moses should be retained, he calls the discussion a question " of words, and names, and of their law." In this manner, any Gentile, circumstanced as he was, would have naturally expressed himself. Of such a controversy he refused to be a judge; "and he drove them from the judgment-seat."

The reason for which he declined to consider questions relative to the law, may thus be explained. Under the government of the Romans, the Jews enjoyed the benefit of a religious toleration. They were permitted to worship the God of Israel, and to observe the ordinances of Moses, not only in Judea, but in the various provinces of the empire. Accordingly, it appears from this history that they had synagogues in the different countries of Asia and Europe, which Paul visited. At the time when he was brought before the tribunal of Gallio, the Christians had not attracted the particular notice of the Romans. Regarding the religion of the Jews with contempt, they did not pay such attention to it, as might have led them, in the infancy of the Church, to discover the difference between the followers of Jesus, and the disciples of Moses. Paul appeared, therefore, to the proconsul, to belong to some Jewish sect, similar to the sects which had long subsisted among that people, under the names of Pharisees, Sadducees, and Essenes. With their internal divisions, the laws of the empire did not interfere, but protected all parties under the general denomination of Jews, and left their differences of opinion to be settled by themselves. On this account, Gallio refused to judge, and seems to have considered himself as having no authority to judge of their religious disputes. He said to them, " Look ye to it ;" intimating that it belonged to them alone to determine such controversies.

The motives of his conduct have been misunderstood. He has been represented as a profane man, who accounted Christianity a question about " words ;" and his name has become the proverbial appellation of a person, careless and indifferent about religion. But, the manner in which he speaks of Christianity, is an evidence not of his profaneness, but of his ignorance. In what other light could the present dispute appear to a stranger, than as a question of words and names? The charge of indifference is equally unfounded. Gallio acted the part of a prudent and impartial judge, who would not pronounce sentence in a cause which he did not understand, and which was not within the sphere of his jurisdiction. While he was ready to do justice between man and man, to redress grievances, and punish crimes, he resolved to preserve inviolate the toleration which the laws of the empire accorded to the Jews. It did not pertain to him as a Roman magistrate, to decide concerning the interpretation of their national law, and the comparative merits of their sects. He has been blamed, therefore, for scrupulously confining himself within the limits of his duty.

It would have been happy for the Christian world, if the conduct of Gallio, instead of being calumniated through ignorance and false zeal, had been imitated by persons in authority. Our religion, which always suffers by the misconduct of those who profess it, would not have been loaded with the reproach of persecution. Let magistrates inquire into every matter of " wrong and wicked lewdness." Let them animadvert, with due severity, upon acts of violence and dishonesty, and secure to their subjects the enjoyment of their rights, and of the fruits of their industry. But, let them remember, that God alone is the Lord of the conscience; and that it is to be governed by the dictates of reason and Scripture, not by the mandates of human authority. With the religion of their subjects they have nothing to do, but to protect them in the exercise of it, and to prevent them from disturbing one another. To maintain that they have a right to interfere any farther, under the pretext of checking heresies and errors, is to destroy the clear and essential distinction between Church and State ; to impose a restraint upon freedom of inquiry; to make civil rulers infallible interpreters of Scripture, while they are not more able to interpret them than the people; and to entrust them with a power, which, the history of past ages authorizes us to say, is less likely to be employed in the defence of truth, than in the support of error.

The indifference with which Gallio witnessed a riot in the court where he presided, cannot be so easily defended. "Then all the Greeks took Sosthenes, the chief ruler of the synagogue, and beat him before the judgment-seat; and Gallio cared for none of those things." A judge should have repressed such an outrage committed in his own presence, and should have severely punished the offenders. We are not, however, so fully acquainted with the circumstances, as to be qualified to pass sentence upon his conduct. It has been supposed, that he permitted the Greeks to beat the rulers of the synagogue, in order to deter the Jews from again troubling him with similar accusations. Be this as it may, by the moderation and equity of the proconsul, the promise made to Paul, that no man should set on him to hurt him, was performed. His life and liberty were preserved; and the Jews, mortified and intimidated by this unexpected check, would not venture again to disturb him in the discharge of his duty.

I shall subjoin the following observations.

First, The success of the gospel does not always correspond with the ideas which have been previously entertained upon the subject. The divine procedure is not regulated by those appearances and probabilities, which are the grounds of our expectations. The Jews who heard the voice of Moses and the Prophets, rejected the gospel; but it was gladly received by the Gentiles, who had lived in profound ignorance of the purposes of grace. The converts to Christianity in Athens seem not to have been so numerous as those in Corinth. Athens, indeed, was full of superstition, and very gross vices prevailed among its inhabitants; but the manners of the Corinthians were still more depraved. Men of learning and reflection are sometimes prompted, by the pride of reason, to treat revelation with neglect and contempt; whereas others of a careless and superficial temper, are led, by particular circumstances, to give such attention to it, as terminates in a firm conviction and cordial belief. Persons of sober habits not seldom appear to be strangers to vital godliness, while sinners of the most worthless character, are "washed, and sanctified, and justified." How shall we account for these things? Are they not so many arguments, in confirmation of the doctrine, which we hold upon the authority of Scripture, that

God dispenses his grace according to his own pleasure, and "hath mercy on whom he will have mercy?"

In the second place, We observe a proof of the wisdom and care of God, in the protection afforded to the Church in its infancy. The Church was destined to undergo severe trials, to contend with the power of the Roman empire, to resist unto blood, in the struggle with Satan and the world; but while it was yet forming, it pleased God to proceed much in the same manner, in which he acted towards the Israelites, immediately after their deliverance from Egypt. "He did not lead them through the way of the land of the Philistines, although that was near; for he said, lest peradventure the people repent when they see war, and they return to Egypt." The disciples of Jesus, indeed, were soon exposed to the malignity of the Jews; but the troubles which these excited, were partial, and of short duration. It was not till the reign of Nero, that the Christians were persecuted by the Roman government; nor till a considerable time after, probably about the beginning of the second century, that express laws were enacted against them. During this interval, they were, in some measure, sheltered under the toleration granted to the Jews. The Church was fully formed, and established, and had spread far and wide, before those formidable attacks were made, which might have proved fatal to it at an earlier period. God proportions trials to the strength of the sufferer; and will not expose his people to any temptations, "which they are not able to bear."

In the last place, Let Christians be careful to conduct themselves in such a manner, that, if they shall be brought before the judgment-seat of their civil rulers, it may not be for any offence against the just laws of the state, but for some question relative to the law of their God. "Let none of you suffer as a murderer, or as a thief, or as an evil-doer, or as a busy body in other men's matters. Yet, if any man suffer as a Christian, let him not be ashamed; but let him glorify God on this behalf." My brethren, if you act according to the spirit and precepts of our holy religion, it is impossible, that you can ever be justly charged with a "matter of wrong, or wicked lewdness;" for your hands will be free from violence and injustice, and your hearts, from the selfish and malevolent passions. The tongue of calumny may impeach you, as it did not spare your blessed Master, and his holy Apostles; "but your righteousness shall go forth as the light, and your judgment as the noon-day."

It was the glory of the primitive Christians, that although they were accused of the foulest crimes, atheism, murder, and incest, their persecutors could prove nothing against them but their steadfast and consistent attachment to the gospel. Even apostates, who are commonly eager, in their own defence, to defame the society which they have abandoned, when interrogated by a heathen magistrate, affirmed this to be the amount of their fault or error, "that they were accustomed to meet upon a certain day, before it was light, and sing a hymn to Christ as God; and to bind themselves by an oath, not to commit any wickedness, but to abstain from theft, robberies, and adulteries, from violating their promises, and refusing to restore what had been committed to their custody."* How honourable was this testimony to the disciples of Christ! What a lustre did it reflect upon his religion! Let a Christian tremble at the thought of being convicted of a crime. May it be the constant care of us all " to preserve consciences void of offence towards God and towards man!" And may the grace of God enable us " by well-doing, to put to silence the ignorance of foolish men!"

---

* Plin. Epist. x. 67.

LECTURE XXII.

PAUL IN EPHESUS.

Chap. xix. 1—20.

The mention of Apollos in the first verse, leads us back to the last part of the preceding chapter, where that eminent minister of the gospel is first introduced to our notice. He was a Jew, born in Alexandria, well acquainted with the Scriptures of the Old Testament, and was possessed of a great share of eloquence. At the time of his appearance in Ephesus, he was imperfectly instructed in the religion of Christ, for he knew only the baptism of John. But, Aquila, and Priscilla who had removed from Corinth to that city, having expounded to him the way of God more perfectly, when he was disposed to pass into Achaia, he was sent to that country with recommendatory letters; and he seems to have been allowed to preach there in the assemblies of the Christians, as well as in those of the Jews. No argument can be fairly drawn from this case, for the right of every person, who is qualified, to commence a preacher of the gospel, although it has been sometimes represented as decisive of the question. The practice of the Jewish synagogue, in which private persons were permitted to explain the Scriptures, and to exhort the congregation, is not a precedent for the Christian Church; and it was only in the synagogue that Apollos preached, during his residence in Ephesus. The sequel of his history is so concise that no considerate person would choose to found upon it the determination of any point in debate. It is certain, that by one Church which was acquainted with his character and qualifications, he was recommended to another, and that in consequence of that recommendation he discharged the duties of a public teacher in the latter. While we perceive some traces of regular procedure in this business, the particular steps are obviously omitted. As those parts of Scripture which are obscure, or defective, should be interpreted by such as are perspicuous and full, we may safely suppose, that Apollos was admitted to the ministerial office, in the ordinary way, by the call of the Church, and the imposition of hands.

"While Apollos was at Corinth, Paul, having passed through the upper coasts, came to Ephesus: and finding certain disciples, he said unto them, Have ye received the Holy Ghost since ye believed?" John baptized his disciples into the faith of the Messiah, as soon to be manifested to Israel. The men whom Paul found at Ephesus, seem to have been disciples of John, who, having acquired some knowledge of Jesus, and of the evidences of his divine mission, believed in him as the Messiah whose approach their Master had proclaimed. But, from circumstances of which we are not informed, the distance, perhaps, at which they lived from Judea, or the want of an opportunity to hear the Apostles or to converse with any of the Christians, they entertained a very imperfect idea of the nature and privileges of the new dispensation; for when Paul asked them, whether they had received the Holy Ghost, they answered, "We have not so much as heard, whether there be any Holy Ghost." In the New Testament, this name sometimes signifies the operations of the Spirit; and in several passages, not his sanctifying, but his miraculous influences. In the latter sense it must, at present, be understood; for Paul did not inquire whether those disciples had been regenerated, but whether the extraordinary gifts, which where then common, had been communicated to them. When they did receive the Holy Ghost by the imposition of hands, we read, that "they spake with tongues, and prophecied."

Unless we consider the question of Paul as referring to the operations of the Holy Ghost, the answer will import, that those men, although disciples of John, and believers in Christ, did not know whether there was such a person as the Spirit. This, however, is an incredible degree of ignorance in Jews, who had often read, in the Scriptures of the Old Testament, of the Spirit of the Lord, by whom the Prophets were inspired. But, according to the explanation we have given of the name, not to know whether there was a Holy Ghost, signifies that they were not apprized of the miraculous dispensation, which had commenced on the day of Pentecost. They had not heard, that the Holy Ghost was restored to Israel, who according to the saying of the Rabbis, departed from it, after the death of Zechariah and Malachi. In like manner, it is said, on a certain occasion, of Samuel, who had been trained up in the fear of God from his infancy, and was then ministering in the tabernacle, that " he did not yet know the Lord ;" ·that is, as we learn from the words which immediately follow, he had not yet been favoured with any vision, or revelation. John, when relating an address of our Saviour to the Jews in the temple, remarks, that " the Holy Ghost was not yet given," or, according to the original, that " the Holy Ghost was not yet," because Jesus was not yet glorified ; undoubtedly meaning, not that the divine Spirit did not then exist, for he had spoken many ages before by the Prophets, but that he was not then poured out upon the disciples in those spiritual gifts, which were so abundantly communicated, after the exaltation of Christ. The words of the Evangelist are analogous to those of the disciples in Ephesus, and illustrate their meaning. They had not heard of the dispensation of the Spirit. Still it is surprising, that a dispensation so extraordinary, which must have given rise to much conversation, and the effects of which were felt in all the Churches, should not have been known to persons, whose faith in Jesus Christ is an evidence, that they had inquired into his character and history. Paul was surprised at their answer, and said to them, " Unto what then were ye baptized ? And they said, Unto John's baptism." They had been baptized by John himself, or by his disciples, and had received no other baptism. Although they believed in Christ, therefore, they were not properly members of the visible Church, into which converts were received by that sacred rite.

From their answer, the Apostle took occasion to point out the nature and design of the baptism of John. " Then said Paul, John verily baptized with the baptism of repentance." It is called the baptism of repentance, because he required from those whom he admitted to it, the confession and renunciation of their sins, and such a change of views and dispositions, as was necessary to prepare them for becoming disciples of the Messiah. For the Baptist, faithful to his commission, used no art to draw the attention of the people to himself, but directed their expectations to Him, who was soon to appear to claim their homage, and to save them from their sins. " He said unto the people that they should believe on him which should come after him, that is, on Christ Jesus." From all quarters, the people flocked to the ministry of John, as no person had for a long time appeared among them, invested with the prophetical character. He was revered for the authority with which he taught, and for the austerity of his manners; and so high did the public admiration rise, that many began to think that he was the Messiah himself. " But he confessed and denied not, but confessed, I am not the Christ." With disinterested zeal he resigned all his honours to his Master.

The following words have been the subject of much controversy. "When they heard this, they were baptized in the name of the Lord Jesus." Some maintain that they are the words of Paul, relating the success of the ministry of John, and import, that many were persuaded to receive baptism from him, not as a rite of initiation into his service, but as a token of their faith in the Messiah, whose superior dignity and near approach he had foretold. It will be acknowledged, I presume, that this is not the sense of the words, which first presents itself to the reader, and it has not, therefore the recommendation of being obvious and natural. Besides, John did not baptize his disciples "in the name of the Lord Jesus," unless this expression be used in some forced and unusual meaning. He merely commanded them to believe in the Messiah, without pointing him out by person, or by name. Others contend, that these are the words of Luke, who records the result of the conversation between Paul and those disciples of the Baptist. As soon as the Apostle had convinced them, that the great design of the ministry of John, was to prepare men for becoming disciples of Christ, not to form a sect or party which should be called by his own name, they submitted to baptism, as a public testimony of their faith in our Saviour, and of their dedication to his service. It is objected to this view of the passage, that it supposes the baptism of John and that of Christ to have been different; and that it furnishes an example in justification of those who assert, that, in certain cases, baptism should be repeated. But, there seems to be no necessity for so identifying the baptism of John and that of Christ, that both could not be lawfully administered to the same individual. John baptized his disciples into the faith of the Messiah as to come; we are baptized into the faith of the Messiah as actually come. The baptism of John was evidently instituted to serve a temporary purpose, in common with all the other parts of his ministry; the baptism of Christ is to continue to the end of the world. The one did not properly belong to the Christian economy, but was preparatory to it;

the other is an ordinance given by our Saviour to his Church to supply the place of circumcision. Christian baptism is administered in the name of the persons of the Trinity; whereas we have no evidence that they were explicitly recognized in the baptism of John. From these considerations, it appears, that the two ordinances differ so much in their form, their design, and their relation to the present dispensation, that they may be considered as perfectly distinct; and, consequently, that a person who had been baptized by John, might have been baptized again by an Apostle. Hence, it is plain, that the case before us affords no precedent for the repetition of Christian baptism. In ancient times, it was customary, in some places, to rebaptize heretics, who returned to the bosom of the Catholic Church; and the same practice is retained by certain sects, in the case of those who accede to their communion, because they account the baptism, which was administered to them in their infancy, to have been unscriptural and void. But, the instance now under consideration gives no countenance to this procedure, because the baptism of the disciples in Ephesus was not a repetition of the same rite, in consequence of an irregularity in the first application of it, but an ordinance, which had not formerly been dispensed to them. They now, for the first time, received the baptism of Christ.

It is unhappy, when we bring to the study of the Scripture, our preconceived notions, our jealousy for favourite opinions, our dread of giving advantage to an antagonist, our anxious care to guard against the dangers, real or imaginary, which threaten our system. In this state of mind, it is impossible that we should be candid and impartial, in the interpretation of it. We must feel a strong inclination to make it express our sentiments, and when it refuses its evidence, to torture it to confess. This is the true source of the forced and unnatural expositions of Scripture, which are too frequent in the writings of all parties. Let the word of God explain its own meaning without any restraint; and if it should not, on every occasion, speak in conformity to our wishes, it will be always consistent with itself.

As soon as the disciples were baptized, "Paul laid his hands upon them, and the Holy Ghost came upon them; and they spake with tongues and prophesied." Imposition of hands was a rite practised in the primitive times, for various purposes, and particularly for the communication of supernatural gifts, which were imparted to qualify the persons for preaching the gospel, or promoting, in a more private manner, the edification of the Church, and to demonstrate to Jews and Gentiles the divine origin of the Christian religion. Those disciples were immediately inspired with the knowledge of foreign languages, and the spirit of prophecy. And thus a proof was given of the great difference between the baptism of John, and that of our Saviour. "For John truly baptized with water; but ye shall be baptized with the Holy Ghost."

Let us proceed to consider the labours of Paul in Ephesus, and the miracles, by which his doctrine was confirmed. Conformably to his usual practice, "he went into the synagogue, and spake boldly for the space of three months, disputing and persuading the things concerning the kingdom of God." He explained the nature of the dispensation of grace, and exerted his holy eloquence to prevail upon the Jews to embrace the gospel as the end and completion of the law. In our times, when the doctrine of the cross is recognised by the Christian world as the foundation of their hopes, to avow our belief of it is an easy matter; and we shall with little difficulty persuade others to concur with us. But, in the Apostolic age, no man could have said, without heroic courage, without having his mind elevated by the love of truth, above the consideration of honour and personal safety, "I am not ashamed of the gospel of Christ." It required boldness to maintain principles, which appeared foolish to the wise men of the world, and drew upon their friends ridicule and persecution. In the synagogue, Paul was surrounded with men, avowedly hostile to the cause which he defended, and, from the violence of their zeal, capable of the greatest excesses. Yet, he dared to proclaim, in their presence, the crucified Jesus to be the Messiah. He "disputed" in the synagogue, replying to the objections of the Jews, and supporting his doctrine by arguments from Scripture. Disputation, however unpleasant, is unavoidable, when we meet with captious and unreasonable opponents. If it often irritates, it sometimes convinces; and, whatever may be its effects upon individuals, it is necessary, for the honour of the truth, that the mistakes, misrepresentations, and sophisms of adversaries, should be detected and exposed.

But, although Paul, we may believe, refuted, in the most triumphant manner, the arguments of the Jews, there were some too proud and obstinate to yield. "Divers were hardened," that is, their tempers were ruffled, and agreeably to the frequent result of disputes they were more than ever confirmed in their opinions; "divers were hardened, and believed not, but spake evil of that way before the multitude." Not content with rejecting his doctrine, they loaded it with opprobrious names, under the influence of passion, or with a view to excite in the minds of the other Jews, the same determined opposition to it. Finding that it would be neither expedient nor safe to continue in the synagogue, the Apostle withdrew with the disciples to the school of Tyrannus, in which he disputed daily for the instruction of those who frequented it. "And this continued for the space of two years; so that all they that dwelt in Asia heard the word of the Lord Jesus, both Jews and Greeks." Asia signifies, in this place, proconsular Asia, which was only a part of what is called Asia Minor. Concerning such universal terms as are used in this passage, we remark, that they are to be understood in a qualified sense, and express not every individual, but a great number. Many of the inhabitants of Asia heard the word during Paul's residence in Ephesus. The fame of his miracles must have spread far and wide, and have excited the public curiosity to see the extraordinary man by whom they were performed, and to hear an account of that religion which they were intended to attest. The city itself was populous, and was the resort of strangers, who flocked to it from all quarters, to worship Diana in her magnificent temple to learn the art of Magic, which was studied there with uncommon ardour, and to pursue the various designs which attract persons to the metropolis of a province.

In this seat of idolatry and magic, the gospel stood in need of the powerful support, afforded by the miracles which God enabled his servant to perform. "And God wrought special miracles by the hand of Paul: so that from his body were brought unto the sick handkerchiefs or aprons, and the diseases departed from them, and the evil spirits went out of them." No person was bound to believe the gospel, till satisfactory evidence of its truth and authority had been produced. The testimony of the apostles themselves was not sufficient to prove that they were messengers from God, because they might be misled by enthusiasm, or might have an intention to deceive, and the same character had been assumed and maintained, with the utmost confidence, by many impostors. The power of working miracles was conferred upon them, to attest their commission, and showed that God was with them, by a proof perfectly decisive, and so perspicuous, that the dull and illiterate might understand it, and feel its force. When we say, that the power of working miracles was conferred upon the Apostles, we do not mean that the laws of nature were so subjected to their will, that they could suspend or change them at their pleasure; but that a promise was made to them, that when they should give the sign by words, or actions, God himself would produce the effect. The miracles were wrought by his arm; and the province of the Apostles was to predict the event, or to announce it immediately before it took place. The Spirit who was always present with them, suggested the proper occasions for giving the sign, so that the power of God was not at their command, but merely cooperated with them to carry on the design in which they were engaged.

In the present case, there was something unusual, as Luke intimates, by saying that God wrought "special" miracles. The way in which the Apostles commonly performed such miracles as are here recorded, was, either commanding, in the name of Jesus Christ, the disease to depart, or by laying their hands upon the patient. But, now handkerchiefs and aprons, which had been applied to the body of Paul, were carried to the sick, who, upon touching them, or applying them to their own bodies, were instantly cured. Virtue proceeded from him in as wonderful a manner as it had proceeded from our Saviour himself, when a woman having touched the hem of his garment, immediately felt herself made whole. This extraordinary scene might have led the spectators to form too exalted an idea of Paul. Dispensing to all who not only approached him, but even at a distance implored, or stood in need of his assistance, the inestimable blessing of health, he seemed to be rather a God than a man; and we should not have been surprised, if the astonished heathens, supposing him to be one of their Deities, who had descended to the earth, had attempted to pay divine honours to him. But, this misconception was prevented by his explicit and uniform declaration, that he was only a minister of God; and by the performance of his miracles in the name of Jesus. On every occasion of this nature, the language of all the Apostles was the same with that of Peter and John. "Look not on us as though by our own power and holiness we had done these things. It is the power of Jesus of Nazareth which has effected them."

The working of miracles by handkerchiefs and aprons, taken from the body of Paul, has been supposed, by superstitious men, to favour their notions, with respect to the virtue of relics. By these are meant the remains of the departed saints, their garments, their bones, and their blood, which have been collected with credulous and undistinguishing avidity. They have been deposited in Churches, and preserved with religious care; pilgrimages have been undertaken to visit them, and the most solemn acts of devotion have been performed in their presence; and a power has been ascribed to them of curing the blind, the deaf, and the lame, of dispossessing demons, and in a word, of performing all the wonders, which are related of Christ and his Apostles. To this extravagance of folly, has grown up, under the fostering care of priests and monks, the veneration which the ancient Christians piously expressed for the bodies of the martyrs. Much of the religion of the Church of Rome consists in respect for relics. But, to this superstition the passage before us gives no countenance. Not to mention, that the most of those relics are supposititious, the things which are imposed upon the unsuspecting multitude as the remains of holy men, having perhaps belonged to a malefactor, a prostitute, or a heathen, it is evident that an extraordinary dispensation does not establish a precedent, which will apply to ordinary cases. All the saints and martyrs did not possess the power of performing miracles, while they were alive, and still less can they be conceived to work them, when lying in their graves. Miracles have long since ceased. The story of their continuance is believed by the ignorant alone, and is supported by a train of scandalous impositions. They are not now necessary, because the truth of Christianity has been fully demonstrated; and we are certain that God will not deviate from the established order of nature, to patronise idolatry, and encourage the most wretched superstition, which ever disgraced the understanding and corrupted the heart.

The success of Paul, in curing all diseases, whether of the body or of the mind, by the name of Jesus, suggested to some Jews, who were pretenders to preternatural powers, the idea of making an experiment of its efficacy. "Then certain of the vagabond Jews, exorcists, took upon them to call over them which had evil spirits, the name of the Lord Jesus, saying: We adjure you by Jesus whom Paul preacheth." I had occasion, when explaining the history of Simon, to make a few remarks upon magic. The object of that science of declusion and imposture, was to cultivate an intercourse with invisible beings, by whose assistance the person should be enabled to cure diseases, and perform other wonderful works. It appears, from the accounts of ancient writers, that in their incantations, the heathens made use of some of the names and titles of the true God, which they had learned from the Jews; for they believed, and some Christians adopted the notion, that there was attached to certain words, a mysterious and sovereign virtue. They were careful, at the same time, to ascertain the names of the particular demons, whose aid they were desirous to obtain; and they employed as charms, a variety of uncouth and barbarous terms.* With these they connected mystical rites, upon the exact observance of which, the success of their invocations was supposed to depend.

This pretended science, which the wiser and better part of the heathens condemned, had, at this time or perhaps earlier, gained credit among the Jews, by some of whom it was studied and practised. This may be collected from the story now under consideraation, and is fully proved by the testimony of Josephus, who relates some of the methods which they used in performing cures, and informs us, that they had books teaching the modes of exorcism and incantation, which they asserted to have been composed by Solomon.† With the name of that wise and illustrious monarch, they attempted to sanctify a profane science, which was expressly forbidden by their law; and to conceal the impure scource from which they had derived it, the superstitious and idolatrous nations around them.

The actors in the present scene, were "vagabond Jews," or persons who strolled from place to place, like the jugglers and fortune-tellers of other nations, to practise their arts, wherever they could find people sufficiently credulous. They are called exorcists, because they adjured evil spirits, or solemnly commanded them, in the name of God, to leave the bodies of the possessed, accompanying the adjuration with magical rites. Their success had hitherto been only apparent through a collusion between them and the other party, or had consisted in certain effects produced upon the imagination of the patient. But, now observing that real dispossessions were effected by the name of Jesus, and that no case was so obstinate as to resist its influence, they were tempted to make trial of its power in preference to the forms of exorcism, which they

---

* Orig. contra Cels. lib. i. 17—20.   † Antiq. Lib. viii. cap. 2.

had been accustomed to use. "We adjure you by Jesus whom Paul preacheth."

Among the Jewish exorcists, "There were seven sons of one Sceva a Jew, and chief of the priests, which did so." But these audacious imposters speedily found, that although there was a mighty efficacy in the name of Jesus, it did not proceed, as they probably imagined, from the sound of the word, but from his divine power, which he could exert or restrain, at his pleasure. He had lent it to Paul, to attest his commission, and to promote the interests of the religion which he published; but he would not lend it, to give countenance to magic. There was no charm in the name itself to drive the demon from his hold; and, accordingly, he treated this impotent attempt to dispossess him, with scorn. "Jesus I know, and Paul I know." "Yes; I know Jesus, and tremble at his power; and I know Paul to be his servant, armed with authority to expel me and my companions from the bodies of men: but who are ye? What right have ye to speak to me in the style of command?" The name of Jesus pronounced by the lips of the profane, and the sign of the cross made by the sons of superstition, are pointless weapons, which the Leviathan of hell accounts mere stubble. The impiety of those magicians was instantly punished; for the man, with the assistance of the indignant spirit, "leaped on them, and overcame them, and prevailed against them, so that they fled out of that house naked and wounded."

I shall not enlarge upon the particulars of the story, but shall content myself with remarking, that the disaster which befel those profligate Jews, served two important purposes, connected with the honour and the success of the gospel. First, it demonstrated the vanity of the magic, by proving the insufficiency of one of its boasted resources, the virtue, which certain names and words were supposed to possess. Of this there could remain no doubt, since a name, which, when pronounced by one person, never failed to expel unclean spirits, had no efficacy, when pronounced by another. It was manifest, that its virtue was not in the sound. Secondly, it afforded the clearest evidence, that the miracles of the gospel were performed by a power superior to magic; for while a demon acknowledged his submission to the one he held the other in the utmost contempt. The name of Jesus was used by those vagabond Jews solely as a magical incantation. It took away, therefore, any pretext for confounding the Christian miracles with the feats of magic, as the heathens maliciously attempted to do; and it might have convinced those who were acquainted with the circumstances of the fact, that the religion which Paul preached was divine, because it was visibly attested by the finger of God himself.

It appears, from the next verse, that the event made a strong and general impression. "And this was known to all the Jews and Greeks also dwelling at Ephesus; and fear fell on them all, and the name of the Lord Jesus was magnified." In particular, it brought magic into discredit with many who had formerly been devoted to it. "And many that believed came, and showed their deeds. Many also of them which used curious arts, brought their books together, and burned them before all men: and they counted the price of them, and found it fifty thousand pieces of silver." In Ephesus, the study of magic was prosecuted with great ardour. Ephesian incantations were proverbial; and the Ephesian letters were certain words, which were believed to have sovereign efficacy in charms and invocations. But, now many who had been deluded by that vain science "showed their deeds," acknowledging their past folly and wickedness, and vowing to renounce it for ever. They abandoned "their curious arts," their inquiries into the names and operations of invisible beings, the modes of invoking them, and the mystical rites to be practised in their service. They collected the books, containing the mysteries of magic, upon which they had expended large sums; and that they might be under no temptation to return to this enticing study, as well as to testify the abhorrence in which they held it, they publicly committed them to the flames. Their value has been differently estimated, according to the coin which is supposed to be meant by a piece of silver; but, perhaps, it amounted to several thousand pounds. It was a sacrifice to the glory of God, consumed in a fire, kindled by the hand of holy zeal. Some persons would have contented themselves with sending the books out of their houses, and would not have scrupled to dispose of them to others, who chose to prosecute the study. But, the converted Ephesians were actuated by more disinterested motives. Those books, over which they had wasted many a guilty hour, should no more minister to unhallowed curiosity, and serve to uphold the impure mysteries of paganism. While their indignation was roused against the impious art, their own loss did not engage their attention for a moment; and they had leisure to think only of the most effectual means of arresting its progress. And in an age, when books were comparatively rare, and copies were slowly multiplied, by the destruction of so many, the study of magic would be rendered less common, and the worthless science would sustain an injury, which could not be repaired without much time and expense.

The narrative is concluded with this remark: "So mightily grew the word of God, and prevailed." It made its way with irresistible force, amidst the obstacles which opposed its progress. It was an evidence of its power, that it prevailed upon so many of the Ephesians to renounce an art, which, from the eagerness of mankind in all nations, and almost in every age, to acquire it, appears to be highly gratifying to the vain curiosity of the human mind; to acknowledge before all men, that what they lately esteemed wisdom was worse than folly; and to present the treasures of their learning as a sacrifice to the honour of religion.

The power of the gospel is as great in our times, as it was in the days of the Apostle. We may not, indeed, often observe it accomplishing a change so sudden and general, in the conduct of a large society; but it continues to produce effects similar and equal, upon the hearts and manners of the individuals who believe it. If it find a man conceited of his understanding, elated by science, full of worldly wisdom, and wedded to opinions inconsistent with the doctrines of revelation, it makes him renounce them as foolishness, and, from a conviction of his ignorance of the things of God, submit with humility to the instructions of Christ. If it find a man engaged in an unlawful employment, or conducting a lawful one, without regard to the principles of honour and justice, it persuades him to forego the gains of iniquity, and to prefer poverty with a good conscience, to the wealth which is the wages of sin. If it find a man pursuing a course of unhallowed pleasures, whatever power they have acquired over his heart, and however long he has been addicted to them, he instantly abandons them in disgust, and is ever after distinguished by sobriety and purity. In short, as an eloquent writer has said, if it find a man passionate, avaricious, sensual, and cruel, it will make him meek, liberal, temperate, and merciful. "For so great is the power of divine wisdom, that it is able to expel at once folly the mother of sin."* The gospel is not like human

---

* Lactan. iii. 25.

discipline, which advances by a slow and imperceptible progress, gaining at one time, and losing at another; but it works a radical change of the heart, and accomplishes such a revolution in its principles, that the effect immediately appears in the reformation of the life. Philosophy may, with much labour, extort from the barren soil, a few dwarfish and sickly plants; but the gospel makes a rich harvest of heavenly graces and virtues spring up in the desert of the soul. It is the word of God, who speaks, and it is done.

Let us, then, by this criterion, determine whether our faith is sincere. If the gospel has humbled our pride, corrected our corrupt inclinations, reclaimed us from errors in principle and practice, and prevailed upon us, after the example of the Ephesians, to part with our favourite but unlawful pursuits, for the glory of God, it has come to us, "not in word only, but in power." But, let that man, who retains his avarice, his dishonest arts, his intemperance, his envy and malice, know, that "his faith is vain, and he is yet in his sins." The word of God "grows mightily and prevails," not when it gives rise to much discussion about religion, and an ostentatious profession, accompanied with no solid fruits of holiness in the life; but when it silently purifies the heart, and gives a new form and direction to the conduct. Those who sincerely believe, pass, like the converted Ephesians, from the service of Satan to that of Jesus Christ. Recognising him as their Lord and Saviour, they submit to his authority; and whatever loss of property and reputation they may incur by the change, they cheerfully acquiesce in it, from a sense of duty, and in the assured hope, that they shall be recompensed at the resurrection of the just.

LECTURE XXIII.

THE UPROAR IN EPHESUS.

Chap. xix. 21—41.

When the seventy disciples returned from their mission, and related to our Saviour, that the devils were subject to them through his name, he said "I beheld Satan, as lightning fall from heaven." The design of his undertaking was to overthrow the empire which the adversary of God had established over the human race, and which was upheld by ignorance and depravity. By the one, he enslaved the understandings of men, and by the other their affections. The gospel which the Apostles preached to Jews and Gentiles, dispelled the darkness of the mind, and conquered the rebellion of the heart. Communicating new and just ideas of God, their duty, and their interest, it made thousands revolt from the degrading servitude of Satan, and seek, in the service of Jesus Christ, happiness and spiritual liberty.

Every art had been employed by the God of this world, to give security and permanence to his kingdom. Amidst his deluded and wondering subjects, he appeared in the character of the true God, affecting to possess his most glorious attributes, and imitating his dispensations, with a bold and impious hand. If Jehovah had his oracles and Prophets in the land of Judea, there were not wanting among the Gentiles the arts of divination, pretenders to the knowledge of futurity, and temples in which the Gods returned answers to the inquiries of their worshippers. If the Almighty displayed his wonders before his chosen people, to confirm their faith, and to assure them of safety under the protection of his providence, the religions of heathenism were supported by fabulous prodigies, and the juggling tricks of magicians. But, the reign of imposture was come to an end. The pagan oracles were silenced by the gospel; the Prophets of idolatry were confounded; amidst the splendid train of miracles, which the Apostles were enabled to perform, the wonders of magic became objects of derision; and the magicians themselves, ashamed of an art which they perceived to be both false and impious, confessed the mighty power of the name of Jesus. This triumph of the truth was displayed in the transactions at Ephesus, which are recorded in the preceding part of the chapter.

But Satan, although defeated, was not subdued. Determined to contend for empire to the last, he employed all his resources to retain that dominion over mankind, which he had long quietly enjoyed. When his frauds were detected and exposed to public contempt, he tried what force could effect. There were still persons in Ephesus attached, from selfish motives, to his cause, by whose aid he hoped to crush the rising interests of Christianity. In the verses now to be explained, we have an account of an attempt to support the reigning system of idolatry by persecution.

Paul was " in labours more abundant ;" not indeed exceeding the measure of his duty, but rising above the proportion with which men of ordinary zeal would have been satisfied; and continuing his activity, after his uncommon exertions might have seemed to entitle him to repose. No sooner was one plan happily executed, than his mind was employed in digesting another. His unexhausted benevolence sought new channels of communication. He wished to add other trophies to those which he had already gained to the cross; to carry the light of the gospel into regions which were yet enveloped in darkness; and to diffuse it more extensively in those, where it had begun to shine. Then only should this indefatigable missionary have thought of desisting from his work, when the whole world was converted, and all the Churches were established in the faith, beyond the danger of falling. We are informed, that when " these things were ended," namely the transactions in Ephesus, related in the preceding verses, " Paul purposed in the spirit, when he had passed through Macedonia, and Achaia, to go to Jerusalem, saying, After I have been there, I must also see Rome." Of the execution of this purpose an account is given in the next chapter, from which we learn, that after the uproar, which is to be the subject of the Present Lecture, had ceased, Paul set out for Macedonia; that he afterwards spent three months in Greece; and then, as we find in another chapter, he returned to Jerusalem. His design to visit Rome was also accomplished, but in a way, which, it is probable, he did not at this time foresee; for having been apprehended in Jerusalem by his countrymen, and retained in custody for a considerable time, by the governors of the province, he was sent a prisoner to the imperial city, to be judged at the tribunal of Nero. He appears to have long entertained a desire to see Rome, and to have met with repeated obstructions. "God is my witness," he says in his Epistle to the Christians of that city, "whom I serve with my spirit, in the gospel of his Son, that without ceasing I make mention of you always in my prayers, making request (if by any means now at length I might have a prosperous journey by the will of God,) to come unto you. Now I would not have you ignorant, brethren, that oftentimes I purposed to come unto you, (but was let hitherto,) that I might have some fruit among you also, even as among other Gentiles." Such being the intention of Paul, he sent Timotheus and Erastus before him to Macedonia; but he himself remained for some time in Asia. It was during this interval, that the tumult took place in Ephesus, which probably made him perform his journey to Macedonia sooner than he had intended.

"And the same time there arose no small stir about that way;" that is, about the gospel which Paul preached, or the new religion which he was propagating. It originated in the alarm of some men at his success, which threatened to deprive them of their gain from the prevailing superstition. Demetrius, by profession a silver-smith, made silver shrines for Diana, who was worshipped in the magnificent temple of Ephesus, and employed several others, in the same lucrative trade. These shrines were small temples, formed after the pattern of the large one, and containing images of the Goddess, which the Ephesians placed in their houses as objects of private devotion, and in the confidence, that they should thus ensure her favour and protection. Amos refers to the same practice among the Israelites, which they had probably learned in Egypt, when he introduces God reproaching them for it in the following words; "But ye have borne the tabernacle of your Moloch, and Chiun your images, the star of your God, which ye made to yourselves." The temples were formed of a precious metal, and were, no doubt enriched with costly ornaments; and the people, mad upon their idols, grudged no expense to procure a treasure, which they probably valued more than all their other possessions. It is an observation worthy of attention, that false religions have commonly been more successful than the true one, in persuading men to devote their substance to sacred uses; not surely because error is, in its own nature, more efficacious than truth, but because the former accords better with the vanity and corrupt propensities of mankind. While the votaries of idolatry and superstition have cheerfully expended immense sums in erecting temples and churches, in framing and adorning images of Gods and saints, and in maintaining a pompous ritual, many of the professed disciples of Jesus are apt to complain of the trifling demands which are made upon them, for the support of the simple institutions of the gospel. A heathen would have given more in one day for the honour of Jupiter or Diana, than some persons who call themselves Christians, will give in a year for the service of their Saviour. Boasting of our superiority to others in purity of faith and worship, we are far surpassed by them in sincerity and zeal.

Although Demetrius was the first who publicly expressed his apprehensions, yet it cannot be supposed, that his brethren had been unconcerned spectators of the success of the gospel. Interest renders men quick to perceive the first symptoms, which threaten their prosperity. He addressed an audience prepared to adopt and anticipate his sentiments, when having called together the workmen of the like occupation, he said, "Sirs, ye know that by this craft we have our wealth." As they all derived profit from the established religion, they would the more readily concur in any measure for supporting it. "Moreover," he adds, " ye see and hear, that not alone at Ephesus, but also throughout all Asia, this Paul hath persuaded and turned away much people, saying, that they be no Gods which are made with hands." Such was, indeed, the doctrine of Paul, who publicly taught that there was but one God, the Creator of heaven and earth; that the Gods of the Gentiles existed only in the imagination of their worshippers, or were dead men and women, or unclean spirits; and that their images, in which they were supposed to be present, were alike unworthy of divine honours, as gold and silver, wood and stone, in the rudest and most unshapely forms. If this doctrine should prevail, as there was reason to fear, from the great number who had already embraced it, those craftsmen would starve for want of employment. The Ephesians would no longer purchase models of a temple, which they considered as profane, and images of a Goddess, whom they had learned to despise.

The opposition which the gospel encountered in the first ages proceeded not from one order of men alone, but from various classes of society. Persons of different ranks and occupations, united in resisting the progress of a religion which was, or seemed to be, hostile to their different interests and views.

Princes and magistrates were alarmed for the safety of the state, which was supposed to be closely and inseparably connected with the established religion. Religious rites were intermixed with all civil and political transactions, and the public prosperity was ascribed to the favour of the Gods. The introduction of a new religion threatened to subvert the foundation, which supported the mighty empire of Rome. Accordingly, we find, that Christianity was accused of being the cause of the wars, earthquakes, tempests, and pestilences, with which the offended Gods afflicted and desolated the provinces.*

Philosophers treated with disdain the doctrines of the gospel, which wanted the ornaments of eloquence, and were repugnant to the principles which they held, upon the subject of God and religion. They were indignant at illiterate men, who presumed to controvert their favourite opinions; and they dreaded the propagation of the new system, as fatal to their interests and their fame. Their wisdom would be derided as folly; their schools would be deserted; and they themselves would be held in contempt, as deserving no other character than that of eloquent babblers.

The priests, the augurs, and the whole train of persons, who were employed in the immediate service of the Gods, were menaced with the total loss of their honours and emoluments. They must fall with the religion of which they were the ministers. The temples would be abandoned; the sacred fire of the altars would be extinguished; gifts and sacrifices would no longer be presented; and they would be disregarded and execrated, as the supporters of a vile superstition, by which mankind had for ages been deluded.

There still remained a numerous class of persons, who contributed by their various occupations to uphold the worship of the

---

* Eusebius has preserved a rescript of Maximin, in which he imputes the late calamities of the empire to the pernicious error of the Christians, and its present prosperity to the zeal which the heathens had recently shown for the worship of the gods. The historian adds this remarkable fact, that while the messengers were publishing the edict in the provinces, there happened an excessive drought, which was followed by famine and pestilence; and that a war soon broke out between the Romans and the Armenians, as if God had expressly interposed to refute the calumnies and proud boasting of the impious emperor. Euseb. Hist. Lib. ix. 7.

Gods, and depended upon it for subsistence. To this class belonged Demetrius and his brethren, the makers of images, the venders of frankincense, and other substances, which were used in the service of the temples, and those who reared and sold animals for sacrifice. The number of such persons must have been very great, as temples and statues were multiplied in every province; and they composed a powerful body, united by a common interest to oppose the reception of Christianity, which would reduce them to beggary.

"Sirs, ye know that by this craft we have our wealth." This was an appeal to a principle, the influence of which is universally felt. About concerns of the greatest magnitude, their religion, their country, the fate of their friends, and the moral improvement of their families, men sometimes discover surprising indifference; but if their temporal interests are endangered, if they are threatened with a reverse of fortune, with the loss or diminution of the affluence and splendour in which they have been accustomed to live, we see them suddenly roused to vigilance and activity, and making every exertion to ward off the impending calamity. But, a regard to our private good, although the spring of many of the common actions of life, as well as of more splendid achievements, is a principle too low to be on every occasion avowed. Our selfishness is concealed from others under a mask of benevolence; and we even wish to hide it from ourselves. If we can contrive to mix our own interests with those of the public, to connect our honour, our emolument, or our power, with the prosperity of our country, or with the defence of religion, we can prosecute our schemes, under this disguise, with more ardour than we should have ventured to display, had they alone seemed to engage us; and we may hope to be applauded for what should have otherwise subjected us to reproach. Demetrius, therefore, artfully added, "Moreover ye see and hear, that not alone at Ephesus but almost throughout all Asia, this Paul hath persuaded and turned away much people, saying, that they be no Gods which are made with hands: so that not only this our craft is in danger to be set at nought, but also that the temple of the great Goddess Diana should be despised, and her magnificence should be destroyed, whom all Asia and the world worshippeth." "The prospect of the loss of employment would justify us in taking measures to defend ourselves; but this is an inferior consideration. Our religion is in danger; and the Divinity who protects our city, and is adored by the surrounding nations, will be abandoned and dishonoured."

On this occasion, Demetrius acted the part of a dexterous politician. He held forth a pretext well fitted to recommend his cause to the attention and favour of the public. The injury sustained by a body of artificers would hardly have roused the whole city of Ephesus, unless their interest had been associated with objects of general concern. At the same time, it is not improbable, that Demetrius was sincere in his zeal for Diana, whom he had long regarded with sentiments of religious respect; and there is no reason to doubt, that the other craftsmen felt for the honour of their tutelar Goddess, as well as for themselves, when they burst forth into the exclamation mentioned in the following verse. The chief motive was a regard to their own interest, but they might not be conscious of its predominant influence. Men are often not more successful in in imposing upon others, than they are in deceiving themselves. The operations of the human mind are exceedingly subtile and refined. Different motives are frequently so blended together, that it is impossible to separate them, and to assign to each its exact share in our actions; and sometimes the motive which exerts the greatest influence, is of all the least perceived. Many a theological polemic, when opposing heresies and errors, has imagined that he was actuated by the pure love of truth, while he was excited solely by pride of understanding. Many a person, who had persuaded himself, that in defending his principles, and the religious society to which he belonged, he had no other intention than to be faithful to Jesus Christ and his Church, has been as much governed by the spirit of party, as the most unblushing supporter of a political faction. The reproof of our Saviour to his two intemperate disciples, is applicable to not a few zealots for religion: "Ye know not what manner of spirit ye are of."

In the present case, we perceive religion serving as a cloak to cover the designs, and as an engine to forward the schemes, of self-interest. The example of Demetrius and his fellows has been diligently imitated. With what apparent zeal for the advancement of piety have establishments been upheld, under which it had long been oppressed, but which rewarded those who defended them, with honours and emoluments? With what clamorous accusations of profaneness and atheism, have they been pursued and hunted down, who attempted to purify the temple of God, by driving out of it buyers and sellers? Have we not heard the cry, "Religion is in danger," raised by men who never bestowed a serious thought upon religion, and, at the moment when they were loudest in its praises, were living in the open violation of its precepts, because they hoped by the magic of the sound, to inflame the passions of the multitude in favour of that system, to which they owed their greatness?

The union of devotion and interest gave full effect to the speech of Demetrius. It produced a phrensy of religious zeal, and the craftsmen, with one voice, exclaimed in honour of their Goddess, whose divinity Paul had dared to deny, "Great is Diana of the Ephesians." They seem to have left the house in which they were assembled, and to have rushed into the street, where they raised this cry, as a signal to the worshippers of Diana to appear in her defence. The expedient succeeded. "The whole city was filled with confusion." The cry was re-echoed from street to street, the alarm became general; the inhabitants deserted their houses; "and having caught Gaius and Aristarchus, men of Macedonia, and Paul's companions in travel, they rushed with one accord into the theatre." The theatres in Rome and in the provincial cities, were commonly large buildings, capable of containing many thousand spectators. They were principally intended to exhibit shows and games for the entertainment of the people; but sometimes public business was transacted in them, and criminals were tried, and executed, by being thrown to wild beasts. The Ephesians dragged Gaius and Aristarchus into the theatre, that they might be judged and punished as accomplices of Paul, in the insult which had been offered to Diana.

At this critical moment, Paul would have gone into the theatre to defend himself and his friends, and to embrace this opportunity of addressing the assembled city, upon the important subject of religion. But, while we must admire the courage of the Apostle, who was not dismayed by the presence of danger, and his generous ardour in willingly exposing his life for the honour of the gospel, and the salvation of souls, we may be permitted, in this instance, to call in question his prudence. How could he expect, that an infuriated multitude should listen to him? Was there not reason to apprehend, that without allowing him to open his lips, they would immediately fall upon him, and tear him in pieces? Such are the reflections which occur to us when considering his conduct; and they are confirmed by the opinion of those, who being upon the spot, were better qualified to judge. It appeared to them to be a rash and hazardous attempt. "The disciples suffered him not; and certain of the chief of Asia, which were his friends, sent unto him, desiring him that he would not adventure himself into the theatre."[*] Being convinced by their representations, he desisted from his purpose.

The next verse contains a just and lively description of a mob suddenly collected. The assembly in the theatre was a scene of absolute confusion. The greater part were ignorant of the cause which had brought them together. The noise in the streets had alarmed them, and seeing others running to the theatre, they had followed. Some cried one thing, and some another. Every man was impatient to speak; every man bawled as loudly as he could; and amidst the universal uproar, no man could be heard.

During this tumult, an attempt was made on the part of the Jews to address the assembly, in order to turn away the torrent of popular indignation from themselves, to Paul and his companions. " And they drew Alexander out of the multitude, the Jews putting him forward. And Alexander beckoned with the hand, and would have made his defence unto the people." Luke, indeed, does not affirm, that this was their design; but it is a construction, which may with some probability, be put upon his words. Alexander was a Jew, he was put forward by the Jews, and he would have made his defence to the people. It is implied in this account, that the Jews had been accused, or at least were conscious that they might be accused, of the same crime, with which Paul was charged. Their doctrine with respect to the theological creed of the heathens, exactly agreed with that of the Christians. They pronounced it to be false and idolatrous; and they had reason, therefore, to fear, that, as they were equally guilty in the eyes of the Ephesians, they should be involved in the same condemnation. From this apprehension proceeded the eagerness which they showed to make their defence, by one of their number. There is no doubt, that, if he had been permitted to speak, he would have endeavoured to save himself and his brethren by some artful explanations and distinctions, and to leave the Christians alone exposed to the rage of the multitude.

---

[*] The chief men of Asia, or the Asiarchs, were officers of religion, or priests, who were appointed to preside over the games, publicly celebrated in honour of the gods. Antonii Van Dale Dissertationes. iii. 3.

Whatever was the intention of Alexander, the assembly in the theatre was too much agitated by the impetuosity of passion, to permit him to address them. He was known to be a Jew, and consequently an enemy to the religion which they had come together to support; and, in a transport of zeal, "they all with one voice, about the space of two hours, cried out, Great is Diana of the Ephesians." By this tumultuous outcry they intended to silence and confound the impious blasphemers of their Goddess. Perhaps, there never was exhibited a more ludicrous scene than the inhabitants of a whole city, vociferating for two hours in succession, the praises of the divinity whom they adored, while for this ebulition of religious fervour no reason could be given, but the attempt of a person of a different persuasion to speak to them. We see to what a height the passions of a multitude may be raised by a trivial incident; with what rapidity the contagion of passion spreads in a crowd; how feeble a barrier truth, justice, and reason oppose to their proceedings; and how ill qualified an assemblage of people without education, without experience, without character, and without responsibility, is, to decide upon questions of politics or religion. The sentences of a mob are passed, as in the present case, by acclamation. The enthusiastic cry, "Great is Diana of the Ephesians," decided the controversy between the living God, and the dead idols of the Gentiles.

The uproar was quelled by the town-clerk, or secretary of the city, a person of considerable authority, in the Asiatic cities, who having obtained a hearing, delivered the speech recorded in the subsequent verses, of which I shall briefly illustrate the several parts.* He begins by expostulating with the people upon the folly of their vehement exclamation in honour of Diana. "Ye men of Ephesus, what man is there that knoweth not, how that the city of the Ephesians is a worshipper of the great Goddess Diana, and of the image which fell down from Jupiter?" They were wasting their time and strength in proclaiming what every person knew, and no man was disposed to deny. No doubt could be entertained of the veneration in which Diana was held by the Ephesians, who were the guardians of her celebrated temple, which was one of the wonders of the world.† He refers to a circumstance which un-

---

* Antonii Van Dale Dissertationes. V. 3.

† The Greek word, translated worshipper, signifies the keeper of a temple; and this title was claimed by other cities as well as Ephesus.

doubtedly contributed to heighten their devotion; the universal belief that the statue of Diana was not the work of any human artist, but was formed by the hand of Jupiter himself, and bestowed as an invaluable gift upon their city. This tale which had been contrived by the priests, to draw numerous worshippers to the temple, was believed by the unthinking superstitious people. An image of celestial origin must have been supposed to possess peculiar sanctity and virtue.

"Seeing then that these things cannot be spoken against, ye ought to be quiet, and to do nothing rashly. For ye have brought hither these men, which are neither robbers of Churches, nor yet blasphemers of your Goddess." The truth of his first assertion was incontrovertible, namely, that Paul and his companions were not sacrilegious persons or robbers of temples; for so the word should have been translated, because Churches signify, in our language, houses in which Christian worship is performed. There were no Churches in Ephesus, nor, perhaps, at that time, in any part of the world. They had not stolen the sacred treasures from any of the temples. If, by affirming that they were not blasphemers of the Goddess, the town-clerk meant only, that they had not indulged themselves in the use of intemperate and scurrilous language against her, this assertion is equally true as the other. Language offending against propriety, and dictated by passion, did not proceed from the lips of the meek Apostles of Christ. Yet, Paul had undoubtedly maintained, that Diana was a pretended Goddess, and that her image was entitled to no religious veneration; and in the opinion of the Ephesians this was blasphemy. It must, therefore, be acknowledged, that the speaker, wishing by any means to soothe and quiet the minds of the people, did not scrupulously adhere to the truth, but gave such a representation as was best calculated to accomplish his purpose.

Of the real cause of this popular commotion, he seems to have been apprized, and to have considered it as originating in a personal quarrel of Demetrius and the workmen with Paul. "If Demetrius and the craftsmen which are with him, have a matter against any man, the law is open, and there are deputies; let them implead one another." Courts of law were appointed to take cognizance of private causes, before which the parties concerned might bring forward their accusations and defences; but these were not subjects of sufficient importance to engage the attention of the citizens at large.

If Paul or any other person was guilty of a public offence, he should be called to account before an assembly convened by lawful authority, and not in an irregular and riotous manner. "But if ye inquire any thing concerning other matters, it shall be determined in a lawful assembly." His last argument he addressed to their fears, reminding them that they were in danger of being punished for their present disorderly procedure; and the penalty might extend not only to the individuals who had caused the insurrection, but to the whole city, which would be subjected to a fine, or deprived of its privileges. The jealousy of the Roman government, which held the sovereignty of the Asiatic provinces by the right of conquest, was ready to repress, with vigour and severity, every symptom of disaffection, and every movement tending to disturb that settled order, which it is the interest of despotism to preserve. "For we are in danger to be called in question for this day's uproar, there being no cause whereby we may give an account of this concourse."

By this speech, which was conducted with much prudence and address, the fury of the people was calmed, and they were persuaded to return peaceably to their homes. Thus God delivered Paul and his companions, from the perilous circumstances in which they were placed. Means and instruments are never wanting, by which he may preserve his faithful servants in the discharge of their duty, without any miraculous interposition. There is no reason to suppose, that the town-clerk of Ephesus was a friend to Christianity. But, he was alarmed, as every wise man will be, at the probable consequence of a popular tumult; he wished no innocent person to suffer, not even the guilty to be condemned without a trial, and to fall victims to the fury of a mob; and while he interposed solely from motives of justice and humanity, and a regard to the public peace, Providence made use of him for the protection of Paul, who had yet many important services to perform.

The passage which has been illustrated, suggests the following reflections.

First, The opposition which has been made in past ages to the gospel, has proceeded from the depraved passions of men, their avarice, their ambition, and their love of earthly pleasures. Its adversaries have not been the sincere friends of truth and virtue, but the slaves of prejudice, and the votaries of vice. The uproar in Ephesus was excited by some mercenary artificers, who worshipped no God with so much ardour as the God of riches. Such opposition, as I have remarked in a former Lecture, reflects honour upon Christianity. Had it been a human contrivance, it would have been adapted, like other impostures, to the corrupt inclinations of mankind. It would have gratified the predominant propensities of the heart; and would have made it the interest of the licentious and the worldly to embrace it. Rejected and calumniated as it has been, it appears to be a pure emanation from that holy Being, whom sinners secretly dislike, although they may profess to love and venerate him. The enemies of our religion, in order to justify their opposition, have advanced many false accusations against it. Malignity has not been sparing of its usual arts, falsehood and misrepresentation. It cannot be justly charged with disturbing the peace of society, which it secures more effectually than the wisest laws, and the most vigilant administration, by impressing upon the heart the purest lessons of morality. It cannot be justly charged with impairing domestic happiness, since, wherever it is sincerely believed, it establishes the empire of love. It cannot be justly charged with impeding the business and the duties of life; for it inculcates active benevolence, and teaches us to acquit ourselves with fidelity in every relation. What, then, is the evil which it has done? It has abolished certain institutions, which originated in the cruelty and licentiousness of mankind; it has overthrown establishments, under which imposture flourished; it has restrained vices, which were the sources of private gratification, and public misery.

Secondly, The sacred name of religion has been prostituted to serve the most infamous purposes. It was the pretext, under which Demetrius and his accomplices concealed their design, to secure the gain which they derived from the folly and delusion of their countrymen. In the name of religion, priests and monks have amassed enormous wealth, and guarded against intrusion those dark retreats, in which they wallowed in the grossest sensuality. In the name of religion, conquerors have desolated the earth, and made havock of the human race to gratify their avarice and ambition. In the name of religion, persecutors have committed cruelties, at which every feeling of our nature revolts. Scaffolds have streamed with blood; fires have blazed with victims; the dwellings of the innocent have been plundered and razed to the ground; and the houseless sufferers have been driven into foreign lands, by demons in human shape, pretending to be actuated by zeal for the glory of God. In the name of religion, Churches have corrupted the doctrines and institutions of the gospel; repealed the ordinances of heaven; imposed their own unhallowed commands upon the consciences of their subjects; and fulminated excommunications against the pious and sincere. The language of all such persons has been, even at the time when they were perpetrating the greatest crimes, " Come, see our zeal for the Lord."

Thirdly, The concurrence of a multitude in support of a cause, is no proof of its justice. Truth is not to be decided by numbers. In the passage which has been explained, we see the whole city of Ephesus defending the honour of their Goddess Diana against the claims of the living God, to be the sole object of their adoration. But, this is not a solitary instance. In the old world, Noah alone was found faithful, while the rest of mankind had corrupted their ways. In the wilderness, all the Israelites rebelled except Caleb and Joshua. When our Saviour appeared upon earth, how few of the Jews acknowledged him to be the Messiah? And in the dark ages, did not "all the world wonder after the beast?" The maxim, that the voice of the people is the voice of God, is, for the most part, evidently false, and, in no case, can be admitted without many limitations. It is, indeed, universally true, that the resolutions and proceedings of the multitude are the will of Providence, which permits and overrules them for its own wise and holy ends, or that they are consistent with the divine decrees, and are the means of executing them: but in this view, the maxim is vague, and of no value, because it implies nothing more than what may be affirmed of the counsels and operations of devils. What, in most cases, is the voice of the people but the voice of thoughtlessness, prejudice, and passion? What is it, in fact, but the voice of a few artful men, who make use of the people as the blind instruments of accomplishing their private designs? They speak as they are directed and act as they are impelled.

Lastly, God reigns, and carries on the designs of his government, amidst the commotions of the world. He rules not only over the unconscious elements, the lightning, the wind, and the rain, but likewise over the passions of men. When these passions are most headstrong and impetuous, he controls their fury, directs their course, and suffers them not to proceed beyond the limits which he has prescribed to them. In the uproar at Ephesus, he preserved the life of Paul and his companions, first by the confusion of the people, and then by the seasonable interference of a person of prudence and authority, who was chiefly influenced by a regard to the peace of the city. Let us not be dismayed, although the pillars of the earth should be shaken, and all things should seem to be out of course. The interests of truth and righteousness are safe, under the protecting care of their Almighty Patron. "The floods have lifted up, O Lord, the floods have lifted up their voice, the floods lift up their waves. The Lord on high is mightier than the noise of many waters, yea, than the mighty waves of the sea."

LECTURE XXIV.

THE LAST INTERVIEW OF PAUL WITH THE ELDERS OF EPHESUS.

CHAP. xx. 17—38.

When Paul had left Ephesus, in consequence of a popular tumult, he went to Macedonia and Greece. On his return from those countries, he landed at Troas, where he spent some days with the disciples, and celebrated the Lord's supper on the first day of the week. In his voyage from Troas, he passed by Ephesus because he wished to arrive at Jerusalem before the feast of Pentecost and would not expose himself to the importunities of his friends, who might solicit him to stay. But, being now to leave this part of Asia for ever, he would not depart, till he had delivered to the pastors and rulers of the Church, his solemn counsels and exhortations. From Miletus, therefore, he sent to Ephesus, and called the elders of the Church.

In the style of the New Testament, an elder does not signify a person advanced in years, but one invested with authority. The title is given to the rulers of the Jews, who are frequently called the elders of the people, and to certain office-bearers in the Christian Church, of whom two classes are pointed out by Paul in one of his Epistles, elders who only rule or govern, and elders who both rule, and labour in word and doctrine. Of the latter description, I apprehend, were the elders of Ephesus, for they are exhorted "to feed" the Church; a duty of the pastoral office, which consists in preaching the gospel for the edification and comfort of the people. "I will give you pastors according to mine heart, which shall feed you with knowledge and understanding." It deserves notice, that the same persons, who here receive the appellation of elders, are called, in the twenty-eighth verse, overseers or inspectors. The word, in the original language, is the same which is translated in other parts of the New Testament, bishops; and it is used in ecclesiastical writings, to characterize an office-bearer of a higher order than elders or presbyters, who exercised authority over the clergy of a whole province or diocese. It is evident, however, that this is a new sense affixed to the term. Although the episcopal form of government is of great antiquity, and traces of it may be perceived not long after the death of the Apostles; yet the distinction between bishops and presbyters, upon which it is founded, did not exist in the primitive times. In the Apostolical style, all the elders of Ephesus were bishops; and according to the genuine Apostolical constitution, there might be several bishops in the same Church.

Paul begins his address to the elders of Ephesus, by reminding them of his manner of life, during the course of his ministry among them. "Ye know from the first day that I came into Asia, after what manner I have been with you at all seasons, serving the Lord with all humility of mind, and with many tears, and temptations which befel me, by the lying in wait of the Jews." Humility was a virtue, by which the Apostle was eminently distinguished. Elevated to the highest rank in the Christian Church, more learned than any of his brethren, and possessed of great natural talents, and of miraculous powers, he was not elated with an idea of his superiority, nor haughty and overbearing in his intercourse with others.

The pious reflection which he introduces in one of his Epistles, was always present to his mind, "By the grace of God I am what I am." He did not dare to be proud of qualifications and privileges which he had not merited, but divine goodness had freely bestowed upon him. His ambition led him, not to assume a lordly dominion over the heritage of God, but to abound in labours for the honour and advancement of the gospel. He treated the disciples as his equals, mingled familiarly with them, meekly instructed the ignorant, and condescended to the infirmities of the weak. "We preach not ourselves, but Christ Jesus the Lord; and ourselves your servants for Jesus sake." His tears were expressive of his tender concern, for the souls of men, of the compassion with which he regarded those who were perishing in their sins, as well as of his sympathy with the disciples, in their common afflictions, and in their sufferings for religion. He was not a man of a stern unfeeling temper; but in him a tender heart was conjoined with a vigorous understanding.

He did not preach the gospel with the indifference of a philosopher settling some abstract question of science, but with all those affections, which its important design and interesting doctrines were calculated to excite. Susceptible of the emotions of love and pity he was not ashamed to melt into tears, at the folly and perverseness of the ungodly. "Many walk, of whom I have told you often, and now tell you even weeping, that they are the enemies of the cross of Christ." Yet the humility and affection, with which he discharged the duties of his office, did not exempt him from persecution. The Jews, the implacable and unwearied enemies of Christianity, were animated with peculiar rancour against Paul, who had once been zealous for the law, but now discovered equal zeal in defence of the gospel. They not only opposed him by their objections and blasphemies, in Ephesus, as they had done in other places; but they seem to have formed plots against his life, to which he refers, when he speaks of "the temptations which befel him by the lying in wait of the Jews." His faith, patience, and courage were tried, or put to the test by the perilous circumstances in which he was placed. But, although those trials were distressful, yet in the end, they redounded to his honour; for he was never induced by a regard to personal safety to shrink from his duty.

Of his constancy and fidelity he has given an account, in the verses which are next to be considered. "And how I kept back nothing that was profitable unto you, but have showed you, and have taught you publicly, and from house to house, testifying both to the Jews, and also to the Greeks, repentance toward God, and faith toward our Lord Jesus Christ." In this summary of Christianity, repentance is of the same import with conversion, and signifies that change of views, disposition, and principles, which takes place when the soul is regenerated, and terminates in the sincere dedication of the heart and life to the service of God. It is this repentance, and not transient remorse for sin, or partial and temporary reformation, which the gospel proposes to accomplish. It calls upon the prodigal son to return to his offended but merciful Father; it teaches him who has strayed in pursuit of the low and polluted pleasures of the world, to elevate his desires to the pure joys of religion. This design it effects by means of faith in Jesus Christ, whom it exhibits as the Mediator, whose blood has reconciled God and man, and opened a friendly intercourse between them. The love of God displayed in the dispensation of grace, melts the heart into genuine penitence; the merit of the Saviour raises it from a state of despondency, and inspires a humble yet confident hope of mercy; and the sinner thus attracted and encouraged, devotes himself to God, with a fixed purpose never again to forsake him. Repentance towards God, or conversion is the end; faith in Jesus Christ is the mean. "I am the way and the truth, and the life: no man cometh unto the Father but by me." Such was the doctrine of Paul, who testified both to the Jews and to the Greeks, that our restoration to the divine favour, and the sanctification of our souls, upon which genuine practical religion is founded, are attainable only by Christ, whom the gospel exhibits as the hope of guilty men.

The instructions of Paul were not confined to a few favourite topics, but comprehended a complete system of necessary truths. "I kept back nothing that was profitable unto you." Those who are influenced by selfish considerations are in constant danger of forsaking the path of rectitude. Instead of preaching those doctrines which would be profitable to others, they are tempted to preach such only as are profitable to themselves. The Apostle was a man of a different spirit. To the suggestions of worldly prudence he paid no attention; his counsellor was conscience; and the source of his actions was a benevolent heart, which sought the salvation of others with an ardour little inferior to that with which it laboured for its own. Contenting himself with the consciousness of upright intention, and the approbation of his Master in heaven, he did not hesitate to bring forward, in the proper season, whatever would contribute to the instruction and establishment of those to whom he ministered. If his doctrine should ultimately be productive of salutary effects, he was satisfied, although, in some instances, it should awaken temporary displeasure. In religion, as in medicine, things are often wholesome which are not agreeable to the taste; and the physician of the soul may occasionally expect, like the physician of the body, to incur the censures of the patient. But, he who is bound by his office, as well as prompted by his feelings, to do good to others, must be superior to every consideration but that of his duty. He must even undertake the ungracious task of endeavouring to serve them in opposition to their wishes, and at the risk of offending them in the mean time; trusting to their wiser thoughts and subsequent experience for the justification of his conduct, or calmly waiting the sentence of God, who, in recompensing his servants, will regard their intention, and not their success.

The diligence of the Apostle was not confined to his public ministrations. He taught the Ephesians "from house to house;" and, we may presume, pursued the same plan in other Churches. In his private intercourse with the disciples, he inculcated the doctrines and duties which he had delivered in their religious assemblies. In their own houses, he could descend to a more detailed exposition, and a more personal application of the truth, than the nature of his public discourses would admit. He could inquire into their spiritual state, their temptations, their perplexities, and their sorrows, and tender such counsels, and reproofs, and encouragements, as the case of individuals demanded. Like a good shepherd, Paul looked well to the state of his flock.

He proceeds to inform the elders of Ephesus of the object of his present voyage. "And now behold, I go bound in the Spirit unto Jerusalem." The expression "bound in the Spirit," has been considered as importing his earnest desire, or his fixed purpose, to visit that city, a purpose from which no ordinary occurrence would divert him. But, it may be understood to signify a strong impulse upon his mind from the Holy Ghost, which will appear the more probable sense, if we reflect, that the Apostles, in choosing places for exercising their ministry, were, in several instances recorded in this book, directed by the Spirit of God. And, when we consider the important consequences of this journey, we shall the more readily believe, that it was undertaken by particular command.

Of the things which should happen to him in Jerusalem, he had received no information. He did not, however, flatter himself with the hope of a favourable reception from his countrymen; but was prepared to expect persecution, in consequence of a general intimation by the Spirit. "Not knowing the things that shall befall me there; save that the Holy Ghost witnesseth in every city, saying, that bonds and afflictions abide me." When Jesus Christ commanded his Apostles to go and preach the gospel to the world, he sent them upon a mission full of difficulty and danger. His religion, although it breathed the spirit of love and peace, kindled war wherever it came. It found an enemy in every man, who was enslaved by his passions, and was unwilling to renounce the pleasures of sin. Peaceable as was the demeanour of his ministers, and benevolent as were their intentions, they were treated as the foes of the human race; and a conspiracy of Jews and Gentiles was formed for their destruction. Of the hardships which they should sustain, and the perils which they should encounter, in the discharge of their duty, the eleven were forewarned by our Saviour himself, and Paul, by a particular revelation. Unlike artful and designing men, who entice others to concur with them, by showing the advantages of the enterprize, while they carefully conceal its difficulties and hazards, our Lord gave them a distinct and full view of the nature of his service, that they might have no cause afterwards to complain of having been deceived, and that no man might become his disciple, but from deliberate choice. It is a proof of the sincerity of the Apostles, and of their firm conviction of the truth of Christianity, that they embraced it with a perfect knowledge of the consequences. We never hear a single word from them, which might lead us to suspect, that they had repented of their conduct; we do not observe one of them discovering an inclination to abandon his post. "None of these things move me, neither count I my life dear unto myself, so that I might finish my course with joy, and the ministry which I have received of the Lord Jesus, to testify the gospel of the grace of God."

This is not the language of one of those lying philosophers, who pretended that pain is not an evil, and affected to smile amidst exquisite tortures. Paul felt as a man, and never attempted to disguise his feelings. But, the afflictions which awaited him in every city, did not so move him as to turn him aside from his purpose. They did not intimidate him, nor cool the ardour of his zeal, nor prevent him from going to any place, to which Providence called him. Although he understood, that new sufferings were reserved for him in Jerusalem, he was resolved to prosecute his journey in obedience to the command of the Spirit. Even life itself he was willing to offer up as a sacrifice to the glory of his Saviour. "All that a man hath," it has been said, "will he give for his life;" but the assertion is not universally true. A coward, a person void of principle and honour, a man of this world, whose views rise no higher than himself, and whose hopes are confined within the narrow boundaries of time, may part with every thing as the price of deliverance from death. But, a Christian would not injure his conscience to preserve his life; he would not save it at the expense of renouncing the service of Christ, or of neglecting the least of his commandments. To a good man, truth, duty, and the approbation of his own mind, will appear incomparably more valuable than a long series of years, spent in the sunshine of prosperity. "I know," said Paul, "the value of life as well as any other man; and I am not insensible to the various blessings with which it is sweetened. But, there is one thing which I prefer to it, the glory of my Redeemer, in whose service I am engaged. My first object is to run my race well, and to finish my course. This is my highest aim; and I shall rejoice, if I can accomplish it, by expiring in the flames, or upon the scaffold." Behold, my brethren, a Christian hero!

The Apostle now proceeds to the great design of his speech; and that the elders of Ephesus, and all those who were present, might give the more serious attention to it, he declares that he is now addressing them for the last time. "And now behold, I know, that ye all, among whom I have gone preaching the kingdom of God, shall see my face no more." That these prophetic words were verified by the event, there is no reason to doubt. Upon his arrival at Jerusalem, as we shall afterwards see, he was apprehended by the Jews, and was sent to Rome, by the governor of the province, to appear before the tribunal of Nero; but, although he regained his liberty, and afterwards spent some time in preaching the gospel, it should seem, that he never returned to Ephesus or Miletus.

At the moment of final separation, the Apostle makes the following solemn appeal to his hearers. "Therefore I take you to record this day, that I am pure from the blood of all men." The language is metaphorical, for Paul is not asserting his innocence in respect of murder, but of the perdition of souls. As the shedding of blood signifies, in the style of the Scriptures, the taking away of the life of another by injustice or violence, the same phrase is used to express the guilt of destroying the souls of our brethren. In this sense, he was free from blood. Individuals had, perhaps, perished in sin under his ministry, but their ruin was entirely owing to themselves. No man could charge him with negligence and unfaithfulness. That minister alone can adopt the same language, who is not accused by his conscience of having omitted any thing, which he might have done for the salvation of his people; who has not lulled them into security by his doctrine or his example, nor flattered them in sin, nor withheld necessary counsels and admonitions, how unwelcome soever they were likely to prove, nor ceased to urge and beseech them to mind "the things which belonged to their peace." "When I say unto the wicked, Thou shalt surely die; and thou givest him not warning, nor speakest to warn the wicked from his wicked way to save his life; the same wicked man shall die in his iniquity; but his blood will I require at thine hand."

But, Paul had warned his hearers, for "he had not shunned to declare unto them all the counsel of God;" and for the truth of this assertion, he boldly appealed to those who had been the objects of his ministry, and the constant witnesses of his conduct. "All the counsels of God," is equivalent to the whole system of revealed truth. The Apostle was not one of those preachers, whose discourses run the perpetual round of a few subjects, which exhaust their poor stock of knowledge, or are selected, because they are easily discussed, and are the best fitted to gain popular applause. As his mind was capable of taking a comprehensive view of the various doctrines and duties of Christianity, so he exhibited them in their order and connexion, carefully adapting his instructions to the diversified characters and circumstances of the members of the Church, and leading them on to perfection. "This scribe who was instructed unto the kingdom of heaven, was like unto a man that is an householder, which bringeth forth out of his treasure things new and old." He was a wise as well as a faithful preacher; and as he never obtruded subjects unseasonably upon the Church, so he did not conceal any truth which he was called to publish, how contrary soever it might be to the ideas and inclinations of those to whom he ministered. What painful study, what profound meditation, what extensive knowledge of the Scriptures, and of other subjects which throw light upon them, what intimate acquaintance with the human heart, and experience of the ways of men, are necessary to enable a minister of the gospel to tread in the footsteps of Paul! "Who is sufficient for these things?" is a reflection which will often occur to the preacher, who has been most diligent and successful in his preparations. What, then, shall we think of those presumptuous intruders into the sacred office, who are not qualified to explain, in a satisfactory manner, a single doctrine of religion?

The Church of Ephesus was no longer to enjoy the instructions and pastoral care of so able and faithful a minister of Christ. On the eve of his departure, therefore, he exhorts the elders "to take heed unto themselves, and to all the flock, over which the Holy Ghost had made them overseers, to feed the Church of God, which he hath purchased with his own blood." They are required first "to take heed to themselves," that they might not be diverted from their duty by the cares and amusements of life, nor through indolence and remissness let slip opportunities of doing good; that they might always perform their functions from pure motives, with a proper sense of their importance, and an ardent desire to accomplish their design; and that their conduct might uniformly serve to illustrate and enforce the doctrines which they taught. The duties of the ministerial office are so various and weighty, the temptations are so great, and the consequences of error and negligence are so fatal, that incessant vigilance is indispensably necessary. It surely concerns those who are the guides of others in religion, to be themselves possessed of a lively faith of the gospel, and to cherish in their own hearts the devotional sentiments which they are daily recommending. This attention to themselves, which Paul enjoined upon the elders of Ephesus, was preparatory to the due care of the Church; for he immediately adds, "Take heed to all the flock." The general injunction is limited to the duty of "feeding" it, by the preaching of the word, and the dispensation of the other ordinances of the gospel, which are the means of communicating spiritual nourishment to the soul. The design of the ministry is "to perfect the saints, and to edify the body of Christ;" to impart instruction and consolation to believers, to assist their progress in faith and piety, and, by this holy discipline, to train them for eternal life. The care which is requisite for these important purposes, must be extended to all the flock, or to all the individuals of which it is composed. Respect of persons is condemned in those who are invested with a public character, and it is peculiarly offensive and incongruous in the Church, because every member of it stands precisely in the same relation to the pastor, and the souls of all are equally precious. If any distinction is made, it should be in favour of those who are the most apt to be overlooked, the humble, the diffident, the weak, and the disconsolate. Jesus Christ has given an example of condescension and tender sympathy to his servants. "He shall feed his flock like a shepherd: he shall gather the lambs with his arm, and carry them in his bosom, and shall gently lead them that are with young."

In this part of his address, Paul introduces several considerations, admirably calculated to excite the elders of Ephesus, and others upon whom the same office has been conferred, to exercise a watchful care over the Church. It is the "Church of God," that is, of Jesus Christ, who is "God over all blessed for ever," as we learn from the last part of the verse, where God is said "to have purchased it with his own blood." It is a society composed of persons intimately related to him, as members of his body; and he claims a greater interest in it than in any other association. God redeemed the Israelites from the bondage of Egypt by his mighty power; but Jesus Christ has redeemed the Church by laying down his life for it. As it is manifest that the Church, purchased with this invaluable price, is unspeakably dear to him, it is a high honour to any man to be entrusted with a charge so precious. With what unremitting activity should he exert himself for its welfare! With what solicitude should he guard it against injury! Over that part of this spiritual society which resided in Ephesus, the Holy Ghost had made the elders whom Paul was now addressing, "overseers,," or bishops. If we suppose him to refer to an extraordinary appointment of those men to their office, by a suggestion or revelation of the Spirit, who said, on another occasion, "Separate me Barnabas and Saul, for the work whereunto I have called them;" their vocation to the ministry was express, and the obligation to perform its duties must have been strongly felt. But, every man, who is duly qualified for the sacred function, and has been regularly set apart to it, may be justly considered as made a bishop by the Holy Ghost; and to consider himself in this light, will be a powerful excitement to unwearied diligence. Let him remember, that there are no sinecures in the Christian Church, and that the names of office are not empty titles of honour. A pastor should feed the flock; an overseer is bound to inspect, with a vigilant eye, the affairs committed to his trust.

Besides these considerations, which are of the same force in every age, there was a particular reason which induced Paul, to enjoin upon the elders of Ephesus strict attention to their charge. He foresaw the approach of perilous times. "For I know this, that after my departing shall grievous wolves enter in among you, not sparing the flock." There is no reference in these words, as some have supposed, to the persecution of Nero, which commenced some years after; but they are an evident prediction of the rise of heresies, by which the Church was very early infested. In the book of Revelation, we read of the sect of the Nicolaitans, whose licentious tenets Jesus Christ abhorred.

Cerinthus, who vented many wild and blasphemous opinions, is said to have been contemporary with the Apostles, or at least with John, who survived his brethren; and when we look into the Epistles of Paul, particularly his Epistle to the Colossians, we observe several allusions to the doctrines which were afterwards propagated by the Gnostics, of all heretics the most impious and absurd. "Also of yourselves shall men arise, speaking perverse things." It has been supposed, that he had particularly in his eye Hymeneus and Philetus, who affirmed that the resurrection was already past, and some other false teachers, who are mentioned in the Epistles to Timothy, which were sent to him, while he was residing in Ephesus. The Apostle calls those heretics "grievous wolves," referring to his former description of the Church under the image of a flock; and it is with manifest propriety that such men are compared to those ravenous animals, because their doctrine is of a pernicious nature, and makes havock of the souls of men. The harmlessness of error is a modern discovery. But, according to our Saviour's representation, they are often "wolves in sheep's clothing," concealing their real character and intentions from the simple and unwary, under the garb of modesty, candour, and piety. Yet, to the attentive and intelligent, they betray themselves by their doctrine, for they speak "perverse things." However specious it may seem, and with whatever arguments drawn from Scripture and reason it may be apparently confirmed, it is a perversion of the oracles of God. It is supported by detached expressions of Scripture, interpreted without regard to the connexion, and to other passages in which the same subject is treated, and by such wresting of the words of inspiration from their obvious sense, as, if attempted upon any other writing, would subject the commentator to the charge of stupidity or dishonesty. By such methods, the divinity and atonement of Jesus Christ, and the personality and operations of the Holy Ghost have been opposed. Finally, it is stated to be the design of the false teachers, "to draw away disciples after them." We know, from the history of the early ages, with how much success their exertions were crowned. The spirit of proselytism is common to all parties; but it has existed, in peculiar vigour, among the teachers of error. The Pharisees "compassed sea and land" to make one proselyte. The missonaries of Rome have travelled into the most distant regions of the earth, to persuade the natives to acknowledge the Pope, and to worship saints, instead of the Gods of their fathers. In ancient and modern times, heretics have signalized themselves by their activity. The solitary enjoyment of their discoveries is not a sufficient reward. Heresy, which is the offspring of pride of understanding, fondness for novelty, and a desire for distinction, courts the attention of the public, and the applause of partisans. Perhaps, in some instances, the mind still hesitating between its old and its new opinions, seeks the decision of its doubts in the suffrages of others. Whatever be the cause which stimulates the zeal of the heretic, scarcely any man whose brain has hatched a new conceit, however silly or absurd, can be content, unless he see a crowd as foolish and giddy as himself, following in his train.

In the prospect of the perils to which the Church should be exposed, the Apostle exhorts the elders to watch. It was not a time for the shepherds to sleep, when wolves were ready to break into the fold. It would not, indeed, be possible, by the utmost care, to prevent the Church from being, in some degree, injured by the doctrines of false teachers; but their mischievous tendency might be, in a great measure, counteracted by timely and vigorous resistance. Paul proposes his own conduct as an example to the pastors of Ephesus, and reminds them of his admonitions and his tears, to excite them to the same fidelity, and the same affectionate concern for the souls of men. "Therefore watch, and remember that by the space of three years, I ceased not to warn every one night and day with tears."

Finally, "he commends them to God, and to the word of his grace, which was able to build them up, and to give them an inheritance among all them that are sanctified." By "the word of his grace," some are of opinion, that Jesus Christ is meant, who is the "Word of God," and may be called the word of his grace, because by him divine grace was revealed to the world. "Grace and truth came by Jesus Christ." And to whom is it so fit, that Christians, whether ministers or people, should be commended, as to him who died for their salvation, and intercedes in heaven, that their faith may not fail? Others think, that "the word of his grace" is the gospel, which in the twenty-fourth verse of this chapter, is called "the gospel of the grace of God;" and it must be acknowledged, that this is the most obvious and natural meaning. There is, indeed, something unusual in commending Christians to God and to the gospel: but, with respect to the latter, nothing more can be understood than a reference to it, or a direction attentively to consider it, as containing the promises, which are the objects of their faith, and the sources of their consolation, and as furnishing the most powerful motives to steadfastness in their profession, and the performance of personal and official duties. It is certain, that the properties which are here ascribed to "the word of grace," do belong to the gospel, which is the instrument of building up the people of God in faith, sanctifying them, and "making them meet to be partakers of the inheritance of the saints in light." The best preparation for an approaching trial, is a serious consideration and firm belief of the truth; for thus Christians are furnished with the evidence of experience, by which the sophistry and allurements of error will be resisted and overcome. He who perceives the excellence of the gospel, and feels its influence in tranquillizing his conscience, and comforting his heart, is in little danger from those who lie in wait to deceive. It would be a hopeless undertaking, to persuade the man who is rejoicing in the light, that darkness is preferable.

The diligence of Paul in ministering to the Church did not proceed from a selfish or mercenary principle. He was entitled, indeed, in justice and reason, to a recompense from those who enjoyed the benefit of his labours; but, in many instances, he chose rather to support himself by his own industry. Let it not be said, that as the first Christians were so poor, that they could not reward their teachers, the generosity of Paul was the effect of necessity. The representation is not agreeable to truth. Some of them had possessions of houses and lands; and the zeal of them all was so fervent, that, like the Galatians, "they would, if it had been possible, have plucked out their own eyes, and have given them to him." But, the Apostle, who was desirous to recommend the gospel by every lawful expedient, willingly declined the exercise of his right, when his self-denial would procure a favourable reception to his doctrine. "What is my reward then? Verily, that when I preach the gospel, I may make the gospel of Christ without charge, that I abuse not my power in the gospel. For though I be free from all men, yet have I made myself servant unto all, that I might gain the more." In this disinterested manner he had acted in Ephesus; and he could say, in the presence of the elders of that Church, "I have coveted no man's silver, or gold, or apparel. Yea, you yourselves know, that these hands have ministered unto my necessities, and to them that were with me."

His conduct was not intended to be a precedent to the ministers of religion in every situation, but was accommodated to the circumstances of the time, and was an illustration by example of those lessons of generosity and love, which he had inculcated upon others. "I have showed you all things, how that so labouring ye ought to support the weak; and to remember the words of the Lord Jesus, how he said, It is more blessed to give than to receive." Charity is incumbent not only upon the rich, but upon those also who earn their subsistence by the labour of their hands; and the latter ought to increase their industry, that out of their greater gain they may be the more able to assist their indigent brethren. This is obviously the meaning of the words, although, when thus understood, they enjoin a degree of active benevolence, rarely exemplified, and I may add, rarely conceived. Who thinks it his duty to labour not for his own advantage alone, and for the maintenance of his family, but to acquire the means of relieving the necesities of others? Where is the man, who, having made ample provision for his personal and relative wants, would pursue business with a design to replenish the source of his liberality, that it might be more widely diffused? How few believe, or, indeed, ever reflect upon the words of our Saviour, "It is more blessed to give than to receive?" As they are not found in any of the Gospels, we may presume, that Paul had learned them by revelation, or from the other Apostles; and being delivered to us by him, they are equally authentic as if they had been recorded by one of the Evangelists. To most men it appears to be more blessed to receive than to give. The increase of their treasures affords them pleasure, and it is with pain that they see them diminished. They are not acquainted with the feelings of a benevolent heart, to which the happiness of others is a source of purer and more exquisite delight than the selfish man can derive from his solitary enjoyments. The influence of the gospel makes the Christian capable of tasting this pleasure. Religion refines our sentiments, and expands our affections. It forms us after the pattern of the divine goodness, and restores the empire of love in the soul. It is more godlike to give than to receive; it is a feature in the character of our heavenly Father, "whose tender mercies are over all his works."

Here Paul closed his address. And now, like a pious and affectionate father, who is about to take the last farewell of his family, he knelt down in the midst of the elders, and in a solemn prayer commended them to God. The historian has said nothing of his feelings on this affecting occasion; but we know that a man of so tender a heart, could not separate, without lively emotions of grief, from those whom he dearly loved. The tears which the disciples shed in abundance, were expressive of their sorrow at parting for ever with a friend, whose sympathy they had experienced in their perplexities and distresses; with a teacher, to whom they had often listened with pleasure and advantage; with a spiritual father, who "in Christ Jesus had begotten them through the gospel." In heaven, pious friends will be re-united; but the interval of separation is gloomy, and nature will let fall some tears, even while the heart feels the cheering influence of hope.

From this portion of the history of Paul, we learn what will give us comfort in the solemn hour, which shall terminate our intercourse with those whom we love. All earthly relations are of temporary duration; the pastor must leave his spiritual flock, and the union, which has been cemented by an interchange of good offices, during many years, must be dissolved. It will alleviate our grief, if when we look back upon our past connexions, our consciences bear witness, that we have faithfully endeavoured to perform the duties belonging to them. A retrospect of our mercies will give us no pleasure, unless they have been improved. The reflection that they have been neglected and abused, will prove a sting in our hearts, which will exasperate our natural feelings, and overwhelm us with sorrow and remorse. How dreadful the thought to a minister of religion, that he has slept over his charge, and suffered immortal souls to perish in ignorance and vice! How would it rend the heart of a father, when looking at the lifeless body of his son, to remember that he had treated him with harshness and cruelty! How much more bitter his anguish, if, at this awful moment, conscience should lift up its voice, and accuse him of having done nothing for the salvation of his child; and if the terrible idea should rush into his mind, that, perhaps, his own offspring, in a state of torment, is cursing him as the cause of his eternal perdition! Happy the dying saint who can say, "I am free from the blood of all men. I have endeavoured with much imperfection, indeed, but with sincerity and diligence, to serve my generation according to the will of God. Lord! thou deliveredst unto me five talents: behold I have gained besides them five talents more."

Farther, The example of Paul shows us in what manner every Christian should study to acquit himself, in the station which Providence has assigned to him. We see a man intent upon the performance of his duty, indefatigable in his exertions, and acting from the purest motives, whose courage was undaunted, and whom no consideration could turn aside to the right hand or to the left. How unlike him are the most of us! Should we not blush to think of our languid and interrupted obedience, of the mixture of selfishness in our actions which have the fairest show of disinterestedness, of our cowardice when danger occurs, of the facility with which we deviate from the path of duty to enter upon some other pursuit! Yet, we serve the same master, whom Paul served, and profess to be equally sincere. We have the same promises of divine assistance, and the same glorious prospects to animate us. Let us be ashamed, that we are so much inferior in zeal and activity. It is a powerful excitement to those efforts which are necessary to the attainment of excellence, to keep constantly in our eye the finest models, the most perfect patterns. Conformably to this plan, the Scripture directs us to contemplate first the example of Jesus Christ, and next that of the most eminent saints. "Being encompassed with a great cloud of witnesses," we are exhorted "to run with patience the race which is set before us." Let us propose for imitation not the dwarfish virtues of the majority of Christians, but the heroic deeds of Paul and other illustrious men, that, if we cannot hope to equal them, we may, at least, rise to higher degrees of holiness than we should have attained, if we had fixed a lower standard. We should account nothing done while any thing remains to be done. "Let us not be slothful, but followers of them, who, through faith and patience, inherit the promise."

LECTURE XXV.

PAUL IN JERUSALEM.

Chap. xxi. 1—32.

The first part of this chapter contains a narrative of the journey of Paul from Miletus to Jerusalem. It would serve no valuable purpose to trace his progress more fully than the inspired historian has done. To engage in a minute detail of the places mentioned in Scripture, of their situation, the character of their inhabitants, and their general history, is justifiable only when the knowledge of such particulars will throw light upon the passages to which they relate; and without this reference, is to give, under the name of a religious discourse, a geographical lecture, which is addressed with manifest impropriety to a worshiping assembly. There were, however, some incidents in his way to Jerusalem, of which it is necessary to take notice, before we procceed to consider what befel him on his arrival in that city.

The first is recorded in the fourth verse, which informs us, that on landing at Tyre Paul found disciples, " who said to him through the Spirit, that he should not go up to Jerusalem." If we understand his words in the preceding chapter, " And now behold, I go bound in the Spirit unto Jerusalem," to import, that he had undertaken this journey by the suggestion of the Holy Ghost, we here encounter a difficulty; for it would seem, that the Spirit had retracted his own order, and that having first commanded, he now forbade, the Apostle to go.

Besides, since Paul, notwithstanding the advice or prohibition of those disciples, did proceed to Jerusalem, must we not pronounce him to have been guilty of the high crime of disobeying a divine command, and, consequently, account the troubles, in which he was involved, the just punishment of his obstinacy? It is impossible, however, on the one hand, to believe, that the Holy Ghost issued contradictory precepts, like an inconstant man, who is of one mind to-day, and of another to-morrow; or on the other, to conceive, that Paul, who, on every other occasion, discovered the profound respect for the will of God, acted in this instance, without any imaginable reason, in direct opposition to it. The conclusion, therefore, to which we are necessarily conducted by these considerations, is, that he was not forbidden by the Spirit himself; but that the disciples in Tyre, forseeing the sufferings which awaited him, if he should go to Jerusalem, presumed to persuade him to desist from his intention. Their knowledge of the troubles which should befal him, proceeded from the Spirit; the counsel to stop in his journey was dictated by the officiousness of friendship. They said to him "through the Spirit" that he should not go up to Jerusalem; that is, they gave this advice, not by the direction of the Holy Ghost, but in consequence of that foresight of the result, which they had obtained by his inspiration. It is a probable apology for their conduct, that they had not been informed of the previous order to repair to that city.

The next remarkable circumstance occurred at Cesarea, where Paul remained for some time with Philip the Evangelist. "There came down from Judea a certain Prophet named Agabus. And, when he was come to us, he took Paul's girdle, and bound his own hands and feet, and said, thus saith the Holy Ghost, So shall the Jews at Jerusalem bind the man that owneth this girdle, and shall deliver him into the hands of the Gentiles." Concerning this prediction, the fulfilment of which is afterwards related, I remark, that although it is said that the Jews should bind Paul, and deliver him up to the Gentiles, yet he was actually bound by the Gentiles, or by the captain of the Roman garrison, who had rescued him out of the hands of the Jews. There is, however, no contradiction between the prophecy and the event, because in the prophetical style, and indeed in the common style of the Scriptures, things are represented to have been done by a person which were done by others at his command, or through his influence, direct or indirect. It was in consequence of the rage which the Jews expressed against Paul, that the Romans seized and bound him. Agabus accompanied the prediction of his sufferings with a symbolical action or an action expressive of their nature. Actions of this kind are frequent among nations in the earlier periods of their history, when the imagination and passions operate with great vivacity, and perhaps the penury of language requires the aid of visible signs; and some of them are retained on particular occasions, after a people is far advanced in civilization. They were common among the ancient Prophets. Isaiah walked " naked and barefoot," to signify, that the Egyptians and Ethiopians should be spoiled, and led into captivity by their enemies; and Ezekiel carried out his household-stuff in the sight of his countrymen, to intimate that Jerusalem should be plundered by the Chaldeans." In the same manner, Agabus bound his own hands and feet with Paul's girdle, to foreshow that he should suffer bonds and imprisonment. It is probable, that when the Prophets first adopted the mode of communicating instruction by appropriate actions, as well as by words, they merely conformed to the manner of their age. It was calculated to rouse attention, to give a distinct and impressive idea of the subject, and, by interesting the imagination, to fix it in the memory.

How was Paul affected by the repeated notices of the afflictions, which he was to endure in Jerusalem? Sometimes, when a man is suddenly involved in perilous circumstances, his mind, by an instinctive effort, rises up to his situation; and, amidst his active exertions to save himself, he has not leisure to take a full and deliberate view of his danger. Few are possessed of such strength of mind, and cool courage, as to look forward with composure to the scene of troubles, through which they are destined to pass. He who is a hero amidst the tumult of a battle, would, perhaps, prove a coward, if he were waiting the slow approach of death in a prison, or on a sick bed. Dark and alarming as was the prospect before him, Paul betrayed no symptoms of fear; but retained his self-command, and the firmness of his resolution. Like his Master, with the cross in his eye, he " steadfastly set his face to go to Jerusalem;" and like him too, he reproved those friends, whose unseasonable kindness would have dissuaded him from his duty. " And when we heard these things, both we and they of that place besought him not to go up to Jerusalem. But Paul answered, What mean ye to weep, and to break mine heart? for I am ready not to be bound only, but also to die at Jerusalem for the name of the Lord Jesus." The concern which the disciples expressed for his safety, was natural. They loved him as a friend, and his life was valuable to the Church. As a proof of their affection, their tears could not but be pleasing to him; but temptation sometimes steals upon us, in the most innocent form, and by a path, which virtue alone was expected to tread. Those tears might melt his soul into unmanly softness. Grief is contagious; and while we sympathize with the sufferer, we would most willingly relieve him. Who could endure the thought of wounding a tender affectionate heart, which trembles for his happiness, and is alive to every injury which he sustains? Who, in opposition to the most earnest solicitations, would persist in an enterprise, the issue of which would overwhelm that heart with sorrow? Paul was too well acquainted with human nature not to be sensible, that he was now exposed to a hazardous trial. He therefore checked the disciples. "What mean ye to weep, and to break mine heart?" "Why do you endeavour, by your prayers and solicitations, to persuade me not to go to Jerusalem? I am ready not to be bound only, but also to die there for the name of the Lord Jesus. Those chains of which you are so much afraid, I shall welcome as an honourable badge of my relation to him; and death itself shall have no terrors for me, if I am required to submit to it, in defence of his cause." The reiterated warnings which he received of his danger, illustrate his magnanimity. We behold a man, who having conceived and resolved upon an important design, pursues it with inflexible perseverance amidst scenes of difficulty and trouble, and is determined to sacrifice even life itself to the attainment of his purpose.

"And when he would not be persuaded, we ceased, saying, The will of the Lord be done." His friends perceiving that he acted under a divine impulse, to which the common maxims of prudence must yield, desisted from their importunities; and their solicitude for his safety gave place to a superior principle, reverence for God. Their conduct affords an example of acquiescence in the dispensations of heaven, which we should imitate, when our friendship and affection are severely tried by a separation from those whom we love. It is the duty of rational creatures to acknowledge, not in words only, but in practice, the supreme authority of their Maker, who has an undoubted right to dispose of them and their affairs according to his pleasure. To this duty Christians are under peculiar obligations, arising from the certain knowledge, that his procedure is always wise and gracious, and that submission to his decrees will be productive of the happiest consequences. Into the hands of our Father and our Sovereign we should surrender what is dearest to us without a murmur. And then only do we render to God the homage, to which he is entitled, when not venturing to prescribe to unerring wisdom, and to limit almighty power, we give our unqualified assent to the arrangements of his providence, and rejoice in the manifestation of his glory, although it should be displayed at the expense of our best earthly enjoyments. "The will of the Lord be done."

Let us now proceed to consider the transactions of Paul in Jerusalem. The day after his arrival, he paid a visit to James and the elders, who were assembled to receive him. "And when he had saluted them, he declared particularly what things God had wrought among the Gentiles by his ministry." It was a narrative of splendid achievements. Without any disposition to boast, Paul could relate a series of flattering successes, of astonishing miracles, of multiplied hardships and perils which he had encountered with heroic courage. Yet, without those emotions of envy which the superior excellence of others is so apt to excite in little, and sometimes even in great minds, the audience listened with pleasure to the detail, and with one voice "glorified the Lord." They were animated by the liberal spirit of Christianity, which engages with such ardour in the cause of religion, and, from a conviction of its importance, is so earnest in wishing its success, that if the work is done, it cares not who is the agent; and is content, if such is the will of God, to labour in obscurity, while others are appointed to act upon a conspicuous theatre.

During the successful labours of Paul among the Gentiles, the gospel had made great progress in Judea. "Thou seest, brother, how many thousands" (the word signifies ten thousands) "of Jews there are which believe, and they are all zealous of the law." The zeal of the unbelieving Jews for the law was founded in the persuasion, that it was the only acceptable mode of serving God; and it excited them to reject Christianity as a false and heretical religion. The Jewish converts, while they received the gospel, believed at the same time, that the law retained its authority; and hence, although they observed the institutions of Christ, they lived, in all other respects, like the disciples of Moses. Some proceeded so far as to maintain, that obedience to the law was necessary to justification. It may be presumed, that an opinion so contrary to the truth, and so expressly condemned by the Council of Jerusalem, was not common among the Christians of that city; but it would be an excess of charity to suppose, that none of them had adopted it.

Among those zealots, a report had been spread, which was calculated to prejudice them against Paul. "They are informed of thee, that thou teachest all the Jews, which are among the Gentiles, to forsake Moses, saying, that they ought not to circumcise their children, neither to walk after the customs. What is it therefore? The multitude must needs come together, for they will hear that thou art come;" and there was reason to fear, that at this meeting, Paul would be publicly accused by the zealots for the law, and much ill humour would be discovered. To guard against such disagreeable consequences, James and the elders proposed the following expedient. "Do therefore this that we say to thee: we have four men which have a vow on them; them take, and purify thyself with them, and be at charges with them that they may shave their heads: and all may know, that those things, whereof they were informed concerning thee are nothing, but that thou thyself also walkest orderly, and keepest the law." The vow which those men had made, seems to have been the vow of the Nazarite, by which an Israelite engaged to drink no wine or strong drink, during the period of his separation, and not to suffer a razor to come upon his head. At the expiration of his vow, he shaved his head, and presented in the temple certain offerings, which the law had prescribed. It appears from the writings of the Jews, not to have been uncommon for persons, who had not come under this vow, to assist the Nazarites in defraying the expense of the customary sacrifices. This the elders advised Paul to do, or to adopt their own words, "to be at charges with the men, that they might shave their heads." The shaving of the head was an expression used to denote the completion of the vow. Thus it would be understood, that there was no foundation for the account which had been circulated concerning him as an enemy to the law; for the Jews would see him giving an unequivocal proof of his regard to it, by the observance of one of its remarkable institutions.

"As touching the Gentiles which believe, we have written and concluded, that they observe no such things, save only that they keep themselves from things offered to idols, and from blood, and from strangled, and from fornication." The elders refer to the decree of the Council of Jerusalem, which exempted the Gentiles from the Jewish law, and subjected them only to the restrictions here enumerated. No blame could be imputed to Paul for having taught that they might be received into the fellowship of the disciples, without submitting to circumcision and the ritual of Moses. His doctrine on this point had the sanction of the highest authority in the Church.

The transaction which has now been explained, is involved in difficulties, and has given rise to objections affecting not only the wisdom but the integrity of all who were concerned in it. Was it not a true report respecting Paul, it has been said, which the brethren in Judea had heard? Did he not teach the Jews to forsake Moses, and tell them, that his law had lost its power of obligation? On what ground, then, can James and the elders be justified in suggesting a plan, the express design of which was to persuade the disciples in Jerusalem of the contrary? Should it be insinuated, that they might not be well acquainted with the doctrine of Paul, a supposition which has little probability, did not the Apostle himself know, that he had taught the exemption of the Jews as well as of the Gentiles from the yoke of ceremonies? Why, then, did he consent to act in such a manner as should make it be believed that "those things whereof the brethren had been informed concerning him were nothing," when in substance they were unquestionably true? Was he ashamed or afraid to profess in Jerusalem, what he had boldly avowed in Greece and Asia? Why did he not with his wonted candour declare, that the Jews were no longer bound to circumcise their children; that in Christ Jesus circumcision was of no avail; and that nothing was required by the gospel, but faith which works by love? It must be acknowledged, that the conduct of all parties in this affair, seems to give ground for these, or similar objections; and to some they have appeared so strong, and so incapable of a satisfactory solution, that their minds have been much perplexed.*

Let us examine the transaction more minutely, and we shall, perhaps, discover, that the conduct of Paul and the elders was not so unjustifiable as at first sight it appears. It may be remarked, that the unfavourable report respecting Paul, which the proposed plan was intended to disprove, was not true in its full extent. He taught indeed, in every place, that obedience to the law of Moses was not necessary to justification, and did not hesitate to declare,

---

* Wits. in vita Pauli. sect. x. 4.

that, in consequence of the death of Christ, and the introduction of the new economy, it was not binding upon the conscience. But, this was very different from asserting, "that the Jews ought not to circumcise their children, neither to walk after the customs." If any believing Jew had chosen not to observe the ordinances of the ceremonial law, the Apostle, I presume, would not have condemned him. But, he did not condemn those, who continued to observe them. He never pronounced the practice of the Mosaic rites, unless it was accompanied, as in the case of the Galatians, with an error in relation to the ground of our acceptance in the sight of God, to be inconsistent with the faith and duty of a Christian. He could not have done so without criminating himself; for we know, that "to the Jews he became as a Jew," conforming their customs, with a view to gain them over to the gospel; and we have seen him, from the same motive, circumcising Timothy. There was properly, therefore, no dissimulation in his joining with the four men who had made a vow, because, on other occasions, "he walked orderly, and kept the law." When he was abroad among the Gentiles, he had entered into the vow of the Nazarite, and shorn his head.

But why, it may be asked, did James, and the elders, and Paul, concur in encouraging the converted Jews, who were zealous for the law, to think, that its obligation continued, although they were aware, that it was abrogated by the death of Christ? Did they not lend their influence to foster a prejudice, which they should rather have exerted their authority to eradicate? It is certain, that the Jews who believed, were emancipated from the Mosaic institute, and might have refused to be any longer in bondage to the elements of the world. But, it appears from the New Testament, that God was pleased, in condescension to the peculiar circumstances of that people, to permit their ancient law to be observed for some time, by those who had embraced Christianity. This permission, I say, was granted from respect to the circumstances of the Jews, whose zeal for the law will not appear surprising to those who attend to the reasons on which it was founded. From their earliest years they had imbibed a sacred reverence for its institutions; and, prior to their conversion, they had regarded it as the only system of religious worship which was acceptable to God. They were fully assured, that its origin was divine, and they had been accustomed to believe it to be of perpetual obligation. To adopt the idea, that this law, so ancient, so venerable, and so sacred, was of no farther use in the service of God, and should, therefore, be laid aside as unprofitable, was a revolution of sentiment too great and violent to be suddenly effected. The change was accomplished by gradual and gentle means. First, the Gentiles were received into the Church without circumcision, and the acceptance of a sinner was declared to depend solely upon faith; next, the Jews were explicitly informed, particularly in the Epistle which Paul addressed to them, that the ultimate design of their ritual was fulfilled in the death of the Messiah; and, when their zeal for the law had been thus insensibly cooled, its abrogation was plainly signified by the destruction of the temple, in which alone its solemn rites could be performed.

After that event, the law was forsaken by all the Jews who professed Christianity, except a few zealots, who having adopted, at the same time, some heretical opinions concerning the person of our Saviour, were expelled from the communion of the Catholic Church. The conduct of the elders and Paul was conformable to this plan of gracious condescension. Respecting the prejudices of the Jews, in favour of the institutions which God himself had delivered to them, and the abrogation of which was not generally understood, they complied with them for a time; and choose rather to expect their removal, by the silent influence of the truth and the progress of events, than to run the risk of irritating their minds, and turning their zeal into inflexible obstinacy, by demanding an immediate renunciation of their ancient habits and attachments.

In this manner the transaction may be explained, so as to preserve our respect for the wisdom and integrity of the persons concerned in it. If, however, there should be some, to whom this explanation does not seem satisfactory, they may be reminded, that while we believe the Apostles to have been inspired, and infallibly directed in the revelations which they made to the world, we do not maintain, that their conduct was, on every occasion, exemp from error. Peter and Barnabas were once guilty of dissimulation from fear of giving offence to the Jews; and if James had been betrayed into the same fault by the same temptation, no conclusion to the discredit of Christianity, or of the Apostolical office, could be drawn from the one case, any more than from the other. We should only have another proof, that the highest attainments in gifts and grace do not raise the possessors to perfection; and that in the present state, man, although placed in the most advantageous circumstances, is still man, a weak and erring being.

Some may be disposed to infer the unlawfulness of the transaction from its unhappy termination, which may be construed into a declaration of Providence against it. It must, indeed, be acknowledged, that we can hardly conceive any scheme to have a more unfortunate issue. The believing Jews were, no doubt, convinced, that Paul was not such an enemy to the law of Moses as they had been led to believe; but this was an object of little importance. With respect to himself, the consequences were of a serious nature; for he was involved in a long series of troubles, was shut up in prison for several years, and was exposed to the risk of closing his invaluable labours, by a premature and violent death. This unprosperous result would almost lead us to suspect, that God was displeased with the measure, did we not know, that the dispensations of providence towards individuals afford no certain criterion of their character and the nature of their actions; and that his servants have often experienced great opposition and incredible hardships, when they were obeying the clearest dictates of his word.

"Then Paul took the men, and the next day purifying himself with them, entered into the temple, to signify the accomplishment of the days of purification; until that an offering should be offered for every one of them." It seems to have been his design, in going into the temple, to give notice to the priests, that he had joined with the four men, and would observe the purity which was required from the Nazarite, for seven days, at the end of which their vow would expire. The temple was surrounded with two courts, separated by a wall of three cubits in height, which was sufficient to mark their boundaries, and, at the same time, permitted those who were in the one court to see what was passing in the other. Into the interior court none but a Jew was permitted to enter; the presence of a stranger would have profaned it. The exterior court was open to the Gentiles; but pillars were erected at proper intervals, with an inscription warning them to proceed no farther, and threatening the impious intruder with death. Some Jews from Asia, who had seen Paul in the streets of Jerusalem, accompanied by Trophimus, a native of Ephesus, hastily concluded, when they again saw him in the temple, that the same person was along with him; and that having formerly spoken, as they affirmed, in disrespectful terms of that holy edifice, he had now polluted it, by introducing an uncircumcised man into its sacred inclosure. This happened, when the seven days of his purification were almost ended. Filled with indignation at his supposed crime, they called aloud to the bystanders to assist in seizing him; and to inflame their zeal, they advanced such charges against him as were peculiarly offensive and provoking to every orthodox Jew. They accused him not only of having profaned the temple by bringing Greeks into it, but of declaiming every where "against the people, and the law, and this place," because he had taught, that the exclusive privileges of the Jews were at an end, and the Gentiles were now to be admitted into the covenant of God; that the Messiah having died upon the cross, the law which prefigured him was to give place to a new and more spiritual system of worship; and that Jehovah, who had for many ages made the temple his peculiar residence, was to be adored, in every land, from the rising to the setting sun.

These accusations produced an instantaneous and violent commotion. "All the city was moved, and the people ran together: and they took Paul, and drew him out of the temple: and forthwith the doors were shut." There is a degree of fury approaching to madness, observable in the proceedings of the Jews against the followers of Jesus, which was the effect of the fierce temper of that people, exasperated by religious bigotry. When the passions of any mob are let loose, law, justice, and humanity present but feeble barriers to their outrages; but a Jewish mob was still more furious and ungovernable, and resembled a number of savage beasts thirsting for blood. It was a principle publicly avowed, and, in the latter period of their history, frequently acted upon, that zeal for the glory of God would justify them in putting transgressors of the law to death, without a judicial trial. In the hands of such men, Paul was in imminent danger; and had not Providence seasonably interposed, he should now have closed his labours and his life. "But as they went about to kill him, tidings came unto the chief captain of the band," or the garrison of Roman soldiers, stationed in a tower which commanded the temple, "that all Jerusalem was in an uproar; who immediately took soldiers, and centurions, and ran down unto them, and when they saw the chief captain, and the soldiers, they left beating of Paul." The Roman commander interfered to suppress the tumult; and finding Paul to be the cause or occasion of it, he rescued him out of the hands of the Jews, and secured him, that if he was guilty of any crime, he might be legally tried and punished. He was the instrument of Providence for the preservation of the great Apostle, who had yet to go through a long course of trials and important services.

It is unnecessary to make any observations upon the remaining part of the chapter. We have seen on what occasion, and by what means Paul was deprived of his liberty, which he did not regain for several years. I shall, in the next Lecture, call your attention to his appearance before the Sanhedrim.

We perceive from the events which have now come under review, that among the disadvantages under which the gospel laboured at its first publication, its contrariety, real or apparent, to the existing religions, was not the least unfavourable to its success. To all the modifications of paganism it was professedly hostile; and it demanded the immediate and unqualified renunciation of the objects and the rites of their worship. Its opposition to the religion of Moses was only apparent; but the appearance was so strong as to alarm the Jews, and rouse them to the most determined resistance. It required them to desist from circumcision, sacrifices, and the other ceremonial ordinances, and to adopt in their room the simple and spiritual institutions of the gospel. Notwithstanding the fickleness which men often discover in matters of taste and fashion, and even in affairs of much greater importance, there are some cases, in which the power of habit operates with so much force, as to render a change exceedingly difficult. Having long acquiesced in a set of opinions and practices, they startle at every proposed alteration, and will not listen with patience to the arguments which are intended to show that it is an improvement. We wonder at the obstinacy, with which the believing Jews retained their ancient usages, although they might have understood that they had lost their meaning and use. It is evident, at the same time, that no people were ever so justifiable in being slow to admit a change, because their religion had been delivered to their fathers by God himself, and was contained in books, which they justly regarded as divine. May we not wonder much more at some persons among ourselves, who entertain the same sacred respect for human dogmas, matters of doubtful disputation, and mere forms, which have nothing to recommend them but the authority of their ancestors, who had no better right to institute forms in religion than their descendants? Let the most trifling variation be introduced in the order of procedure to which they have been accustomed; let an alteration be made in modes manifestly indifferent, and times arbitrarily fixed; let a human appendage to a divine ordinance be removed; and they are as much alarmed and displeased, as if an attempt had been made to subvert the foundations of our faith. Such persons would do well to consider, that, in the same spirit, they would have been as ready, if they had lived in the days of Paul, to exclaim against his doctrine, as the most furious zealots for the law, among the believers in Jerusalem.

Let us remark with pleasure, in the triumph of the gospel over every kind of opposition, a proof of its divinity, and an earnest of its future victories. Heathenism, with all the assistance which it received from the secular power, and the strong interest which it possessed in the corrupt passions of mankind, was not able to stand against it. Judaism yielded to its superior influence. Myriads of the Jews embraced Christianity. That religion, indeed, still subsists; but in what condition? Is it not divested of its glory, without its temple, its priests, and its sacrifices? Has it not degenerated into an absurd and contemptible superstition, which is retained only by the outcasts of mankind? It is the meagre and lifeless image of what it once was; and while it points its impotent malice against Christianity, it involuntarily does it homage, by bearing testimony to the truth of its predictions, in every region of the earth.

My brethren, our hearts are ready to despond when we consider the formidable obstacles, which oppose the diffusion of evangelical truth. Heathen idolatry and Mahometan superstition are established throughout a great part of the earth. In other regions, Antichristian delusion have spread far and wide their baleful influence, and infidelity boasts of its numerous disciples. Ignorance, dissipation, and the love of worldly things have alienated the minds of most men from serious subjects. But meditate now upon the works of the Lord, and remember the years of his right hand. Have we forgotten the victories, which it has gained? Do we suspect that it has lost its vigour, or that God will never again pluck it out of his bosom? If his power seems at present to slumber and sleep, it is that it may awake with greater energy than ever. "Behold, I create new heavens, and a new earth: and the former shall not be remembered, nor come into mind." Let us not perplex ourselves about the means of effecting that mighty revolution in human affairs, which is announced by prophecy. He will provide them, " who calls the things that are not as though they were." All nature is obedient to his voice; and if, in the whole compass of creation, nothing should be found fit for his purpose, there is an unfailing resource in his Almighty power. When he says, " Let there be light, there shall be light."

LECTURE XXVI.

PAUL BEFORE THE COUNCIL.

CHAP. xxiii. 1—10.

WE have seen, in the last Lecture, to what danger Paul was exposed, not long after his arrival at Jerusalem. He was saved from the fury of the Jews, who intended to put him to death for the supposed crimes of blasphemy against the law, and profanation of the temple, by the commander of the Roman soldiers, who kept guard in the castle of Antonia. In the end of the twenty-first chapter, we are informed, that, after some conversation with that officer, he was permitted to address the people; and in the twenty-second chapter, we have an account of his speech. He begins by assigning the reason, which had induced him, who was once zealous for the law, and a persecutor of Christianity, to become its friend and advocate. The sudden and surprising change is attributed to a miraculous appearance of our Saviour, which convinced him, that he was the true Messiah, and not an impostor as he had hitherto believed.

There is one fact, not recorded in any of the preceding chapters, the mention of which gave great offence to his hearers, and was the occasion of the abrupt termination of his speech. I shall relate it in the words of the Apostle. " And it came to pass, that when I was come again to Jerusalem, even while I prayed in the temple, I was in a trance, and saw him saying unto me, Make haste, and get thee quickly out of Jerusalem: for they will not receive thy testimony concerning me. And I said, Lord, they know that I imprisoned and beat in every synagogue, them that believed in thee. And when the blood of thy martyr, Stephen, was shed, I also was standing by, and consented unto his death, and kept the raiment of them that slew him. And he said unto me, Depart: for I will send thee far hence unto the Gentiles." It was impossible for an unbelieving Jew to hear this account without the utmost indignation, because, it charged him and his brethren with the guilt of obstinately rejecting the Messiah, and represented the Gentiles as chosen to enjoy those privileges, of which the Jews had proved themselves to be unworthy. This statement was so contrary to the pleasing idea, that they were the favourites of Heaven, and to the contempt in which they held the nations of the world, that nothing can be conceived more mortifying to their pride, and more calculated to inflame their resentment against the speaker. Accordingly, although they had listened with calmness to the narrative of his conversion, "they now lifted up their voices, and said, Away with such a fellow from the earth; for it is not fit that he should live. And they cried out, and cast off their clothes, and threw dust into the air."

The chief captain, who could not comprehend the cause of the uproar, either because he did not understand the Hebrew language, in which Paul delivered his speech, or because he was ignorant of the points in dispute between the Christians and the Jews, "commanded him to be brought into the castle, and bade that he should be examined by scourging, that he might know wherefore they so cried against him." He ordered Paul to be scourged, that the severity of pain might extort a confession of his crime; for, at present, there was no proof of his guilt, and the only presumption against him was the general clamour of the multitude. The barbarous practise of subjecting an accused person, to torture, was, in certain cases, permitted by the Romans, and has been adopted by some modern nations, in contradiction to the plainest dictates of justice and common sense. It is evidently unjust to punish a man, who, for aught his judges know, is innocent; and there is not a more precarious method of discovering the truth than the confession of a person in pain, who cannot be supposed to be master of his own thoughts, and may be induced to make any declaration, which shall procure immediate relief from his sufferings. "But as they bound him with thongs, Paul said unto the centurion that stood by, Is it lawful for you to scourge a man that is a Roman, and uncondemned?" The law forbade a Roman citizen to be scourged; and Paul inherited this character by birth, although his parents were Jews. Tarsus, the place of his nativity, was favoured by Julius Cesar and Augustus; and it is probable, that the right of citizenship was one of the privileges which the latter had conferred upon its inhabitants. The rank of citizen of Rome was an honour to which the most illustrious persons aspired. The chief captain had obtained it with a great sum; and knowing with what jealousy it was guarded by the laws against every insult and violation, he dismissed those who should have examined the prisoner by torture. Paul, although willing to suffer and die for the gospel, had not imbibed that enthusiastic passion for martyrdom, which impelled some Christians in the following ages, to court torments and death, by voluntarily accusing themselves at the tribunals of the heathen magistrates. Acting upon this sober and rational principle, that, if we can avoid sufferings without deserting our duty, we ought to avoid them, he pleaded his civil rights, as a defence against the cruelty of the men, into whose hands he had fallen. But, as there was no law forbidding a Roman citizen to be imprisoned, he was detained in the castle till the next day, when the great council of the nation was summoned to meet.

The assembly, before which Paul appeared on this occasion, was that which was commonly known by the name of the Sanhedrim, and was the highest court in the nation. The Jewish writers affirm, that it subsisted during all the ages of their commonwealth, and was instituted in the wilderness, when seventy elders of Israel were chosen to assist Moses in the government. The Sanhedrim was composed of the same number of members. Some, however, are of opinion, that its commencement can be traced no farther back than the return from the Babylonian captivity. It was a court to which appeals were made from the sentences of inferior judicatories; but there were some causes of greater difficulty and importance, in which it claimed a sole right to judge. When our Lord said, that "it could not be that a Prophet should perish," that is, should die by a judicial sentence, "out of Jerusalem," he seems to have referred to the Sanhedrim, which met in that city, and assumed the exclusive authority to try the pretensions of the Prophets, and to punish those who were found guilty of imposture. In the degenerate times, which preceded the downfal of the Jewish state, a true Prophet was more likely to be condemned, than to be recognised and honoured by men, who were corrupted by false notions of religion, and by the vices of the age. The Council was now summoned by the chief captain, as it had been called together, at the birth of our Saviour, by Herod. Its independence was lost, and its jurisdiction was abridged, during the reign of that king, to whom it was an object of jealousy. The Roman commander brought Paul before the Sanhedrim, because he appeared, from the clamours of the people, to have been guilty of some offence against their laws; and, probably, that court asserted its right to judge him as a blasphemer of Moses, and of their sacred institutions.

In the presence of this august assembly, Paul was not abashed and intimidated. Alone in the midst of enemies, who had both the inclination and the power to injure him, he surveyed them with an undaunted countenance; supported by consciousness of innocence, and the expectation of that assistance, which Jesus Christ had promised to his disciples, when they should be brought before governors and kings for his sake. Instead of endeavouring to disarm their resentment, and to court their favour by any mean concession, or any retractation of his principles, he dared to assert the purity of his motives, and the rectitude of his conduct. "And Paul earnestly beholding the council, said, Men and brethren, I have lived in all good conscience before God, until this day."

The import of this declaration is easily understood, from the frequent occurrence of the same language in ordinary conversation. When a person affirms, that he said or did any thing with a good conscience, he means, that he was not influenced by improper motives, but by a conviction of duty; and that his own mind was so far from condemning him, that it approved of his conduct. In this sense, Paul could truly assert, that he had lived in all good conscience before God, not only since his conversion to Christianity, but also prior to that remarkable change of his views. "I verily thought with myself," he says, in his speech to king Agrippa, "that I ought to do many things contrary to the name of Jesus of Nazareth." When opposing him and his religion, he was fully persuaded, that he was performing an acceptable service to God, because he sincerely believed our Saviour to be an impostor. Still he was "a blasphemer, a persecutor, and an injurious person; but he obtained mercy, because he did it ignorantly, in unbelief." His activity did not originate in malice, but in a mistaken idea of duty. That he acted with the same integrity in the subsequent period of his life, it is impossible to doubt. It was upon the most satisfactory evidence, that he embraced the religion which he had persecuted, and from the purest motives, that he underwent so much toil and suffering in propagating and defending it. "This was his rejoicing, the testimony of his conscience, that in simplicity and godly sincerity, not with fleshly wisdom, but by the grace of God, he had his conversation in the world." The design of the declaration which he now made, was to assure his judges, that whatever construction they were disposed to put upon his conduct, it was not from caprice, or with an interested view, that he had passed over to Christianity, but from the unbiassed dictates of his mind; and that he was now as firmly convinced of its truth, as he had ever been of the divine authority of the law.

Ananias, the high-priest, offended at the presumption of Paul, who had spoken before leave was granted by the court, and still more at this bold testimony to the goodness of the cause in which he was embarked, commanded those who stood by him, to "smite him on the mouth." Among the Jews, this seems to have been a customary mode of expressing reproof and contempt. Zedekiah, a false Prophet, "smote Micaiah a Prophet of the Lord on the cheek, and said, Which way went the Spirit of the Lord from me to speak unto thee?" and when our Saviour stood before Caiaphas, the officers "smote him with the palms of their hands, saying, Prophesy unto us, thou Christ, who is he that smote thee?"

"Then said Paul unto him, God shall smite thee thou whited wall." A whited wall, or a wall daubed with plaster, which gives it a goodly appearance, is an expressive figure to denote a man, whose real dispositions are different from the character which he assumes. "They are sordid and base," says a heathen philosopher, speaking of some persons who made a false show, "but outwardly they are adorned after the similitude of their walls." From the high-priest and the president of the Sanhedrim, the strictest regard to justice might have been reasonably expected; but the conduct of Ananias too plainly showed, that he was liable to be transported by passion, beyond the bounds of decorum, and was capable of violating the law, when he could do so with impunity. "Sittest thou to judge me after the law, and commandest me to be smitten contrary to the law?" It was contrary to the law, which forbade the judges "to do any unrighteousness in judgment," and directed them, when a person was accused, "to inquire, and make search, and ask diligently," before they passed sentence upon him, to order a man to be smitten, who had not been proved guilty of a crime. "God," says Paul, "shall therefore smite thee." These words ought not to be considered as a passionate exclamation, or an imprecation of vengeance, because the Apostle had learned the lessons of patience, meekness, and forgiveness, in the school of Jesus Christ, was, on all other occasions, an illustrious pattern of those graces, and, as we have reason to believe, from the promise of our Lord to which we lately referred, was now particularly assisted by the Spirit. They may be understood as an intimation founded upon the threatenings of Scripture, of the punishment which a man guilty of such injustice, should sooner or later incur, unless he repented. We may even suppose Paul to have been under the impulse of the prophetic Spirit, and that by his inspiration he now foretold the fate of Ananias. The supposition has great probability, because he undoubtedly enjoyed, at this time, the presence of the Holy Ghost, by whom he was enabled, in many other instances, to predict future events. "God is about to smite thee, thou hypocrite." As Ananias is said to have suffered a violent death, the correspondence between the event and the plain import of the words, favours the idea, that they were intended as a prophecy. To this view of them, it may, indeed, be objected, that the Apostle, as we shall afterwards see, did not know Ananias. But, he knew him to be unworthy of the station which he held as a member of the Sanhedrim; and as the organ of the Spirit, he might have denounced his doom, although he had been totally unacquainted with his person and character.

To the by-standers, the language of Paul seemed unguarded and indecent. He had reproached a man, whose character should be held sacred on account of his office. "Revilest thou God's high-priest?" Paul answered, "I wist not brethren," or I did not know, "that he was the high-priest: for it is written, Thou shalt not speak evil of the ruler of thy people." This was a wise law, founded in the principles of justice and expediency. Not only is respect for our superiors necessary to the support of their authority, which is weakened by want of confidence in their talents and virtues; but when we consider that they are but men like ourselves, whose judgments are not infallible; that they may err with the best intentions, and while they have no object in view but the public good; and that they are often surrounded with persons whose interest is to deceive and mislead them; we shall perceive the equity of requiring us to be candid in forming an opinion of their proceedings, and cautious in our language, when it is necessary to blame them.

The answer of the Apostle is attended with some difficulties. How was it possible, it has been said, that Paul should not have known Ananias, since he had now been several days in Jerusalem, and had frequented the temple, where the high-priest would be often seen? Besides, as he was president of the council, and wore certain badges of his office, must he not have been distinguished, at a single glance, by his seat and his dress? Two methods have been adopted for removing this difficulty. The first supposes, that Paul did know Ananias, but refused to acknowledge him to be high-priest; the second presumes that he was ignorant of both his person, and his official character. Those who think, that the Apostle knew him, consider his words, "I wist not," as equivalent to "I do not acknowledge," and they assign the one or the other of the following reasons why he did not acknowledge him; either that the Jewish priesthood was now abolished by the death of Jesus Christ, who had assumed the character of high-priest of the Church, and had an exclusive right to it; or that Ananias was in truth not the high-priest, but had intruded himself into the office, or purchased it with money; and Paul had learned from Gamaliel, that a person who had procured an office by bribery, should not be recognised as a judge, and was not entitled to respect. Neither of these comments upon the words of the Apostle, and least of all the first, will recommend itself to such as love simplicity, and believe, that on this, as other occasions, he studied plainness and candour in expressing his sentiments. Both represent him as using the word "to know," in an equivocal sense, which is hardly consistent with honesty. Others think, that Paul having been long absent from Jerusalem, might really not know Ananias to be high-priest, especially as the office was not now held during life, but passed, at the will of the Romans, from one person to another in such quick succession, that three are said to have possessed it, in the short space of a year; that the Sanhedrim having probably been assembled, not in the usual place, but in the castle, he might not have appeared in his official dress, nor in his ordinary seat; or that, upon the supposition that Paul did know him and his dignity, he might not observe among so many judges, who commanded him to be smitten, and the high-priest was the last man, whom he should have suspected to be guilty of so gross a violation of the law. Any of these solutions may be considered as satisfactory; but more, I apprehend, has been said upon this subject than was necessary. The difficulty, if not created, has certainly been magnified, by the elaborate attempts to explain it. Paul was a man so little disposed to conceal his sentiments on the most trying occasions, so little liable to be driven to any mean shift or evasion by the presence of danger, that we might have contented ourselves with his simple assertion, "that he wist not that Ananias was the high priest."

But, if Paul had known the rank of the person, who commanded him to be smitten, would he have refrained from speaking as he did? Does not this seem to be the import of his reference to the law, "Thou shalt not speak evil of the ruler of thy people?" And if his language admitted of correction, where was the promise of the Saviour, "that he would give a mouth and wisdom to his Apostles, which all their adversaries should not be able to gainsay nor resist?" This is a greater difficulty than the other, although it has attracted less attention; but it may be satisfactorily explained. Paul, I apprehend, does not quote the law, with a design to convince his accusers, that as he distinctly remembered it, he could be charged only with an unintentional transgression. Ignorance of the person of the high-priest would not have acquitted him from a breach of the precept, which was equally violated by reviling the other members of the Sanhedrim, who were all invested with the dignity of rulers. Nay, to speak evil of any man, although the lowest and most obscure member of society, was contrary to the law of love, which has, indeed, received new enforcements from the gospel, but was binding under the Mosaic dispensation. The question to be considered is, whether Paul was actually guilty of reviling Ananias; and it may be confidently answered in the negative. If, as we have already supposed, he was under a prophetic impulse, his language, however different from the style, in which ordinary men are bound to address their civil and ecclesiastical superiors, was not disrespectful. In truth, the words were not his own, but the words of God, who pours contempt upon the wicked princes of the earth, and counts them as vanity. A Prophet claimed superiority to the greatest of men; and it was the prerogative of his office to reprove magistrates and kings, and to denounce against them the judgments of Heaven. Our Lord, who never "rendered railing for railing," and "when he was reviled, reviled not again," called Herod the tetrarch, "a fox," on account of his cunning and cruelty.

We are next to consider, by what expedient Paul defeated the design of the Sanhedrim, which, we may confidently affirm, from our knowledge of the implacable enmity entertained by the unbelieving Jews against the disciples of Jesus, had assembled with a premeditated resolution to condemn this ringleader of the Christian heresy. It was by dividing his enemies, and inducing one party to espouse his cause from opposition to the other. "And when Paul perceived, that the one part were Sadducees, and the other Pharisees, he cried out in the council, Men and brethren, I am a Pharisee, the son of a Pharisee: of the hope and resurrection of the dead I am called in question." The Pharisees and the Sadducees were the chief religious sects among the Jews, with the one or the other of which all the persons of learning, and rank, and fashion, were connected. The Sadducees acknowledged the divine origin of the Jewish religion, and of the Scriptures of the Old Testament, for there is no satisfactory evidence that they received only the five books of Moses; but they interpreted the promises in a temporal sense, and maintained, that obedience was rewarded, and sin was punished, only in the present life. They denied the existence of any spirit besides God, or of any separate spirit; for they rejected the immortality of the soul, and asserted that it died with the body. It is not easy to conceive on what ground they could controvert the existence of angels, who are so often represented in the sacred books of the Jews, as appearing, and speaking, and acting; but it is probable, that they imagined them to have been transient appearances, or temporary emanations of divine power. Having discarded from their system the immortality of the soul, and a future state of retribution, they were necessarily led to deny the doctrine of the resurrection. "The Sadducees say, that there is no resurrection, neither angel nor spirit: but the Pharisees confess both." The religious creed of the latter was more consonant to Scripture, to the suggestions of conscience, and to the expectations of the human race. They believed not only that angels were real beings, but that the soul should survive the body, be reunited to it at a future period, and share in its happiness or its misery. The tenets of the Sadducees were embraced chiefly by the rich and the great, who wished to enjoy the pleasures of life, without the dread of a future reckoning; while those of the Pharisees were espoused by the lower orders, and by all the sober part of the community. From the opposition of their principles, and a competition for power, the two sects regarded each other with jealousy and aversion.

When Paul perceived that the one part of his judges were Sadducees, and the other part were Pharisees, he cried out in the council, "Men and brethren, I am a Pharisee, the son of a Pharisee: of the hope and resurrection of the dead I am called in question." Some may be disposed to consider this declaration of his sentiments as an artifice or stratagem, scarcely consistent with simplicity and manliness of conduct. But, Paul asserted nothing but what was strictly true; for he had once belonged to the sect of the Pharisees, and he still retained so much of their creed as related to the resurrection of the dead, and the subjects connected with it. He was now standing before the Sanhedrim, because he had affirmed the resurrection of Christ, which was not only a proof of his Messiahship, but is the grand evidence of our future triumph over the power of death. It will, perhaps, be objected, that there was a great difference between the doctrine of the Pharisees upon this point, and that of Christianity; for, that according to Josephus, they did not hold the resurrection of the same body which had died, but the transmigration of souls, or their passage from one body to another. But, in this instance, we may suspect his accuracy, or his fidelity. He has either ascribed to the whole sect an opinion which was entertained only by a few; or with the same disregard to truth which has led him to accommodate other parts of his history to the taste of the Gentiles, he has not scrupled to render the doctrine of the resurrection more palatable to them, by representing it as nearly allied to the notions of Pythagoras and other philosophers. There is no doubt, that the ideas of the Pharisees were in substance the same with those of the Scriptures. Paul knew them as well as Josephus, and would not have ventured to misrepresent them, in the presence of the chief men of the sect.

No blame can be justly imputed to the Apostle for this avowal of his sentiments, although it was made with a design to divide the members of the council. Our Lord has recommended to his disciples "the wisdom of the serpent," as well as "the harmlessness of the dove;" not the practice of deceit and wicked policy, but the enlightened prudence, which knows how to improve favourable opportunities, and to avoid danger without a desertion of duty. No man is required to die for religion, unless he cannot live, but by renouncing and dishonouring it. If a seasonable declaration of the truth would save the life of Paul, by what law was he bound to be silent? And, if by so innocent an expedient he could turn the hostility of the adversaries of the gospel against one another, while

---

* De Bello Jud. lib. ii. cap. 12.

during the contest he should escape, was he not perfectly justifiable in making use of it? It will throw additional light upon his conduct to remark, that he was now before judges, from whom he had no reason to expect an impartial trial. The high-priest had already commanded him to be smitten contrary to the law; and he foresaw from this commencement, with what violence and disregard of justice the business of the court would be conducted. He was, certainly, at liberty to employ any means, consistent with truth and honour, to deliver himself from so iniquitous a tribunal.

The plan which he adopted was successful. "And when he had said so, there arose a dissension between the Pharisees and the Sadducees; and the multitude was divided." In the ninth verse we are farther told, "that there arose a great cry: and the Scribes that were of the Pharisees part arose, and strove, saying, We find no evil in this man; but if a spirit or an angel hath spoken to him, let us not fight against God." How powerful is the influence of party-spirit in forming our opinions, and swaying our affections! It confounds our moral perceptions, and incapacitates us for judging impartially of either our enemies or our friends. Those who have yielded up their understandings to its government, see every object through a deceitful medium; and in their eyes, the characters of others change from bad to good, and from good to bad, according as they approach or recede from the arbitrary standard of excellence, which they have presumed to establish. When Paul was introduced into the presence of the Sanhedrim, he was regarded by all the members as a heretic and a blasphemer. But, no sooner has he declared himself in favour of the Pharisees, than he is pronounced by them to be an innocent person. What! could they find no evil in the man, who had openly apostatised from Moses, and preached through Jesus the resurrection of the dead? No; the thought instantly occurs to them, that an angel or a spirit may have spoken to him, and, his doctrine may be a revelation from heaven; and they gravely admonish the court to beware of opposing him, lest they should be found guilty of contending with God himself. And what was the cause of these new and liberal sentiments respecting Christianity? Whence do the Pharisees begin to suspect it to be true? Some have been inclined to put a charitable construction upon their conduct; but there does not appear to be any sufficient reason for attributing it to conviction, and it may be accounted for by a less honourable principle. Paul had avowed one of the pec liar doctrines of the Pharisees in the presence of their rivals, whom they were always eager to humble; and the merit of this action atoned, in their eyes, for all the heresies which he was said to have propagated. They were willing to allow, not from a change of their views, but from opposition to the Sadducees, that the gospel might be true, because it lent its aid to support one of the distinguished articles in their creed.

In this way, I think, their conduct should be explained. But, by whatever motive they were influenced, the contest between them and the Sadducees became so vehement, and was carried on with so much noise, that the Sanhedrim could not proceed in the trial. The chief captain being afraid lest Paul should fall a victim to the violence of the parties, "commanded the soldiers to go down, and to take him by force from among them, and to bring him into the castle." In this manner, the design of the Jews against him was defeated; and he was preserved, as the Lord told him the following night, to bear testimony to the gospel in Rome, as he had already done in Jerusalem.

To this discourse I shall subjoin a few practical inferences.

First, We learn how desirable it is to enjoy the testimony of a good conscience, particularly in the season of adversity and trial. A well-grounded persuasion of the goodness of the cause in which we are engaged, and consciousness of the purity of our motives, will support our minds under reproach, and arm us with courage in the midst of dangers. A conscience enlightened by Scripture and purified by faith, will prove a source of satisfaction, into whatever difficulties we are brought by our religious profession; whereas the man whose heart accuses him of insincerity, must blush at his own baseness, even when his hypocrisy is rewarded with the most flattering commendations A good conscience is a preservative from remorse and fear, two inmates which torment the soul in which they reside. What embarrassment and anxiety should the Apostle have felt in his present circumstances, had he been acting the part of an impostor? But, we have seen him collected and undaunted; and being at peace with himself and with God, he did not dread the power of the Jewish rulers, who had condemned his Master, and were actuated by the same hostile sentiments towards himself. "If our heart condemn us not, then have we confidence towards

God;" and when we can look up to him as our friend and guardian, " we shall not fear what flesh can do unto us."

Secondly, Let us be careful to discover a meek and quiet spirit, when we are injured and ill treated by others. We, indeed, hear Paul, when Ananias commanded him to be smitten on the mouth, saying, " God shall smite thee, thou whited wall." But we should consider that the actions of other men which were right, are to be imitated by us, only when we are in the same circumstances; and that it is an abuse of examples, to make a general and indiscriminate application of them. The disciples wished to be permitted to bring down fire from heaven upon a Samaritan village, as Elijah had done to the bands of armed men, which were sent by the king of Israel, to seize him; but they had not the spirit of Elijah. Paul, we have reason to believe, was moved by the Spirit of prophecy; and words spoken under a divine impulse, however severe, were not inconsistent with Christian charity. Our rule is plain, " not to render railing for railing, but to bless them that curse us, and pray for them that despitefully use us, and persecute us." Above all other examples is that of Jesus Christ, who instead of upbraiding his murderers with their wickedness, and denouncing the vengeance of Heaven against them, said, when he hung upon the cross, and felt their cruelty in every member of his body, " Father forgive them: for they know not what they do."

Lastly, How easily can God defend his own cause! By a word spoken in season, the designs of the Jewish Sanhedrim against Paul were defeated. When the enemies of the truth are united to oppose it, they are but men; and God says to his Church, " Who art thou, that thou shouldest be afraid of a man that shall die, and of the son of man which shall be made as grass?" At his command, their breath goes out, or their power and their wisdom strangely fail, so that " their hands cannot find their enterprise." Besides, although in their conspiracy against religion, they seem to be in perfect concord, yet they are influenced by very different motives, which may happen to clash with one another; and in the common affairs of life, they are divided by envy, jealousy, resentment, and an interference of pursuits. There is no true friendship among the wicked; it is merely a temporary connexion of interest, or a combination of mischief. With how much ease can Providence turn their union into open hostility, as in the case of the Ammonites, the Moabites, and the inhabitants of mount Seir, who having invaded the land of Judah, in the days of Jehoshaphat, perished by one another's sword; or in that of the Pharisees and Sadducees, who spent the fury, which was ready to burst forth upon Paul, in mutual clamour and contention? Let no good man ever act the part of a coward. God is with him; and who shall harm him, if he is a follower of that which is good? Let no good man despair of the interests of religion. Is not the arm of Omnipotence able to protect the cause of truth against every adverse power? "Why do the heathen rage, and the people imagine a vain thing? The kings of the earth set themselves, and the rulers take council together, against his anointed, saying, Let us break their bands asunder, and cast away their cords from us. He that sitteth in the heavens shall laugh: the Lord shall have them in derision. Then he shall speak unto them in his wrath, and vex them in his sore displeasure."

LECTURE XXVII.

PAUL BEFORE FELIX.

Chap. xxiv.

We have seen what courage and prudence Paul displayed in the presence of the high-priest and the rulers of the Jews, and by what expedient he defeated the purpose, for which the counsel was assembled. A few words seasonably spoken, revived the hostility of two rival sects, which were united for a moment in the prosecution; and so violent was the contest, that the Roman commander was obliged to interfere, and to carry back the prisoner to the castle.

By this disappointment, the malice of his enemies was exasperated. Paul had been marked out as a victim to their zeal; his death was deemed necessary to vindicate the honour of their religion; and if it could not be accomplished under the forms of law, which have often given the colour of justice to the most iniquitous deeds, it was determined, that he should perish by the hands of assassins. We are informed in the preceding chapter, "that when it was day, certain of the Jews banded together, and bound themselves under a curse, saying, that they would neither eat nor drink, till they had killed Paul." Such a conspiracy must excite our detestation, whether we reflect upon the purpose for which it was formed, or upon the solemn bond, by which the members pledged themselves to execute their plan. Having resolved upon the death of the Apostle, they guarded against the influence of their cooler thoughts, and the feelings of compunction or pity which these might have awakened, by engaging under a dreadful imprecation speedily to perpetrate the murder. Their own lives were staked upon the success of the enterprise; and the God of mercy and justice was invoked, to witness and to ratify a combination of blood. From this transaction we learn how much conscience may be debauched the principles of a false religion. Superstition will sanctify the foulest actions in the eyes of its deluded votaries. There is no atrocity, however revolting to the natural feelings, and the unsophisticated moral sentiments of mankind, to which the mind may not be reconciled, if it have been previously persuaded that the deed will be acceptable to God. The horrors of the inquisition, and the barbarous cruelties exercised upon the friends of truth by the Antichristian Church, are examples of crimes committed in the name of God, and mistaken for acts of holy zeal. Men have imagined, that they never stood higher in the favour of Heaven, than at the moment when they were displaying the malignity of demons, and the ferocity of savages.

There is a particular account, in the preceding chapter, of the manner in which this conspiracy was discovered by the chief captain, and of the plan which he immediately adopted for the security of Paul. He sent him under a strong guard to Felix the governor of Judea, who resided in Cesarea, and gave orders to his accusers to follow him. The chapter now before us relates the proceedings at this new tribunal.

Let us attend, in the first place, to the speech of Tertullus, an orator, whom Ananias and the elders had chosen, on account of his eloquence and address, to conduct the prosecution. Felix, before whom he was appointed to plead, was a freedman of the emperor Claudius, by whom he had been entrusted with the government of Judea. The accounts of his conduct in this high station, which have been transmitted to us by both Jews and Romans, are exceedingly unfavourable. He had, indeed, dispersed and destroyed some bands of robbers who infested the country, and to this very proper exercise of his authority Tertullus seems to allude, when he says, "By thee we enjoy great quietness;" but from the general history of his administration, he appears to have been a man void of all regard to justice and humanity. Under his government the people were subjected to innumerable vexations and injuries, and their property and lives were wantonly sacrificed, to gratify his avarice, or his revenge. Impatient of control, he procured the assassination of Jonathan the high-priest, whose only crime it was, that he had freely remonstrated against his tyrannical proceedings. In a word, relying upon the influence of his brother Pallas, who was in high favour with the emperor, "he exercised royal authority," to adopt the words of Tacitus, "with the spirit of a slave, and indulged himself in every species of cruelty and lust."*

After this description of the character of Felix, with what surprise must we read the speech of Tertullus! "Seeing that by thee we enjoy great quietness, and that very worthy deeds are done unto this nation by thy providence, we accept it always, and in all places, most noble Felix, with all thankfulness." What! was this man a stranger in Judea? Had he never heard the complaints and curses of the people against their unrighteous governor? Tertullus was one of those orators whose talents are exposed to sale, and are purchased by the highest bidder; a venal pleader, prepared to espouse either side of a question, and to employ, without moral discrimination, the means which seemed best adapted to ensure success. In order to obtain the condemnation of Paul, he endeavoured to gain the favour of the judge by flattery, than which nothing more readily steals upon the heart, and renders it more pliant and accommodating. The flattery was certainly gross, and had scarcely the semblance of truth; but Tertullus had, perhaps, studied human nature so well as to know, that none are more eager to grasp at the praise of virtue, than those who least deserve it. To them, indeed, it is most necessary, because, in the want of the reality, they may derive some advantage from the name. Eloquence, exerting its powers in giving a luminous and impressive statement of truth; in portraying the charms of virtue, and exhibiting the deformity of vice; in defending the innocent against oppression and calumny, and dragging forth the wicked to execration and punishment; eloquence employed in these important offices, and uniting with the clear deductions of reason and experience, all the energies of language, and all the ornaments of an ardent and cultivated imagination, is undoubtedly one of the noblest and most enviable talents, which a mortal can possess. It may uphold the religion and morals of a nation, and may save a sinking state from ruin. But, when it aims at exciting the passions, without enlightening the understanding; when, with its false colouring, it makes the worse appear the better cause; when it corrupts the imagination, and undermines the principles of morality; when like a base prostitute, it offers its services to every person who solicits its assistance; when it substitutes flattery for honest reproof, and condemns what it ought to applaud and

---

* Tacit. Hist. v. 9.

defend; it is more noxious than the pestilence which taints the air that we breathe, or the lightning which blinds us with its overpowering splendour, and overwhelms us with its irresistible force.

Tertullus proceeds to exhibit the grounds of accusation against the prisoner at the bar, which were three, sedition, heresy, and profanation of the temple. The charge of sedition is contained in these words. "We have found this man a pestilent fellow, and a mover of sedition among all the Jews throughout the world." From our knowledge of the history of Paul, we may boldly pronounce this charge to have been unfounded. But, as it was more likely than any other to prejudice a judge so jealous and suspicious, the unprincipled orator did not hesitate to advance it with all the confidence of truth. He is accused of heresy, when he is called "a ringleader of the sect of the Nazarenes;" an appellation given from contempt to the followers of Jesus, who lived in Nazareth, out of which no good thing was expected to come. The new religion was deemed a heresy, to which the Jews affixed the ideas of faction, error, and apostacy. Lastly, he is represented as "having gone about to profane the temple," because it was supposed that he had brought Trophimus, an uncircumcised Gentile, into its sacred inclosure. These were serious charges, which, had his enemies been able to substantiate them, would have subjected him to punishment, according to both the Jewish and the Roman law. Tertullus includes with an insinuation against Lysias, the chief captain as having obstructed the course of justice, by violently carrying off Paul, when the Sanhedrim was met to judge him. He says nothing respecting the intention of the Jews to put him to death, when he was found in the temple, or the conspiracy which some of them afterwards formed to assassinate him, and by the discovery of which, Lysias was induced to send him to Cesarea. With the art of an orator, he sets the conduct of his clients in the fairest light, and suppresses every circumstance unfavourable to their cause.

With this tissue of flattery and falsehood, let us contrast the simple and honest defence of the Apostle. "Forasmuch as I know, that thou hast been of many years a judge unto this nation, I do the more cheerfully answer for myself." This is not, like the introductory address of Tertullus, an insincere and undeserved compliment to Felix. Paul does not call him a righteous governor, and praise the mildness and equity of his administration; but merely expresses his happiness in having an opportunity to plead for himself before a judge, who having lived several years in Judea, was acquainted with its laws and usages, and with the temper and manners of the people. To him, the vehemence with which Paul was accused would not appear a proof or even a presumption of his guilt, as he was aware of the bitterness of Jewish zeal, and the intolerance which they displayed in their religious disputes. By his residence in the country, he had also acquired some knowledge of Christianity; and being a disciple neither of Moses nor of Christ, he was able to decide with coolness and impartiality, whether Paul was worthy of blame for having espoused and propagated the new faith.

The Apostle proceeds to reply to the several accusations in their order. The charge of sedition he expressly denies, and challenges his adversaries to prove, that he had been found in the temple, in the synagogues, or in any part of the city, engaged in disputation, or attempting to sow the seeds of disaffection to government. "Because that thou mayest understand, that there are yet but twelve days since I went up to Jerusalem for to worship. And they neither found me in the temple disputing with any man, neither raising up the people, neither in the synagogues, nor in the city: neither can they prove the things whereof they now accuse me." Paul, indeed, declined no proper opportunity of preaching the gospel, and defending it against its adversaries; but he always conducted himself with meekness and prudence. His behaviour as well as that of the other Apostles, was strictly conformable to the duty of good citizens. He exemplified the precept which he inculcated upon others, to be subject to the higher powers. In the primitive ages, Christianity was not propagated by exciting insurrections among the people, by inflaming their minds against the government, and by the overthrow of civil institutions; but by a simple manifestation of the truth, and by leaving it silently to work a change in the sentiments of mankind. The Christians cheerfully obeyed the laws, as far as was consistent with obedience to God; and when conscience forbade them to comply, they patiently submitted to sufferings. No bitterness of spirit was mingled with the disputes in which they were compelled to engage; no intolerant zeal was displayed against the most unreasonable and malignant opponents of truth. Like their blessed Master, "they did not cry, nor lift up, nor cause their voice to be heard in the streets."

To the charge of heresy he pleads guilty. "But this I confess unto thee, that after the way which they call heresy, so worship I the God of my fathers, believing all things which are written in the law and the Prophets." Christianity was stigmatized as a heresy. But, with whatever odious name it might be branded by the Jews, it was not an apostacy from the ancient religion of the country, for Paul continued to worship the God of his ancestors; and the doctrines which he had embraced, although they were represented by his accusers as novel and blasphemous, were contained in their own sacred writings. The law prefigured, and the Prophets foretold, Jesus Christ and redemption through his blood. He adds, "And have hope towards God, which they themselves also allow, that there shall be a resurrection of the dead, both of the just and unjust." The reason for specifying this article of his faith, seems to have been his former avowal of it in the presence of the Sanhedrim, which, having caused much contention among the members of the court, had probably been misrepresented to Felix. "If I have declared my hope of the resurrection of the dead, they cannot consistently blame me, since the same hope is entertained and professed by themselves." The resurrection of the body is not a doctrine peculiar to Christianity, but has always been an article in the creed of the Jews. It was rejected, indeed, by the Sadducees; but while in point of number they were an inconsiderable sect, their naked and comfortless system was at variance with the faith of the nation, founded upon the promises of God, and was regarded with detestation by the devout and sober minded part of the community. With the greater part even of the orthodox Jews, this hope was nothing more than a speculative opinion; but the life of Paul was an illustration of its practical effects. "And herein do I exercise myself, to have always a conscience void of offence toward God, and toward men." In the view of the retribution which will take place at the resurrection of the just and the unjust, it was the constant study of the Apostle, to act such a part, that his conscience should bear testimony in his favour, and anticipate the approbation of his judge. Whatever opinion, therefore, Felix might entertain of the grounds of his hope, he could not condemn him for adopting a principle, which exerted so salutary an influence upon his conduct. A heathen might deem it a delusion; but it was a pardonable one, since it was favourable to the practice of virtue.

To the last charge of profaning the temple he answers in the following words. "Now after many years, I came to bring alms to my nation, and offerings. Whereupon certain Jews from Asia found me purified in the temple, neither with multitude, nor with tumult: who ought to have been here before thee, and object, if they had ought against me." He did not return to Jerusalem, after a long absence, for the purposes of sedition or impiety, but on an errand of charity, to bring alms to his countrymen, or those contributions which he had collected for the relief of the poor. So far was he from showing any disrespect to the temple, that having joined with some others in a religious vow, and purified himself according to the law, he went into it to offer the customary sacrifices. During the time which he spent in it, he was guilty of no disorder, and did nothing inconsistent with the sacred nature of the place. Those who saw him there, could not justly charge him with any offence; Paul complains that they were not present to be confronted with him, that he might have an opportunity to establish his innocence. At the same time, he boldly challenges those who were present, the high-priest and the elders, to point out any fault in his conduct, when he appeared before the council, "except this one voice, that he cried standing among them, Touching the resurrection of the dead, I am called in question by you this day." To this declaration of his faith, they could not reasonably object. The Pharisees believed the resurrection of the body: and the Sadducees must have allowed, that Paul had the same liberty to assert, which they had to deny, it.

Such is the defence which the Apostle made for himself, simple, distinct, dignified, and in every part of it, strictly conformable to truth. We may remark the courage which he displayed, when standing alone before his accusers and his judge; his calmness in replying to misrepresentation and falsehood; and the confidence with which he maintained his innocence. Instead of shrinking from an investigation of his conduct, he claimed it as his right.

Felix resolved to delay giving judgment, till Lysias, the chief captain should arrive, from whom he expected a full and impartial account of the matter. It is remarked by Luke, "that he had more perfect knowledge of that way;" or that in consequence of having lived several years in Judea, he was acquainted with the history and doctrines of the Christian religion. He probably considered it as a harmless superstition, and suspecting, perhaps, that this prosecution had originated in bigotry, he was not disposed to give implicit credit to the accusations of the Jews. He could not, however, dismiss Paul from his tribunal, because he had yet heard only strong assertions of his guilt, on the one hand, and of his innocence, on the other; but he ordered him to be treated with kindness, and allowed him as much liberty as a prisoner could enjoy.

The knowledge of the new religion which the governor, who seems to have been no careless spectator of what was passing around him, had already acquired, excited his curiosity to hear an accurate detail of its principles from Paul, who was one of its most eminent teachers. "And after certain days, when Felix came with his wife Drusilla, which was a Jewess, he sent for Paul, and heard him concerning the faith in Christ." Drusilla was the daughter of the Herod whose tragical end is related in the twelfth chapter of this book. She was first married to Azizus king of Emesenes, who had consented for her sake to embrace the Jewish religion; but not long after she deserted him, and was married a second time to Felix, who had seduced her affections. Her conduct gave great and just offence to the Jews, who detested her as an adulteress, and a traitress to her religion, which condemned her for entering into this relation with a Gentile.* Such were the persons before whom Paul was summoned to give an account of the Christian doctrine; and when we recollect what has been already said with respect to the unjust and oppressive administration of Felix, we shall perceive his reason for selecting the topics, upon which he discoursed in their presence.

Paul having been requested by Felix to explain "the faith in Christ," willingly embraced this opportunity to give a summary account of the doctrines and institutions of his religion. To preach Christ "as the power of God unto salvation to every one that believeth, to the Jew first, and also to the Greek," was his favourite employment. He was not ashamed of this subject, however strange and foolish it might seem to men whose minds were preoccupied by the maxims of a vain philosophy, and the tenets of a corrupt theology. His heart warmed with love and gratitude to the Saviour, rendered his tongue eloquent in commending him to the world. But, Paul was too wise and too faithful a preacher, to suppress any part of the truth, when circumstances required him to publish it. He adapted his discourses not to the taste, but to the character and

---

* Joseph. Antiq. lib. xx. cap. 5.

situation of his hearers. Reflecting that he now stood before two persons of profligate manners, to whom the doctrine of salvation would be uninteresting, unless their consciences were alarmed, he entered upon an illustration of those duties, in which they were chiefly deficient, and announced the awful sanction, by which Christianity confirms them.

A courtly preacher, when addressing such auditors, would have contented himself with representing the gospel as a new theory of religious opinions, and with a vague declamation upon virtue and vice, more calculated to amuse than to reform. Paul, dismissing the arts of accommodation, as, in the present case, inconsistent with the fidelity which he owed to God and to the souls of men, selected a subject, which, although not grateful to the feelings, through the divine blessing, would be profitable. He reasoned on justice and temperance in the presence of Felix, who openly lived in the neglect of those virtues. He held up a faithful mirror before him, which exhibited his features in all their deformity. A lecture on justice and temperance was a direct reproof of the man, who had often abused his power to oppress those whom he ought to have protected, and who in order to gratify his sensual appetites, had invaded the most sacred domestic rights, and broken the dearest bonds of society.

It is possible to declaim against vice in terms so soft and gentle, that our words, like pointless arrows, shall not penetrate the conscience. It may be represented as a failing or impropriety, which a regard to decorum requires us to correct, and as productive of such consequences to our reputation, our health, our worldly interest, and our domestic comfort, as it will be prudent to avoid. Paul thundered against it with the honest indignation of a virtuous mind, and with the authority of a messenger from God, commissioned to denounce the punishment which awaits the guilty and impenitent. To Felix and Drusilla, to whom also a part of his discourse was directed, he gave warning of the judgment to come, at which the great and the small, without distinction of persons, shall appear before God, and be recompensed according to their deeds. The principles of morality are exposed, without defence, to the inroads of our impetuous passions, if they are not exhibited in connexion with a future retribution. A perception of the beauty of virtue and the deformity of vice, which has been represented as sufficient to excite us to our duty, and to guard our hearts against temptation, is a romantic theory, founded in ignorance of human nature, and inattention to experience. The moral sense, of which philosophers talk, can mean nothing but conscience; and, without a reference to a higher tribunal, conscience has no authority. It is only by powerful appeals to our hopes and fears, that the heart will be interested, and the sinner, fascinated by the syren song of pleasure, and hastening to seize forbidden joys, will be rescued from the illusions of sense, and induced to abandon his purpose. The doctrine of a judgment to come gives a force to the commands of religion, which the boldest sinners have found themselves unable to resist.

The power of the word of God appeared in the impression which it made upon Felix. "As Paul reasoned of righteousness, temperance, and judgment to come, he trembled." Conscience reminded him of his crimes against the laws of God and man, and summoned him to a more awful tribunal than that of the Roman emperor. What a surprising spectacle is now presented to us! The Apostle, whose liberty and life depended upon the will of Felix, dares to address him in the language of truth, without being deterred by the thought, that so wicked a man was more likely to be offended than reformed. Felix sitting as his judge, surrounded with his guards, and invested with supreme power in the province of Judea, trembles at the words of a poor unfriended prisoner. They have exchanged situations. Felix is the criminal, arraigned and convicted; and Paul is the judge, or rather the accredited deputy of the Sovereign Judge of heaven and earth.

But, although Felix felt a momentary conviction of guilt, his heart was not changed. Truth was an unexpected and unwelcome visitant, whose presence troubled him, and interrupted those pleasures to which he was still attached; and he made haste, therefore, to dismiss it. "Felix trembled, and answered, Go thy way for this time; when I have a convenient season, I will call for thee." What! was any other business more urgent than the reformation of his conduct, or more important than the salvation of his soul! The governor would have found leisure to listen to Paul, if he had relished his doctrine, and been as deeply affected as the jailor of Philippi, who exclaimed, "What must I do to be saved?" but an hour, or a minute, appears too long, when we are compelled to hear those practices exposed and condemned, which we cannot justify, and are resolved not to forsake.

We do not find that a convenient season ever occurred to Felix, for hearing Paul on the same subject. The governor, indeed, sent often for him; but he confined him, we may presume, to general topics, and cautiously avoided the repetition of those truths, which had given him so much uneasiness. He was a base, unprincipled man. Convinced of the innocence of Paul, he retained him in custody, expecting that his friends would purchase his liberty with money. Felix would not do justice without a bribe. As a bribe was never offered, Paul remained in prison, till Felix was recalled, when he left him in bonds, to please the Jews; trusting, that by this instance of attention to their wishes, they should be so much gratified, as to forgive the crimes of his administration. In this hope, however, he was disappointed, for soon after his return, the chief men of the nation followed him to Rome with their complaints, and he narrowly escaped the just punishment of the wrongs with which he had afflicted Judea, by the intercession of his brother, who was, at that time, in favour with the emperor.

From the history of what passed between Felix and Paul, when the latter reasoned before him concerning righteousness, temperance, and judgment to come, we may draw the following instructions.

First, We conceive what power the word of God can exert upon the conscience. There is, indeed, no greater virtue in the terms in which his will is expressed, than in those of ordinary language, nor can the sound of them, like the pretended incantations of magic, produce any mysterious effect upon the hearers. The letter is dead; it is the Spirit who gives life. When the secret influence of its Author accompanies the simple words in which it is delivered, the impression made upon the mind is more wonderful than human eloquence was ever able to effect. Felix might have been quite composed, and might have even been entertained, by the elegant declamation of a philosopher against vice; but when a plain Apostle preaches, without a nice selection of terms, and without rhetorical ornaments, the governor trembles. He sees, or seems to see, the God of justice and purity seated on his throne of judgment; he hears a voice accusing him of his crimes, and demanding his punishment. "Is not my word like as a fire? saith the Lord; and like a hammer that breaketh the rock in pieces?" It is the word of Him, who can impress upon the soul such a sense of his majesty and holiness, as shall disturb and terrify it amidst the most profound security. Its efficacy, however, does not arise solely from the momentous and awful nature of its doctrines, but from the divine power which accompanies it, and operates, not blindly and necessarily, but under the direction of sovereign wisdom.

I remark, therefore, in the second place, that those to whom it is addressed, are not all affected by it, in the same manner. Felix trembled, when Paul reasoned of righteousness, temperance, and judgment to come; but we do not read that Drusilla experienced a similar agitation. She seems to have retained the utmost composure, during a discourse which should have alarmed her as well as her husband. Perhaps, she supported her courage by the thought, that although an adulteress, she was guilty of none of those acts of injustice with which Felix was chargeable, for in the estimate of some persons, a less degree of wickedness is positive virtue; perhaps, she was a more hardened and determined sinner than he; perhaps, being a Jewess, she contrived to persuade herself, that as one of the chosen people, she should find favour with her Maker, notwithstanding the disorders of her life. It is impossible to enumerate or to conceive the various methods, by which sinners fortify themselves against the influence of the word of God. Their success in the art of deceiving themselves is manifest, from their indifference to the most solemn and momentous truths. While one man startles at his danger, and makes haste to escape from it, another hears the doctrines by which he is awakened, with consummate listlessness. Salvation is equally necessary to all, but few seek it with earnestness. "Many say, Peace and safety, although sudden destruction is coming upon them, as travail upon a woman with child; and they shall not escape."

In the third place, impressions and emotions, which seemed to prognosticate conversion, frequently pass away, without producing any lasting effect. Who would not have augured good from the fears of Felix? But the fit of terror was transient; he exerted himself to put a stop to it, by dismissing the preacher; and he immediately returned to his former course of injustice and profligacy. Often have men exclaimed, in a moment of alarm, What must we do to be saved? who never honestly and resolutely engaged in the work of salvation. Sinners contrive a variety of expedients to recall the hopes which had fled from them, and again please themselves with their own delusions. Starting up, like a man who is roused from sleep by a loud noise, they continue awake for a short time, and are restless; but they gradually sink into their usual state of insensibility. They quiet their consciences, perhaps, with the opiate of pleasure. Plunging into folly and dissipation, they forget the cause of their uneasiness; and turning away their eyes from the danger which alarmed them, they persuade themselves that it is removed. Let us not be deceived by occasional appearances of religion in others, or in ourselves. Although the spring should open with a fair promise of fruit, yet a fatal blast may, in a single night, disappoint our expectations.

Lastly, Let us beware of trifling with the word of God, by dismissing it, when it solicits our attention, and deferring the duty which it immediately demands, to a future opportunity. "Go thy way for this time; when I have a convenient season, I will call for thee." In this disrespectful manner, it is often treated, when it is pressing upon the attention of men the concerns of their souls, and has begun to exert its power upon their consciences. But, they promise to themselves, that the business which is neglected to-day, shall be attended to to-morrow. It is a promise which they have no serious intention to perform; for if they were sincerely resolved to engage in the work of salvation, they would presently enter upon it. It would be of such magnitude in their eyes, that the delay even of an hour would seem too long. They would dread impediments, which the progress of time might create; and would be urged on by the uncertainty of life, the unexpected termination of which might send them down into the grave with their resolutions unexecuted. "Whatsoever thy hand findeth to do, do it with thy might; for there is no work, nor device, nor knowledge, nor wisdom, in the grave whither thou goest."

Procrastinating sinners, why is the present not a convenient season? Do you expect, that as you advance in life, your hearts will grow softer, and the influence of the world upon them will decline? Ah! how much are you deceived? The result will be totally different; for your hearts will become callous, and earthly cares will twist themselves more closely about them. Is any business more interesting than the well-being of your souls, which are far more precious than ten thousand worlds, and through your neglect, may be lost for ever? Are you at this moment in no danger of eternal perdition? Is there no sentence against you in the word of God, the execution of which is deferred only by his patience, upon the continued exercise of which you cannot reckon? Are your lives more certain now, although you enjoy all the vigour of youth, than they will be at any subsequent stage of your existence? Alas! that men, whose eternal fate may depend upon the determination of the present day, and to whom salvation is offered, perhaps, for the last time, should permit themselves to be imposed upon by arguments, which would not dissuade them from immediate attention to their secular interests, and which are so evidently fallacious, that they condemn all but themselves, who allow their conduct to be influenced by them. The present is a convenient season; other opportunities may be less favourable, but will not be more advantageous. Should you not consider, that the same motives from which you delay till to-morrow, will prevail upon you to-morrow to delay till the next day; and that you may go on in this course of guilt and folly till life is exhausted, and death has set its inviolable seal upon your doom? Disregard not therefore, the voice of God, nor say to him, "We will afterwards hear thee," lest provoked by this insult, which would excite the indignation of a human superior, he should refuse to listen to your prayers, when you shall call upon him in the day of distress. Remember his awful words, which are full of terror to every careless sinner. "Because I have called, and ye refused, I have stretched out my hand, and no man regarded; but ye have set at nought my counsel, and would none of my reproof: I also will laugh at your calamity, I will mock when your fear cometh; when your fear cometh as desolation, and your destruction cometh as a whirlwind; when distress and anguish cometh upon you. Then they shall call upon me, but I will not answer; they seek me early, but they shall not find me: for that they hated knowledge and did not choose the fear of the Lord. They would none of my counsel; they despised all my reproof. Therefore shall they eat of the fruit of their own way, and be filled with their own devices."

LECTURE XXVIII.

PAUL BEFORE FESTUS AND AGRIPPA.

Chap. xxvi.

Felix, whose character and conduct were reviewed in the last Lecture, was one of those in whom conscience has not entirely lost its authority, but whose sinful habits and propensities are so strong, as to counteract the force of its commands. He was convinced that Paul was innocent of the crimes laid to his charge, and was, therefore, bound in justice to set him immediately at liberty. But he retained him in bonds from a motive of avarice; and when he was recalled from the government of Judea, he left him in prison, in the hope that by this instance of complaisance to the Jews, he should prevent them from carrying their complaints of his cruelty and extortion to the emperor.

Felix was succeeded by Festus, who a few days after his arrival in the province, went up from Cesarea to Jerusalem. The hatred of the chief priests and rulers against Paul was implacable. Time had not abated its violence, nor had his sufferings during an imprisonment for at least two years, inclined them to relax the severity of their measures. Hence, they now endeavoured to persuade Festus to send for him to Jerusalem, that he might there undergo a trial; under this apparently reasonable and harmless request, concealing a most nefarious design. During the long interval which had elapsed since they resolved upon the assassination of Paul, they had not repented of their purpose. Often, we may believe, it had been the subject of reflection and conversation in their confidential meetings; but the only sentiment which ever arose in their minds was regret that they had been prevented from accomplishing it. A false zeal for God had perverted their moral judgment and feelings. Religion, misunderstood, and corrupted by the influence of human passions, justified, in their eyes, one of the most atrocious deeds of injustice and cruelty. In cases of this nature, no remedy can be expected from conscience, which sometimes arrests the wicked man in his career, because it is preoccupied by an erroneous idea of duty, and prescribes, in the name of God, actions which it ought, in the most explicit manner, to condemn. The chief priests and elders had concerted, that Paul should be murdered in the way; and they might have accomplished their design without detection, because the country was infested with bands of robbers and lawless persons, to whom the guilty deed would have been imputed.

With this request Festus refused to comply; and the enemies of Paul were obliged to repair to Cesarea, where he successfully defended himself against their accusations. As the governor, however, in consequence of fresh solicitations, or with a view to conciliate the favour of the Jews, at the commencement of his administration, now discovered an inclination to transfer the judgment of the cause to Jerusalem, the Apostle found it necessary to appeal to Cesar. This appeal to a foreign judge was not made with a view to reflect upon the laws of his country as insufficient for the security of innocence, but from his certain knowledge, that he had no justice to expect from the partial and hostile tribunal of the Sanhedrim. As a Roman citizen, he had a right to claim the protection of the Roman laws; and it was the privilege of a citizen, to carry his cause from an inferior judicatory to the emperor himself, not only when a sentence, by which he deemed himself aggrieved, had been pronounced, but at the commencement, or at any stage of the process. This expedient was calculated to secure an impartial execution of the laws. It was a check upon those magistrates of cities, and governers of provinces, who were disposed to abuse their power; and it afforded an accused person the benefit of a second trial, before a court where the partialities and prejudices arising from local circumstances, which frequently obstruct the course of justice, would not operate to his disadvantage. Paul expected fairer treatment from a heathen emperor than from the supreme council of the Jews; and was willing to submit his cause rather to Nero than to the high priest.

By the appeal to Cesar, the proceedings were stopped; and the Apostle was remanded to prison, till an opportunity should occur of sending him to Rome. In the mean time, Agrippa and his sister

Bernice came to Cesarea on a visit to Festus. Their father was the Herod, who killed James, the brother of John, with the sword, and died, as this historian relates, by the judgment of God. At the death of his father, Agrippa was too young to succeed him in the throne; but he received from the emperor Claudius the kingdom of Chalcis, which was afterwards exchanged for other dominions. Bernice was first married to her uncle Herod, king of Chalcis, and after his decease, to Polemon, king of Cilicia, with whom her connexion was not of long continuance; for she soon returned to her brother, and was now living with him, under suspicion of an unlawful familiarity between them.* Festus having mentioned the case of Paul to Agrippa, the king expressed a desire to hear him. His curiosity would be gratified by seeing a man who had rendered himself so remarkable, first by his zeal for Judaism, and afterwards by his conversion to Christianity, and by receiving from him a true and particular account of the new religion, which was the subject of so much conversation and discussion.

When the court was assembled, Paul having been permitted to speak for himself, began by expressing his happiness in being called to plead his cause, before so competent a judge as Agrippa. He does not, indeed, insinuate, that he expected him to be more candid than Festus, nor does it appear, that the governor entertained any prejudice against him, and was disposed to favour his accusers. But, Agrippa, who had been educated in the knowledge of the law of Moses, and of the writings of the Prophets, was better qualified to decide upon the merits of the question than Festus, who had lately come into Judea, and was not acquainted with its religion and customs. "I think myself happy, king Agrippa, because I shall answer for myself this day before thee, touching all the things whereof I am accused of the Jews; especially because I know thee to be expert in all customs and questions which are among the Jews." The man who addresses an audience, to whom the subject of discourse is new, and who are ignorant of the principles, without which it cannot be understood, is placed in disadvantageous circumstances. When delivering the most important truths, he may seem to utter crude fancies, and the reveries of a disordered brain. Festus thought Paul mad, when he was stating

---

* Joseph. Antiq. lib. xx. cap. 5.

some of the great doctrines and facts of Christianity. But, in the presence of Agrippa, the Apostle could illustrate the harmony between the gospel and the law, with the hope of producing conviction, or at least of proving that the new religion was not so irrational and impious, as its malignant enemies represented it. Accordingly, the king acknowledged that the arguments had made a favourable impression upon his mind.

After this introduction, Paul proceeds to give an account of himself prior to his conversion, in order to pave the way for the relation of that event. " My manner of life from my youth, which was at the first among mine own nation at Jerusalem, know all the Jews which knew me from the beginning, (if they would testify,) that after the most straightest sect of our religion I lived a Pharisee." The Jews were divided into several sects, differing widely in their sentiments and practices, although they were united in the same religious fellowship. Of all those sects the Pharisees were the strictest. Professing a sacred reverence for the law, they were scrupulously punctual in observing the ceremonial duties which it enjoined, and the traditions of the elders, in which religion was supposed chiefly to consist. Josephus informs us, that they were accounted more pious than others, and more exact in the interpretation of the laws. To this sect Paul was attached in the preceding part of his life. He adopted its peculiar tenets, rigidly conformed to its institutions, so that "touching the righteousness which was in the law, he was blameless," and imbibed the vehement zeal, which distinguished the Pharisees, and usually characterises those sects, which affect pre-eminence in orthodoxy and purity.

His connexion with the Pharisees he had now renounced, as well as some of their tenets, which were contrary to the Christian faith; but he retained such of them as were agreeable to Scripture. For why did he now stand a prisoner at the tribunal of Festus? Had he committed any crime against the state, or was he guilty of any offence against religion? No; he was persecuted by his countrymen, for his steadfast adherence to the promises of God, which they also professed to believe. " And now I stand, and am judged for the hope of the promise made of God, unto our fathers: unto which promise our twelve tribes, constantly serving God day and night, hope to come; for which hope's sake, king Agrippa, I am accused of the Jews." The promise made to the fathers is the promise of the Messiah, or, as some suppose, that of the resurrection of the body to eternal life. Paul, however, was not blamed for simply teaching the resurrection of the dead, which was expected by all the Jews, with the exception of the Sadducees, but for asserting that it would be affected by the agency of Jesus of Nazareth, and that God had given an example and earnest of it, by restoring him to life. The subject of dispute, between him and his adversaries was confined to the ground of our hope; and in this discussion the truth of Christianity was involved.

If the question which follows, be considered as addressed to Agrippa, it is not easy to perceive the propriety of it. " Why should it be thought a thing incredible with you, that God should raise the dead?" The resurrection of the dead was not deemed incredible by the Jews, in whose Scriptures it is expressly taught, and who entertained such conceptions of the power of God, as removed the difficulties with which it seems to be encumbered. They did not disbelieve the resurrection of our Saviour, because they judged it to be impossible, but because they counted him an impostor, in whose favour it was absurd and blasphemous to suppose God to have exerted his miraculous power. I consider the question, therefore, as addressed to the Gentile part of the audience, to whom the resurrection did seem incredible. As it was a doctrine of great importance in the Christian system, Paul was careful in this stage of his discourse, to obviate an objection against it, which arises from the complete destruction of the body in the grave. How can it be believed that its parts, which are separated, decomposed, and in appearance annihilated, shall be collected together, and arranged in their original order; and that it shall live again, after an interval of hundreds or thousands of years? He reminds the Gentiles that, however strange it may seem, the event ceases to be improbable, as soon as we reflect upon the agent, to whose power no limits can be assigned. He who created the body of man, is undoutedly able to restore it, after it had been blended with its native elements. Nothing which may be done, is impossible to omnipotence; no effect, how much soever it may surpass the common operations of nature, should be acounted too wonderful to be believed, when God has declared his intention to produce it. "Ye do err," said our Lord to the Sadducees, not knowing the Scriptures, nor the power of God."

Paul returns to his own history. While he lived a Pharisee, he had conceived an implacable hatred against Jesus Christ, which was displayed in many acts of violence and cruelty, of which his disciples were the objects. He dragged them to prison, consented to their death, scourged them in the synagogues, in which the Jews were wont to inflict corporal punishment upon offenders against religion, compelled them to blaspheme, or made every effort to force them to deny Christ, and, perhaps, in some instances, succeeded through the frailty of the sufferers, and in the excess of his rage, pursued them to strange cities, to which they had fled for safety. In persecuting the Church, Paul acted from conscience. He never doubted that Jesus was an impostor, and consequently, that the means which he employed to check the progress of his religion, were acceptable to God. "I verily thought with myself, that I ought to do many things contrary to the name of Jesus of Nazareth." We learn, by the way, that the standard of our duty is not conscience, which sometimes calls good evil, and evil good, but the perfect and unchangeable law of God; and that it will not be a sufficient apology for our errors of practice, that we can plead its dictates, because there is a higher authority, by which its commands are controlled. We perceive, too, that sincerity, of which some men speak, as if it were the only virtue, or as if it would atone for almost every mistake, is of no value, unless we be sincere in what is right. No man was ever more sincere, or more fully convinced of the lawfulness of his proceedings than Paul, when he persecuted the disciples of Christ; but notwithstanding this persuasion, he afterwards reflected upon his conduct with shame and detestation, and pronounced himself to be the chief of sinners. We may farther see the difference between false and true zeal. False zeal is a hateful compound of pride, passion, and injustice. It seeks the injury and destruction of those against whom it is directed, and, like a torrent, sweeps away every thing before it. The man of enlightened zeal, entertains a much stronger hatred of sin than the false zealot, and opposes it with honest indignation; but he pities the sinner, is desirous to reclaim him, and is far from thinking, that to torture his body is the best expedient for saving his soul. Saul, the persecutor, is not, surely, a pattern to Christians, although many of them have found it more congenial to their proud and impatient temper, to imitate his furious zeal against the gospel, than to comply with the exhortation delivered by him, in the character of an Apostle, "in meekness to instruct those that oppose themselves, if God peradventure will give them repentance to the acknowledging of the truth."

Paul proceeds to account for his subsequent conduct, in endeavouring to propagate the religion which he had laboured to destroy. "Whereupon as I went to Damascus, with authority and commission from the chief priests, at mid-day, O king, I saw in the way a light from heaven, above the brightness of the sun, shining round about me, and them that journeyed with me. And, when we were all fallen to the earth, I heard a voice speaking unto me, and saying in the Hebrew tongue, Saul, Saul, why persecutest thou me? It is hard for thee to kick against the pricks. And I said, who art thou, Lord? And he said, I am Jesus whom thou persecutest." As the conversion of Paul was the subject of a former Lecture, it is not necessary now to give a particular illustration of it.* Yet, the repeated references to it in his speeches, and the miraculous manner in which it was accomplished, will justify me in making a few remarks in this place, upon an event, from which many important instructions may be drawn.

The first remark relates to its extraordinary nature. Paul was not brought to the knowledge of the truth, by the ordinary means, but by an unusual, and what we may strictly call a miraculous, dispensation. We do not know of a similar interposition in favour of any other person, although it would, perhaps, be presumptuous to affirm, that God has never again stept aside from his established method, for the salvation of a sinner; but we are certain, that it is not by visions and voices from heaven, that men are commonly converted. From his character and circumstances, Paul seems to have been beyond the reach of the ordinary means. Yet, it was not properly for his own sake, that this singular plan was adopted, for in the sight of God, Saul of Tarsus was of no more importance than any other Jew, but to make his conversion at once a striking proof of the truth of Christianity, and an illustrious display of the sovereignty of divine grace.

I remark, in the second place, that at the time of his conversion, his mind was in a state highly unfavourable to a change. Had he been a man of loose manners, an open transgressor of the law of God, his conscience might have been easily alarmed, so that he should have willingly listened to the gospel, proclaiming pardon to

---

* Lect. xii.

the guilty. But, he was a Pharisee, elated by a proud confidence in his own righteousness, who treated the humiliating doctrine of salvation by grace with contempt. Had he been a calm and moderate man, he might have candidly examined the evidence in favour of Christianity, and have been convinced by it. But, his prejudices were strong; they were wrought up, according to his own confession, to madness; and agreeably to the usual process of the passions, his hatred of the gospel became the more virulent, the more it was indulged. His case was hopeless without a moral miracle, analogous to the power displayed in making water flow from a solid rock, and life return to a dead body in the grave. The conversion of Paul demonstrates the immediate agency of God, " who quickeneth the dead, and calleth those things which be not as though they were."

In the third place, this event affords a striking illustration of the grace of God, or of the free, unconditional exercise of his mercy. It elucidates and confirms the doctrine, that salvation is not of works, but of grace. Much has been said concerning certain qualifications which a sinner must possess, that he may be a proper object of the favour of his Maker; but to this idea the case before us gives no countenance. In Paul, at the time of his conversion, there was no qualifications, which could recommend him to divine mercy, or render it congruous and equitable, that it should be extended to him in preference to others. He was actuated, in a high degree, by all those passions, which are just objects of abhorrence and punishment, pride, rage, enmity to the truth, and implacable hatred against good men. There was no relenting of heart, nor so much as a doubt in his mind with respect to the propriety of his conduct; he was decided in his opposition to the gospel, and bent upon the extirpation of it from the earth. It was at this moment, the most unlikely of all to be the season of gracious visitation, that Jesus whom he persecuted, chose to appear, not to punish but to pardon his crimes, and to employ the blasphemer and persecutor in his service. Was not Paul, without controversy, saved by grace? And with this example in his eye, why should any man, however unworthy, despair of obtaining salvation, when he seeks it by faith?

In the last place, the conversion of Paul was sudden and complete. It may be said, indeed, of every convert, that he passes at once from a state of nature to a state of grace, because a middle state between condemnation and pardon, between the bondage of sin and spiritual liberty, is inconceivable. But, in most cases, there is a previous process, of which the steps are distinctly marked. Serious thoughts arise in the mind of the sinner; remorse for past offences, and fear of punishment disturb his peace; tears are shed, and prayers are multiplied; and the duties of religion are diligently and anxiously performed. The conversion of Paul, like the creation of light, was accomplished in an instant. He who but a moment before breathed threatenings and slaughter against the disciples of Jesus, lies prostrate before him, and says, "Lord, what wilt thou have me to do?" This was not the transient effect of a fit of terror, the deceitful language of distress, which is forgotten as soon as the cause which extorted it is removed. The sincerity of his conversion is manifest from his subsequent conduct. The conviction of the truth of Christianity which now took possession of his mind, lasted during the remainder of his life, and called forth his vigorous and well-supported exertions in its service. Jesus Christ did not appear to him, solely for his own salvation, but to employ him in preaching the gospel to the nations of the world; and, accordingly, he gave him the following commission. " But rise, and stand upon thy feet, for I have appeared unto thee for this purpose, to make thee a minister and a witness both of these things which thou hast seen, and of those things in the which I will appear unto thee; delivering thee from the people and from the Gentiles, unto whom now I send thee, to open their eyes, and to turn them from darkness to light, and from the power of Satan unto God, that they may receive forgiveness of sins, and inheritance among them which are sanctified by faith that is in me."

The office with which Paul was invested was of the most honourable nature; and such it seems to every Christian. But, in the state of the world at that time, it subjected him to the contempt and hatred of all classes of men. By the Greeks he was accounted a babbler, and by the Jews an apostate and a heretic; and we shall, perhaps, form an idea of his situation tolerably exact, by supposing it to have been similar to that of the ringleader of some illiterate and enthusiastic sect in our own age, whom high and low, learned and unlearned, never mention but in terms of scorn and detestation, with this difference, however, that while our laws protect every man in the exercise of his religion, the life of the Apostle was exposed to perpetual danger. Paul was perfectly aware of the consequences of accepting the office; but he neither declined it at first, nor did he afterwards discover any inclination to resign it. "Whereupon, O king Agrippa, I was not disobedient unto the heavenly vision: but showed first unto them of Damascus, and at Jerusalem, and throughout all the coasts of Judea, and then to the Gentiles, that they should repent and turn to God, and do works meet for repentance. For these causes, the Jews caught me in the temple, and went about to kill me. Having therefore obtained help of God, I continue unto this day, witnessing both to small and great, saying none other things than those which the Prophets and Moses did say should come: that Christ should suffer, and that he should be the first that should rise from the dead, and should show light unto the people, and to the Gentiles." The alacrity with which he engaged in the service of Christ, and the undaunted courage, which he displayed in performing his duty, are proofs of his full persuasion of the truth of the gospel, and of the complete change of views and principles which he had experienced, in consequence of the appearance of our Saviour, in the way to Damascus.

While the Apostle was relating the manner of his conversion, and the doctrines which he had since preached to Jews and Gentiles, he was interrupted by Festus, who exclaimed, "Paul, thou art beside thyself: much learning doth make thee mad." If we reflect upon the character and circumstances of Festus, we shall not be surprised, that Paul appeared to him in the light of a madman. The governor was a heathen, who probably knew little about the Jewish religion, and had scarcely heard of Christianity, before he came into Judea. To such a man, how strange must every thing relative to it have seemed! What could he think of Paul's miraculous conversion! How different from his views of religion, was the account which the apostle gave of the design of his ministry, to open the eyes of sinners, to deliver them from the dominion of Satan, and to sanctify them through faith; and of the grand facts on which Christianity is founded, the death and resurrection of its Author! These were subjects which the governor could not comprehend, and which excited no distinct notions in his mind. The discourse which he had heard, seemed to be a jumble of waking dreams, a collection of extravagant fancies, more resembling the ravings of an insane person, than the thoughts of a man in his senses. At the same time, as Paul had referred to the writings of Moses and the Prophets, and had probably cited a variety of passages from them, Festus concluded, that he was a man of learning, whose mind intense study had disordered, and who was bewildered by the multitude of his ideas. "Much learning doth make thee mad."

To this abrupt and indecent charge Paul replied with temper and politeness. He remembered the respect due to the supreme magistrate of the province, and displayed the meekness, which should characterise a Christian, upon every occasion. A passionate answer would have been unsuitable to his present circumstances, and to the spirit of religion, which he was endeavouring to vindicate and recommend. "I am not mad, most noble Festus; but speak forth the words of truth and soberness." In support of this assertion, he appealed to Agrippa. "For the king knoweth of these things, before whom also I speak freely: for I am persuaded that none of these things are hidden from him; for this thing was not done in a corner." To Agrippa, a professor of the Jewish religion, the writings of the Prophets, which foretold the sufferings and glory of the Messiah, were familiar. He could not be ignorant of the history of Jesus of Nazareth, and of the report of his resurrection, which was publicly and confidently asserted by his disciples. He had undoubtedly heard of the conversion of Paul, which, whether we consider the character of the man, or the suddenness of the change, must have been a subject of general conversation. With respect to both these events, it was true, "that this thing was not done in a corner." The conversion of the Apostle was soon made known by his appearance in the character of a preacher of the gospel; and, besides, the men who accompanied him to Damascus, were witnesses of the miraculous interposition by which it was affected. The resurrection of Jesus was a fact of public notoriety. The Roman soldiers, who were stationed to watch the sepulchre, saw the angel descend, and roll away the stone which closed the entrance to it; the body could not be found; the disciples appeared in the streets and in the temple, affirming that their Master was risen; and many miracles were performed in confirmation of their testimony. It is an argument of great weight in favour of the gospel, that it was published at the time, when the events which it records, are said to have happened; that it was submitted to the examination of those, who, had it been a human contrivance, could have easily convicted it of imposture; and that it stood this severe test, and prevailed, in circumstances which would have proved fatal to every thing but truth.

After this indirect appeal to Agrippa, Paul turns from Festus to the king himself. "King Agrippa, believest thou the Prophets? I know that thou believest." Agrippa and all the Jews, believed that the Prophets were divinely inspired, and consequently, that their predictions should be punctually fulfilled. But, no man who held this belief, and understood the prophetical writings, could refuse to acknowledge Jesus to be the Messiah, because his character and the events of his life are so clearly described in them. The argument from prophecy was sufficient for the conviction of the Jews; and accordingly, we observe, that the mind of Agrippa was strongly affected by it. He said to Paul, "Almost thou persuadest me to be a Christian."

It is evident, that in this summary of his speech, Luke merely gives an account of the general source, from which the arguments were drawn. Paul had endeavoured to show the exact correspondence between ancient prophecy and the history of our Saviour; and Agrippa acknowledged that there was such a degree of probability in the reasoning, as almost induced him to admit the conclusion, that Jesus was the Christ. But he stopped here, either because his humble life and ignominious death were contrary to the notions of the pomp and splendour of the Messiah and his kingdom, which a Jew was accustomed to entertain; or because he was restrained, by worldly considerations, from candidly declaring his sentiments. The remains of his Jewish prejudices, or a dread of the consequences, if he should avow his convictions, and embrace Christianity, arrested his progress. It would have been no easy matter, in that age, for a king to profess the despised and offensive doctrine of the cross. The rage of the Jews against him would have been without bounds; and he would have incurred the displeasure of the Roman emperor, and probably have been degraded from his royal honours. Whatever was the motive which prevented him from becoming an entire convert to the religion of Christ, his conscience compelled him to acknowledge, that there were strong presumptions of its truth.

The reply of the Apostle breathes the spirit of benevolence, by which a genuine Christian is influenced even towards his enemies. "I would to God, that not only thou, but also all that hear me this day, were both almost, and altogether such as I am, except these bonds." This wish or prayer might have seemed ridiculous to those, who considered only the external circumstances of the Apostle, a poor man and lightly esteemed, precluded by his character and profession from the pleasures of the world, and constantly exposed to its most formidable evils. But Paul makes an exception of the chain with which he was bound. He was content to be a solitary sufferer, and desirous that his hearers should participate in his advantages, without having a share in his troubles. He would have rejoiced to see them all enjoying the peace which dwelt in his own bosom, the consolation by which he was sustained, and the blessed hope, which cheered him in the dark scenes of adversity, and makes even the valley of death shine with celestial light. The best prayer which a Christian can offer up for another man, is, that he may be associated with him in his spiritual privileges. Let the men of the world wish health, long life, riches, and honours to their friends. These are the only blessings of which they know the value; and if they sincerely desire others to be as happy as themselves, possessed of all the good things which they so much esteem, what more can we expect from them? He who has tasted the higher pleasures of religion, will wish that grace, mercy, and peace may be multiplied to those in whom his heart is interested. He will say with the generous spirit of Paul, " May God make them what his grace has made me, and much better! May they have all my joys, without any of my sorrows!"

When Paul had closed his defence, his judges withdrew, and having consulted together, were unanimously of opinion, that he had done nothing "worthy of death or of bonds." Agrippa was almost convinced of the truth of Christianity; and Festus regarded it as a harmless superstition. There was nothing, therefore, to hinder him from being set at liberty but his appeal to the emperor, which, perhaps, he had not power to withdraw, and an inferior court could not set aside. We may, therefore, be disposed to regret that Paul had made this appeal, as he might have been immediately dismissed from the bar of Festus, and have returned to the free exercise of his Apostolical office, which had been so long interrupted. It is evident, however, that it was a measure absolutely necessary at the time, to preserve him from falling into the hands of the Jews, who were resolved upon his destruction. By the Head of the Church, it was overruled as the occasion of sending him to Rome, the centre of concourse to all the nations of the earth, where he preached the gospel, which he had already published in many of the chief cities of the empire; and while this journey was subservient to the interests of religion, it was attended with no worse consequence to himself than his continuance for some time longer in bonds.

This chapter would furnish a variety of useful remarks; but I shall conclude with a few reflections, suggested by the impression which the speech of Paul made upon Agrippa. "Almost thou persuadest me to be a Christian." We learn from this example, that there may be convictions of the truth, which are prevented by certain causes from terminating in conversion; or that particular persons may make such approaches towards religion, as in the language of our Saviour, "not to be far from the kingdom of heaven," and yet may not fully submit to its authority.

Perhaps, there may be found, among professed infidels themselves, some persons, the state of whose minds much resembles that of Agrippa. They are secretly convinced that Christianity is true, or the evidence in its favour appears so strong, that they entertain suspicions and presumptions of its truth; but they are hindered from pursuing the inquiry, and avowing their sentiments, by pride, by the prevalence of corrupt propensities, by a dread of the reproaches of their companions in unbelief, or by some other base consideration, which counteracts the suggestions of conscience. Their hearts misgive them, when they seem to be boldest in expressing their contempt for religion, and they tremble while they pretend to set its awful sanctions at defiance. How unhappy must such persons be! There is a frequent and painful struggle in their breasts between inclination and a sense of duty; they are desirous to taste and they venture to pluck, the forbidden fruit; but they have not yet been able to fully persuade themselves, that the threatening is only an imaginary terror. Of religion they know as much as disturbs them in their pleasures, but not so much as to prevail upon them to give their cordial consent to it. While they hate the light and refuse to come to it, lest their deeds should be reproved, what a dreadful load of guilt do they accumulate? No man can despise religion without sin; but how great, how inexcusable is the sin of those, who affect to despise it, although their hearts secretly bear witness to its truth and excellence!

Again, Among the members of the Church, there are persons, who believe the gospel to be true, and profess an attachment to it, but, at the same time, are only almost persuaded to be Christians. Their faith is a cold and careless assent, which has little or no influence upon their hearts. They do not feel themselves interested in religion. They hear its awful and comfortable doctrines without emotions of fear or joy; they observe its institutions without devout affections; they obey its precepts without any liking to the duties which they enjoin. Conscience will not permit them to do less; but why are they content with so little? If the gospel is true, is it not worthy of all acceptation? If Jesus Christ is the Saviour of sinners, is he not entitled to their highest gratitude and love? Consider, ye lukewarm friends of Christianity, that if you are not in earnest about religion, it can serve no valuable purpose to make a profession of it. "I would," said our Lord to the Church of Laodicea, "thou wert cold or hot." He requires you to take a decided part, to be either for him or against him; and he would rather that you should openly avow your hostility, than that under a show of regard, you should harbour a contemptuous indifference.

Lastly, There is a third class of persons, to whom the words of Agrippa may be applied. They have not only the form, but they seem also to have experienced the power, of religion. They trust, as they flatter themselves, in the mercy of God, and hope for eternal life; they take delight in hearing the doctrines and promises of salvation; they engage in the exercises of devotion with fervour, and punctually perform many of the common duties of life. Yet, their religion is a false show; there is nothing real under those specious appearances. They are not, indeed, deliberate hypocrites, studying for fame or gain to impose upon others; but they are themselves imposed upon by their own feelings. There is no radical change of their principles; they are not new creatures in Christ Jesus; they are almost, but not altogether persuaded to be Christians. Remember the account given by our Saviour, in the parable of the sower, of some "who receive the word with joy, and continue for a season, but have no root in themselves." It, therefore, deeply concerns the professors of religion to examine the emotions of their minds, and the attainments which they suppose themselves to have made, by the criterion of Scripture. No man should, upon slight evidence, or by a hasty induction, produce a sentence in his own favour. Let him reflect, that the heart is deceitful above all things; and that there may be a strong movement of the affections, and even a reformation of the conduct, while it remains under the dominion of sin. It is by the grace of God, that a man becomes altogether a Christian. This new character cannot be assumed at pleasure, nor produced merely by the force of arguments, and the influence of favourable circumstances. It is the image and superscription of our heavenly Father, impressed upon the soul by his own hand; for " we are born, not of blood, nor of the will of the flesh, nor of the will of man, but of God."

LECTURE XXIX

PAUL IN MALTA AND ROME.

Chap. xxviii.

This chapter begins with showing us Paul and his company safely landed in the Island of Melita. He had been sent by sea, with other prisoners, to Italy; and the incidents of the voyage are related in the preceding chapter. After stopping at several places, and encountering adverse winds, they were overtaken by a tempest, which drove them upon an unknown coast, were the vessel was stranded. Of this disaster Paul had given early notice, not by his skill in maritime affairs, but in consequence of a divine revelation. The centurion to whose charge he was committed, was more disposed to believe the master and the owner of the ship, who seemed to have suspected no danger; and the voyage was continued. When the storm arose, an angel was sent to inform Paul, that the lives of all the company, consisting of sailors, soldiers, and prisoners, should be preserved. The next day, he communicated this information, which was intended not only to comfort his own mind, but by exhibiting him as a man who enjoyed intercourse with Heaven, to recommend him to the favour of the centurion. Accordingly, he was held in such esteem by that officer, that for his sake, he would not permit the soldiers to murder the prisoners, as they had proposed to do, in order to prevent their escape. The prediction of Paul was exactly fulfilled; for, notwithstanding the wreck of the vessel at some distance from the shore, of two hundred and seventy-six persons, not an individual perished, but by different expedients they all got safely to land.

It is worthy of observation, that although Paul expressly foretold, that there should be no loss of lives during the voyage, yet when the sailors were attempting to escape by means of the boat, he said to the centurion, "Except these abide in the ship, ye cannot be saved." How shall these things be reconciled? If God had determined to save Paul and his companions, should not his purpose have been accomplished, whether the seamen had left the ship or had remained in it? Are the divine decrees dependent upon circumstances, and liable to be reversed by the volitions and actions of men? The objection is not peculiar to the present case, but has been advanced against the doctrine of predestination in all its extent. If the counsels of God are absolutely fixed, it has been said, they will be executed, whatever may happen; and, consequently, exhortations to duty are preposterous, and the use of means to avoid one thing, and obtain another, is idle labour. The objection has a specious appearance, which dazzles superficial thinkers; but it is founded in mistake, or intentional misrepresentation. It proceeds upon the idea, that the decrees of God are determinations respecting certain ends or events, without a reference to the means; and thus it attributes a procedure to Him who is wonderful in counsel, which would be unworthy of any of his creatures, endowed with only a small portion of reason. The objection first separates things, which cannot, in fact, be disjoined, the means and the end; and then holding up the doctrine of the decrees in this mangled and distorted light, pronounces it to be absurd. With whatever parade and confidence, therefore, it has been brought forward, it has no relation to the subject, and is only of use to destroy an extravagant and senseless theory, which has been substituted in the room of the genuine doctrine of Scripture.

When God decreed an event, he, at the same time, decreed, that it should take place in consequence of a train of other events, or as the result of certain previous circumstances. Thus, he did not propose to save Paul and his companions unconditionally, by means of the seamen remaining on board to manage the ship, till it should be driven on the coast of Melita. In the same manner, he has not determined to save sinners, let them live as they will; but he has chosen them to salvation, "through the sanctification of the Spirit, and belief of the truth." To say, therefore, that unless the means be employed, the ends will not be accomplished, is to assert a very simple and self-evident truth, that the purposes of God will not be fulfilled, unless they be fulfilled. Had Paul and his company been preserved without the aid of the sailors, the decree of God would not have been executed; nor would it be executed, if it were possible for a sinner to escape eternal perdition, without faith and repentance. The same event is supposed in both cases; but it is effected in a different way from what God had ordained Let us always remember, that the means make a part of the divine decrees as well as the end. The system of things is like a chain composed of many links, upon each of which the union and consistence of the chain depend. If one link were broken, the chain would be destroyed. This view of the decrees of God does not make them dependent upon the mutable will of man, and liable to be frustrated by its capricious movements.. Providence is not an occasional interference, but a constant agency of the Creator, directing and controlling events in subservience to his own designs, and, at the same time preserving inviolate the nature of his creatures. The hearts of men are in the hand of the Lord, who turns them as the rivers of water, without infringing their liberty. None of his purposes, therefore, can be defeated, because the means of carrying them into effect are provided, and will be brought into operation, in the proper season. The importance of the subject will justify these remarks, although they have detained us from entering upon the consideration of the passage, which it is the design of the present Lecture to explain.

" And when they were escaped, they knew that the island was called Melita." There were two islands bearing this name in ancient times; the one belonging to Dalmatia, and the other lying in the Mediterranean, between Sicily and Africa. The course which Paul was steering, and several circumstances in the history of his voyage, has given currency to the common opinion, that the island upon which he was shipwrecked, was Malta, which has lately attracted our notice, as the scene of our military operations, and is now a part of the British dominions.* The tradition of the country favours this opinion; and the inhabitants still show a place upon their coast, which they call " the port or haven of St. Paul."

The island was originally peopled by strangers from Africa or Phenicia. If the term, barbarous, is used to denote a people rude

---

* Bochart, Phaleg. part ii. lib. i. cap. 26. It is, however, the opinion of some learned men, that it was the other island, called Melita Illyrica, and situated in the Hadriatic. within the limits of which Malta cannot be properly included.

and uncivilized, it could not be justly applied to the inhabitants of Malta; but Luke seems, on this occasion, to have adopted the style of the Greeks, who called those barbarians who did not speak their language, and gave this appellation to the Egyptians and Indians who were as learned as themselves, and to the Persians, in whose mighty empire laws were established, and the arts of life flourished. In the present case, however, the epithet is not expressive of contempt; for the historian immediately remarks, to the honour of those islanders, " that they showed Paul and his company no little kindness: for they kindled a fire, and received them every one, because of the present rain, and because of the cold." Pity was excited by their sufferings, and what unaffected hospitality could do to alleviate them, was cheerfully done.

While the inhabitants of Malta were sympathizing with the unfortunate strangers, their attention was directed to Paul, by a very extraordinary incident. "And when Paul had gathered a bundle of sticks, and laid them on the fire, there came a viper out of the heat, and fastened on his hand. And when the barbarians saw the venomous beast hang on his hand, they said among themselves, No doubt this man is a murderer, whom, though he hath escaped the sea, yet vengeance suffereth not to live." The conclusion was such as would naturally occur to persons, persuaded that a moral government is exercised over mankind, but whose views were not corrected and enlarged by Scripture, or by accurate observation and extensive experience. They were right in believing, that God who knows the actions of men will recompense them according to their desert, and that he sometimes interposes, in a visible manner, to punish atrocious crimes. But, they erred in supposing such interpositions to be so regular, as to afford certain grounds for interpreting the design of every calamitous event. When a viper issuing from the fire fixed upon Paul's hand, they immediately inferred that he was a murderer, whom the vengeance of Heaven had overtaken. They were more ready to consider him as a criminal, because he was a prisoner; and they probably charged him with murder, because it has been observed, that of all crimes, it most rarely escapes with impunity. They did not reflect that this world is not the place of retribution; that although there are occasional manifestations of justice, the exercise of it is for the most part delayed; that notorious transgressors sometimes live long, and die in peace; and that the lot of good men is often full of affliction and sorrow.

These reflections, which arise from a very slight view of human life, seem not to have occurred to the unenlightened inhabitants of Malta. How great was their surprise, when they saw Paul shake off the viper into the fire; and having expected "that he should have swollen, or fallen down dead suddenly, they perceived no harm come to him?" They were, no doubt, well acquainted with the properties of the animal, and had frequently observed the deleterious effects of its poison. But, they did not know, that this man was a servant of the Lord of the universe, who had said concerning those who believed, "that they should take up serpents, and that if they drank any deadly thing, it should not hurt them." Astonished at the event, they passed from one extreme to another, and concluded that Paul was a God. Those poor heathens, who had long been accustomed to believe that their Deities sometimes assumed the human form, supposed him to be one of them, who, for some unknown reason had descended to the earth. We see in this instance, a true picture of man, who judges by appearances and equivocal signs, and changes his opinions as often as the scene around him fluctuates. If he has pronounced a first sentence rashly, the second is, perhaps, more foolish and extravagant. Paul was not a murderer; but he was still less a God. He was only a minister of Jesus Christ, who had destined him to important services, and honoured him with his particular protection.

We are informed of other miracles, which Paul performed during his stay in the island. "In the same quarter were possessions of the chief man of the island, whose name was Publius, who received us, and lodged us three days courteously. And it came to pass, that the father of Publius lay sick of a fever, and of a bloody flux: to whom Paul entered in, and prayed, and laid his hands on him, and healed him. So when this was done, others also which had diseases in the island, came and were healed." The first miracle had so astonished the ignorant inhabitants, that they supposed Paul to be a God; but this honour he would reject with indignant zeal. We have seen in what manner he and Barnabas acted, when the inhabitants of Lystra having fallen into the same mistake, on a similar occasion, were preparing to offer sacrifice to them, in the characters of Jupiter and Mercury. The Apostle was, no doubt, equally careful to undeceive the Maltese, and to instruct them in the knowledge of the Creator, who alone is God, and is exclusively entitled to religious worship. There was, however, an inferior honour due to the Apostles, which the miracles were the means of procuring. By these they were pointed out as the servants of God, who had a claim not only to the offices of friendship from those with whom they conversed, but also to respectful attention and implicit faith, when they professed to deliver his will. Miracles were not designed to aggrandize them as men, but as ministers of the Messiah, to authenticate their commission, and to convince both Jews and Gentiles, that they should act a safe and prudent part, in submitting to them as their guides in religion. To this purpose they faithfully devoted their supernatural powers, never, in a single instance, employing them to draw admiration to themselves, or to promote their secular interests. Notwithstanding the silence of the history, we may confidently affirm, that Paul made the miracles which he performed in Malta, subservient to the cause of Christ. A man so eager to do good, who, although a prisoner, does not seem to have been under restraint, would not remain inactive during the three months which he spent in the island; and as his wonderful works had gained him the favour of the people, he enjoyed a very favourable opportunity to instruct them in the knowledge of the gospel. And thus, what we should call an accidental event, the shipwreck of Paul upon an unknown coast, was overruled by Providence as the occasion of introducing Christianity into Malta, where it still exists in the corrupted form, which it has assumed in countries, subject to the authority of the Pope.

The kindness which the inhabitants showed to the strangers, who had escaped the perils of the sea, when they were first cast upon their coast, was continued to Paul and his friends, from respect to his character, and gratitude for the favours which they had received from him. "Who also honoured us with many honours, and when we departed they laded us with such things as were necessary." When our Lord conferred miraculous powers upon the Apostles, he enjoined a free and generous exercise of them. They were not to set a price upon their cures, but to heal the sick, and cast out devils, without demanding or expecting a reward. By this injunction, however, they were not restrained from accepting the gifts which should be presented to them, by those who esteemed them "for their work's sake." It was reasonable, that they should be recompensed by the persons to whom they devoted their time and labour; and a man of the purest generosity, who would scorn a bribe as the motive to his duty, will be pleased with tokens of affection from the objects of his beneficence, and estimate them far above the value which sordid self-interest would attach to them.

When winter was past, and the season became favourable for the prosecution of their voyage, the centurion with the prisoners under his care, sailed from Malta, in a ship of Alexandria; and having passed the island of Sicily, arrived at Puteoli, a city of Italy, not far distant from Naples. From this place Paul proceeded to Rome by land. In the way he was met by some Christians from that city, who, having heard of his appoach, went to meet him as far as Appii Forum, and the Three Taverns, two cities at the respective distances of fifty, and thirty miles from the capital. They had probably never seen the Apostle, but they had heard his fame, and enjoyed the benefit of his instructions; for he had sent an Epistle to their Church, which makes a part of the sacred canon of the New Testament. The present circumstances of Paul were not calculated to induce strangers to court an acquaintance with him. Associated with a number of prisoners who were accused of different crimes, he was on his way to the tribunal of Nero, by whose sentence he might be deprived of his life. No honour could result from a connexion with such a man; and his friends might be involved in trouble and danger, by the suspicion and jealousy of government. But, it was the glory of the disciples of Jesus in those early ages, that they were united in the bonds of affection, which the severest trials were not able to dissolve. They did not selfishly and pusillanimously abandon him, who was singled out to encounter the hostility which the world entertained against them all. They gathered around him in the hour of adversity, to sustain his courage, and to alleviate his sorrows, by their presence and their counsels. When Jesus Christ was sick and in prison, in the persons of his faithful servants, they accounted it both a duty and a privilege to visit him.

This unexpected visit had an agreeable effect upon the mind of the Apostle. "When he saw them, he thanked God," who had disposed those brethren to show him kindness in the time of danger; "and he took courage," or felt his resolution confirmed in the prospect of the troubles, which might befal him in Rome. "Iron sharpeneth iron, so a man sharpeneth the countenance of his friend." By the simple presence and approving looks of his friends, as well as by their exhortations, a sufferer shall be sustained, in the severest trials of his patience and fortitude. As it is a common cause, in which Christians are embarked, every man is bound to contribute to its success by his personal exertions when they are wanted, or by supporting his brethren who are actually engaged in the conflict, and there is not a saint of the highest order, who may not be assisted by the prayers and counsels of those, who are much inferior to him in talents and attainments. The courage of the great Apostle of the Gentiles was invigorated, by the presence of some private Christians from Rome.

Upon his arrival in the city, the centurion delivered the prisoners to the captain of the guard, or the commander of the pretorian bands, which were stationed in Rome, to guard the person of the emperor, and to retain that mighty capital in subjection. But, Paul was permitted to dwell by himself, or as we learn from the thirtieth verse, in a house which he had hired. This favour was probably obtained by the intercession of the centurion, who had conceived a friendship for him, and would be more readily granted, because he had not come to Rome properly in the character of a criminal, but rather as a man, who had been compelled to appeal to Cesar, by the injustice of his countrymen. He was attended by a soldier to whom he seems to have been fastened, according to the custom of the Romans, by a chain fixed to the right hand of the prisoner, and the left hand of his guard. " For the hope of Israel," he says I am bound with this chain."

These words were addressed to the chief men of the Jews, whom Paul had called together three days after his arrival in Rome. " And when they were come together, he said unto them, Men and brethren, though I have committed nothing against the people or customs of our fathers, yet was I delivered prisoner from Jerusalem into the hands of the Romans, who, when they had examined me, would have let me go, because there was no cause of death in me. But when the Jews spake against it, I was constrained to appeal unto Cesar, not that I had ought to accuse my nation of. For this cause, therefore, have I called for you, to see you and to speak with you: because that for the hope of Israel I am bound with this chain." It was evidently the design of this speech, to remove the prejudices which the Jews might have conceived against him, that they might be prepared to listen patiently, when he pleaded in defence of Christianity. He had not violated the laws of his country, nor was it his intention to accuse his own nation to the emperor.

The appeal proceeded simply from a regard to his personal safety; his innocence had been declared by the Roman governors of the province of Judea; and the true cause of his present confinement, as well as of his past sufferings, was his faith in the Messiah, whose advent they, and their brethren in every region of the earth, were anxiously expecting.

The Jews answered, "We neither received letters out of Judea concerning thee, neither any of the brethren that came, showed or spake any harm of thee." It is surprising that the priests and elders at Jerusalem, who persecuted Paul with implacable hostility, had not endeavoured by letters or messengers, to prejudice their brethren in Rome against him. As their sentiments had not undergone a change in his favour, their silence may, perhaps, be accounted for, by the want of an opportunity to send information to Rome, in consequence of the lateness of the season, when Paul set out on his voyage. "But we desire," they add, "to hear of thee what thou thinkest: for as concerning this sect, we know that every where it is spoken against." Christianity made its first appearance under the disadvantage, of a bad name, which was principally owing to the malignant industry of the Jews, as we learn from an ancient writer, who informs us, that they sent messengers from Jerusalem to their synagogues in foreign countries, announcing that an impious and lawless sect had been formed by a certain impostor, Jesus of Galilee.* No means were neglected to repress what they considered, or affected to consider, as a pestilent heresy. But, while the malice of the Jews was chiefly to be blamed for the unfavourable character which was attached to Christianity, truth requires us to add, that the Gentiles were fully disposed to adopt and circulate their slanders, and to load our holy religion with other opprobrious charges, invented by themselves. These are recorded and completely refuted by the Fathers. "The sect was every where spoken against." What other fate could it expect! It offended the prejudices of men of all religions; it condemned their vices, and even many of their virtues; it taught doctrines from which corrupt reason revolted; it enjoined duties, to which the depraved heart was unwilling to submit. It was received, therefore, with a general outcry, like the screams of the birds of night, when the light which they abhor, bursts into their dark and foul habitations.

---

* Just. Martyr. Dialog. cum Tryph.

Notwithstanding the reports to the disadvantage of the gospel, the Jews, with whom Paul was now conversing, had not come to a final determination to reject it. They were willing to hear both sides. Having seen it attacked, they also wished to see it defended. A day being fixed, "there came many to him into his lodging: to whom he expounded and testified the kingdom of God, persuading them concerning Jesus, both out of the law of Moses, and out of the Prophets, from morning till evening." The discouse was long, because the subject was ample, much reasoning was necessary, and probably many objections were proposed. The Apostle "expounded the kingdom of God," or explained the nature of the new dispensation of religion, and proved that Jesus was the Christ, by testimonies from the law of Moses, and the prophetical writings. In an address to the Jews, no other mode of proof could have been attempted with propriety. If an appeal had been made to the evidence of miracles, they would have replied, that their law expressly forbade them to hearken to a Prophet, who should endeavour, by signs and wonders, to entice them from the religion of their fathers. I do not mean, that there was any defect in this evidence, which that of prophecy was necessary to supply. It was by the miracles of the Apostles, that the Gentiles, who did not know the books of the Prophets, were convinced. But, since God had provided another species of proof, in the harmony between the old and the new dispensation, and had directed the Jews to look for it, no reasoning, in which this essential part was omitted, could have justified them in receiving the gospel as a divine revelation. It was necessary to demonstrate, that Jesus of Nazareth was the person whose character and actions are described by Moses, David, and Isaiah; and that his religion possessed all the properties of the new covenant, which God had promised to make with his people in the latter days. Our Lord adopted this plan in his discourses to the Jews; and we see from many occurrences in this book, that his ministers followed his example.

Among the Jews whom Paul addressed, there were, no doubt persons of different dispositions, and different degrees of information; some, who had considered the prophecies with more attention than others; and some, who being less prejudiced against the notion of a spiritual Messiah, would not be so averse to recognise him in the person of the crucified Jesus. At the same time, it should be remembered, that the grace of God is the efficient cause of the success of the gospel; and that, while the eyes of one man are opened to perceive its truth, another remains under the blinding influence of corrupt reason, and earthly affections. "Some believed the things which were spoken, and some believed not."

The assembly being divided, a discussion ensued, in which the one part maintained the doctrine of Paul against the other. Before they separated, he reminded them of a prophecy in the book of Isaiah, the application of which to the unbelieving part of his audience was obvious. From the frequent mention of it in the New Testament, and, in particular, from the words of the Evangelist John, it appears to have been ultimately intended to represent the character and conduct of the Jews, at the commencement of the Christian dispensation. It begins with foretelling, that they should be delivered up, in the righteous judgment of God, to a blinded mind, and a hardened heart; or, at least, that they should discover the most surprising stupidity and insensibility, so as not to understand what was plainly told, nor to see what was placed before their eyes. "Well spake the Holy Ghost by Esaias the Prophet, unto our fathers, saying, Hearing ye shall hear, but shall not understand; and seeing ye shall see, and not perceive." The exact fulfilment of this part of the prophecy, is evident from their obstinate rejection of our Saviour as an impostor, notwithstanding the splendid train of miracles, by which his mission was attested, and the manifest accomplishment of ancient predictions in his death, and the various circumstances in his life. The prophecy goes on to account for their conduct. "For the heart of this people is waxed gross, and their ears are dull of hearing, and their eyes have they closed; lest they should see with their eyes, and hear with their ears, and understand with their heart, and should be converted, and I should heal them." This description of their spiritual taste seems to be taken from a man addicted to gluttony and drunkenness, whose mental faculties are benumbed, whose very senses are blunted, and who, oppressed by the effects of intemperance, sinks into a profound sleep. The unbelief of the Jews was not the consequence of involuntary and invincible ignorance, but of the predominance of sinful affections. They were not willing to understand and perceive. Jesus Christ, in his humble form, had no attractions for men, who desired nothing so much as the honours and pleasures of the world. They would not believe that he was the Messiah, because they were displeased with the lowliness of his character, and the spiritual salvation which he offered to bestow. Hence, they are said " to have closed their eyes," as a person does, to whom the light is offensive, or who wishes not to see a disagreeable object. The chief seat of unbelief is the will. It is not from want of evidence that the gospel is rejected, but from disinclination of heart. Its mysterious doctrines would meet with no opposition from our reason, if it were not prejudiced and corrupted by our passions. In the parable of the marriage supper, the conduct of those who refused the invitation, is ascribed to the influence of the cares and enjoyments of the present life. We have, then, before our eyes an awful example of men, who, by the neglect of their privileges, had provoked God to withdraw his Spirit, and to leave them to the uncontrolled dominion of carnal affections. Such was the moral condition of the Jews in the Apostolic age; and such it has continued for more than seventeen hundred years. It administers a solemn warning to us, to take heed lest we also be hardened " through the deceitfulness of sin."

To this prophecy Paul directed the attention of the unbelieving Jews, as a subject of serious consideration. It was calculated to alarm them all, and might, through the blessing of God, rouse some of them from their spiritual lethargy, which was an awful prognostic of eternal death. He concluded with a declaration, which was always mortifying to the Jews, but which he now made, not with a design to irritate them, but to provoke them to jealousy. When better motives failed, the dread of being superseded in their privileges, might render them cautious of rashly and perversely rejecting the gospel. Although they should resist its evidence, yet the Gentiles would believe, and be admitted into the place which they had long held in the favour of God. " Be it known unto you, therefore, that the salvation of God is sent unto the Gentiles, and that they will hear it."

" And when he had said these words, the Jews departed, and had great reasoning among themselves." The gospel was the subject of their private conferences, in which the arguments on both sides were canvassed. Those who were convinced of its truth, would be eager to convert their unbelieving brethren; and we may conceive the unbelievers to have been equally earnest to reclaim them from heresy. How those reasonings terminated we are not informed; but it may be presumed, that while some were at last brought to see the Christian religion to be worthy of all acceptation, the effect of opposition upon others, was to render them more decided and obstinate in rejecting it.

The chapter closes with a short account of Paul during the period of his imprisonment. He was permitted to dwell in his own hired house, to which every person, who chose to visit him, had access, and to preach the gospel without restraint. Although the Apostle was in chains, the word of God was not bound. He was likewise employed in writing letters to the Churches in different parts of the world. The Epistles to the Ephesians, the Philippians, and the Colossians, and the short letter to Philemon, bear internal marks of having been composed during his confinement in Rome. Whether the second epistle to Timothy should be dated from his first or his second imprisonment, is a question, about which learned men are not agreed. The Epistle to the Hebrews, which is ascribed with more probability to Paul than any other person, seems to have been written after he was loosed from his bonds. He was restored to liberty, in consequence of a full proof of his innocence, or through the intercession of some friends in the household of Cesar, who had embraced the Christian religion. The accounts of the subsequent part of his life, of the places which he visited, and the time which he spent in his Apostolical labours, are, for the most part, uncertain and conjectural. We know, however, that he was again imprisoned in Rome, and in that city, sealed with his blood the doctrine which he had long and faithfully preached.

I have traced, as far as any authentic records remain, the history of this illustrious servant of Jesus Christ, whose exertions in the cause of the gospel, were adequate to the high expectations which might have been entertained, from the extraordinary manner in which he was called to the Apostolical office. By immediate revelation he was furnished with a profound knowledge of the mysteries of redemption ; and in natural abilities he was, perhaps, superior to his brethren, in supernatural endowments, certainly not behind the chief of the Apostles. Transferring to the service of religion the activity and ardour of mind which he inherited from nature, he declined no labour, and shrunk from no danger, in endeavouring to advance the glory of his Saviour, and the best interests of the human race. It was his most delightful employment to preach the doctrine of salvation by the cross, without being at all discouraged by the ridicule of the Greeks, and the persecuting zeal of the Jews. His life was a life of faith upon the Son of God, the constraining influence of whose love he constantly felt, and whose grace sustained him in a series of duties and difficulties, by the pressure of which the unassisted strength and courage of any man would have been overwhelmed. The close of his life might seem unfortunate to those, who looked only at his bodily sufferings; but it was cheered by the peaceful recollections of a good conscience, and the triumphant hope of an everlasting recompense. "I am now ready to be offered up, and the time of my departure is at hand. I have fought a good fight, I have finished my course, I have kept the faith. Henceforth, there is laid up for me crown of righteousness, which the Lord the righteous judge shall give me at that day." In his conversion, he exhibits an instance of divine grace, which should preserve the unworthy from despair; in his Apostolical character, he is a pattern to Christian ministers of diligence and fidelity, of entire devotedness to the service of the Saviour, and the most ardent love to the souls of men; as a willing martyr for religion, he inculcates this important lesson upon us all, that the truth should be dearer to us than our lives, and that we should resolve to follow our Redeemer to prison and to death.

I have now brought to a conclusion this course of Lectures on the Acts of the Apostles. After tracing the history of the Church, from the ascension of Christ to the meeting of the first Christian Conncil in Jerusalem, I have surveyed the principal events in the life of Paul, to which the subsequent narrative confines our attention. Although he seems to have been "in labours more abundant," yet we are not to suppose, that the other Apostles were inactive, or that their transactions furnished nothing unworthy to be known. Invested the same commission, actuated by the same zeal, endowed with the same supernatural powers, and assisted by the same Spirit, they, undoubtedly, exerted themselves, with unwearied diligence, to diffuse the knowledge of the gospel; but, with the exception of some particulars, it has seemed good to the Holy Ghost to pass over their history in silence. After the list of their names, which is inserted in the first chapter, most of them are never again mentioned in any part of these inspired memoirs.

Five years are elapsed since this course of Lectures commenced;

and five years are no inconsiderable portion of the life of man. At the close of any period of time, it is our duty to inquire, whether we have improved our opportunities and privileges, and what progress we have made in wisdom and holiness. This inquiry is particularly necessary at the conclusion of a series of religious instructions, the professed intention of which was to enlighten and purify us. If these illustrations of the Apostolical history have accomplished the design with which they were delivered, you have been led to admire the wisdom and power of Jesus Christ, displayed in the establishment, the protection and the enlargement of the Church. Your belief of the divine origin of our holy religion has been confirmed by the many proofs which you have seen, of the presence of God with those who first published it; and your conviction of its transcendent excellence has been strengthened, by a view of its beneficial effects in reclaiming mankind from idolatry, and its attendant vices. You have felt yourselves animated with the same contempt for the blandishments and terrors of the world, which so strongly characterised the conduct of the primitive Christians. You have resolved, after their example, to glory only in the cross of Christ and to consecrate yourselves to his service. While you beheld the grace of God to the Gentiles, whom he visited by the ministry of his holy servants, to bless them through his Son, " the desire of all nations," you have been thankful, that whether the gospel was preached to the inhabitants of Britain by any of the Apostles, or not, the joyful sound has been heard in this island; and that, at the distance of seventeen centuries from the age in which they lived, you reap the fruits of their pious labours.

Remember, that it is the Holy Spirit only, by whom the pen of Luke was guided in composing this history, and the other sacred writers were inspired, who can open your understandings to understand the Scriptures, and dispose you to receive the word of God, with reverence and love. May he bless what has been spoken, according to his own will, that our preaching and your hearing may not be in vain! I conclude with the words of Paul to the Church of Thessalonica. " Therefore, brethren, stand fast, and hold the traditions which ye have been taught, whether by word, or our epistle. Now, our Lord Jesus Christ himself, and God even our Father, which hath loved us, and hath given us everlasting consolation, and good hope through grace, comfort your hearts, and stablish you in every good word and work." Amen!

Other Solid Ground Titles

PAUL THE PREACHER: *Sermons from Acts* by John Eadie
THE COMMUNICANT'S COMPANION by Matthew Henry
THE CHILD AT HOME by John S.C. Abbott
THE LIFE OF JESUS CHRIST FOR THE YOUNG by Richard Newton
THE KING'S HIGHWAY: *10 Commandments for the Young* by Richard Newton
HEROES OF THE REFORMATION by Richard Newton
FEED MY LAMBS: *Lectures to Children on Vital Subjects* by John Todd
LET THE CANNON BLAZE AWAY by Joseph P. Thompson
THE STILL HOUR: *Communion with God in Prayer* by Austin Phelps
COLLECTED WORKS of James Henley Thornwell (4 vols.)
CALVINISM IN HISTORY *by Nathaniel S. McFetridge*
OPENING SCRIPTURE: *Hermeneutical Manual by Patrick Fairbairn*
THE ASSURANCE OF FAITH *by Louis Berkhof*
THE PASTOR IN THE SICK ROOM *by John D. Wells*
THE BUNYAN OF BROOKLYN: *Life & Sermons of I.S. Spencer*
THE NATIONAL PREACHER: *Sermons from 2nd Great Awakening*
FIRST THINGS: *First Lessons God Taught Mankind* Gardiner Spring
BIBLICAL & THEOLOGICAL STUDIES *by 1912 Faculty of Princeton*
THE POWER OF GOD UNTO SALVATION *by B.B. Warfield*
THE LORD OF GLORY *by B.B. Warfield*
A GENTLEMAN & A SCHOLAR: *Memoir of J.P. Boyce* by J. Broadus
SERMONS TO THE NATURAL MAN *by W.G.T. Shedd*
SERMONS TO THE SPIRITUAL MAN *by W.G.T. Shedd*
HOMILETICS AND PASTORAL THEOLOGY *by W.G.T. Shedd*
A PASTOR'S SKETCHES 1 & 2 *by Ichabod S. Spencer*
THE PREACHER AND HIS MODELS *by James Stalker*
IMAGO CHRISTI: *The Example of Jesus Christ* by James Stalker
LECTURES ON THE HISTORY OF PREACHING *by J. A. Broadus*
THE SHORTER CATECHISM ILLUSTRATED *by John Whitecross*
THE CHURCH MEMBER'S GUIDE *by John Angell James*
THE SUNDAY SCHOOL TEACHER'S GUIDE *by John A. James*
CHRIST IN SONG: *Hymns of Immanuel from All Ages* by Philip Schaff
DEVOTIONAL LIFE OF THE S.S. TEACHER *by J.R. Miller*

Call us Toll Free at 1-877-666-9469
Send us an e-mail at sgcb@charter.net
Visit us on line at solid-ground-books.com
Uncovering Buried Treasure to the Glory of God

www.ingramcontent.com/pod-product-compliance
Lightning Source LLC
Chambersburg PA
CBHW080540230426
43663CB00015B/2651